ATONEMENT, LAW, AND JUSTICE

ATONEMENT, LAW, AND JUSTICE

The Cross in Historical and Cultural Contexts

Adonis Vidu

Baker Academic
a division of Baker Publishing Group
Grand Rapids, Michigan

Published by Baker Academic
a division of Baker Publishing Group
P.O. Box 6287, Grand Rapids, MI 49516-6287
www.bakeracademic.com

Printed in the United States of America

Library of Congress Cataloging-in-Publication Data

Vidu, Adonis.
 Atonement, law, and justice : the cross in historical and cultural contexts / Adonis Vidu.
  pages cm
 Includes bibliographical references and index.
 ISBN 978-0-8010-3919-5 (pbk.)
 1. Atonement—History of doctrines. 2. Jesus Christ—Crucifixion. 3. Law and gospel.
 I. Title.
 BT265.3.V53 2013
 232′.3—dc23   2014007212

In keeping with biblical principles of creation stewardship, Baker Publishing Group advocates the responsible use of our natural resources. As a member of the Green Press Initiative, our company uses recycled paper when possible. The text paper of this book is composed in part of post-consumer waste.

14 15 16 17 18 19 20   7 6 5 4 3 2 1

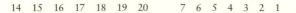

For Anthony C. Thiselton,
my *Doktorvater*, with gratitude for all your
writing, teaching, and friendship

Contents

Acknowledgments

This book was written during a sabbatical leave from Gordon-Conwell Theological Seminary. I would like to thank the Trustees, President Dennis Hollinger, and the administration of the seminary for granting me this opportunity and for supporting our sabbatical program. I would also like to thank my colleagues in the Division of Christian Thought for endorsing my sabbatical application, and in particular my colleagues in the systematic theology department for shouldering the teaching load.

As a systematic theologian I often felt out of my league in having to write on historical theology. I was fortunate enough to find invaluable help and advice from my colleagues in the church history department, Gordon Isaac, Gwenfair Adams, and Frank A. James III. My colleagues in the department of systematic theology, Richard Lints, Patrick Smith, Don Fairbairn, and especially Jack Davis and David Wells read various parts of the manuscript and provided much needed feedback. I would also like to thank Sean McDonough for taking time to read part of the manuscript, and for our many and always stimulating conversations. My gratitude also goes to Jens Zimmermann and to an anonymous reader at Baker Academic for their comments on earlier drafts. My editors at Baker Academic Robert Hosack, Robert Hand, Jeff Reimer, and Bethany Murphy are to be commended for their expert attention and patience.

Thanks are also due to a number of students who have contributed to this project as it was unfolding. Two of my research assistants proved extremely reliable: Robert Frazier and Andrew R. Johnson. Former students Larry Locke and Matthew Wong also made helpful comments.

I am also deeply grateful to my colleague Meredith Kline for locating and obtaining countless inter-library loans and for suggesting a number of additional resources on the atonement.

None of my work would have been possible without the unflinching support and encouragement of my wife, Adriana, and our daughter, Hannah. I look forward to ways of atoning for depriving them of my mental and physical presence during the past two years.

This book is dedicated to my doctoral supervisor at the University of Nottingham, Prof. Anthony C. Thiselton. The writing of this project, in addition to other pressing deadlines, sadly prevented me from adding to a *Festschrift* presented to Tony by colleagues and former doctoral students in celebration of his extraordinary career and personal impact. I am still discovering the many ways, some visible, some subtle, in which I am indebted to him.

Abbreviations

Anselm

CDH *Cur Deus Homo*

Augustine

C. Faust *Contra Faustum*
De Trin. *De Trinitate*
Enchir. *Enchiridion de fide, spe, et caritate*

Calvin

Comm. Exod. *Commentary on Exodus*
Comm. Isa. *Commentary on Isaiah*
Comm. Rom. *Commentary on Romans*

Irenaeus

Ad. Haer. *Adversus Haereses*

Gregory of Nyssa

Or. Cat. *Oratio Catechetica*

Ritschl, Albrecht

JR *The Christian Doctrine of Justification and Reconciliation: The Positive Development of the Doctrine*, ed. H. R. Mackintosh and Alexander Beith Macaulay (Clifton, NJ: Reference Book Publishers, 1966)

Thomas Aquinas

ST *Summa Theologiae*

Introduction

Atonement theory has been undergoing something of a renaissance over the past decade or so. While some excellent monographs have been written, few writers have embraced the task of writing a history of atonement theories. This is somewhat understandable, given the already-existing reliable and penetrating analyses from the likes of Ritschl and Dillistone, and more recently Fiddes, Schmiechen, and Weaver,[1] in addition to a number of notable edited volumes.[2]

There are some gaps in these histories, though. With the exception of Weaver, none of these authors engages with the last thirty years or so of the conversation. The initial motivation of this work was to provide an introduction to the bewildering variety of recent proposals about the atonement. Another gap is that none of these histories have been written from a position sympathetic to the theory of penal substitution. While the reader will notice that I do not hesitate to critique certain aspects of this tradition, I am in broad agreement with a penal substitutionary model.

Nevertheless, the reader should not expect to find an exhaustive history of atonement thinking in the following pages. That task is quite clearly above

1. Albrecht Ritschl, *The Christian Doctrine of Justification and Reconciliation: The Positive Development of the Doctrine*, ed. H. R. Mackintosh and Alexander Beith Macaulay (Clifton, NJ: Reference Book Publishers, 1966); F. W. Dillistone, *The Christian Understanding of Atonement* (Philadelphia: Westminster, 1968); Paul S. Fiddes, *Past Event and Present Salvation: The Christian Idea of the Atonement* (Louisville: Westminster John Knox, 1989); Peter Schmiechen, *Saving Power: Theories of Atonement and Forms of the Church* (Grand Rapids: Eerdmans, 2005); J. Denny Weaver, *The Nonviolent Atonement*, 2nd ed. (Grand Rapids: Eerdmans, 2011).

2. Charles E. Hill and Frank A. James III, eds., *The Glory of the Atonement: Biblical, Theological, and Practical Perspectives* (Downers Grove, IL: InterVarsity, 2004); Ivor Davidson and Murray Rae, eds., *God of Salvation: Soteriology in Theological Perspective* (Aldershot: Ashgate, 2011).

my own expertise as a philosophical and systematic theologian. What I am trying to offer is, quite simply, a *critical reading of the history of atonement theories*. As opposed to a history as such, a "critical reading" engages with selected patterns, recurrent concepts, and attempts to discern broader themes, all from a critical perspective. My own angle is quite clearly connected to my theological sympathies.

I suggest that *the history of atonement thinking could be read as an ongoing conversation with the history of thinking about justice and the law*. Not that this should come as a surprise for the theologically astute reader. Numerous commentators have pointed out the influence of contextual theories of justice on atonement theologians. However, as far as I am aware, there has been no book-length study of this topic.[3] A few studies of the relationship between atonement and the law have indeed been written,[4] but most of them are apologies for penal substitution and thus do not apply themselves to other theories of atonement.[5]

This book sets out to fill that gap. I have discovered that the cross-fertilization between the two intellectual discourses is quite extraordinary. I will attempt to tell the story of atonement thinking by connecting it to the development of law-and-justice theories. Let me make it very clear that I am not trying to *explain* the development of atonement theory by showing how it was influenced by changing juristic contexts. While such historical explanations are theoretically possible, they are extremely risky, not least because, as I will show, the pollination goes both ways. Not only are theologians influenced by the legal philosophies of their day, but theology also inevitably influences and changes legal structures and ideologies.

Yet *explanation* is not the only possible benefit of such a critical reading. Awareness of this ideational traffic yields a better *understanding* of atonement thinkers by situating them in their intellectual contexts (especially the juridic and philosophical dimensions of those contexts). In addition, exploring the way in which atonement theology influences the legal culture throws light on the *significance* of atonement thinking for important aspects of practical life

3. Some articles, though, deserve mention: Jeffrey C. Tuomala, "Christ's Atonement as a Model for Civil Justice," *American Journal of Jurisprudence* 38 (1993): 221; James E. Gregg, "Penology and Atonement," *The Biblical World* 49, no. 4 (1917): 203–8; Jerome Hall, "Biblical Atonement and Modern Criminal Law," *Journal of Law and Religion* 1, no. 2 (1983): 279–95.

4. John McLaughlin Armour, *Atonement and Law: Or, Redemption in Harmony with Law as Revealed in Nature* (Philadelphia: Christian Statesman, 1885); Albert Barnes, *Atonement in Its Relations to Law and Moral Government* (Philadelphia: Parry & McMillan, 1859).

5. One exception is Horace Bushnell, *Forgiveness and Law: Grounded in the Principles Interpreted by Human Analogies* (New York: Scribner, Armstrong, 1874). Also of notice is Robert C. Moberly, *Atonement and Personality* (London: John Murray, 1901).

(politics, law, penal systems, etc.). Clearly there is a dialectic here, for an understanding of "use" and "significance" at least contributes to—if it doesn't entirely determine—an understanding of "meaning."

The uniqueness of this book, then, is that it offers an interdisciplinary reading of the development of atonement theory from the perspective of its engagement with intellectual discourses relating to law and justice. This is not entirely unrelated to my own theological bias in favor of penal substitution. It is no accident that most of the books that have tackled this relationship defend this particular understanding of the cross. The doctrine of penal substitution belongs to a family of theories that prioritizes the place of justice in the understanding of the atonement. Both Anselm (satisfaction theory) and Calvin (penal substitution) argue that God could not simply gratuitously forgive us without compensating his justice in some way.

As my study will show, all atonement theories want to affirm that God preserves his justice in the process of redemption. But not all theologians operate with the same understandings of justice. Theories of justice and attitudes to law constantly develop and change. I propose to follow both of these intersecting trajectories.

But this project is not simply descriptive. It also asks: Have these writers properly described the action of God in Christ? I will very briefly summarize the constructive dimension of this project and then explain how the book unfolds.

Atonement theology seeks to ascribe a particular action to God. To put it differently, it seeks to assign responsibility for a particular action. We more or less know the Easter events, but the question is, What precisely is God doing in those events? Does he send Jesus to the cross? If so, does he punish Jesus through the cross? Does he intend his death more like a ruse to fool the devil? Or perhaps Jesus goes to the cross as a demonstration of his love for God and God's love for us? The conflicts among these theories arise over assigning value to the facts. In other words, the conflict is over ascribing responsibility to God.

What these theologians are doing is not unfamiliar. We witness such exercises daily in criminal courts. Prosecutors and defense attorneys both try to make a case for or against the responsibility of a defendant for a particular act. Without getting into a philosophical discussion of responsibility, I would like to isolate one inevitable dimension of this confrontation. That is, *the assigning of responsibility for a particular action is partly based on knowledge of the agent's character*. In other words, both prosecution and defense try to make it either plausible or implausible, respectively, that *this* agent could have done *this* deed. When a connection needs to be established between an act and an agent, we naturally correlate the quality of the act with the qualities we know the agent to possess. To take a mundane example from criminal cases:

Is the defendant violent, does he have a history of harmful acts, and does he have it in him to kill someone? To establish this, we draw on everything else we know about him. We try to bring to bear his whole personality and character in order to establish whether he might have been *capable* of such a deed.

Clearly these are not the only considerations that go into assigning responsibility. But they are a necessary dimension of this process. Now, atonement theologians engage in a similar process. They have the "facts," so to speak. But how are these facts to be interpreted? What are the *actions* within these events? What is God doing in this "killing"? So theologians seek to correlate various actions (God deceives Satan; God punishes Jesus; God accepts a satisfaction; God establishes a moral example or a moral influence; God deconstructs systems of scapegoating; and so on) with the known character of God.

And so atonement theology becomes the doctrine of God. Conflicts over the meaning of the cross are in fact conflicts about the very nature and moral character of God. This again reveals the bearing of the law-and-justice conversation. Is God just? What kind of justice characterizes his being? How does this justice correlate with his love? Which is the more fundamental?

There is, however, an important disanalogy between God and human agents. Descriptions of human character will inevitably reveal persons that are more powerful than wise; more just than loving; more or less patient, true, honest, constant, faithful, charitable, and so on. Both prosecution and defense will seek to marshal their view of the balance of an agent's attributes to buttress their case.

But God is not that kind of agent. Divine attributes are not more or less balanced. They do not exist in a certain *combination*. They don't because, as the church has traditionally affirmed, *God's being is simple*. God does not *have* attributes: he *is* his attributes. This matters a lot when we're trying to understand divine agency. I will argue that God is the perfection of agency. As a result, God will be understood to stand in the background of his actions in a very different way (though not unrelated) to the way in which human agents stand in the background of their actions. To put it more simply: God is present in his actions in a different way than we are present in ours. Moreover, divine actions have a quality not shared by human actions.

In short, I will be appealing to the doctrine of divine simplicity and to the extraordinary import it has on the doctrine of the atonement. Thus the constructive dimension of this project consists in pointing out that understanding the "perfection of divine agency," or divine simplicity, strictly qualifies the way in which we may ascribe actions to God. In relation to my own sympathies for penal substitution, divine simplicity rules out certain caricatures of this doctrine, both friendly and unfriendly.

A final word about the structure of the book. I have divided the whole history of the atonement into five different periods, or paradigms, if you will: patristic, medieval, Reformation, modernity, and postmodernity (for lack of a better term). I am not claiming that these periods are self-contained paradigms, totally unique in relation to one another. There is a tremendous amount of continuity between them. I am not denying that. Yet at the same time the material has to be divided into manageable segments. I therefore readily accept that there is a fair amount of generalization going on. I am betting on the heuristic value of such a procedure, but I am also aware of the risks involved.

For discussion I have also selected a number of individual theologians from each period, rather than attempting a less detailed overview of the whole period. Thus there are sustained discussions of certain well-known contributors to atonement theology, but also of theologians, while not less known, less discussed in relation to the atonement. Unfortunately, choosing to go in-depth with certain thinkers means that not all important contributors to this conversation can be accounted for.[6] Nevertheless, my aim was not to write an exhaustive history, but to test in various writers the cross-pollination between atonement, justice, and law.

It should also be clarified that, strictly speaking, this is not a work of constructive theology. I do not enter detailed debates about the biblical justification of each theory. While I explain how various authors anchor their theories scripturally, I focus my attention on their interaction with their legal context. Since this is primarily a critical reading of the history of a particular doctrine, I do not spend time on the Old Testament or New Testament development of key atonement concepts. I take that to be the "data" these theologians attempt to unpack and interpret, precisely in light of their cultural presuppositions.

The first chapter engages with patristic theories of the atonement in their relationship to ancient conceptions of justice and law. The significant factor in relationship to this first period is that God and the pagan gods are regarded as being above positive law. The interests of the gods in relation to justice are not first and foremost the preservation of the law. Laws are very much secondary to a justice understood primarily as order. This will be seen to cohere very well with the thought of both Gregory of Nyssa and Augustine.

Chapter 2 reveals a momentous shift that took place in understandings of justice and law. Scholars call this the legal revolution of the twelfth and thirteenth centuries. In both law and theology, justice comes to be approximated as law. Law is now regarded as defining the framework for human and

6. I would have liked, for instance, to include discussions of Irenaeus, Athanasius, Faustus Socinius, Hugo Grotius, Richard Hooker, Karl Barth, and many others. Also missing are much-needed discussions of global theories of the atonement, especially in an African context.

divine relationships. Not surprisingly, atonement theologians like Anselm and Thomas Aquinas in particular reflect this renewed interest in law. This is not to say that the legal revolution yields a uniform effect on atonement theory. Operating from within the same legal revolution, the work of Peter Abelard and John Duns Scotus will reflect their own unique understandings of justice.

The time of the Reformation consolidates the legal revolution began in the twelfth century, but with different emphases. The medieval theology of merit upon which both Anselm's and Aquinas's respective theories of the atonement were built is eroded. But Luther and Calvin display conflicting attitudes toward law. On the one hand, Luther tends to see the law as God's "alien work." Thus Christ's work is not to be understood as serving a logic of the law, but rather as transcending it. On the other hand, Calvin tends to identify law with the very nature of God, leading to the classic doctrine of penal substitution. Thus the third chapter is an extended discussion of Luther's and Calvin's theologies of the cross.

The fourth chapter tackles three modern theologians/philosophers: Immanuel Kant, Friedrich Schleiermacher, and Albrecht Ritschl. Modernity is shown to be a departure from the framework of medieval understandings of justice. The primordial emphasis here becomes moral transformation, especially as expounded by Kant. Both Schleiermacher and Ritschl craft their theological proposals in critical conversation with Kant's philosophy of law and justice.

The penultimate chapter tackles so-called postmodernity. The distinctive characteristic of this period, of tremendous relevance for our topic, is its generalized suspicion of law, especially the ability of law and legal institutions to mediate justice. God himself, then, must not be understood as acting within and thus legitimizing such human systems of justice. Postmodern atonement theories are primarily concerned with nonviolence, including a rejection of the violence of any law. I discuss several theologians in this chapter, from the work of René Girard and S. Mark Heim, to John Milbank's work on the atonement, to the work of Asian American scholars (namely, Andrew Sung Park), to feminist and postcolonial theologians.

The final chapter also serves as a constructive conclusion. I argue that the concept of divine simplicity is particularly relevant for our atonement theories. It both rules out certain theories that prioritize one or another of the divine attributes (whether love or justice), and cautions us about the way we think about the unity of the divine action in Christ. While my conclusions are in general sympathetic to penal substitutionary theory, the way I tell the story of penal substitution will not always be familiar. In other words, I am not arguing that the theory of penal substitution is "the one ring to rule them all," but I would insist on the sine qua non of its main intuitions.

Justice, Law, and the Cross in Patristic Thought

Justice in Ancient Greece and Rome

Ancient Greek and Roman reflection on justice and law is one of the determinative contexts for understanding patristic theories of the atonement. As I pointed out in the introduction, it is not that Hellenistic and Roman jurisprudence and moral philosophy *explain* the emergence of particular atonement theories, in the sense of determining its development. I will show that Christian theologians were not uncritical with respect to this context. Instead, an understanding of such contexts provides us with an insight into the *plausibility* of such contextual atonement theories.

It is a well-known fact that patristic reflection on the cross did not normally take the form of a full-fledged theory of penal substitution, or of a theory of moral example or influence. While some would like to trace the doctrine of penal substitution precisely as understood by Calvin all the way back to Athanasius, Irenaeus, or Augustine, this is usually done at the cost of grossly distorting their thought.[1] Nobody in this period gives any thought

1. See, for example, Steve Jeffery, Michael Ovey, and Andrew Sach, *Pierced for Our Transgressions: Rediscovering the Glory of Penal Substitution* (Wheaton: Crossway, 2007). We can

to the *necessity* of God's prosecuting his retributive justice as a *condition* of his forgiveness. The thought that God could not gratuitously forgive becomes a major assumption of atonement theories only after Anselm's *Cur Deus homo* in the eleventh century. While some in the patristic era held that there were other roadblocks in the way of divine victory, no such obstacle stood in the way of divine forgiveness. God's forgiveness is purely gratuitous (Isa. 43:25; Rom. 5:8, 20) in the sense that he is above any constraints placed on his being from the outside in the exercise of his love. This means that the goings-on at the cross need not be seen as a case of divine punishment administered on the human Son, as a satisfaction of God's retributive justice, which is a necessary condition of the full manifestation of divine love.

A Christian Innovation?

In this gratuitousness of divine love, some authors see a radical departure from the religious and cultural assumptions, typically encapsulated in the principle of *lex talionis*, eye for an eye (Exod. 21:23–24; Lev. 24:20; Deut. 19:21). Such retributive justice, with its assumed necessity of punishment as physical harm proportionate to the crime, is assumed to have been the cultural norm. In such a context, it is argued, the Christian doctrine of love of the enemy appears utterly dissonant. This, then, is supposed to be the great difference that Christianity makes. In a context of reciprocal killing in the name of justice, it offers a vision of justice understood as love and peace.

This case has most recently been made by Nicholas Wolterstorff, who argues that Christianity's greatest contribution, in terms of thinking about justice, is the idea that forgiveness as refusal to demand punishment does not contradict or undermine justice.[2] While ancient culture had an account of "lenient punishment," sometimes praising the importance of equity and mercy in the treatment of the criminal, "nobody in pagan antiquity proposed that it is right sometimes to forgo imposing the appropriate penalty. Some were dubious about equity as opposed to abstract *dikē* in determining proper punishment; nobody was in favor of forgoing the proper punishment."[3] This interpretation tends to focus all attention on a contrast between ancient pagan retribution

---

distinguish between penal substitutionary theory and penal substitutionary themes, the latter of which are undoubtedly present in these early writers, as I shall point out.

2. Nicholas Wolterstorff, *Justice in Love* (Grand Rapids: Eerdmans, 2011). See also his "Does Forgiveness Undermine Justice?," in *God and the Ethics of Belief: New Essays in Philosophy of Religion*, ed. Andrew Dole and Andrew Chignell (Cambridge: Cambridge University Press, 2005). Wolterstorff draws significantly on the work of Martha Nussbaum, "Equity and Mercy," *Philosophy and Public Affairs* 22, no. 2 (1993): 83–125.

3. Wolterstorff, *Justice in Love*, 226–27.

(sometimes tempered by equity) and Christian love and forgiveness, with the implication that Christianity rejects an account of retributive justice *in favor of* love, forgiveness, and peace.

A closer look at "pagan antiquity," however, shows a much messier picture, which in fact greatly reduces the contrast sketched by Wolterstorff. In the first part of this chapter, what I shall endeavor to show is that pagan antiquity did not exclusively favor retribution, as Wolterstorff argues, but that alongside retribution there was precisely the idea of a (divine) gratuitous forgiveness, precisely in the name of peace and order (and thus justice). Pagan antiquity, on the contrary, witnessed a contest between rival conceptions of justice, one of which was precisely that which Wolterstorff thinks was inaugurated by Christianity and Judaism. The plausibility structure of ancient culture, within which the patristic writers operated, clearly contained the idea of gratuitous divine forgiveness. Whether or not this explains the failure of these writers to see retribution in the cross—precisely because they did not necessarily expect God to exact it—is a matter I cannot settle here. But the undeniable fact is that the idea of divine forgiveness that is both unconditional and just (Rom. 3:26) was not at all foreign to ancient culture.[4] It is now time to unpack this historical claim.

I will focus on four distinct writers or schools to demonstrate my case: Homer, Aeschylus, the philosophers Plato and Aristotle, and Roman juris-prudential thought. Needless to say, this does not represent an exhaustive or even fair representation of all the ancients had to say about law and justice. My purpose is much more modest. On the one hand, I wish to substantiate my assertion that gratuitous forgiveness was not absent from ancient culture; on the other, I hope to highlight those jurisprudential and moral principles that patristic writers also embraced or rejected.

We readily think of justice as an attribute of God (Jer. 50:29; Isa. 45:21; Deut. 32:4; Col. 3:25; 2 Thess. 1:6; Heb. 6:10), of human beings, of society, or of actions. Indeed, as our study progresses, one will notice that much of the debate over the atonement is in fact a debate over how justice may be defined, how it applies to God, and how it relates to other divine attributes. It is not by any means an exaggeration to say that the doctrine of the atonement is a consequence of one's understanding of the divine nature.

But before "justice" was thought to be *a quality* that applied to God, it wasn't even a clear concept. The great Hellenist scholar Eric A. Havelock points out that prior to the invention of *dikaiosynē*, that is, until Greek culture matured, justice was not objectified, or reified, into a thing. "*Dikē* and *dikaios*

---

4. Supporters of penal substitution may wish to make an even stronger claim: that the differ-ence and contribution of Christianity consists precisely in its account of how God can forgive without doing violence to justice (namely, by exercising retributive justice).

refer to the maintenance of reciprocal relations of right: they connote 'rights' rather than 'righteousness'; they were indexes of a purely external behavior, whether of gods or of men. With the appearance of *dikaiosynē*, it occurred to some that this kind of reciprocal propriety corresponded to personal virtue, the *property* of an individual."[5] The process we shall chart does indeed lead from Homer to Plato, *from propriety to property*, from justice understood as order to justice internalized as a virtue of the soul.

The Justice of Homer

Homer (9th–8th cent. BC) illustrates much of this early notion of justice as order, as Alasdair MacIntyre notes:[6] To behave according to *dikē* is to fulfill one's role in society. Goodness is predicated of a person simply on the basis of a *fitting performance*. There is no interest in whether motivations for the act are pure or impure but simply in external form, on the propriety of the action. A person can neither demand praise for a good intention nor request forgiveness: "You cannot avoid blame and penalty by pointing out that you could not help doing what you did, that failure was unavoidable."[7]

Often, in such a world, the causes and motivations of one's actions are not simply natural. The gods play an active part in prompting people to certain actions. Importantly, however, this does not nullify responsibility. I am responsible for the external quality of my actions, no matter what inward or supernatural compulsion led to those actions. Hugh Lloyd-Jones makes the same observation. People, he argues, may blame the gods for prompting them to wrong action, but they may never disclaim responsibility for their decision.[8]

The fundamental prerogative of the gods is to preserve the order. As Havelock points out in the same context, "*Dikē* means basically the order of the universe, and in this religion the gods maintain a cosmic order."[9] The gods are not the creators of this order, but they merely enforce it and preserve it. While some authors, such as Demosthenes, ascribe the laws that govern this order to the gods, saying that "every law (*nomos*) is an invention and gift of the gods,"[10] the general

5. Eric A. Havelock, "*Dikaiosynē*: An Essay in Greek Intellectual History," *Phoenix* 23, no. 1 (1969), 51.

6. Alasdair MacIntyre, *A Short History of Ethics: A History of Moral Philosophy from the Homeric Age to the Twentieth Century* (London: Routledge, 1998), 7.

7. Ibid.

8. Hugh Lloyd-Jones, *The Justice of Zeus* (Berkeley: University of California Press, 1983), 161.

9. Ibid.

10. Quoted in Rémi Brague, *The Law of God: The Philosophical History of an Idea* (Chicago: University of Chicago Press, 2007), 21.

assumption in ancient Greece is that the gods only govern and enforce this order, without having created it. According to Rémi Brague, "The laws are imposed on the gods rather than produced by them."[11] "To be sure," Brague points out, "the gods are invoked as guaranteeing sworn rights, and they punish the guilty. But they are not the source of law. A god never issues a commandment."[12]

This is highly significant because it suggests a necessity pressing on the gods themselves. The necessity, however, does not apply to the enforcement of the laws, but to maintaining the order. In other words, while the gods are "sworn" to uphold order among human beings, they do not uphold that order by strict enforcement of the law. This brings us to a tension running throughout legal history between justice—here defined as order—and the laws that govern the affairs of human beings. The gods, as will be shown, sometimes maintain order and peace precisely by choosing to neglect certain laws. This Olympian relaxation of laws, however, should not be mistaken for grace, much less love. For, as Lloyd-Jones points out, while Zeus condescends to punish crimes, "he is not their [human beings'] creator, nor their benevolent father in heaven. . . . The gods govern the universe not in men's interest but in their own, and have no primary concern for human welfare."[13]

According to Homer, the gods prefer to settle disputes by peaceful means rather than legal procedures. While, as we have shown, a notion of retributive justice is clearly in place, it is by no means thought to exhaust the sense of justice. There isn't only one way of dealing justly with a crime, namely, exacting a proportionate amount of harm from the criminal. While such a response to crime is indeed sometimes appropriate, *more often the way of arbitration and peaceful settlement best serves the cause of justice.*

David Luban takes a very hard line on Homer's sense of justice. In *Hymn to Hermes*, Homer's Zeus is concerned above all with harmony and friendship among the Olympians, and not with punishment. While this may seem to pit justice against peace, Luban observes that this dilemma does not arise for the Homeric age because *dikē* was accomplished through peaceful settlement, not legal action.[14] *Dikē*, as Michael Gagarin notes, is society's system for settling disputes peacefully. The legal process in early Greece is thus one of peaceful arbitration.[15]

11. Ibid., 20.
12. Ibid., 22.
13. Lloyd-Jones, *Justice of Zeus*, 161.
14. David Luban, "Some Greek Trials: Order and Justice in Homer, Hesiod, Aeschylus and Plato," *Tennessee Law Review* 54 (1986): 279–326 (here, 280).
15. Michael Gagarin, "*Dikē* in Archaic Greek Thought," *Classical Philology* 69, no. 3 (1974): 186–97.

In Homer, yet also in Aeschylus and Plato, Luban finds the origins of the legal system understood as *an instrument of compromise, as opposed to a dispenser of justice.* Thus, far from operating with a strict conception of retributive justice, Homer in fact greatly weakens the concept, preferring instead modes of settlement that do not involve punishment. We shall find this preference all across Greek culture, all the way up to Plato's explicit repudiation of retributivism.

Hubert Dreyfus and Sean D. Kelly also point out that "Homeric culture repressed the natural tendency toward blood loyalty."[16] The repressed, however, is not necessarily altogether absent. The *Iliad* makes all kinds of cries for a justice of a retributive kind. Achilles fumes over the injustice of Briseis's being taken away from him by Agamemnon, refusing the latter's proposed settlement in a cry for retribution.

> Not if his gifts outnumbered the sea sands
> or all the dust grains in the world could Agamemnon
> ever appease me—not till he pays me back
> full measure, pain for pain, dishonor for dishonor.[17]

In the Greek moral universe, argues James Boyd White, this speech marks the breakdown of the honor world.[18]

Aeschylus's Defense of Peaceful Settlement

By the time of Aeschylus's *Oresteia* (5th cent. BC), the repressed impulses toward vengeance return with a vengeance. The trilogy tells the story of the trial of Orestes, for the crime of matricide. The story, however, begins long before that, with a series of reciprocal killings. As Agamemnon prepares to go to war with Troy, he sacrifices his daughter Iphigenia as a gesture intended to favorably dispose the gods toward him. Clytemnestra, his wife, avenges the death of her daughter by killing Agamemnon upon his return home. While at it, she also kills his mistress, the beautiful Cassandra, a slave brought home from the war. As Orestes himself returns, he finds out about the murder of his father. He is now confronted with a choice. He can either kill his mother in the name of the Furies, as a vengeance demanded by the law

16. Hubert Dreyfus and Sean D. Kelly, *All Things Shining: Reading the Western Classics to Find Meaning in a Secular Age* (New York: Free Press, 2011), 92.

17. Homer, *The Iliad*, ed. Robert Fitzgerald (Oxford: Oxford University Press, 2009), 154.

18. James Boyd White, *When Words Lose Their Meaning: Constitutions and Reconstitutions of Language* (Chicago: University of Chicago Press, 1984), 48–49; see Luban, "Some Greek Trials, 289.

of blood, or he can kill her as a just retribution in the name of the new gods and their universal law, with its stipulations against regicide.[19] He decides for the latter.

The Furies are predictably enraged and seek to take Orestes's life for his crime of matricide. The cycle of violence seems destined to go on and on. It is precisely at this point that Athena intervenes and sets up a court for the purpose of trying Orestes. In the end, Athena manages to save Orestes's life, despite his obvious crime against his mother.

There are all kinds of levels of discourse in the *Oresteia*. One of these is the conflict between two rival conceptions of justice. On the one hand, justice is understood retributively, as *lex talionis*, operating on the principle of vengeance. The Furies (or the Erynies) stand for this principle. Their authority had been denied in the Homeric world. They are understandably outraged.

> We are strong and skilled;
> we have authority; we hold
> memory of evil; we are stern
> nor can man's pleading bend us.

What we have here is an unflinching principle of retribution for each and every crime. Homer's gods, on the one hand, are willing to relax the law in the interests of peace. The Furies, on the other hand, are willing to take the whole world down in the interests of law.

Havelock notes an interesting aspect of this tension. The Furies' complaint is precisely against the younger gods, as opposed to the older gods of revenge and blood feuds: "Their power exceeds their justice."[20] The complaint is precisely that such gods, in being willing to forgive, and able to forgive—that is, in imposing their desire for Orestes not to be punished—are acting unjustly. Thus, one might say, the conflict between the Furies and the younger gods is precisely a conflict over the moral nature of divinity. It is a contest between the gods' power and their justice, long before the thirteenth-century debates between voluntarism and intellectualism.

The appearance of the Furies on the theater stage was recorded as being frightening. It was so horrific that pregnant women witnessing the play were said to give premature birth. There seems to be something demonic about the Furies. On the one hand, they are neither human nor quite divine. But they are a force to be reckoned with even by the gods. While Athena wishes to forgive

---

19. For more on this, see Dreyfus and Kelly, *All Things Shining*, 94.
20. Eric A. Havelock, *The Greek Concept of Justice: From Its Shadow in Homer to Its Substance in Plato* (Cambridge: Harvard University Press, 1978), 285.

Orestes, she knows that she cannot simply dismiss the Furies. Moreover, they are ruthless and will stop at nothing in pursuit of their mission. The Furies also act as great prosecutors, reminding people and gods of trespass and demanding punishment. One may even say that their role is similar to the role of the Satan in the Bible. They are both prosecutors and tormentors. But there is an ambivalence here. While they are truly frightful, they also claim to represent justice. They prosecute in the name of a law sanctioned by the gods themselves. Because the law is their authority, they seem to be entitled to what they are doing. The gods' willingness to relax the law is thus taken as an injustice, which has to be spoken against and opposed. Thus, while the Furies sometimes oppose the gods, they do so in the very name of the gods themselves. They see themselves as the true upholders of the law, which it is the duty of the gods themselves to uphold.

But there is a second, rival conception of justice in the *Oresteia*, and it is this conception—namely, the Homeric sense of justice as propriety—that ultimately prevails. This conception of the law is, according to Luban, "an instrumentalist conception of legal argument and legal institutions."[21] The point of the courts is not to uphold the law for the sake of law but to mediate and arbitrate between competing interests. Public settlement is preferable to private vengeance. Havelock points out that the *Oresteia* signifies a return to a Homeric sense of justice as reciprocal courtesy.[22] He sees the sense of justice as propriety and order to be in contrast with the personified sense of justice that figures earlier in the play as "narrowly punitive."[23]

> The drama thus opposes justice to justice; the language employed leaves this in no doubt. One part of the action—the major part—celebrates justice as applied in a legal procedure, and dramatizes its effects. A second part—communicated in the language of the chorus and also their acts—celebrates a justice which is injured, perhaps destroyed, in the course of the same events.[24]

Only on pain of neglecting some important evidence could one claim, then, that ancient Greek justice did not make room for forgiveness. On the contrary, at least up to Aeschylus, as Orestes himself puts it, "Justice collides with justice."[25] But it is undeniable that the gods are regarded as being more

21. Luban, "Some Greek Trials," 312.
22. Havelock, *Greek Concept of Justice*, 288.
23. Ibid.
24. Ibid., 286.
25. Aeschylus, *Choephori* 461. In *Principalities and Powers: A Study in Pauline Theology* (Oxford: Clarendon, 1956), G. B. Caird argues that "five centuries before Paul came to Athens

than willing to relax the law, precisely in the interest of justice (as peace and order).

Plato and Aristotle

As Greek culture matures in the thought of the philosophers, justice becomes a virtue of the soul. Plato (4th cent. BC) is unsatisfied with the Homeric moral discourse, which was content to address justice as it emerged in particular situations. As MacIntyre notes, "Part of his strategy is to expel the Homeric inheritance from the city-state."[26] Havelock too comments on Plato's astonishing hostility to poetry, to Homer, and in particular to Greek drama. "Plato has in fact stated that justice must occupy a dimension, not previously sanctioned by tradition, which will ever afterward confer on it a bifocal meaning: the justice of a community, a social morality, and the justice of the soul, a personal morality."[27] Plato's great discovery is that morality cannot attach simply to the exterior form of action. One may accomplish one's duty in society out of fear, or out of some kind of ulterior purpose. Those motivations, while hidden from the public eye, are relevant to the moral life. To Havelock's social morality corresponds the notion of a public justice, which Plato still very much understands as order. But people will not be regarded as just persons simply on account of carrying out their proper role. Only insofar as they possess the quality of justice can they be regarded as just.

Aristotle (4th cent. BC) retains Plato's insight that, as the application of law serves the interests of justice, it must maintain these distinctions. His criminal law distinguishes between different types of acts precisely in terms of the subjective attitudes that accompany them. Such attitudes could be either negligence, accident, or tort. Torts themselves are divided into those committed by passion and those resulting from free choice. For Aristotle, as well as Plato, such factors may call for leniency in the application of the law.

For Plato, justice remains clearly associated with order, but that order is both outward and inward. Wolterstorff describes this position: "Justice is present in society, on the right order way of thinking, insofar as the society measures up to whatever is the standard for the rightly ordered society. The Greek tradition inherited by Plato thought of the gods as having established an order for human beings that the Greeks called justice. Injustice is a departure from

---

Aeschylus in the *Prometheus Vinctus* and the *Oresteia* had made Greece aware of the conflict between divine goodness and divine justice" (50).

26. Alasdair MacIntyre, *After Virtue: A Study in Moral Theory* (Notre Dame, IN: University of Notre Dame Press, 1985), 131.

27. Havelock, *Greek Concept of Justice*, 312.

dikē, departure from cosmic order."[28] Plato is quite explicit that the social and outward order must be reflected in an inner equilibrium:

> In reality, justice pertains not to the outward action (performed) upon one's (concerns), but to the inner, that which really pertains to oneself and to the self's concerns; the individual avoids allowing the elements in the soul to mind each other's business and get involved with each other: he actually makes a proper disposition of (what is) personal to him: he personally assumes command and organizes himself and becomes friend to himself.[29]

What is the function of law within such an account of justice as fundamentally inner order? Will Plato retain Homer's preference for peace and friendship, or will he revert to the Furies' legalistic punishment? In fact, while Plato and Aristotle ascribe importance to law, neither regards the law as a universal fit for every person and situation. Instead, both advocate the importance of discerning the particulars of each situation in the name of equity.

Plato regards the fundamental function of the law as being primarily educational. Positive law cannot conflict with the idea of justice. The aim of the law is to make people good. For Plato, the concepts of justice and goodness are related to that of order. As Carl Joachim Friedrich explains, "Plato later returned to the traditional Greek doctrine according to which a good order of the *polis* could be secured only by the making of a basic law or *nomos*. But this *nomos* is seen by Plato as a participation in the idea of justice, and through this participation it, in turn, participates in the idea of the good."[30] What this means is that "law is, like all things in this world, merely a phantom bridge for the wise in their search for eternal verities and values."[31]

Aristotle adds to this educational function that of maintaining peace and arbitrating controversies. Thus, although law is connected to justice, and justice is understood fundamentally as order, *neither Plato nor Aristotle approaches a legalism that demands retribution in the name of a universal principle*. The law is nothing but a means, a historically conditioned means, for the achievement of virtue. Neither philosopher goes as far as to say that law is nothing but a servant of the interests of the ruling class (legal positivism), but neither do they describe the law as the absolutely binding norm, whose trespass automatically must be punished, on pain of injustice.

28. Nicholas Wolterstorff, *Justice: Rights and Wrongs* (Princeton: Princeton University Press, 2010), 30.

29. Plato, *Republic* 443c.9, quoted in Havelock, *Greek Concept of Justice*, 322.

30. Carl Joachim Friedrich, *The Philosophy of Law in Historical Perspective* (Chicago: University of Chicago Press, 1963), 17.

31. Ibid., 18.

The fundamental aim of the law being primarily education, and sometimes arbitration, it is only just that the law may sometimes be relaxed, if this will better serve these purposes. Aristotle pleads for an attention to the particulars of each case:

> It is equitable to pardon human weaknesses and to look not to the law but to the legislator, not to the letter of the law but to the intention of the legislator, not to the acts themselves but to the moral purpose, not to the part but to the whole, not to what a man is now but to what he has been always or generally, to remember good rather than ill treatment and benefits received rather than those conferred, to bear injury with patience, to be willing to appeal to the judgment of reason rather than to violence, to prefer arbitration to the law court, for the arbitrator keeps equity in view, whereas the judge looks only to the law.[32]

Plato too is quite explicitly rejecting a conception of justice as paying back in kind. Such a conception is articulated by Polemarchus in *The Republic*: "It is just to do good to your friends when they are good and harm to your enemies when they are evil."[33] Socrates objects that such an application of the law would make your enemy even more evil. In other words, such an application of justice, although it may be in strict conformity with the law, will not contribute to the development of the virtue of justice in the soul of one's enemy. Socrates replies: "To injure a friend or anyone else is not the act of a just man, but of the opposite, who is the unjust."[34] Doing harm to a friend or enemy would only be just if it created the quality of *dikaiosynē* in him. Thus retribution for retribution's sake, in the name of the application of a universal law, is not justice. The larger aim of rehabilitation and education has to be kept in mind.

Retributive justice fails, according to Plato, since "what's done can't be undone."[35] In the *Protagoras* Plato argues that "he who desires to inflict rational punishment does not punish for the sake of a past wrong which cannot be undone; he has regard to the future and is desirous that the man who is punished, and he who sees him punished, may be deterred from doing wrong again."[36] The only possible purpose of punishment is rehabilitation. In this

---

32. Aristotle, *Rhetoric* 1.13.13 (trans. W. Rhys Roberts [New York: Dover, 2004]).

33. Plato, *Republic* 1.335 (in *Dialogues of Plato*, trans. Benjamin Jowett, vol. 2 [Cambridge: Cambridge University Press, 2010]).

34. Plato, *Republic* 1.335.

35. Plato, *Laws* 933d–34a.

36. Plato, *Protagoras* 324b (in *Protagoras, Philebus, and Gorgias*, trans. Benjamin Jowett [New York: Prometheus, 1996]).

no effort should be spared: "We may absolutely use any means to make him hate injustice and embrace true justice."[37]

To conclude our commentary on Plato and Aristotle, it is evident that both philosophers steer clear of legalism and retributivism. Both, moreover, affirm a concern for the equitable treatment of the criminal. Sometimes this involves reformatory punishment, and sometimes forgiveness. So much are they willing to place the interests of peace and friendship over those of just retribution that Luban feels compelled to talk of "the triumph of instrumentalism" in Plato.[38]

The Stoics and Roman Law

There is an important continuity between the Greek and Roman conceptions of law and justice. Brague observes that

> Rome's conception of "divine law" was similar in sentiment to the Greek. It even presupposed something like a desacralization: divine law was not law revealed by the gods but was rather the right of humans to establish with the gods a system of predictable relations. When Rome and Hellenism combined forces, they both considered (or would have considered) ridiculous the Jewish idea of the gods dictating a path of action to be followed and behavior to be observed—the *halakhah* of the Jews or the *sharia* of Islam—as a matter of principle and in all circumstances.[39]

For both Romans and Greeks, argues Brague, the law is not the invention of the gods. It is not a product of the will of the deity, but of reason. Thus the law is transparent; it can be read off of nature. Brague makes the interesting comment that for the Greeks, and Sophocles in particular, anything that is written cannot be divine.

Robert W. Shaffern echoes the same sense of continuity between Greece and Rome: "Most of the formulations which we encounter [in Roman law] are in fact those which had already been set forth by Plato and Aristotle, and yet there is an important difference between the legal conceptions of the Roman jurists and those of Plato and Aristotle."[40] He goes on to explain that "the Stoics [ca. 300 BC onward] exploded the framework of the polis which had

---

37. Plato, *Laws* 862d, quoted in Leslie Rubin, *Justice v. Law in Greek Political Thought* (Lanham, MD: Rowman & Littlefield, 1997), 257.

38. Luban, "Some Greek Trials," 313–21.

39. Brague, *Law of God*, 22–23.

40. Robert W. Shaffern, *Law and Justice from Antiquity to Enlightenment* (Lanham, MD: Rowman & Littlefield, 2008), 27.

been beyond argument for Plato and Aristotle and proclaimed mankind as the all embracing community."[41]

Julius Stone adds a second distinction: "Greek law scarcely survived as a system because it never found its class of legal specialists, or abandoned its lay administrators or its popular tribunals of grotesque size; while Roman law developed through the efforts of jurisconsults and praetors into a permanent heritage of Western society."[42] One might say that while for the Greeks the law was subordinated to the aims of the city, as supervised by the philosopher kings, in Rome law managed to acquire sufficient autonomy (and power) and therefore developed as a sui generis enterprise, created its own class of scholars, and managed a whole bureaucratic system. The West was quickly emerging, under the rule of the Roman Empire, as a judicial society under the rule of law. As the Roman Empire was expanding, the old Roman civil law, which was primitive and based on clan organization, became unusable and had to be transformed in the process and adapted to the new demands. Stone points out that this process of adapting was centered on the attempt to discover the common universal principles under all laws. Moreover, "in the background of this practical achievement was the naturalization into Roman intellectual life of Stoic philosophy, as a result of the close contacts with Greek philosophical thought which accompanied the spread of Roman domination."[43]

Stoicism regarded law as an expression of the immanent divine (*logos*), present in the world and animating it. It gave enormous impetus to the idea of a natural law, a law "not prosecuted as the expression of an explicit will," whether a divine command or the will of the rulers, "but rather as issuing from the intimate depths of things, as an emanation of what is most inherent in them."[44]

Greek ideas of equity and mercy remained influential in Roman law. This is evident from a cursory reading of the *Digest*.[45] Jurists like Ulpian and Papinian insisted that equity, leniency, and liberality inform all judicial proceedings. They also insisted on due attention being paid to the spirit of the law as well as to its letter. Moreover, generosity was to inform all legal proceedings. Thus, for instance, "in a case where the wish of the manumitter is uncertain, preference is to be given to liberty," which is more desirable than anything. In respect

41. Ibid., 28.
42. Julius Stone, *Human Law and Human Justice* (Stanford, CA: Stanford University Press, 1965), 39–40.
43. Ibid., 40.
44. Brague, *Law of God*, 29.
45. The *Digest* is the lengthiest part of the *Corpus iuris civilis*, a codification of Roman law commissioned by Justinian I (527–65), and it contains fragments from the second-century classical jurists. The other parts of the "Civil Law" were the *Institutes*, the *Code*, and the *Novels*. For an excellent introduction, see Shaffern, *Law and Justice*, 68.

of punishments, these "should be as lenient as justice permitted. In doubtful cases, the more generous view is always to be preferred."[46]

The Justification of Divine Deceit in Gregory of Nyssa (ca. 335–ca. 395)

As we have seen, the cultural milieu of patristic Christianity was freighted with reflection on justice, the place of law in relation to justice, and the relation between the divinity and human justice. I have argued that far from embracing a clearly retributive vision of justice, classical thought wrestled with competing understandings of what it means to rightly respond to wrongdoing. What predominates in the writers canvassed, rather, are the peaceful, restorative, and reconciliatory aims of justice, to the detriment of strict retribution demanded by the law. While Aeschylus gives a voice to the repressed notion of vengeance and automatic punishment, such impulses are rationalized into an Athenian legal institution that incorporates fear but whose main aim remains peaceful settlement of conflict. *The Greeks did not have a problem with the relaxation of laws as a way of achieving peace, even as they remained fully aware of the repressed cries for retribution.* One of the reasons why retribution was not automatic is the influence of the passions, of all kinds of compulsion pressing on the free will of the moral agent. Orestes murders his mother at the incitement of Apollo. While his action remains free and responsible, he acts under the influence of a pressing demand of a particular bond (blood relation to father, duty to obey the gods), against the demand of another one (his blood relation to his mother, duty to and fear of the Furies). Indeed, in Greek drama humanity is often described as existing at the intersection of cosmic forces that impose conflicting desires and ideals on men. Aeschylus is one of the first to give voice to these (sometimes inward) passions, intentions, and deliberations; and Athena's verdict validates them as morally relevant. Plato, then, while rejecting the form of moral discourse he finds in Homer, nevertheless retains its main thrust and abstracts these narrative directions into clear and distinct ideas. Justice continues to serve the interests of peace, with equity and mercy being important components of the very concept of justice, rather than being opposed to it.

Satan as the Avenger of Justice

It is not at all surprising that the dominant patristic conception of the atonement, the so-called ransom theory, would be at home in such a culture.

---

46. All of the above, from Shaffern, *Law and Justice*, 83, who quotes from the *Digest*.

Several historians have noted this parallel. F. W. Dillistone connects the idea of ransom—which, loosely described, is the idea that the atonement consists in Christ's paying a ransom (Mark 10:45) that frees us from the domination of Satan—with the fear and apprehension that were characteristic of life in the Mediterranean world.[47] Alden A. Mosshammer, in a wonderful piece on the thought of Gregory of Nyssa in the context of Hellenistic culture, also notes the tension in pre-Hellenistic thought between freedom and necessity, fundamentally the tension between human freedom and external necessity. He points out that "every action of the Homeric epic is the result of an interplay between human purpose and divine purpose," and thus the conflict arises because "men are free, purposeful beings who are denied the power to realize their own nature. So profound is this sense of frustration that the Greeks depict even the gods as subject to the whimsical dictates of fate."[48]

Patristic atonement theories are therefore cast on a cosmic canvas of "the powers of this dark world" and "the spiritual forces of evil in the heavenly realms" (Eph. 6:12). The relevant actors are not simply the sinner and the Triune God. Satan is himself one of the protagonists. The context is dualistic, and the role of Satan is very complex. Much like that of the Furies, the role of Satan is ambivalent. Gustaf Aulén, the theologian who has perhaps done the most to resurrect interest in what he calls "the classic" view of the atonement, identifies this "double-sidedness" as essential to the classic view: the powers over which victory is won are at the same time the executants of God's judgment (Job 1:6; Luke 4:6; 1 Cor. 5:5; 1 Tim. 1:20) on sinful humanity.[49] Not only is the devil, the prince of death and destruction, the enemy that must be defeated, but also his claims are not groundless. This ambivalence about Satan, however, is also an ambivalence about God. Aulén does not shy away from this conclusion: "God is at once the author and the object of reconciliation; He is reconciled in the act of reconciling the world to Himself."[50] As John Chrysostom has it in his commentary on Col. 2:14: "The devil held that bond that God made with Adam."[51] He thus had the right and the power, assigned to him by God, of punishing humanity with death.

47. F. W. Dillistone, *The Christian Understanding of Atonement* (Philadelphia: Westminster, 1968), 92.

48. A. A. Mosshammer, "Gregory of Nyssa and Christian Hellenism," *Studia patristica* 32 (1997): 170–95 (here 173).

49. Gustaf Aulén, *Christus Victor: An Historical Study of the Three Main Types of the Idea of the Atonement*, trans. A. G. Hebert (New York: Macmillan, 1969), 56.

50. Ibid.

51. John Chrysostom, *Homily* 6, on Col. 2:6–7 (in *Nicene and Post-Nicene Fathers of the Christian Church*, series 1, ed. Philip Schaff [1885–89; repr., Peabody, MA: Hendrickson, 1994], 13:286).

This aspect is extremely significant, and in fact it indicates that the medieval and Reformational emphasis on propitiation is simply another conceptualization of an intuition shared with the ancient Christian theologians.[52] These patristic theologians, however, were reluctant to pursue this intuition too deeply. Most of the time they were content to externalize the wrath and retributive justice of God onto Satan. They stressed that Satan had "rights"—that is, he was in some respect entitled to his destructive actions—much like the Furies were both entitled to theirs and yet could still be detested by the gods, represented here by Apollo: "Heaven loathes you. . . . No god loves such as you!"[53]

Some, like I. A. Dorner, go even further, suggesting that "the idea of substitution is common to all the fathers" and "the necessity of mortal suffering is always brought in some way, directly or indirectly, into connection with the divine justice."[54] Indeed, sin is precisely what justifies Satan to act in his retributive role as the one "who holds the power of death" (Heb. 2:14). But it is highly significant that the office of avenger of justice is precisely Satan's and not God's. Surely such pretense could only resist for so long before the demand for greater precision exposed its inadequacy. Satan is only the executant of God's justice, and thus the fundamental problem of the atonement cannot be about the defeat of Satan *simpliciter*, as if his office did not have divine sanction. Dorner points out that it is ultimately God who remains sovereign and that the satanic bondage is ultimately tied to sin and guilt: "For it is only guilt and sin, personal or inherited, which justly incurs God's displeasure. Further, it is only through God's displeasure that Satan possesses power over men, while this power again is displayed in death, which is inflicted by Satan, as well as in the dominion of sin."[55] It will be primarily thinkers in the West, beginning with Augustine, who will increasingly do justice to this fundamental feature. Until the Middle Ages, as Dorner comments, "the central-point of the ruin from which deliverance is necessary" was Satan.[56] The early fathers either did not perceive this connection between satanic dominion and divine retribution, or they were reluctant to follow it through and thus minimized it. They remained singularly focused on the dominion of Satan and of death.

Dorner goes so far as to argue that this is the reason for the persistent dualism of the classic theory. The fathers realized the importance of the penal

52. For an excellent analysis of the trajectories of patristic soteriological thought, see Donald Fairbairn, "Patristic Soteriologies: Three Trajectories," *Journal of the Evangelical Theological Society* 50, no. 2 (2007): 289–310.
53. Aeschylus, *Eumenides* 168–98.
54. I. A. Dorner, *A System of Christian Doctrine* (Edinburgh: T&T Clark, 1890), 4:8–9.
55. Ibid., 4:10.
56. Ibid., 4:11.

dimension but were reluctant to describe God as directly punishing the Son, since this would have jeopardized divine love. Thus they used Satan as a proxy. "But when punitive justice was placed in Satan, outside God, it was made to appear as if justice were not an objective determination of the divine essence, as if God might be reconciled with sinners without further ado, provided Satan's right and power were out of the way."[57]

If one equates justice with retributive justice, as Calvin in particular does (and Dorner following him), then Dorner might be right that, in the classic view, justice would be rendered an inessential attribute of God. But if our description of the ancient thinking about justice is right, then strictly speaking it is only retributive justice that is thus removed from God's very essence, not justice as such. In this case the fathers were simply echoing, as one should expect, a common understanding of justice, which pushed retribution into the background while foregrounding peace and forgiveness.

Defeating Satan

While the most common view among the fathers was that the devil had rights, some dissent is also recorded. Augustine denies this and affirms that Satan's power was delegated. Then there was also the view of the devil as a usurper. On the whole, however, the devil was regarded as having some rightful dominion over us. Athanasius subscribes to this position, and so does Irenaeus. The latter stresses the limited but real suzerainty of Satan and that this limited the options for how he should be defeated. In one voice, the fathers stress the importance of human responsibility in this. Irenaeus encapsulates this conviction: "The devil could not be justly arraigned for a disaster in human affairs to which man himself had given his assent."[58]

For Irenaeus, it was essential that God's victory over Satan would use means completely opposite to Satan's grasp of power over humanity. This could not happen "by violent means, as the [apostasy] had obtained dominion over us at the beginning, when it insatiably snatched away what was not its own, but by means of persuasion as became a God of counsel, who does not use violent means to obtain what he desires; so that neither should justice be infringed on, nor the ancient handiwork of God go to destruction."[59]

With violence being excluded as an option, some bargain had to be struck with the devil. While Irenaeus affirms that Christ appears incognito, it is

---

57. Ibid., 4:13.
58. Quoted in Dillistone, *Christian Understanding of Atonement*, 95.
59. Irenaeus, *Haer.* 5.1.1 (in *Ante-Nicene Fathers*, ed. Alexander Roberts and James Donaldson [1885–87; repr., Peabody, MA: Hendrickson, 1994], 527).

unclear whether Irenaeus envisaged a transaction with the devil.[60] Origen, however, does not have any reservations. He takes the metaphor of ransom literally, asking to whom the ransom was paid and answering that a transaction with Satan took place, in which Satan, unaware of Christ's divinity, asked for the blood of Christ and therefore was deceived into committing the ultimate suicidal act. The devil was therefore intentionally deceived by an incognito Christ. Origen does not bother to justify this act of divine deception, even though he clearly implies that God was responsible for it.

Here, then, we have one of the most popular motifs of the ransom theory, the idea of the divine ensnaring of Satan. Dillistone tells us that "the hook and bait motif [Job 40:24–41:1 (40:24–25 MT); Ps. 22:6] is the most popular of all" motifs used by the church. There were other such images: the cross as a net for catching birds, the cross as a mousetrap, and so on. These provided what some would call the backbone and others would regard as ornaments of a theory that survived with "little serious criticism"[61] until its disassembly by Anselm in the eleventh century. It provided countless artists with primary motifs, and it inspired generations of worshipers.

The divine deception motif received its most explicit defense from Gregory of Nyssa. Briefly summarized, the theory holds that Satan is tricked by God into accepting the body of Christ in return for the souls of human beings, which he held under his control. Satan accepts the ransom and kills Christ, oblivious to the fact that he had no right to kill a sinless person. Having thus committed the ultimate sin, and having overextended his authority, he is rightfully deprived of it.

The Morality of Divine Deceit

It is understandable that such a theory would eventually run up against serious criticism. Nor is it hard to anticipate what the critiques will focus on. Dorner argues that "the deceptive craft, although represented as military strategy, fails to harmonize with the divine holiness."[62] Numerous such critiques have been formulated.[63] More charitable interpreters fasten on the

---

60. Laurence William Grensted, *A Short History of the Doctrine of the Atonement* (Manchester: Manchester University Press, 1920), 34.

61. Aulén, *Christus Victor*, 48.

62. Dorner, *System of Christian Doctrine*, 4:12.

63. Hastings Rashdall calls Gregory of Nyssa's theory "childish and immoral" (*The Idea of Atonement in Christian Theology* [New York: Macmillan, 1919], 364). Also see J. A. MacCullough, *The Harrowing of Hell: A Comparative Study of an Early Christian Doctrine* (Edinburgh: T&T Clark, 1930), 205; Aulén, *Christus Victor*, 47; Georges Florovsky, *The Eastern Fathers of the Fourth Century* (1933; repr., Belmont: Notable & Academic Books, 1987), 195. For a more

patently metaphorical nature of the idea. Colin Gunton, for example, insists that there is still some value in this kind of language, provided it is not taken literally. Not only is the idea of divine deceit problematic, but the very language of the demonic raises questions: "The language of possession by demonic forces, then, is used to express the helplessness of human agents in the face of psychological, social, and cosmic forces in various combinations."[64] Aulén, a fan of the classic model, is clearly embarrassed. The language can only be redeemed if we penetrate "to that which lies below the outward dress, and look for the religious values which lie underneath."[65] He does not know how to respond to the charges except by appealing to the larger religious point, as opposed to taking the expressions literally: "Behind all the seemingly fantastic speculations lies the thought that the power of evil ultimately overreaches itself when it comes into conflict with the power of good, with God himself. It loses the battle at the moment when it seems to be victorious."[66] Finally, Hans Boersma argues that what justifies divine deception is the saving intent of God.[67]

Interestingly, all of these sympathetic critics seem to be at a loss to properly justify this procedure of the divine victory, thus failing to explain the immense success and popularity of the idea. It is not as if patristic writers like Gregory of Nyssa were not interested in the idea of divine justice or divine holiness. In fact, as other critics point out, this was precisely one of their main concerns. Hence the best way to defend the procedure of divine deceit is to show that it was fully consonant with the notion of justice as understood by the Greeks. The theologians who did not bother to justify it may have not felt the need for this, having taken the idea for granted. Moreover, theologians like Gregory of Nyssa, who does make an attempt to justify it, appeal precisely to those aspects of justice that we have canvassed in the previous section.

In an important article, Nicholas Constas convincingly shows that divine deception was certainly not a problematic concept in Hellenistic culture. "Since classical antiquity," he writes, "the use of deception was sanctioned as an acceptable pedagogical, strategic, and therapeutic device." This "blended readily

thorough list, see Nicholas P. Constas, "The Last Temptation of Satan: Divine Deception in Greek Patristic Interpretations of the Passion Narrative," *Harvard Theological Review* 97, no. 2 (April 2004): 139–63 (here 145–46); repr. from *Greek Orthodox Theological Review* 47, nos. 1–4 (2002): 237–74.

64. Colin Gunton, *The Actuality of the Atonement: A Study in Metaphor, Rationality, and the Christian Tradition* (New York: Continuum, 2003), 66.

65. Aulén, *Christus Victor*, 47.

66. Ibid., 55.

67. Hans Boersma, *Violence, Hospitality, and the Cross: Reappropriating the Atonement Tradition* (Grand Rapids: Baker Academic, 2004), 193.

with the popular Platonic belief that the world of truth was different from the world of appearances (1 Cor. 2:7; 2 Cor. 3:6). The world of appearances was a world of change and flux. It was an empire of signs, inherently unstable, ambiguous, dissembling, and transitive. It was, in a word, deceptive, and any figure incarnate in that world was just as likely to conceal the truth as to reveal it."[68] Constas goes on to observe that when Plato is questioned about whether the greatest Homeric hero is the honorable Achilles ("true and simple") or Odysseus the liar ("wily and false"), he gives the crown to Odysseus, "arguing that only the liar knows what the truth is." Moreover, "given their Olympian grasp of eternal verities, there was no end of lying and trickery among the Greek and Roman gods, and disguise and deceit is typically not a human but a divine strategy, a divine deception."[69]

Constas may be a bit heavy-handed in his projection of the Platonic theory of forms onto the Christian theology of Gregory of Nyssa. While the sensible world is indeed one of flux, the fact of the incarnation also means that this world is capable of receiving a revelation of divine truth. Indeed, while Jesus conceals his identity from Satan, he does not conceal it from his disciples. Thus, if there is an intended deception, it is not an inescapable one, due somehow to the finite medium of revelation. Nevertheless, Constas does us an invaluable service in pointing out the plausibility and acceptability of divine deception in the ancient world.

Justice and Power

Not only is divine deception reasonably unproblematic in Hellenistic culture, but Gregory of Nyssa also expends considerable effort to provide further justification for it. So much so, in fact, that critics like Anthony Meredith interpret Gregory's God as "hampered by the consideration of human justice." He goes on to observe that "what is remarkable is that nowhere does Gregory appeal to the sovereign power of God in his account of the redemption of the world. Gregory's God must always work within the rules established by the harmony of the four attributes, that is, by his known and inferable nature."[70] Ironically, Dorner's assessment is exactly opposite; he judges that the power of God, rather than justice, dominates the patristic accounts of ransom, Gregory included. "This application, although starting from the idea of justice, makes the divine majesty and power, not justice, finally decide the victory of Christ;

---

68. Constas, "Last Temptation of Satan," *Greek Orthodox Theological Review* 47:241.

69. Ibid. Alasdair MacIntyre (*Short History of Ethics*, 4) also remarks that in the *Odyssey*, cunning is treated unambiguously as a virtue.

70. Anthony Meredith, *Gregory of Nyssa* (London: Routledge, 2003), 84.

and the deceptive craft, although presented as a military strategy, fails to harmonize with the divine holiness."[71]

So which is it? Gregory is in fact explicit about the necessity of the atonement's proceeding according to justice. First, Gregory echoes the restrictions against divine violence we saw in Irenaeus above:

> If any one out of regard for the person who has so sold himself should use violence against him who bought him, he will clearly be acting unjustly in thus arbitrarily rescuing one who has legally been purchased as a slave. . . . On the same principle, now that we had voluntarily bartered away our freedom, it was requisite that no arbitrary method of recovery, but one consonant with justice, should be devised by Him Who in His goodness had undertaken our rescue.[72]

As a matter of principle, therefore, God's actions must be consonant with justice.

But what is justice? Gregory defines it clearly: "The essential qualities of justice and wisdom are before all things these; viz., of justice, to give to everyone according to his due; of wisdom, not to pervert justice, and yet at the same time not to dissociate the benevolent aim of the love of mankind from the verdict of justice, but skillfully to combine both these requisites together, in regard to justice returning due recompense, in regard to kindness not swerving from the aim of the love of man." The idea of "to each his own due" spells out a distributive theory of justice, perfectly consonant with the Platonic ideal of order. Thus, "he who practised deception receives in turn that very treatment, the seeds of which he had himself sown of his own free will."[73]

Constas also notices the consonance between this deception and the principle of distributive justice. "Gregory argues that it was only right that an act of deception should be undone by an act of deception, a notion that accords with the 'riddling definition of justice used by the poets' outlined by Plato in the *Republic*."[74] Constas then mentions, in addition to this fit, that this divine deceit was also enacted for therapeutic purposes, Satan himself being ultimately redeemed. The reader, however, should not get the impression that what justifies divine deceit is simply the "riddling definition of justice," to each his due. In fact, as we have seen, Plato, through the voice of Socrates, explicitly disclaims such a vision of justice. Returning to each in kind will sometimes fail to create

---

71. Dorner, *System of Christian Doctrine*, 4:12.
72. Gregory of Nyssa, *Oratio catechetica magna* 22.
73. Ibid., 26.
74. Constas, "Last Temptation of Satan," *Greek Orthodox Theological Review* 47:243.

in that person the virtue of justice, which alone would morally justify that act. Thus Satan's ultimate redemption is not simply a bonus consequence of an already-just act (deceiving the deceiver), but the very condition required for the moral acceptability of that deceit.

Thus some of the fundamental attributes of God cohere in his saving work: "His choosing to save man is a testimony to his goodness; His making the redemption of the captive a matter of exchange exhibits his justice; while the invention whereby he enabled the enemy to apprehend that of which he was before incapable, is a manifestation of supreme wisdom."[75] God's wisdom is displayed in his employing a principle that appears both necessary, "in order to secure that the ransom in our behalf might be easily accepted by him who required it,"[76] and acceptable according to the canons of justice.

It is not hard to see why such a position would give rise to such antithetical reactions. On the one hand, theologians more inclined toward the retributive and the forensic, like Dorner, are dissatisfied by the absence of the divine retributive element from this theory. This is precisely what makes it so appealing to feminist-inclined thinkers like Frances Young, for example: "By stressing God's redemptive love . . . and rationalizing his wrath, [Origen and Gregory of Nyssa] produced a theory of atonement which was on the face of it more consistent, avoiding the notion of propitiation and stressing God's victory over evil."[77] On the other hand, "moral example" fans like Hastings Rashdall argue instead that excessive attention is paid precisely *to* the satisfaction of divine justice, leading to such horrible conclusions and abominable imagery.

For this latter group, the most troubling aspect of Gregory's theory is the equal stress he places on divine goodness/love, on the one hand, and divine justice, on the other hand. To these moral exemplarists,[78] imposing such a correlation on divine love and divine justice, to which one may add a whole series of divine attributes (holiness, wrath, mercy, wisdom, etc.) represents an ultimately Platonic influence that must be excised from theology. In fact, Meredith is attempting to describe Gregory as a Platonist who is more influenced by a Platonic than by a Pauline understanding of God. Talking about his theology of the divine attributes, he finds it important that "in his treatment of these issues the terms of the debate are dictated by an idea of the Deity which owes as much to Plato and Origen's adaptation of Plato in, for example, his *Contra Celsum* 3.70, as it does to any specifically Jewish or Christian account

75. Gregory of Nyssa, *Or. cat.* 23.

76. Ibid., 24.

77. Quoted in Morwenna Ludlow, *Gregory of Nyssa: Ancient and (Post)Modern* (Oxford: Oxford University Press, 2007), 112.

78. I am calling them moral exemplarists quite loosely, as chap. 4 (below) will clarify.

of the Godhead." By contrast, Meredith points to Paul and Augustine: "For neither of these writers is God, as it were, 'hampered' by the consideration of human justice. For them the thought of philosophically conceived justice as outlined, for instance, in book 5 of the *Nicomachean Ethics* of Aristotle, seems not to affect their perception of the idea of the divine justice and election."[79]

Augustine's Teaching on the Cross (354–430)

Does the pattern of a nonretributive justice hold up in Augustine? The Western and Eastern traditions have often been distinguished from each other by characterizing the West as having a more juridical emphasis. On one level this is certainly true. But it can also be misleading if it is taken to mean that Eastern theology did not equally prioritize justice. What we find instead is that both traditions regard God as just—and indeed, both generally prioritize justice—but they employ competing definitions and emphases of justice. The judicial apparatus in the East differs from that in the West, with the West developing as its hallmark a whole class of jurists and an institution of law that will persist through the centuries following the sacking of Rome, eventually to be rediscovered around the twelfth century.

Human and Divine Justice

While both traditions are concerned to affirm that "the LORD is a God of justice" (Isa. 30:18), Augustine does make a departure from the assumption that divine justice is mappable onto human justice. If one could say about Gregory of Nyssa, with a certain caution, that he sees continuity between divine justice and human understandings of justice, and that divine justice is transparent to human reason, Augustine is much more cautious on this point. He affirms the continuity between divine and human justice on one level, but denies it on another. On the one hand, Augustine affirms a distributive notion of justice according to which each must receive their due. This is manifested both in the just retribution that is due all humankind in virtue of Adamic sin (Rom. 5:12) and in the practice of penance, which is predicated on the assumption that God will eventually save those who persevere (Phil. 2:12), that is, those who ultimately do what lies within them to do. Both of these theological loci presuppose a continuity with human intuitions of justice: first, we deserve to be punished for our transgressions; and second, God is ultimately justified in

79. Meredith, *Gregory of Nyssa*, 75. For a defense of Gregory, see Andrew Radde-Gallwitz, *Basil of Caesarea, Gregory of Nyssa, and the Transformation of Divine Simplicity* (Oxford: Oxford University Press, 2009).

accepting us partly on the basis of our own effort in transforming ourselves. This takes place through the practice of penance, although it presupposes the priority of divine grace.

This brings us to the dissonance from human conceptions of justice, for Augustine's doctrine of election is explicitly intended to contradict these. He rejects the Ciceronian understanding of justice as giving "to each their due." Commenting on the parable of the vineyard laborers (Matt. 20:1–16), Augustine shows that God's justice does not consist in his rewarding people's merits but in fidelity to his promise of grace.[80]

The political consequences of Augustine's departure from Cicero are also important for our study. The latter had defined the state as "a multitude bound together by a mutual recognition of rights and a mutual cooperation for the common good." Justice, for Cicero, is the actual ordering of society so that it will reflect this "common interest" and this "mutual recognition of rights." As such, justice depends simply on a rational recognition of this *iuris consensus*. In critiquing Cicero's political thought, Augustine offers one of the first realist critiques of politics. He argues that actual states can and have been formed around much less lofty ideals than justice. In fact, he argues, there has never been the kind of republic that Cicero describes. Men unite not only around ideal virtues but also around utilitarian interests that may have nothing to do with justice. Mary T. Clark captures this Augustinian realism:

> The philosophers, however, were unrealistic—not in their highlighting of the indispensable role of justice in society, but in naively believing that men without love for one another can rise to justice. As a realist, Augustine, was acutely aware that men naturally tend to shade things in their own favor. To make this extreme tendency for self-preference serve the interests of society, something more than the precept to "give to others what is their due" is needed.[81]

The thing lacking is love. Unless men and women's relations to each other are ordered by love, their pride and self-assertiveness will get in the way of creating a just society.

When the love of God is instilled into our souls, when we are properly submissive to God as the origin of the order in the universe, then such mutual cooperation is possible. As Alister McGrath puts it, "Whereas Cicero taught that *iustitia* was based on *ius*, arising from the *iuris consensus*, Augustine

---

80. See Alister McGrath, *Iustitia Dei: A History of the Christian Doctrine of Justification*, 3rd ed. (Cambridge: Cambridge University Press, 2005), 52.

81. Mary T. Clark, "Augustine on Justice," *Revue des études augustiniennes* 9, no. 1 (1963): 92–93.

argued that *ius* itself must be regarded as based on *iustitia*. Thus for Augustine, there can be no *res publica* without there being true *iustitia* within the community—that is, a right ordering of all its relationships in accordance with the divine purpose."[82] Such a right ordering, therefore, is not in itself achievable apart from the gracious action of God, his fulfillment of his promises of grace.

This, again, is the point of dissonance: God elects to work out his promises of grace for some individuals and not others (Rom. 8:30). This grace does not depend in any way on the merit of the elect; it is purely gratuitous (Rom. 9:13–18). God's election does not make him less just since justice is defined fundamentally as the divine preservation of this order.

Robert Dodaro's *Christ and the Just Society in the Thought of Augustine* is a wonderful explanation of the cohesion between Augustine's political theology and his soteriology. Dodaro observes that Augustine repeatedly compares the philosophical conception of justice to Pelagian theology. Both presume that virtues have their source within ourselves, rather than being gifts from God. Against this assumption, on the basis of Romans 10:3, Augustine insists that all virtues come from God and are mediated by Christ. On account of our humanity, however, true justice is never completely present this side of eternity. Dodaro explains that

> since true virtue resides in God and is not proper to the soul, even Christians who seek virtue in the love of the true God can, because of original sin, know this virtue only imperfectly. . . . They experience peace, for example, as consolation in the midst of misery, rather than as true beatitude that is known only after death. "True justice" for pilgrim members of the city of God consists in sharing with others the forgiveness of sins, rather than in the achievement of a perfected virtue.[83]

Let me summarize some of our discoveries so far. (1) Augustine emphasizes the distinction between Creator and creation and the difference between human and divine justice. (2) He dismisses the Ciceronian account of justice since it is predicated on the ability of the human person to truly seek justice; it is idealistic and naive and fails to understand the pervasiveness of human sin. (3) True justice is to be equated with God's faithfulness to his promises. It consists in the ordering of creation according to God's will. (4) Only once the soul is thus ordered is human justice possible as a faint resemblance of

82. McGrath, *Iustitia Dei*, 52.
83. Robert Dodaro, *Christ and the Just Society in the Thought of Augustine* (Cambridge: Cambridge University Press, 2004), 111.

ultimate divine justice. (5) This ordering of the soul is not to be achieved through human effort, but it is to be received as a gift from God.

With this summary in mind as we discuss Augustine's view of the atonement, we shall see the manner in which Christ mediates that gift to us.

Retribution in the Just Society

Augustine offers a bifocal understanding of the just society. On the one hand, Augustine is careful to affirm secular governments. The role of these systems of justice, as we shall see, is limited. On the other hand, the existence of the church alone, as the community of grace, makes possible a just state. The church acts as a constant check on the power and pride of the state, reminding it that all human beings are sinful. This Augustinian realism softens the rigidity of Stoic universal law and can be understood as a curbing of its legalism. Legalism starts in pride, in the presumption that the power for virtue lies within the human person and, additionally, that humans can complete this virtue in their present existence. The church acts as a constant reminder that we can only faintly reflect justice as a community of forgiven persons. As Dodaro puts it, "The just society is penitential."[84]

Augustine never developed a specific legal philosophy, but as Friedrich notes, "he shows a particularly striking tendency which is part of legal philosophy, namely, . . . to see the political order as dominated by the purpose of peace. The reason is that the political order has now been reduced to the negative function of maintaining peace, for it merely serves the purpose of enabling the faithful to occupy themselves with the more lasting task of eternal salvation."[85] Jean Bethke Elshtain concurs: "Augustine doesn't give us the complete architecture of the form of rule most compatible with his understandings of love and justice. It seems safe to say, however, that it would be a type of governance that builds in barriers to cruel and capricious behavior on the part of earthly rulers."[86]

Peace and love, which form such a central part of the Christian conception of justice, ought to find their way into the penal system as such. Numerous letters Augustine wrote to several secular rulers demonstrate his concern for a merciful application of law. He repeatedly responds to such rulers that it would be contrary to justice to pardon offenders. Here again we encounter the theme of a conflict between the demands of mercy and those of justice. Augustine makes it clear that the mercy and the intercession of the bishop to the secular authorities is not contradictory to justice. While it is good that criminals

---

84. Ibid., 112.
85. Friedrich, *Philosophy of Law*, 37.
86. Jean Bethke Elshtain, *Sovereignty: God, State, and Self* (New York: Basic Books, 2008), 10.

should fear the severity of punishment (Rom. 13:3), there is also goodness "in our intercession which works to restrain your severity."[87] His correspondences with Marcellinus and Volusianus show the extent of his concern to curb the violence of punishment and his preference for forgiveness:

> But our desire is rather that justice be satisfied without the taking of their lives or the maiming of their bodies in any part, and that, by such coercive measures as may be in accordance with the laws, they be turned from their insane frenzy to the quietness of men in their sound judgment, or compelled to give up mischievous violence and betake themselves to some useful labour. This is indeed called a penal sentence; but who does not see that when a restraint is put upon the boldness of savage violence, and the remedies fitted to produce repentance are not withdrawn, this discipline should be called a benefit rather than vindictive punishment?[88]

A rehabilitative understanding of punishment thus forms the centerpiece of Augustine's penal philosophy. A strictly retributive vision of justice, not tempered by the recognition of universal sinfulness, is based on pride (Matt. 18:23–25). Gaylon Caldwell notes that "the quality of justice will vary directly with the quantity of pride in the public officers, since pride makes judgments punitive; but when pride does not obscure this illumination, any man will realize that," as Augustine puts it, "evil is removed, not by removing any nature, or part of nature, which has been introduced by evil, but by healing and correcting that which has been vitiated and depraved."[89] Caldwell further concludes that "Augustine's criticism of human justice centers on the failure of its practitioners to recognize that they are sinners judging sinners and their consequent inability to make their judgments restorative rather than retributive."[90]

Several writers have noted the impact of such a political theology on the development of the Western legal system. Harold Berman points out that, among other things, Christianity "introduced a concept of equity into legal rights and duties generally, thereby tempering the strictness of general prescriptions."[91]

---

87. Augustine, *Letter* 153.16, in Oliver O'Donovan and Joan Lockwood O'Donovan, eds., *From Irenaeus to Grotius: A Sourcebook in Christian Political Thought, 100–1625* (Grand Rapids: Eerdmans, 1999), 127.

88. Augustine, *Letter* 133.1, to Marcellinus (in Schaff, *Nicene and Post-Nicene Fathers*, series 1, 1:470). For similar ideas in favor of the necessity of leniency, see also *Letter* 139, to Marcellinus (in Schaff, *NPNF*, series 1, 1:488–90).

89. See Gaylon Caldwell, "Augustine's Critique of Human Justice," in *Augustine and Modern Law*, ed. Richard O. Brooks and James B. Murphy (Aldershot: Ashgate, 2011), 102.

90. Ibid., 102–3.

91. Harold Berman, *The Interaction of Law and Religion* (Nashville: Abingdon, 1974), 54.

Berman also acknowledges that Christianity was not the only influence in this respect; indeed, we have noticed similar tendencies in Hellenistic and Latin thought. Nevertheless, it remains instrumental in "providing the main ideological justification."[92] Kevin Uhalde makes another observation in relation to this influence. Christianity did not affect "the devices, techniques, and procedures that supplied and controlled justice in real life. The single most outstanding factor of change in the way elites handled justice and the way ordinary people experienced it was the rise in the person of the bishop as an official who bridged the theory and practice of justice."[93] Often, as we have noted, this influence weighed heavily in the direction of mercy and forgiveness.

It should not be thought that Augustine rejects all aspects of retributive justice. As I will show below, there is a place for just retribution, though punishment does not exhaust the content of rectifying justice. In due time I will return to this retributive dimension and its part in the story of atonement. For now it is safe to conclude that Augustine has his suspicions regarding a narrowly retributive justice on the human plane. The fundamental reason for this suspicion is that, as fellow sinners, we cannot presume an absolute position from which to judge. Such a position is occupied exclusively by God (Deut. 32:35; Rom. 12:19), whose punitive judgment remains just (Gen. 18:25; Ps. 103:6; Rom. 3:5). But at the same time when he has made retribution a necessary component of justice, Augustine has also made it secondary to rehabilitation and restoration. As it will transpire, while human beings justly deserve punishment, the elect are nevertheless spared, by virtue of the atoning work of Christ. The question is, What exactly is it about this atoning work that effectively removes humanity's liability to punishment? Is it the fact that Christ has been punished on our behalf, or is it the fact that he restores us to a life pleasing to God? This discussion concerns us in what follows.

Augustine on the Divine Attributes

An important question is whether there is a possible conflict between God's love, his desire to see us through, and his justice, whether there is a felt tension between the demands of this love and those of his justice. Clearly Augustine does not understand divine justice as commensurate with human justice.

Thomas Talbott, writing about the "Augustinian tradition of separating justice and mercy," argues that, up to Milton, it is as if introducing this separation

92. Ibid.
93. Kevin Uhalde, *Expectations of Justice in the Age of Augustine* (Philadelphia: University of Pennsylvania Press, 2007), 8.

would introduce a conflict within God himself. While Talbott is right about the tradition, he wrongly insinuates that it originated with Augustine. Our discussion of Aeschylus in particular has shown that there is a long-standing contest about the nature of the divinity and the claims of justice on God. Sometimes, as with the tradition stemming from Origen and Gregory of Nyssa, the tension was externalized onto the person of the devil. Augustine refuses to kid himself with this idea. While the devil retains some of that role, as we shall see, Augustine fully understands that the problem of humanity is that of facing a wrathful God, whose justice demands retribution (Deut. 32:35; 2 Chron. 6:23; Isa. 34:8; 59:18; 2 Thess. 1:8), yet whose love aims for our salvation. This tension is on full display in Augustine, but he did not invent it. Much less did he borrow it from Plato. On the contrary, as I hope to show, it marks a clear difference from Hellenism.

Talbott, continuing his critique of this tradition of the separation between justice and mercy, argues that, if Augustine really held such a view, it would contradict his doctrine of divine simplicity. In Talbott's reading, this doctrine entails that God's "justice requires exactly the same thing his love requires: the absolute destruction of sin; it requires that sinners repent of any wrong they have done to others and that they be reconciled to one another."[94] The doctrine of simplicity, then, must be defined such that mercy and justice are two different names for God's only moral attribute: his love. Mercy and justice are therefore synonymous (Ps. 33:5; 89:14).

Let's overview what Augustine himself says about this doctrine. In *The City of God* (11.10) he writes that "those things which are essentially and truly divine are called simple, because in them quality and substance are identical, and because they are divine, or wise, or blessed in themselves, and without extraneous supplement." According to the most basic understanding of simplicity, in God, being and existence are the same thing (Exod. 3:14; John 5:26). God's attributes are his being and nothing more than that. This doctrine is admittedly puzzling and controversial. But, as I will show in the final chapter, I do not think Augustine ever intended to argue that all of God's attributes are identical. Sometimes, it is true, Augustine is less careful than others, as when he argues that these different qualities "have one meaning; in order that our aim may not be distracted by a multiplicity of objects"; and "it is the same thing in God to be righteous that it is to be good or blessed."[95] Just as careless is this one: "Or do goodness, again, and righteousness, differ from each other in the nature of God, as they differ in his works, as though they were two diverse qualities of God—goodness one

94. Thomas Talbott, "Punishment, Forgiveness, and Divine Justice," *Religious Studies* 29, no. 2 (1993): 151–68 (here 168).
95. Augustine, *Trin.* 15.5.8.

and righteousness another? Certainly not; but that which is righteousness is also itself goodness; and that which is goodness is also itself blessedness."[96]

When Augustine states that these qualities "have one meaning," he does not *mean* it in the post-Fregean sense that we are accustomed to. Rather, he means that these attributes do not refer to different objects, like Platonic universals existing independently of God. Instead, they have one meaning in the sense of having the same reference: the very nature of God. What Augustine does not intend to say is that predicating goodness of God is the same as predicating justice of God, and so on. The doctrine of divine simplicity is not intended as an apophatic sublation of all talk of divine nature. Rather, it is intended as a caution, as an apophatic reserve, if one may put it this way. It affirms that when we predicate qualities of God, we do not thereby ascribe to God a universal that has an existence apart from his being. That is what it means to say that his being is not composed of parts.

The point of simplicity is not that the attributes are identical, but that they are inseparable from each other. Each attribute names, identifies, or picks out an aspect of God's being. Thus Kevin Vanhoozer comments:

> When we conceive of God's being in terms of communicative act, we see more easily how God can be simple yet complex, not in the sense that his being is composed of parts but rather that it requires several concepts in order to do justice to its richness. . . . In describing God's being-in-communicative-act from different perspectives, we are not describing various "parts" of God. On the contrary: *each perfection refers to the whole of God's being-in-communicative-act, though each describes only one aspect of it.*[97]

Here is not the place to dwell on Vanhoozer's creative proposal about divine communicative act and its manifold descriptions. His clarification in regard to divine simplicity, however, is spot on.

Oliver Crisp also takes Talbott to task for misunderstanding the doctrine of divine simplicity. The concept does not entail that all attributes are subordinated to divine love (1 John 4:8), but that they are all the same. God's love is the same as his justice, writes Crisp. "For perfect-being theologians like Augustine, Anselm and Aquinas, the simplicity of the divine nature means that *God, as actus purus,*

---

96. Ibid., 15.5.7.

97. Kevin Vanhoozer, *Remythologizing Theology: Divine Action, Passion, and Authorship* (Cambridge: Cambridge University Press, 2012), 275–76. For other excellent discussions of simplicity, see Stephen Holmes, "'Something Much Too Plain to Say': Towards a Defence of the Doctrine of Divine Simplicity," *Neue Zeitschrift für systematische Theologie und Religionsphilosophie* 43 (2001): 137–54. See also chap. 6 (below) for a discussion of simplicity in relation to atonement in general.

is just and benevolent at one and the same time. But since they do not construe justice as perfect in forgiveness, deeming instead that it is perfect in retribution, they do not maintain that justice requires forgiveness in every instance."[98]

From this discussion of divine simplicity, we can reasonably conclude that, while the doctrine as employed by Augustine remains puzzling, we can rule out a certain way of caricaturing his thought. Talbott comes at least close to this caricature. That is, the charge sometimes caricatures the Augustinian position as depicting a God who is torn between his attributes. His justice demands one thing, while his love seems to demand something else. Sometimes the very same caricature appears in presentations of the doctrine of penal substitution that do not carefully engage either with the doctrine of simplicity or with what it means to make any kind of predication about God. In fact, as Lewis Ayres and Michel René Barnes show, the language of simplicity is intended precisely as a metalinguistic caution: "The application of the language of simplicity and of 'Being itself' to God is not intended as descriptive of a comprehensible object. Such language serves to shape our talk of God and to help us articulate the revealed principles of Trinitarian theology, but God remains outside our grasp, drawing us toward the sight that will replace faith at the judgment."[99]

Thus, when we portray a tension in God between his love and his mercy, we should be careful lest we construe this precisely in the way the doctrine of simplicity is intended to foreclose. Namely, these are not attributes and compulsions that press on God from outside, as it were. Neither should God be regarded as a kind of a schizophrenic deity, caught between warring inner impulses. *It is precisely such capriciousness, on the one hand, or impotence, on the other, that the concept of simplicity expressly denies.*

A certain dose of apophaticism is certainly a much-needed corrective, as long as it doesn't entail the impossibility of meaningful predication about God. Without giving apophaticism full reign, we can still affirm that the Christian doctrine of simplicity, unlike in Platonism, preserves the ontological gap between creation and Creator. While for Plato, and for Stoicism, God's being is transparent to our reason, thus allowing us to map our justice onto divine justice, Christianity makes any such smooth transition problematic.

This gap between divine justice and human justice, then, is the contrast between the Hellenistic (and pre-Hellenistic) doctrines of God and Christian

---

98. Oliver Crisp, "Divine Retribution: A Defense," *Sophia* 42, no. 2 (2003): 48. Although Crisp maintains that all attributes are the same, he does not mean that there is no difference between the attributes.

99. Lewis Ayres and Michel René Barnes, "God," in *Augustine through the Ages: An Encyclopedia*, ed. Allan D. Fitzgerald, OSA (Grand Rapids: Eerdmans, 1999), 389.

theology. It would have been absurd for the Greek gods to issue any laws, because the laws are obvious. The idea of a positive divine law would be preposterous to them. The law (and sometimes fate) is above the gods. So a god only enforces something that is pressing upon his own being. The Jewish and Christian God, however, does legislate. There is no law, no justice, over and above his being to which he merely tips his hat. God's being is identical with his attributes, including his love and his justice. There can be no deduction of these attributes independently of revelation. The doctrine of simplicity is intended to safeguard precisely this principle. It is a rejection of a Hellenistic philosophical conception of God, even as it is expressed in the Hellenistic philosophical language of substance and attributes.

Further, Augustine's doctrine of simplicity is consonant with his quasi-voluntarism. Although Stone regards Augustine as being "clearly a voluntarist,"[100] he argues that Augustine "based divine law on both God's will and reason."[101] Thus divine justice is accessible by both faith and reason. Augustine thus understands God as the supreme and perfect Being whose justice is not complete except in love, and every other attribute; whose love is only perfect in his justice, and every other divine perfection. There is no compulsion on this Being other than his own will. The question, then, is whether there is any tension between Augustine's voluntarism and what remains of his retributivism. For that we need to turn to an exposition of his doctrine of the atonement as such.

Augustine's Doctrine of Penal Substitution?

Several scholars are quick to identify Augustine's theory of the atonement as belonging to the penal substitutionary type. They point to Augustine's use of such concepts as punishment, propitiation, the wrath of God, and so on, then conclude that he has all the main components of the penal substitutionary theory.

It is true that Augustine comes very close to such an understanding of the atonement. Besides the use of familiar expressions and concepts, other key assumptions seem to dispose him to this particular theory. Let me rehearse some of them.

1. Augustine's doctrine of original sin leaves us in no doubt about the necessity for the canceling of sin as debt and guilt. Augustine does not make much of guilt as a moral concept. He prefers to speak of it as liability to punishment. But salvation needs to entail precisely this blotting out of

100. Stone, *Human Law and Human Justice*, 44.
101. Ibid., 45.

our liability to punishment. Although salvation does include elements of moral transformation (see below), it necessarily must also include forgiveness as a forgoing of the punishment that is a consequence of original sin.

2. Atonement is conceived as being primarily Godward. While Augustine retains some of the framework of the ransom theory, with its talk of the rights of the devil, for him it seems to be more a matter of language than anything else. Not that the influence of the devil is unimportant. Quite the contrary. But Satan is ascribed a clearly subordinate role. His dominion is completely under the control of God, and he has authority only insofar as God allows it. Augustine goes to the very heart of the problem in identifying the basis of the devil's authority in the problem of sin. Thus demonic torments and temptations, Satan's threat of death, ultimately depend on our liability to such evil due to our sin. It is not the devil as such that has to be defeated, but rather the basis of his claim on us, and that is precisely the wrath of God. Augustine clearly recognizes that the crux of the problem is the relationship between humankind and God. This is a clear penal substitutionary element since no other family of theories takes God to be the object of the work of Christ on the cross.

3. Finally, the centerpiece of the work of Christ is not the incarnation as such but precisely his death on the cross. Even more than the resurrection, it is Christ's death that represents a fitting sacrifice, which propitiates God.

What Aulén has called the classic theory does not incorporate the final two assumptions, though it does not explicitly deny the first one. But classic theories, especially in their Eastern subsequent development, make less of sin, understood as human guilt and debt, as a fundamental barrier to God. The Russian theologian Vladimir Lossky illustrates this difference.[102] The fact of sin does not so much represent a chasm that has to be bridged as it does an obstacle that must be circumvented. Sin only means that God needs to change his pedagogical methods, given its reality. This is not to say that all Eastern theologians share this view and minimize the legal dimension of sin. But in the ancient world the cosmic framework of demonic forces made it very easy for these theologians to shift both human responsibility for sin, and divine wrath

102. See, among other examples, Vladimir Lossky, *Mystical Theology of the Eastern Church* (Crestwood, NY: St. Vladimir's Seminary Press, 1976), 135, but especially Lossky, *Orthodox Theology: An Introduction* (Crestwood, NY: St. Vladimir's Seminary Press, 1978), 113.

against it, onto Satan's shoulders. While human beings do remain responsible for their sin, it is more the responsibility of a young, ignorant, but growing child who has free will but is unable to use it wisely. In the West, however, the predominance of juristic modes of thought has helped focus the issue of the ultimate responsibility and the incurred liabilities.

With Augustine holding to the three assumptions outlined above, it can be very easy to jump to the conclusion that his is a theory of penal substitution. This conclusion, moreover, is sometimes tempting for scholars eager to buttress the historical pedigree of their own theories. There are, however, several items in Augustine's thought that make any such attribution problematic. This is where our groundwork in Augustine's conception of justice begins to throw some light onto his theology of the atonement.

First, although Augustine clearly incorporates retributive elements—I will address this in much greater detail below—there is a clear distinction between divine and human justice in his thought. This distinction alone should give us pause before we claim that what happens on the cross is the execution of a divine sentence through a human justice system. Advocates of penal substitution sometimes do make precisely such an identification, which in turn has often led critics to charge that the theory lends credence to corrupt systems of justice. Instead of portraying such human systems as under the divine judgment, the identification of the two helps preserve and legitimize an unfortunate status quo. Augustine, however, is clearly aware of the distinction between the two justices. While he does see the punitive hand of God at work in human governments, he also sufficiently exposes the limitations of secular government to make us ask: Can ultimate divine justice be carried out through a human court?

Further, and continuing with the previous point, it is precisely on account of the ontological difference between creature and Creator, which entails a discrepancy between human and divine justice, that Augustine significantly weakens the retributive demands of human justice. For Augustine, a restorative conception of human justice is always to be preferred over a retributive one. In fairness, it should also be pointed out that Augustine continues to affirm the importance of retribution, but he stops short of making it the sine qua non of justice. The question is whether Augustine's restorative conception of human justice entails anything about God's justice. Is divine justice perhaps premised on the necessity of punishment? We shall deal with this problem in a bit.

The second item, which suggests further dissonance with penal substitution, is the high value Augustine put on the practice of penance. Protestant theologians are all too aware of this fact, but they tend to regard it as being organically disconnected from his theory of the cross, arguing that while Augustine got his atonement theory right, his theology of penance contradicted it. Augustine's theory of the atonement is of a piece with his anti-Pelagian affirmation of the priority of grace. Both affirm a basic human inability to obey God, and both stress the sufficiency of Christ's work for the absolution of our guilt. But Augustine restricts the work of the atonement to the cancellation of our liability to punishment for original sin. For every actual and postbaptismal sin we commit, an act of penance is required. If, however, he did not interpret the atonement in a strictly penal substitutionary way, an underlying congruity with his theory of penance might be revealed.

I argue that Augustine in fact puts forward a theory of representative sacrifice that clearly includes an element of retribution. The language of substitution is obviously present in this quotation from Augustine's De trinitate: "And thence he proceeds to his passion, that he might pay for us debtors that which he himself did not owe."[103] Rashdall correctly notes that Augustine directly uses the word "punishment."[104] Indeed, Augustine explicitly states that "Christ, though guiltless, took our punishment, that He might cancel our guilt, and do away with our punishment."[105] And again: "The believer in the true doctrine of the gospel will understand that Christ is not reproached by Moses when he speaks of Him [Christ] as cursed, not in His divine majesty, but as hanging on the tree as our substitute, bearing our punishment."[106]

Neither does Augustine hesitate to use language of propitiation: "Since men are in this state of wrath through original sin—a condition made still graver and more pernicious as they compounded more and worse sins with it—a Mediator was required; that is to say, a Reconciler who by offering a unique sacrifice, of which all the sacrifices of the law and the prophets were shadows, should allay that wrath."[107] The fundamental problem is that of reconciliation between God and humanity, and Augustine sees the reconciliation as working both ways. "Thus by the single sacrifice, of which the many victims of the law were only shadows, the heavenly part is set at peace with the earthly part and the earthly reconciled to the heavenly."[108] This is clearly penal substitutionary language.

Although Augustine talks about propitiation, he is careful to avoid notions of a Father who, on account of the sacrifice of his Son, turns from wrath to love:

103. Augustine, Trin. 13.14.
104. Rashdall, Idea of Atonement, 331.
105. Augustine, Faust. 14.4.
106. Ibid., 15.7; cf. Gal. 3:10.
107. Augustine, Enchir. 10.33.
108. Ibid., 16.62, referencing Col. 1:19–20.

Pray, unless the Father had been already appeased, would He have delivered up His own Son, not sparing Him for us? Does not this opinion seem to be as it were contrary to that? In the one, the Son dies for us, and the Father is reconciled to us by His death; in the other, as though the Father first loved us, He Himself on our account does not spare the Son, He Himself for us delivers Him up to death. But I see that the Father loved us also before, not only before the Son died for us, but before He created the world. . . . Nor was the Son delivered up for us as it were unwillingly, the Father himself not sparing Him. . . . Therefore together both the Father and the Son, and the Spirit of both, work all things equally and harmoniously; yet we are justified in the blood of Christ, and we are reconciled to God by the death of His Son.[109]

Careful theories of penal substitution do not pit an angry, vengeful Father against a loving, sacrificing Son. Often, though, they replace this with another equally problematic notion of the Father as punishing the Son. Not Augustine. He is equally careful to avoid any notion that breaks the unity of the work of the Trinity. It is therefore crucial to understand precisely what the role of Jesus's punishment is in the atonement. Several questions will need to be answered: first, as to the justice of the death of Christ; second, as to who punished Jesus; and third, as to the function of the punishment in the larger scheme of the atonement.

First, Augustine does not tire of reminding us that the death of Christ is properly a manifestation of God's justice (Rom. 3:25–26). Augustine does, however, stop short of claiming that no other mode of salvation was possible for God. Unlike Anselm later on, and much like Aquinas, he emphasizes the fittingness and appropriateness of this mode of salvation:

Those then who say, What, had God no other way by which He might free men from the misery of this mortality, that He should will His only-begotten Son, God co-eternal with Himself, to become man, by putting on a human soul and flesh, and being made mortal to endure death?—these, I say, it is not enough to refute, as to assert that that mode by which God deigns to free us through the mediator of God and men, the man Christ Jesus, is good and suitable to the dignity of God; but we must show also, not indeed that no other mode was possible to God, to whose power all things are equally subject, but that there neither was nor need have been any other mode more appropriate for curing our misery.[110]

Augustine hints at the possibility of God's simply using his power to save us. In saying this, Augustine seems to be backtracking on his own doctrine of

109. Augustine, *Trin.* 12.2.15.
110. Ibid., 13.10.13.

divine simplicity, implying that God could have, even in principle, saved us by divine fiat, and thus bracketing justice. Indeed, the mutual conditioning of the divine attributes seems to be a matter of divine pleasure and will, rather than necessity. Augustine expresses this unity in terms of the divine pleasure: "It pleased God, that in order to the rescuing of man from the grasp of the devil, the devil should be conquered, not by power, but by righteousness; and that so also men, imitating Christ, should seek to conquer the devil by righteousness, not by power. Not that power is to be shunned as though it were something evil; but order must be preserved, whereby righteousness is before it."[111]

There are two senses in which Augustine can speak about the justice of this arrangement. On the one hand, it was just (a matter of righteousness) that the devil would be stripped of his power not through force but through a kind of trick. Augustine does not shy away from using the metaphor of deceit. On the other hand, the death of Christ was a matter of justice in the sense that he endured the death justly deserved by human nature. He doesn't connect the two ideas. This may not be accidental because there is an apparent incompatibility here. On the one hand, the devil could have been stripped of his power by force; but on the other hand, could humanity have been forgiven without the payment of its just penalty? While the just defrocking of the devil can be shown to have a positive didactic effect on humanity (that humans should also seek to conquer him by righteousness), would Augustine also affirm that God could have chosen to forgive sinners without exacting any kind of punishment? He certainly does not seem inclined to affirm the latter. Over and over he stresses the justly deserved death that humanity has incurred on account of its sin. To put it differently, it is not always clear what is driving the mechanism of the atonement. Is it the fact that we have been rescued from the influence of Satan—and this through a death that in theory could have been prevented? Or is it through the fact that, as Augustine says elsewhere, "as Christ endured death as a man, and for man; so also, Son of God as He was, ever living in His own righteousness, but dying for our offences, He submitted as man, and for man, to bear the curse which accompanies death." Clearly, the devil continues to play an important part in Augustine's argument, but the priority of justice seems to be much stronger when he talks in terms of the just curse of death, which Christ endured on our behalf. Again, the question is, Could God have granted us his forgiveness without Christ's having to undergo the punishment of death, especially since Augustine claims that God could have defeated Satan simply by power? It is not clear to me what Augustine's answer might be.

111. Ibid., 13.13.17.

Oliver Crisp suggests an interpretation of Augustine according to which "God's justice does not permit him to forgive a person their sin without retributive justice being served."[112] Crisp alludes to the following passage in the *Enchiridion* as justification for this interpretation: "And he also sees that those who are saved *had to be saved on such terms* that it would show—by contrast with the greater number of those not saved but simply abandoned to their wholly just damnation—what the whole mass deserved and to what end God's merited judgment would have brought them, had not his undeserved mercy interposed."[113] Two things may be pointed out on the basis of this quotation alone. First, the necessity to which Crisp refers seems to have more of a demonstrative, one might say even pedagogical, role. The manner of God's salvation had to be such that the just deserts of sin would be *evident*. Thus, strictly speaking, this is not a necessity placed on divine forgiveness as such. Only if this divine forgiveness is also intended to have a particular pedagogical function must it, of necessity, take a particular form. Second, we might also observe that such a demonstration of deserts could conceivably be accomplished in any number of different ways. Augustine's explanation of the necessity of the death of Christ in relation to the requirements of divine justice is not sufficiently clear.

Let us, then, move on to the next question: Who punished Jesus? Affirming that humanity justly deserves its fate in death, Augustine stops short of saying that God punished Christ. Throughout his works, Augustine ascribes to the devil the role of the enforcer of divine justice. At the same time he attempts to distinguish God from death (Wis. 1:13), while affirming its justice. Talking about the death of the sinner, he writes that God "was not Himself the cause of death; but yet death was inflicted on the sinner, through his most just retribution. Just as the judge inflicts punishment on the guilty; yet it is not the justice of the judge, but the desert of the crime, which is the cause of the punishment."[114] In other words, death due to sin is self-inflicted. It is not God who metes out punishment, but we who bring it upon ourselves.

While Christ dies the death that is due as punishment to human nature, in his case it cannot be regarded as a punishment, since punishment requires a hard treatment against one's will: "Herein lies the punishment in the death of the body, that the spirit leaves the body against its will, because it left God willingly."[115] But Christ laid down his life willingly and freely (John 10:17–18; 15:13); thus "the spirit of the Mediator showed how it was through no punishment of sin

112. Crisp, "Divine Retribution," 37.
113. Augustine, *Enchir.* 25.29.
114. Augustine, *Trin.* 4.12.15.
115. Ibid., 4.13.16.

that He came to the death of the flesh, because He did not leave it [the flesh] against His will, but because He willed, when He willed, as He willed."[116]

This is a significant point, for it implies that Christ was not punished by God. If Christ were in fact punished by God, the claim that the devil overextended himself in killing Christ could no longer be made! And it is precisely this claim that Augustine resolutely drives home throughout book 4 of *De trinitate*. The devil "stripped himself" of authority by claiming a sinless Christ over whom he had no authority. And again in book 13, "What, then, is the righteousness by which the devil was conquered? What, except the righteousness of Jesus Christ? And how was he conquered? Because, when he found in Him nothing worthy of death, yet he slew Him. And certainly it is just, that we whom he held as debtors, should be dismissed free by believing in Him whom he slew without any debt."[117] The death of Christ was perpetrated by the devil, who unjustly thought Christ was within his reach (1 Cor. 2:8; Col. 2:15).

Clearly, then, this death is a miscarriage of justice. Why, then, could such an unjust death be at the same time a demonstration of divine justice and pleasing to God (Isa. 53:10)? I think the short answer, from Augustine's perspective, is that Christ's death was pleasing to God not as death *simpliciter*, but as the extent of Christ's obedience to the Father, even in the face of an unjust and cruel death.

This brings us to our final question: the role of this death in the economy of the atonement. Let me state my conclusion from the outset: the necessity of Christ's death is consequent upon the necessity of his having become man and thus assuming a mortal humanity. What pleases God is not primarily that Christ died but that on behalf of humanity, and as a complete human being, he offered a sacrifice even in the face of death.

In Augustine, J. N. D. Kelly identifies the presence of a variety of atonement motifs, from hints of a "physical doctrine" to the ransom theory. While these themes are important and sometimes worked out in quite some detail, especially the Christus Victor theme, his "central thought" is that "the essence of redemption lies in the expiatory sacrifice offered for us by Christ in his passion."[118] Kelly, however, tends to blur the distinction between sacrifice and punishment: "Its fundamental rationale, as we might expect, is that Christ is substituted for us, and being Himself innocent discharges the penalty we owe."[119] It is, however, important not to confuse this with the later logic of

116. Ibid.
117. Ibid., 13.14.18.
118. J. N. D. Kelly, *Early Christian Doctrines*, rev. ed. (San Francisco: HarperSanFrancisco, 1978), 392.
119. Ibid., 393.

penal substitution, even though Augustine does talk explicitly about the importance of Christ's bearing our punishment, and he also uses the language
of substitution. Christ's death is certainly penal in the sense that all death is
penal, not in the sense that the Son is therefore punished by the Father. There
are no traces of that idea in Augustine.

Kelly also points out that "Augustine's teaching stresses the exemplary aspect of Christ's work in a way that is without precedent."[120] Throughout his
discussions of the atonement, Augustine emphasizes the unobligated nature
of Christ's death, his prioritization of righteousness to power. This sharply
contrasts both the ambitions and pride of Satan, and human behavior. Christ
takes on human nature and demonstrates in his divine-human person what
it means to be a child of God. He demonstrates perfect obedience and, to
use Irenaean language, recapitulates what humanity was originally meant to
be. In this he satisfies God. But taking on the human condition also entails
living in the face of death. Despite having the power to avoid death, Christ
chooses to face death. It is precisely his attitude to his death that satisfies and
propitiates God.

Augustine distinguishes between physical death and spiritual death (Rev.
20:6), or the death of the spirit. Part of what the atonement is supposed to
mend is the pathological human attitude to death, "because men strove more
to shun that which they could not shun, *viz.*, the death of the flesh, than the
death of the spirit, *i.e.*, punishment more than the desert of punishment (for
not to sin is a thing about which either men are not solicitous or are too little
solicitous; but not to die, although it be not within reach of attainment, is
yet eagerly sought after)."[121] Christ demonstrates another approach to death:
"the Mediator of life, [makes] it plain that death is not to be feared, which by
the condition of humanity cannot now be escaped, but rather ungodliness,
which can be guarded against through faith."[122]

If one looks for a single logic within Augustine's doctrine of the atonement, one will have a hard time finding it. There are interlocking arguments,
not always logically integrated. We have come upon another such strand here.
What makes the death of Christ pleasing to God is not so much the fact
that it represents the punishment due to humanity but that Christ's human
attitude in proximity to his death is exemplary. He is a fitting and pleasing
sacrifice on account of his obedience even in the face of death. This is what
propitiates God.

120. Ibid.
121. Augustine, *Trin.* 14.12.15.
122. Ibid.

Such a demonstration is not simply intended for God, but it has an actual effect in the lives of his followers (1 Pet. 2:21; 4:1, 6). This brings us to the moral example theme. Augustine's choice to put justice (righteousness) before power speaks to our temptation to assert ourselves and elbow our way as far from death as possible. "And righteousness was therefore made more acceptable in humility, because so great power was in His Divinity, if He had been unwilling, would have been able not to suffer humility; and thus by Him who died, being thus powerful, both righteousness was commended, and power promised, to us, weak mortals."[123] This is clearly a moral example theme. Robert Dodaro makes much of this: "Christ's ability to take upon himself the despair of the members of his body is matched by his capacity to transfer back to his members the virtues that are proper to himself." And, "Augustine describes as a 'wondrous exchange' (*mira commutatio*) this transfer by which Christ assumes the fear of death that all members of his body experience, while he communicates back to them his own hope as consolation."[124]

To recapitulate, one significant strand of Augustine's atonement theory interprets the death of Christ as being especially pleasing to God not because it represents a divine punishment. Rather, God is pleased that the Son, having assumed the human condition with everything it entails, including fearsome death, is utterly obedient to him even in the face of the destruction of the body. One may read this theory of the atonement as having a main thread, represented by the idea of sacrifice. But *the idea of punishment is decidedly submerged here, though without disappearing completely*. Christ becomes man so that he may offer himself back to God in the same manner in which humans were always intended to: in self-abnegating obedience (Phil. 2:8). The death that Christ suffers is indeed a punishment, because it belongs as the just desert of the human condition, which Christ assumed. This idea is absolutely essential, and it has the logical consequence that Christ removes our liability for punishment. But God takes delight not so much in seeing Christ punished as he does in beholding the attitude of the Son in the midst of our cursed condition.

For Augustine, there is no representation without retribution. There is no incarnation without the cross. For to take on human flesh is to participate in the desolate experience of mortality. This mortality is indeed a just divine retribution. But the propitiating aspect of Christ's work is not so much the pain of Christ as his response to it. The result is a life that commends righteousness and gives hope against death.

123. Ibid., 13.14.18.
124. Dodaro, *Christ and the Just Society*, 106.

Summary

1. An analysis of ancient conceptions of justice shows that there is no inhibition with regard to gratuitous forgiveness on the part of the gods. Justice is understood primarily as order. The duty of the gods is to preserve peace, with arbitration and amicable settlement as the preferred responses to wrongdoing.

2. Ancient thought regarded positive law, including specific laws regulating relationships between the gods and humanity, with suspicion. A concept of natural law is affirmed, but the overall attitude is that God (or the gods) are not restrained by principles of legality. The preservation of order is not by the necessary upholding of the laws. Considerations of equity temper the cold application of legality.

3. Although there is an element of retribution, in many writers it is directly challenged. The overall picture, then, is that of a contested conception of justice, between a legalism that demands vengeance and punishment, and an instrumentalism that regards the ultimate aim of law as order.

4. Neither Plato nor Aristotle approach a legalism that demands retribution in the name of an abstract principle. They critique retributive conceptions of justice in the name of a rehabilitative function of punishment. Stoicism and Roman law emphasized the notion of equity and the importance of paying attention to particular circumstances, which thus opened the way for the eventual internalization of justice as a virtue of the soul.

5. In the Christian context, the idea of divine retribution, set against a cosmic background, is externalized onto the person of Satan. Thus God's essential benevolence is insulated from divine wrath (until Augustine). This happens despite Gregory of Nyssa's explicit endorsement of divine simplicity. Thus it is not so much that Gregory does not affirm a doctrine of divine simplicity, but that he does not realize its significance for the correlation of the divine attributes of love and wrath. Gregory does indeed affirm that justice belongs to the very being of God, but echoes the hesitation of his generation to also project wrath unto the person of God.

6. Yet justice remains a constant concern for patristic theologians. God's dealings with Satan have to be just. Divine deceit is not an arbitrary act of God but a justified response to the devil's actions.

7. Augustine denies that divine justice is mappable onto human justice. He critiques the Ciceronian version of this continuity, which will eventually become the norm again. Nevertheless, Augustine does initiate a strand

in Western thought that will always be suspicious of this continuity. It will be picked up again by John Duns Scotus and by Luther.

8. Augustine does, however, seem to be influenced by Plato's internalizing of *dikaiosynē*. He thus conceives of justice as a right ordering of the soul. However, this virtue cannot be achieved through human law. Augustine has a dim view of the law, restricting its function to the tempering of libido. It can only curb sinfulness, but law itself does not create a virtuous Christian nature. Such a moral transformation can only happen supernaturally, through the infusion of divine love.

9. Augustine's emphasis on love further yields a rehabilitative understanding of punishment and leads him to see the role of the church as a tempering of the retributivism of the secular city.

10. These reservations with regard to punishment are reflected in Augustine's understanding of the atonement. Although he makes use of the language of substitution and propitiation, he continues to use the bait motif, and he stops short of affirming the necessity of Christ's death. Christ offers himself as what I have called a "representative sacrifice."

11. The moral exemplarism of Augustine is undeniable as well. Christ does not so much restore a balance of abstract justice (a kind of legalism), but reorders the soul by infusing it with love. This alone satisfies God's justice.

Medieval Atonement and the Legal Revolution

The Reemergence of Law

Law is not much of a factor in atonement theories from the patristic age. Since God is above the law that he gave to Moses (John 1:17; Rom. 10:4; Gal. 3:24), it was quite natural to think that he might overlook it in dispensing his forgiveness. Any set of positive human laws could not be approximated to divine justice. God's absolute transcendence precluded any such easy commensuration. This is not to say that God's being was not identified with justice (Deut. 32:4; 2 Thess. 1:6), but since justice is one of God's absolute attributes, it cannot be known, much less approximated to human justice.

Both Platonic notions of divine transcendence and Christian convictions about the pervasiveness of sin enter into Augustine's understanding of human justice. His critique of Ciceronian justice remains highly influential for the early Middle Ages, although as we shall see, Ciceronian conceptions are not altogether absent. But it is Augustine's rather dim view of the political that decisively marks early medieval attitudes toward the law. Since the earthly city can never reach divine justice, it can at most aim for a function of law as tempering "libido," the drive to power and manipulation. Christians should still be good citizens, but by this Augustine means that Christians should humbly

45

acquiesce to the authority of legitimate rulers. The Christian's engagement in the public square, through politics and law, is not an essential part of reaching one's end. Nature is not perfected in the political associations of the earthly city, but only by grace, in the city of God.

Law and Peace

If the purpose of law cannot be to establish justice, then the former can only assume the role of tempering the desires of the flesh. The aim of law, then, is the maintenance of peace. It is not chiefly concerned with objective righting of wrongs but with arbitration and management of conflict, with the aim of reestablishing peace. *Pax Romana* remains the ideal of human justice. In Augustine we do not have any theological motivation for the transformation and redemption of human laws. These are a necessary condition of fallen human nature, but they cannot be taken as being revelatory of anything divine.

While for the Eastern fathers Greek ideals of friendship, peace, and order were primordial, similar Roman ideals remained influential up to the eleventh century. As I have suggested, the various ransom metaphors remained useful precisely because theology had assigned law a minimalist function between God and humanity. Laws apply between humans, but they are not binding on God. Laws are an unfortunate necessity for fallen humanity.

It is not a coincidence that the ransom model began to fade precisely when Western culture rediscovered the law, human law, in its universal, rational, and indeed divine character. This chapter recounts snippets of the story of the reemergence of law from the eleventh to the fifteenth centuries, by focusing on the principal theologians of the atonement from the Middle Ages: Anselm of Canterbury, Peter Abelard, Thomas Aquinas, and John Duns Scotus. Despite their many differences, these thinkers are united in their high evaluation of human laws as well as the divine law (*lex divina*), which *provides the framework for divine-human relationships*.

Augustine died in AD 430, not long after the barbarian conquest of Rome (AD 410). The gradual conquest and disintegration of the Roman Empire ushered a period of significant social transformations, not least in terms of legal institutions. Although "at no time during the Middle Ages did study of the Roman Law entirely cease," the decline of the empire brought with it an eclipse of its legal structures. Its universal law, which Justinian codified in the sixth century, gave way to a dissipation and fragmentation of legal authority that was primarily guided by customary law, both written and unwritten. Folk law, with all its superstitions and irrational practices, became normative all across Europe. Christianity had neither the desire nor the ability (for a certain period of time) to reform such a system. If anything, the law did become more humane, anchored in real social bonds between people, rather than an objective and rigid structure. As the great historian of law and religion Harold J. Berman puts it, prior to the eleventh century, law is not "dissembedded from general custom."[1] There is no perception of law as a body of rules and concepts universally applicable, rational, and indicative of normative divine justice.

Berman insists on the complicity of Christianity with feudal and folk systems of law. Not only did it not challenge them, but it also provided added theological justification to some of its practices. For example, the Germanic legal institutions of ordeal and compurgation[2] were supported by a Germanic and Christian theology of indwelling supernatural powers: "It was presupposed both by Germanic religion and by the Christianity which initially replaced it that supernatural powers were immanent within the natural sphere."[3] It was assumed that since God is on the side of the innocent, he would step in and vindicate the person who was in the right. Although these practices were already falling out of favor by the ninth century, they indicate the state of the medieval and Germanic legal institutions.

Anselm of Canterbury straddles the border between early medieval conceptions of law that came to be seen as obsolete and the revolutionary ideas that swept over Europe in the eleventh and twelfth centuries. From the twelfth-century Renaissance onward, the new conception of law was firmly in place.

The Legal Revolution

A full account of the historical and political factors leading to this revolution cannot be attempted here. Europe was slowly beginning to emerge from barbaric fragmentation. There was significant population growth by the mid-eleventh century, especially in the cities, bringing with it a revival of long-distance trade. This change alone is significant enough to warrant calling it a real commercial revolution. By the late eleventh century, the recovery of Europe was well on its way, with the consolidation of France and the taking back of Spain from the Moors. One might also mention the monastic reforms that were taking place at Cluny, or those through the order of the Cistercians,

---

1. Harold J. Berman, *Law and Revolution: The Formation of the Western Legal Tradition* (Cambridge, MA: Harvard University Press, 1983), 78.
2. Methods of proving the truth of the testimony of a witness in lawcourts. These involved testing either the witnesses or the accused through some kind of physical, usually dangerous and painful, ordeal. If the wounds healed, the subject was thought to be innocent, or trustworthy. Examples of ordeals include trial by water and by fire. Duels were also practiced.
3. Ibid., 64.

which systematized and uniformized monastic practice and law throughout the church. The upsurge of trade and the population of urban centers triggered both a rebirth of learning and a rediscovery of ancient sources, particularly Aristotle. As we shall see, this rediscovery was to have radical consequences for the understanding of theological rationality and indeed for our ability to reflect on the depths of divine justice.

All of these changes, when taken together, "created the need for a legal order whose mechanisms were better suited to the demands of an urban mercantile society than the legal practices then current in the West."[4] It seemed as if scholars all over Europe were turning to ancient legal sources. The then-recent availability of the full text of Justinian's *Code* and *Digest* triggered a renaissance of Roman law. The rebirth of logic and the rediscovery of Aristotle provided a new breed of legal scholars with the tools for the systematization of law. As Berman notes, "Since Roman legal norms were true and just, they could be reasoned from apodictically, to discover new truth and justice. But since they contained gaps, ambiguities, and contradictions, they had to be reasoned from dialectically as well; that is, problems had to be put, classifications and definitions made, opposing opinions stated, conflicts synthesized."[5] As governments become increasingly centralized, Roman law, adapted and interpreted in new schools of law and by the newly founded profession of "lawyers," slowly but surely replaced feudal and customary law.

The primary beneficiary of all of these changes was going to be the Catholic Church. The investiture controversy—in which the church acquired its independence from the state by condemning simony, the practice of buying a bishop's seat from the local feudal lord—would prove to be the watershed moment in the history of both the church and European state. The Roman papacy succeeded in affirming that it alone had the right to award such positions of authority. Thus, in the late eleventh century, precisely the period in which Anselm of Canterbury was writing, the papacy was engaged in a struggle with feudal lords and kings. Anselm was directly involved in this struggle, on the side of the church. Rome's victory over the state ultimately ensured the victory of law. As Rémi Brague comments, "The major intellectual event that returned the idea of law to the center of Christian thought in the Middle Ages was the elaboration of a coherent system of canon law, beginning with the 'papal revolution' of the late eleventh century."[6]

---

4. James Brundage, *The Medieval Origins of the Legal Profession: Canonists, Civilians, and Courts* (Chicago: University of Chicago Press, 2008), 77.

5. Berman, *Law and Revolution*, 141.

6. Rémi Brague, *The Law of God: The Philosophical History of an Idea* (Chicago: University of Chicago Press, 2007), 217.

Everything changed after this historical moment. The church (and theology) became synonymous with law. As the noted medievalist Gillian Evans points out, for the central-medieval mind (twelfth and thirteenth centuries), there was no contradiction between one's being a servant of the law and one's being a servant of the church. Law and theology were often blended in a way that sounds so foreign and often scandalous to the modern mind.[7] James Brundage is right to claim, "It was probably no coincidence that, for example, Lanfranc (d. 1090) and Anselm (d. 1109), the powerful archbishops of Canterbury at the height of the Reform movement, were both men of substantial legal training, coupled with a strong determination to see that the kings they served observed the prescriptions of canon law."[8]

What is the significance of this shift? How important is it? Here the opinions vary, from the enthusiastic Berman, who sees a radical new beginning and emphasizes the discontinuity with pre-eleventh-century notions of justice, to Anton-Hermann Chroust, who argues that Augustine's ideas about justice remain fully in force throughout the Middle Ages.[9] It is perhaps wise to emphasize both the continuity and what I think were undeniable shifts. We shall do that as we tackle individual medieval authors.

According to Berman, after the eleventh century, law develops as a sacred, self-sustaining, self-evolving being. Contrary to Plato, who is skeptical of human ability to approximate divine justice, eleventh- and twelfth-century lawyers believe law can be mapped onto divine justice. The concept of natural law, so important for medieval theology, provided scholars with an epistemically accessible standard according to which they could critique human positive laws. The Platonic and Augustinian distinction between the two orders is no longer embraced. Instead, medieval thinkers become quite confident of a number of theological propositions.

1. Human justice participates in divine justice. We can and we should probe the depths of divine justice.

2. It is therefore possible to approximate this divine justice in human positive law.

3. The authority of human law derives from its faithfulness to natural law. If a discrepancy should appear, the positive law would cease to have the attribute of legality, and therefore its claim to authority would be nullified.

7. G. R. Evans, *Law and Theology in the Middle Ages* (London: Routledge, 2001).
8. Brundage, *Medieval Origins*, 80.
9. Anton-Hermann Chroust, "The Function of Law and Justice in the Ancient World and the Middle Ages," *Journal of the History of Ideas* 7 (1946): 298–320.

4. Law is the framework for the divine-human relationship, a claim we shall unpack in what follows.

Variations will certainly appear in the interpretation of these propositions. For instance, the particular relation God has to his own law will come up for debate in the thirteenth century. The derivation of the authority of human laws will also be contested in that same century. Even if not all our authors will have the same degree of enthusiasm about these statements, it can be modestly stated that they encapsulate an emerging new confidence in the ability of law both to mediate divine-human relationships and to set the framework for the achievement of human ends and goods. *The view of justice generally is shifting from a reconciliatory to a law-based approach, in which justice operates as an independent body free from emotions or social bonds, is rationally mappable, and perhaps most importantly is commensurate with divine justice.* As Bernard of Clairvaux will argue in the twelfth century, there would be law even if everyone were just. The law of God is that by which God himself lives (*quod ipse ex ea vivat*).[10]

Anselm of Canterbury (1033–1109)

Anselm is not afraid to speculate about divine justice. A Platonist and a realist (categories that will acquire some significance later on), he sets theology firmly on a new logical and rational foundation. We can and we should speculate about the attributes of God, which are ultimately one (the doctrine of divine simplicity); and indeed, we can test positive law for correspondence to natural law. Although, as we shall see, he maintains a strict distinction between human and divine justice, the two are related. There is such a thing as human justice insofar as it participates in divine justice. Moreover, divine justice operates in human affairs through the institution of government.

Neither of these ideas is necessarily new. In fact, Anselm's critics are quick to point out that his whole understanding of the atonement is predicated on a feudal, Germanic understanding of justice. While that statement is not without justification, the reality is that *Anselm's thought spans ancient conceptions of justice and atonement, then-current contextual juridical factors, and an utterly novel preoccupation with law.* It is important to highlight both the elements of continuity with the past (and present) and Anselm's creative way of moving beyond the terms of the current discussion in a way that will decisively alter future theology. Christus Victor elements are still clearly present

10. See Evans, *Law and Theology*, 13.

in his thought, together with an as-yet-partial emphasis on retribution. Both reconciliatory and retributive ideas of justice play clearly delimited parts, but, as we shall see, *Anselm manages to relegate the retributive element to a very precise role in the divine plan*, such that ultimately the divine salvific action is not about punishment but about rehabilitation.

Anselm, Augustine, and Legalism

Although the process would only be completed in the thirteenth and fourteenth centuries, theology was by this time decisively engaged in a process of legalization involving the gradual formation and assertion of canon law, but also the monastic practice of penance. Adolf von Harnack, along with many other critics, comments that Anselm makes the practice of penance the principle of his new theology, rendering his theology purely legalist. While this is a caricature, the practice of penance does indeed play a significant part in his theology, in particular its provision of clear penances for sins. A principle of equivalency and proportionality between sin and atonement is undeniably present in Anselm. Sin ceases to be a supernatural, transpersonal, and demonic force and becomes almost a quantifiable thing. Again, while this is a less than charitable reading of Anselm, the fact remains that, however sympathetic we may wish to be, for him, law (as order) forms the context for any meaningful relationship, both among people and between people and God. As Berman notes, "In *Cur Deus homo* Anselm's theology is a theology of law."[11] Nevertheless, to state my conclusion from the outset, it would be simplistic to talk about a cold Anselmic legalism.

In fact, Anselm never talks about law as such.[12] He prefers to talk about the will of God, although his correspondence demonstrates that he treats these terms synonymously. He does not have a similar hesitation with regard to the concept of justice. Here Anselm remains thoroughly Augustinian. The justice of God is shown not by rewarding people according to their deserts, but by doing what is appropriate to the divine nature, what is appropriate to God, considered as the highest good. Alister McGrath challenges any facile interpretation of Anselm's debt to his legal context: "Far from endorsing prevailing secular accounts of justice, as some less perceptive critics suggested, Anselm aims to disconnect the theological discussion of redemption from preconceived human patterns of distributive or retributive justice."[13] Thus Anselm's

11. Berman, *Law and Revolution*, 180.
12. Brague, *Law of God*, 216.
13. Alister McGrath, *Iustitia Dei: A History of the Christian Doctrine of Justification*, 3rd ed. (Cambridge: Cambridge University Press, 2005), 76.

main interest is the formulation of a theory of justice consonant with divine nature itself. But once he has arrived at that conception, it is such that God himself needs to abide by it, in virtue of his own nature. It is this dimension of necessity that is peculiar to Anselm, as a departure from Augustine, but it is a dimension that will never be quite at home in the Middle Ages.

Crouse also points out the Augustinian background to Anselm's notion of *iustitia*. The fundamental definition of justice is rectitude of will. As we shall see, this is a fundamentally ethical, personal understanding of justice. Nevertheless, Anselm reads it through the legal categories of his day, in particular "satisfaction." This does not mean that Anselm's whole conception is legalist in that sense. We should not allow the analogies he is using from positive law (from feudal courts) to obscure the ultimate theological orientation of his argument.

Sin, as a failure to render to God what is his own, incurs a debt. This debt has to be repaid to God, without there being any possibility of gratuitous forgiveness of this debt. Since this particular debt cannot be paid, there are two options left for the sinner/criminal: *aut poena, aut satisfactio* ("either punishment or satisfaction"). This is a very brief summary of the first part of Anselm's argument. Anselm will then argue that Christ is the only one able to offer a fitting satisfaction to God. We shall engage this argument in detail, but for now let us observe two distinct dimensions of this first part of the argument. First, as observed, Anselm operates with an intensely personal notion of justice as rectitude of will. Once that rectitude of will is lost, as Adam failed to maintain it and thus incurred an original debt, God will necessarily be engaged in the process of restoring this rectitude to humankind. Second, the process of restoration cannot bypass the moment of the repayment of the debt. Here the feudal (or Roman?) conception of satisfaction comes into the picture. And this is where, to most critics, the genuinely personal discussion of justice acquires the cold, arithmetic abstractness and objectivity of legalism. For here we are talking about strict equivalences, proportionality, infinity, and so on. We move from personal to physical categories. Indeed, salvation is ultimately transmitted by a quasi-physical (or metaphysical) participation in the merits of Christ.

To repeat, there is an apparent tension in Anselm between his discussion of justice—not without its critics, to be sure—and his elaboration of the divine solution to human debt. Both of these discussions betray elements of both continuity and discontinuity between ancient theories and the new age in whose formation Anselm was so instrumental.

Let us take the notion of justice first. In *Cur Deus homo*, Anselm selects from a number of competing definitions of justice the following: justice is action directed toward the highest good. As McGrath comments, here the fundamental notion is that of rectitude, with justice as the moral dimension of rectitude.[14] In *De veritate*, Anselm maintains the same notion: justice is uprightness (*rectitudo*) of will kept for its own sake.[15] Thus justice is not the unreflective or perhaps even unintentional keeping of the order but the free willing and affirmation of the order for its own sake. Stones are not just because they maintain the order (they fall to the ground when dropped). It takes a rational nature to be just. But the reasons for which we do certain things are also relevant to the justice of those actions. At this point, as Brower points out, Anselm pioneers a deontological account, anchoring justice in actions not done for some utility (eudaemonism) but for their own sake.

What this notion of justice entails, however, is the concept of a divinely intended order of things. Here the personal dimension is already qualified by a metaphysic. Justice is not independent of knowledge but presupposes it. One must know the rightful order of things (natural law) in order to freely affirm it. Two kinds of critiques are possible at this point.

First, it has been suggested that Anselm is engaging in a "Platonic fantasy,"[16] which absurdly entails that only the philosophers can attain to justice and morality, since it is only they who can know the forms (and thus the order). But we are well and truly beyond Platonic dualism, for with Anselm any person has a knowledge of the natural law. Any person knows right from wrong. Justice is when we choose right for the sake of rightness itself. Anselm's cosmos is a well-ordered construction, populated with free, rational individuals who, ideally, freely affirm the current order of reality. Reality has a transparent, knowable order and structure. It is not difficult to see how such an ontology also requires catalogs of rights and wrongs. It may be this emphasis on the accessibility of natural law that leads to the accusation of legalism, but it should not be forgotten that this is never the complete picture. *The moral quality of an act does not consist simply in the action but also in the orientation of the will in that particular action.* Thus we have both a clear objective standard, a law, and the necessity of the will in acquiescing to that standard. We indeed are not far from legalism, but Anselm is certainly not a legalist.

This brings us to the second critique. Several authors have lamented the way in which Anselm's philosophy simply affirms the status quo. In his theology Anselm simply reproduces the hierarchical feudal order as the natural order of things: the gravity of a crime, for instance, was considered proportionate

---

14. Ibid., 56.

15. Anselm, *De veritate* 12.

16. Sandra Visser and Thomas Williams, *Anselm*, Great Medieval Thinkers (Oxford: Oxford University Press, 2009), 202–7.

to the social status of the victim. Colin Gunton argues that Anselm's position is not oppressive, and Gunton maintains that Anselm merely stood for the duty of the feudal order to uphold the order of rights and obligations, without which society would collapse. But Timothy Gorringe objects to precisely the idea that this preservation ought to take place through retribution. The identification of justice with retribution, he argues, only takes for granted an order and a set of equivalencies between crime and punishment that is in itself unjust. "Abstractions about the need for justice then, as now, have always underwritten oppression."[17]

This certainly is a forceful critique. It is especially poignant today, as we shall see in our penultimate chapter. Yet it does not seem to touch the main principle of Anselm's argument—namely, that there is an underlying order of things—but only his empirical point that feudal society stands for that order. Moreover, it is not even clear that Anselm intended to make this empirical point, only that he utilized a social analogy to make a point about the relationship between the status of the victim and the gravity of the crime. The only hierarchy Anselm really needs for his argument to work is the "ontological difference" between God and humanity. Thus, although Anselm uses an analogy from private law, it "has been broken through completely in the use to which it is put."[18]

Not only is Anselm's approach to justice specifically theological, but his emphasis on law (as order)—which imposes constraints on God himself, not from outside his own nature of course—also marks a decisive transition beyond both Roman and Germanic conceptions of justice. This brings us back to the continuity between these two frameworks (Roman and Germanic), which ought not be forgotten. According to Anton-Hermann Chroust, "The medieval thinkers essentially professed a theological version of the traditional lego-philosophical view that law and justice have as their true purpose the harmonious preservation of the *status quo* in the interest of common peace and order."[19] Indeed, although from the eleventh century onward law becomes universal and unavoidable, its main purpose of arbitration and reconciliation still lingers, until it will be definitively eclipsed at the time of the Reformation and the formation of modern states. Berman corroborates this point in relation to Roman criminal law, which "especially in the earlier period, but also at the time of Justinian, was not greatly concerned with the moral

17. Timothy Gorringe, *God's Just Vengeance: Crime, Violence and the Rhetoric of Salvation*, Cambridge Studies in Ideology and Religion (Cambridge: Cambridge University Press, 1996), 101.

18. John McIntyre, *Anselm and His Critics: A Re-interpretation of the Cur Deus Homo* (Edinburgh: Oliver & Boyd, 1954), 80.

19. Chroust, "Function of Law and Justice," 320.

quality of the specific criminal act; it was concerned, rather, with what is called today the protection of interests and the enforcement of policies."[20] In other words, there was no stringent reaction to crime, no outrage to demand a necessary retribution. The point I have been trying to make is that there is no hesitation about forgiveness in the High Middle Ages, as is sometimes asserted. The difficulty is in trying to capture the essence of a period of transition, where the old still lingers (predominance of arbitration, reconciliation, and peace) as the new emerges and becomes established (the predominance of law). This process will not be completed until the time of the Reformation, where crime becomes an act not simply against private individuals but against the law itself, and thus truly beyond forgiveness. Shailer Matthews's claim that there is an "inhibition to forgiveness" in the Middle Ages either assumes a concept of forgiveness that is inhibited in any possible historical age, or is just a plainly mistaken historical evaluation. Both the newly rediscovered Roman law as well as feudal and Germanic practices actually preferred arbitration.

Anselm's genius is to sense (partly) that an objective law demands an objective righting of the wrong. In tempering and containing the idea of retributive justice (to temporal sins), he decisively advances beyond the medieval consensus.

Sin, Crime, and Punishment

Central to Anselm's doctrine of atonement is his theology of original sin. Sin is simply failure to render to God his due. What is due to God is our obedience and affirmation of the divinely given order, as accessible through natural law. Adam's sin is the failure to preserve this *rectitudo* for its own sake. Thus the essence of original sin is the inherited lack of moral rectitude in the will of fallen humankind. Humans are no longer capable of freely submitting their rational natures to God. The original uprightness of Adam is something that was given to him, something that cannot be acquired. But once given, it became his responsibility to maintain it.

Even in this dimension, Anselm is going much beyond the current Germanic consensus, as Berman points out:

> Sin had formerly been understood to be a condition of alienation, a diminu-
> tion of a person's being; it now came to be understood as specific wrongful
> acts or desires or thoughts for which various penalties must be paid in tem-
> poral suffering, whether in this life or the next. What specific wrongful acts
> or desires or thoughts were to be punished, and by what kinds of degrees of

20. Berman, *Law and Revolution*, 192.

temporal suffering, was to be established primarily by the moral law revealed by God first in Scripture (divine law) and second in the hearts and minds of men (natural law); but it was to be further defined by the positive laws of the church.[21]

The contrast could not be clearer: in pre-eleventh-century theology (and Eastern theology), sin is something that we have to be healed from. Furthermore, penance is an act not of retribution but of discipline and rehabilitation. From the eleventh century onward, penance acquires distinctively retributive overtones. But Anselm restricts retribution to temporal sins. For the sins we commit in our lives we can be punished. Not so for original sin, for which there is no adequate punishment short of complete annihilation.

Berman highlights the contrasting understanding of sin and crime in Anselm and the regnant conceptions:

> The new concepts of sin and punishment based on the doctrine of the atonement were not justified in Germanic terms of reconciliation as an alternative to vengeance, or in Platonic terms of deterrence and rehabilitation, or in Old Testament terms of the covenant between God and Israel—though elements of all three of these theories were present. The main justification given by Anselm and by his successors in Western theology was the concept of justice itself. Justice required that every sin (crime) be paid for by temporal suffering; that suffering, the penalty, be appropriate to the sinful act; and that it vindicate ("avenge") the particular law that was violated.[22]

Thus it is unlikely that Anselm could be explained simply in terms of Germanic or feudal terms. His conception of sin and the appropriate response to it transcends these cultural expectations.

We are about to move on to a discussion of Anselm's doctrine of the atonement as such. Up to this point I have described the prelude to this doctrine, namely, Anselm's understanding of divine justice as that which is appropriate to God's nature, and human justice as rectitude of the will. Human blessedness, for which we have been created, is a gift from God. After the fall, God can no longer give this gift as long as humanity owes God this debt: "man cannot and ought not by any means to receive from God what God designed to give him unless he return to God everything which he took from him."[23] But the purposes of God cannot fail. It would be contrary to the very nature of God to create something and then watch it be destroyed, or to destroy it himself in response to

21. Ibid., 171.
22. Ibid., 183.
23. Anselm, *Cur Deus Homo* [hereafter *CDH*] 1.23.246; see also 1.24.250.

its sin. Punishment—of the kind appropriate to an infinite offense—is never an option for Anselm. His doctrine of creation and of the divine purposes commits him to a view of God as binding himself to the execution of his plans. Once he has created us as the kinds of creatures we are—namely, people destined to achieve blessedness—God has to save us. Thus a certain necessity obtains, but it is important to understand that this necessity is tied in to the nature of God, as well as to his will: once God sets out to create such beings, he is committing himself to seeing them reach their ultimate end.

Standing in the way of God's achieving his purposes is historic human debt. Here we come to the second part of Anselm's doctrine of the atonement, the one that seems most unsatisfactory, for a variety of reasons. His explanation of this part of the doctrine of the atonement may be broken down into discrete constituent parts.

The Impossibility of Gratuitous Divine Forgiveness

One option might be, as Anselm's student Boso suggests, for God to simply forgive and erase the debt. Anselm quickly brushes this suggestion aside. If the foregoing is correct, Anselm is not simply the child of an age suffering from an inhibition to forgiveness. It would have been rather easy for Anselm to invoke extreme circumstances as calling for God's forgiveness, especially since this would preserve the status quo, the order and the peace of creation. His reasons for rejecting this option are theologico-philosophical. The chief stumbling block in the way of such an option is his conception of the nature of God. What emerges from this argument is an understanding of divine nature that is identical to supreme justice.

If God were to simply blot out the transgressions, without receiving a satisfactory compensation, God would cease to be the "controller of sin" (ordinator peccatorum). God would thus be exposed to a contingency that would disrupt and diminish his purposes for the world. This is an impossibility. Again and again, in responding to Boso's reasons, Anselm argues from what is "fitting" about God. We'll return to that theme immediately below. Another similar argument against gratuitous forgiveness goes as follows: justice being regulated by law (notice his appeal to law as being coextensive with justice), for "if sin is neither paid for nor punished, it is subject to no law." But this "makes injustice like God. For as God is subject to no law, so neither is injustice."[24] God alone is not determined or constrained in his actions and thoughts by any external law. If injustice (Anselm's term for any departure

24. Anselm, *CDH* 1.12.218.

from God's ordinances) does not inexorably lead to the repayment of the debt, it is equivalent to God, being subject to no law.

To say that God is subject to no law only means that God is not subject to any law external to his own nature and being, existing eternally alongside God. Anselm might equally have said that God is not bound by any law, save the law of his own being, supreme justice. In determining what God may or may not do, Anselm is not shy to invoke the principle of what is or is not fitting for God: "If God desires a thing, it is right that he should desire that which involves no unfitness."[25] It is a contradiction in terms to claim that God desires something that is unfitting. Therefore, just as it is unfitting for God to desire to lie (and therefore he does not lie), it is unfitting for God to exercise the kind of compassion that does not involve the repayment of debt. As we meditate on and seek to understand the divine attributes, we must probe these in their relationships to each other. In this case, divine compassion must not be seen to interfere with his dignity.

> We ought so to interpret these things [God's liberty and choice and compassion] as that they may not seem to interfere with his dignity. For there is no liberty except as regards what is best or fitting; nor should that be called mercy which does anything improper for the Divine character. Moreover, when it is said that what God wishes is just, and that what He does wish is unjust, we must not understand that if God wished anything improper it would be just, simply because he wished it.[26]

This is a consistent argument throughout his works. In the *Proslogion*, he restates it almost identically: "If God ought not to pity, he pities unjustly."[27] However we define the individual attributes of God, we must not forget that they qualify each other: "Though it is hard to understand how thy compassion is not inconsistent with thy justice; yet we must believe that it does not oppose justice at all, because it flows from goodness, which is no goodness without justice; nay, that it is in true harmony with justice."[28]

Anselm's vision of God and the universe is that of a harmonious whole, ordained by God in light of what is most fitting. There is no contradiction between what is most fitting to God and what appears to reason to be most fitting. Faith shows itself to be consistent with reason and with our intuitions about justice. Anselm reaches these conclusions *remoto Christo*; in other words, he

25. Ibid., 1.12.219.
26. Ibid., 1.12.205.
27. Anselm, *Proslogion* 9.60.
28. Ibid., 9.62.

intentionally leaves out the testimony of Scripture, precisely in order to demonstrate the rationality of Christian faith to the infidel. And it is law, under the guise of fittingness, that provides the linchpin between human order and divine order. In his relations to humanity, God binds himself to his own law. This law and this justice are nothing other than God's very being, as Anselm comments elsewhere.[29] It is God's very nature that makes gratuitous forgiveness impossible.

Either Punishment or Satisfaction

The same argument about what is (intuitively) fitting about God leads Anselm to argue that the fall of humanity into sin, which frustrates the divine plan, has to be in some way reversed, rectified. God created humanity for blessedness and happiness. This happiness is a gift that comes from God as a reward for humanity's being just. God intends to give this gift to humanity, but he cannot simply give it as long as we owe him this great debt. There are only two options left if God is to act "according to the method of justice." Either God punishes the souls of humanity with eternal damnation, or an adequate satisfaction is made for the crime.

Eternal punishment is the only punishment proportionate to the crime, since the crime is committed against the infinite nature of God. There is no wiggle room and no negotiation here. But in doing this, God would thus have created humans only to obliterate them. Given the "fittingness" argument, this cannot stand. It is not fitting for God's being to have created something only to have it destroyed later on. God would not be the supremely wise being.

The only other open option is that of satisfaction. In feudal society, as in Roman law, and indeed in the Old Testament, and also in the canonical practice of penitence, there must exist equivalents to punishment. This need for proportionality fits the legal image I have been describing. The aim of jurisprudence in the Middle Ages is still arbitration, still finding the least avenging course of action. The notion of satisfaction fits precisely such a precedent.

Just satisfaction involves not only returning to the victim what has been taken from her but also giving something more. This is not an alien concept even to our contemporary generation. The concept of reparations is our modern way of doing justice to precisely the same intuitions in the notion of satisfaction. The balance is not righted simply by giving back what has been taken. Indeed, some things cannot be replaced. The sentimental value of an object, for instance, cannot be readily attached to the object's replacement. That sense of irreplaceable loss is precisely what the surplus involved

29. Anselm, *Monologion* 15.65.

in acts of satisfaction addresses. Satisfaction, then, has to be proportionate to the crime.

But what is the crime, and what kind of satisfaction does it demand? The crime is sin. Sin is a failure to render to God his due, by failing to maintain the rectitude of will given by God. God, Anselm argues, stakes his honor on humanity's being able to withstand the temptations of the devil. God's honor consists in his demonstration that this finite creation will remain faithful to God even under temptation, unlike the fallen Satan, who at his own initiative disobeyed God. Humanity dishonors God by caving in to the temptation of Satan. The dishonor consists in the fact that God's purposes are no longer accomplishable (under present conditions), for humanity cannot be given happiness as long as God is owed a debt. Anselm summarizes this argument: "Man being made holy was placed in paradise, as it were in the place of God, between God and the devil, to conquer the devil by not yielding to his temptation, and so to vindicate the honor of God and put the devil to shame, because that man, though weaker and dwelling upon earth, should not sin though tempted by the devil, while the devil, though stronger and in heaven, sinned without any to tempt him."[30]

What was taken from God was nothing more than the possibility of the divine victory over the devil. Notice how Anselm reverses the ancient picture: humanity is no longer described as the impotent weakling under the inescapable influence of the devil. Humans indeed put themselves in this position, but justice demands that humans themselves extricate themselves from this situation. Thus it is impossible for humanity to be reconciled to God "unless man first shall have honored God by overcoming the devil, as he dishonored him in yielding to the devil."[31]

This is the extent of the devil's role in Anselm's scheme of atonement. This conflict is between humanity and God. Creation and humanity belong to God, and God cannot be held hostage to anyone's demands. The older view of the atonement found no sympathy in Anselm. As Richard Southern comments, "He had too uncompromising and too unitary a view of God's dominion over the whole creation to accept any view which diminished God's majesty in the smallest way."[32] There are clear benefits and some challenges to this strategy. Among the benefits we might mention are the due attention to the gravity of sin. Older views did not always adequately account for the personal dimension of sin as the essence of the bondage, but tended to evacuate humanity

30. Anselm, *CDH* 1.22.244.
31. Ibid., 1.22.245.
32. Richard W. Southern, *Anselm: A Portrait in a Landscape* (Cambridge: Cambridge University Press, 1992), 209.

of the responsibility for dealing with it. But there are also clear challenges. Anselm raises the stakes tremendously by deigning to offer an *explanation* of the mechanism by which God saves us. What possible transaction took place between humanity and God, and how might it be explained? The drive for an explanation also brings Anselm into the vicinity of necessity. Some common scheme must equally apply to God as well as to humanity, if such an explanation is at all possible. Older views easily fell back on a narration of a cosmic victory. This did not explain much. The scholastic drive, on the contrary, is to probe the depth of this mystery for its reasonableness.

Christ's Satisfaction for Sins

The next step in the argument, once Anselm has established the necessity of satisfaction as the only alternative to utter destruction, is to demonstrate the impossibility of human satisfaction, despite its necessity. Humanity already owes to God everything it might offer as a gift to God. What is required is a gift that would satisfy the honor of God. Yet humanity cannot offer this, both on account of our sinfulness and because "the price paid to God for the sin of man [should] be something greater than all the universe besides God."[33] Naturally, such a thing is not in the possession of any person, since "he who can give God anything of his own which is more valuable than all things in the possession of God, must be greater than all else but God himself."[34] It seems that humanity cannot make such an offer; only God can do so. Yet it is precisely humanity that must make satisfaction. This brings Anselm to the affirmation of the necessity of the God-man.

Most of book 2 of *Cur Deus homo* is taken up with the demonstration of the necessity and sufficiency of Christ's satisfaction. Christ, as the God-man, offers to God that which he does not owe God, namely, his death. This gift is of infinite value because of Christ's divinity. God, in turn, rewards Christ for this gift, making salvation available, not for Christ who does not need it but for whomever he chooses to bestow it on. Christ, in effect, has acquired exceeding merit, and this merit is transferable to the saints.

Christ did not assume a fallen human nature. Hence, he was not born a mortal. Since death is a consequence of sin, and since he remained steadfast in perfect obedience to the Father, it was within his power not to die. Yet Christ chose to lay down his life in utter obedience to the Father. This "gift of his life surpasses all the sins of men"; it more than sufficiently compensates for the damaged honor of God.

33. Anselm, *CDH* 2.6.258.
34. Ibid.

In return, God bestows a reward that Christ does not need for himself, but which he gives to his followers. Without this reward, Christ's exemplary death in obedience to God would be of no avail. There were other examples than Christ. It is not for lack of examples that humanity found itself crippled and in such a predicament. Rather, it was the debt that could not be removed saved by this means. Thus, despite Anselm's clear inclusion of an exemplary function of the life and death of Christ, he deals a deathblow to any theory of atonement that makes Christ's example the main mechanism of the atonement:

> For surely in vain will men imitate him, if they be not also partakers of his reward. Or who could he more justly make heirs of the inheritance, which he does not need, and of the superfluity of his possessions, than his parents and brethren? What more proper than that, when he beholds so many of them weighed down by so heavy a debt, and wasting through poverty, in the depth of their miseries, he should remit the debt incurred by their sins, and give them what their transgressions had forfeited?[35]

Peter Abelard (1079–1142)

Both the dramatic theory and the satisfaction theory are usually described in theology textbooks as objective understandings of the atonement. The principal benefit of the atonement consists in some good that obtains irrespective of its appropriation by believers. Both describe the work of the atonement as something that is complete and, while it does need to be appropriated in the life of the believer, can be defined without appeal to the latter's subjectivity.

In Abelard we encounter a so-called subjective theory. One should not take these distinctions too rigidly, however. The designation is justified inasmuch as Abelard stresses the example that Christ sets as well as his moral influence. Yet objective elements are not entirely lacking in his thinking. Indeed, there are several traditional elements present in his work, and these should not be overlooked. Moreover, all of the three theories discussed so far involve a transaction of sorts, and this entails something complete made available for reception. The dramatic theory presents a completed victory of Christ, which needs to be appropriated by the believer; the satisfaction theory adduces the merits of Christ, in which we ought to participate; finally, the moral influence theory presents the demonstrated love of Christ, with which we are to be infused.

35. Ibid., 2.19.299.

Nominalism and Ethics

Abelard's specific position on the atonement is determined both by his distinctively Catholic soteriology (his understanding of justification, infusion of love, and sacraments), and by his nominalism and ethics. His work in these fields gave him a distinctive approach to the matter.

Abelard could be described as a moderate nominalist. That is to say, he denies the objective existence of universals. Universals are words (*voces*), and it is only individual things that have existence. This does not mean that we ought to cease speaking about them, but logical rigor demands that we not confuse them with things and that we remain aware of what we are talking about when we do draw on such concepts. This development raises some interesting complications for the doctrine of the atonement. On the one hand, justice is no longer a universal in which human justice participates. It is not a "thing" with a self-contained existence. Neither is human nature a substance in which we participate as humans. There are only individual human beings. The same goes for sin: it is not a substance that gets transmitted through birth.

These categories are not erased so that they may no longer be used in theology, but Abelard's clarification of their nature prevents them from being used in the same traditional ways. Thus human nature is not something that can be abstractly "healed." Nor is original sin something that either has dominion over us (see the dramatic and Eastern personalization of sin) or that burdens us from our mothers' wombs. Human nature, sin, and even justice are realities of the mind. For a nominalist mind it is much more difficult to appreciate our common participation in the humanity of Adam, as well as our common being in Christ.

This denial of universals moves Abelard in a decidedly individualist direction. But it is not so much that Abelard wants to deny all realities other than individual things. The point is that our ways of accounting for these realities, as well as the activity taking place where these realities exist, are logically flawed. There are such things as transindividual relations, but we ought to talk about them in natural, acceptable, and rational terms. One could indeed try to understand his theological project as an apologetic, a purification of the conceptual apparatus of theology. Concepts such as universals, such as human nature, are second-order tools that have run out of steam. We need to employ new and commonsense tools in order to illuminate the realities that these terms were also seeking to describe. Abelard's genius would be to look for a natural explanation of, in this case, the transmission of sin and the infusion of divine love.

Abelard's nominalism is consistent with the jurisprudential trajectory we have been examining. His nominalist check on abstract justice did not block the drive toward law. Quite the contrary, a nominalism hugely influenced by Abelard, according to Berman, "played an indispensable role in the movement to systematize law."[36] As Berman further notes, an abstract conception of justice would have made it difficult to derive particular legal rules and institutions. Nominalism, with its exploration of the logical links between concepts and words, provided the infrastructure for the creation of new positive law and institutions.

It is interesting to note that Abelard's opposition to the satisfaction theory takes place against the background of many shared premises about law. We need to imagine the unified trajectory toward the resurrection of law as being crisscrossed by many different discourses nuancing and contextualizing this larger drive. While the twelfth century participates in the emergence of law, it also elaborates on the relationship between law and self. Jean Porter argues that the whole trend of the twelfth century was to move beyond a wooden legalism.[37] Our theologian is a clear representative of that movement, as his ethics demonstrates. Nevertheless, Abelard's nominalism was not an attack on the notion of the law as such. Such an attack would surely come, but we have to await our contemporary intellectual landscape to witness it.

Abelard distinctly values the divine moral law. God's law is good (Pss. 19:8; 93:5; Rom. 7:13–16), and reason attests to this. While there is another law at work in my body (Rom. 7:23), namely, the law of sin and desire, God's law remains perfect and holy. Porter explains that while Abelard's famous argument ties sin to consent of the will (not to desire, or emotions, or disposition), he still thinks in terms of the strictures of the law, which reflect objective relations of obligation and right, rather than the irreducibly private expression of individual emotions. What he has in mind here is the long tradition of locating sin and guilt in the passions. Thus the inner consent that constitutes merit or sin takes its value from its objective character as an act of respect or contempt for God the lawgiver.[38] His ethical emphasis on consent does not therefore compete with his extraordinary valuation of the objective law.

Sin

Abelard's conceptualization of ethics is one step further in than Anselm's. If Brower is right to catalog Anselm's ethics as deontological, then Abelard's

36. Berman, *Law and Revolution*, 141.

37. Jean Porter, "Responsibility, Passion, and Sin: A Reassessment of Abelard's *Ethics*," *The Journal of Religious Ethics* 28, no. 3 (2000): 367–94.

38. Ibid., 389.

might be described as situational.[39] Whereas Anselm locates the moral value of an act in the disposition of the will, which is clearly vitiated after Adam's fall, for Abelard, it is the conscious assent to this inclination that is the morally relevant factor. For Anselm, it is the very disorientation of the will, as demonstrated in its misguided desires, that is sinful. What mediates between us and God is a catalog of morally upright acts. Abelard does not deny the existence of objective moral obligation, but he pushes this obligation inward, defining it in terms of obedience to or contempt of God. "All actions are in themselves indifferent," he writes; "the intention, only, gives them moral worth."[40]

If the moral worth of an action does not reside in the deed itself, nor in the passions, but in the intention, then the doctrine of original sin will have to be reworked. And Abelard does not hesitate to rework it. We endure not the *guilt* of Adam's sin, but only the punishment for it. This is of a piece with his nominalism: guilt cannot be transmitted unless there is an identity of substance. We do inherit the liability for Adam's sin, which is God's punishment of the human race, our alienation from God, including the agonies of both temporal and eternal death. We also inherit the disordering of our reason, which is now "overshadowed by sin." Our soul is no longer able to rule over our lower nature. Our will is misdirected.

Yet it is not the misdirectedness of our will that is in itself sinful. It is our conscious assent to that misdirection. This is the reason why we cannot be said to inherit the guilt of Adam's sin, for the deterioration and immoral inclination of our being is something to which we have to assent in order for it to be sinful. Abelard is quick to note that all humans commit actual sin and that sin is thus a universal condition of humanity. To summarize: we inherit not the guilt of Adam but the corruption and the punishment of death inflicted by God on his descendants.

The Logic of Divine Love

In one swift move, therefore, Abelard has removed Anselm's traditional understanding of original sin as creating an infinite debt of humanity before God. He also challenges the Anselmian idea that God might be bound by some kind of necessity, which he calls "extraneous to his nature." Supreme justice, which Anselm had equated with the nature of God, is not seamlessly embodied in revealed law. We are beginning to witness the nominalist erosion of the identity between God and law.

39. See R. E. O. White, *Christian Ethics* (Macon, GA: Mercer University Press, 1994), 117.
40. Quoted in ibid. See also Peter Aberlard, *A Dialogue of a Philosopher with a Jew, and a Christian*, trans. Pierre J. Payer (Toronto: Pontifical Institute of Medieval Studies, 1979), 111, 158. See also Abelard, *Abailard's Ethics*, trans. J. Ramsay McCallum (Oxford: Blackwell, 1935), 42.

While Abelard values the law that God gave to Moses as good and perfect, it must not be understood as a perfect manifestation of his nature, since it does not fully manifest God's nature as love. The law functions on the principle of fear: it steers people to right action on the basis of their fear of consequences. It does not operate out of love. He contrasts the Old Testament and New Testament ages: the former "is said to be of slavery, the latter is of freedom; the former of fear, the latter of love; the former imperfect, the latter perfection."[41] By arguing that the law is imperfect and that God cannot be bound by the law that he has given to us, Abelard weakens the link between God and law. Such a law has a very well-defined function, and it is superseded by Christ, who fulfills it. Love is the ground of the divine-human relationship.

The love of God still imposes a necessity of salvation on God. He could not have not saved us, for it is in his very nature to be love. Richard Weingart contrasts this "necessity inherent in divine nature" with an Anselmian "external necessity."[42] The contrast is not convincing, since for Anselm divine law is not external to his own nature, per the doctrine of divine simplicity. Abelard similarly restricts what God can or cannot do: his power is limited by his goodness. God cannot do what is not good, or fail to do what is good.[43]

An essential difference still remains between Abelard and Anselm on the question of divine necessity. Anselm's affirmation that law is binding on God ties the latter to a particular, necessary course of action (leading ultimately to Christ, Anselm's objective). Abelard's God is not bound by any prescribed course of action, but only by his love. God might conceivably have manifested this love in salvation in many different ways, yet he chose this particular method.

It is not immediately clear whether Abelard specifically objects to Anselm's theory of atonement. If he does, then he is grossly caricaturing Anselm, as Weingart also shows.[44] Both thinkers, however, share a critique of the *ius diaboli*. Moreover, Abelard seems to be adopting Anselm's main line of reasoning, in addition to which he invokes the Ciceronian notion of justice.

Despite their common elements, the two systems could hardly be more different. Abelard fundamentally disagrees on the nature of the problem. This is not a judicial debt, but a disorientation of desire. It is this deterioration of human will that has to be mended. The process of mending, moreover, has to take place along human, natural lines.

41. Quoted in Richard E. Weingart, *The Logic of Divine Love: A Critical Analysis of the Soteriology of Peter Abailard* (Oxford: Clarendon, 1970), 70.
42. Ibid., 92.
43. Ibid., 93.
44. Ibid., 89–91.

It is not that he denies there being an objective aspect to the problem. Our liability to punishment is real. The subjective dimension is that we have a strong inclination to obey our misdirected desires. What Christ has to do is precisely to heal this disorientation. Hastings Rashdall argues that in this Abelard is "inspired no doubt by Origen." Moreover, he castigates the "immorality of anything which makes forgiveness arbitrary. He [Abelard] sees that God can only be supposed to forgive by making the sinner better, and thereby removing any demand for punishment."[45] Rashdall's criticism gets at the (very Catholic) distinctive of Abelard's doctrine of the atonement: God's forgiveness is justified by his creation in us of a different habit, which is nothing but divine love in us.

Abelard's Doctrine of Penal Substitution?

This subjective dimension of the atonement, while it is indeed at the center of Abelard's thought and is his most original contribution to the doctrine of the atonement, does not deny the necessity of our being absolved of our liability for Adam's crime. While he rejects Anselm's schema of *aut satisfactio aut poena*, he actually places more emphasis than Anselm on Christ's undergoing punishment on our behalf. Thomas Williams's conclusion that "Abelard explicitly teaches a theory of penal substitution" is not far off the mark. Liberal historians have been rather embarrassed by this, dismissing it as being inessential to his thought, a mere vestige of an older language, or mere metaphors devoid of accompanying theories. Without engaging in this interpretative dispute, it should be pointed out that Abelard does vigorously reject satisfaction theories of the atonement, which run on tracks parallel to penal substitution. He also explicitly denies that God might or should be appeased by the death of his Son. Nevertheless, he also talks about Christ as expiator of sins. "He has removed from us the punishment of sin by which even the righteous were previously held." Moreover, as Weingart comments, Christ also voluntarily submitted to God's wrath against sin. Because Christ is sinless, he saved us from divine wrath.[46]

What are we to do with these texts? On the one hand, one might surmise that Abelard is forced to comment on specific texts, in particular Rom. 4:25 and 8:30, on which occasion he reverts to traditional language, yet without logically integrating them into his theory. On the other hand, he could in fact be proposing a multidimensional explanation of the work of Christ.

45. Hastings Rashdall, *The Idea of Atonement in Christian Theology* (New York: Macmillan, 1919), 359.
46. Weingart, *Logic of Divine Love*, 145.

There is no necessary contradiction between the idea that Christ submitted himself to divine wrath and the conviction that God's attitude toward
us must not change. As I will show in the last chapter, there is a way of
telling the story of penal substitution in a way that neither eclipses other
images nor involves God in anthropomorphic caricatures. Nevertheless,
Abelard certainly does not believe the focus of Christ's work on the cross
is on its canceling of our liability to punishment. What, then, is the cross
fundamentally about?

Abelard's Positive Theory

The following well-known passage from Abelard's Romans commentary encapsulates the essence of his thought: "By the faith which we have
concerning Christ love is increased in us, because, by virtue of the conviction that God in Christ has united our human nature to himself, and by
suffering in that same nature has demonstrated to us that supreme love."[47]
All his central ideas about the atonement are captured in this text. Christ,
in dying for us, does not (fundamentally) pay a penalty on our behalf. It is
not God who sends Jesus to his death, but Jesus goes to these lengths out
of his obedience to God and his dedication to his vocation. Such a demonstration of love has the power to evoke in us a similar love. "Each one is
also made more righteous after the Passion of Christ than before; that is,
he loves God more, because the completed benefit kindles him in love more
than a hoped-for benefit."[48]

The presence of this infused love is what ultimately justifies the sinner
before God. Abelard assumes a Justinian concept of justice as rendering to
each his or her due. It is impossible for human beings to stir this love within
themselves. It must be achieved on their behalf. This theory, then, is quite
explicitly not mere exemplarism, but an actual infusion. The divine love is
instilled in us, infused in us, by the force of Christ's example. At the same
time, Abelard's belief in the freedom of the will prevents him from going all
the way with Augustinian predestinarianism. This love has to be consented
to, acted on. The grace of God, made available in Christ, has to be received
in faith, hope, and love. While the elect are determined by God's free choice,
it still depends on them to embrace the offer of grace.

The passion of Christ is directly related to the moral transformation of the
believer. "Therefore, our redemption is that supreme love in us through the
Passion of Christ, which not only frees us from slavery to sin, but gains for

---

47. Ibid., 79; Abelard, *Romans* 162.
48. Abelard, *Romans* 168, *questia* on Rom. 3:26.

us the true liberty of the sons of God, so that we may complete all things by his love rather than by fear."[49]

Against the accusation that this is a mere Pelagian exemplarism, Abelard argues that the infusion of this divine love, through Christ's example, does not take place independently of the work of the Spirit. It is ultimately the Spirit who enables the predestined to acquire this divine love, through God's prevenient grace.

> The Spirit creates light first through the inspiration of faith, then hope, and finally love, by so perfecting man in works of love that he loves not only for himself but also for others. Not only is he good for his own advantage, but he also makes others good by the example of his works, by the benefits offered, and by the doctrine which he preaches. Therefore the creation of light signifies the illumination of faith. The Holy Spirit, inspiring those whom he pleases, begins the spiritual building of the soul from this foundation.[50]

Such grace is what enables the human response to this incredible demonstration of love, turning the sinner toward God in love. This perfect love casts out fear. It sets us on a renewed relationship with God, based on new terms.

Thomas Aquinas (1225–74)

The thirteenth century witnesses the apogee of the legal revolution that started in the eleventh century. The doctrine of the atonement, then, naturally takes a further step in the direction of its legalization. The rediscovery and rehabilitation of the works of Aristotle as compatible (in principle) with Christian doctrine contributed both to the consolidation of the doctrine of human nature and to confidence in the doctrine of the being of God. Aristotle had not written specifically on law, but the translation into Latin of his *Ethics* and *Politics*, an event that took place during the lifetime of Thomas Aquinas, proved immensely significant for the future course of Christian theology. Aquinas in particular, more than any other Christian medieval theologian, proved instrumental not only in making Aristotle acceptable but also in synthesizing his thought with the theology of the church.

Political Theology

Aquinas's political theology is also a watershed in the history of theology. While he does not uncritically borrow from Aristotle, it can be said that, as far

49. Ibid., 168.
50. Quoted in Weingart, *Logic of Divine Love*, 166, from Abelard, *Expositio in hexameron*.

as it goes, Aristotle's theory of nature is the cornerstone of his political philoso-phy. Nevertheless, the "non-Aristotelian flavor of the Thomistic teaching"[51] can definitely be seen in Aquinas's supplementation of it with a Christian theism.

Humanity is inherently political and social. It belongs to our very nature to be in community. Social life represents one of the ends of human nature, and as such it belongs to its very essence. This represents a step beyond the dismissive politics of Augustine, for whom the state and the polis do not stand for positive, much less appropriate, goals of the human being. Aquinas adopts the Aristotelian idea of the social and political realization of human nature without hesitation. The purpose of the city, moreover, is the cultivation of virtue among individual citizens. A city is good and just if it succeeds in this cultivation of virtue.

But cities need to be ruled, and they require regimes of power that impose such a rule. Essential to the life of the city are the laws by which those in power justly rule. Thus, as Ernest Fortin comments, "Laws are the privileged instrument of politics and stand in relation to the works of man as universals to particulars. It is through them more than through any other agency that the ruler promotes justice and moral goodness among the citizens. Moral virtue is acquired precisely by the repetition of those acts which the law prescribes, or by habitual living and education under good laws."[52] Thus laws do not have a merely "restrictive" function but are also the positive means for the inculcation of virtue among individuals. To be a social and political being is to be a being under law. Not only does law retain its primacy for Aquinas—as the context for the proper relation between people and between God and humanity—but law is also given a positive specification, as the means ordained by God for the moral education of humanity.

The theological supplement consists in the idea that there is a personal, divine, and thus transpolitical realm that legitimates and judges the justice of the city. This goes beyond the purely immanent logic of Aristotle, according to which the ultimate standard is human excellence. The laws of the city not only have to promote human excellence, but also have to reflect "natural law," namely, the divinely given order of nature. In other words, the city must be conducive to an appropriate realization of human nature. It follows that any departure from human law, inasmuch as this law is faithful to natural law, ultimately represents an offense against God. Each of these offenses incurs a debt of punishment, to which we shall return momentarily.

51. Ernest L. Fortin, "Thomas Aquinas," in *The History of Political Philosophy*, ed. Leo Strauss and Joseph Cropsey, 3rd ed. (Chicago: University of Chicago Press, 1987), 264.
52. Ibid., 257. See also Thomas Aquinas, *Summa theologiae* [hereafter *ST*] 1.2, Q 92, art. 1: "Lawmakers make men good by habituating them to good works."

Fortin summarizes these points well: "Within this context man's whole moral life acquires a distinctively new orientation; it ceases to be understood solely in terms of human completeness or fulfillment and becomes in the final instance a matter of willing and grateful compliance with a divinely authorized and unconditionally binding law."[53] Aquinas, it seems, remains within an understanding of justice as right order. His notion of justice, as McGrath comments, consists in a rectitude of order within the interior disposition of humans.[54] For Aquinas, in other words, justice is a virtue of the soul. Human positive laws, when right, are conducive to the creation of this virtue.

The Function of Law

Law isn't merely the constraint of a prior relationship to God (old covenant) that has to be overcome but is also the continued condition (although modified) of the Christian's relationship to God. As we shall see, for Aquinas, Christian life consists in the acquisition of merit, which alone satisfies the justice of God. Humanity must cooperate with divine grace in the production of such merit, on pain of temporal and future punishment. The important point to remember is that law forms a constant background for divine-human relationships.

This does not mean that there is only one law. Thomas recognizes five types of laws. (1) The eternal law (*lex aeterna*) is the very mind of God, the divine providence and ordering of reality. (2) The natural law (*lex naturalis*) represents the imprint in human nature of this design. All people have access to the most fundamental features of this natural law, namely, its basic precepts, although their significance for particular actions is not always transparent to all. (3) Human law represents those laws enacted and promulgated by human authorities. These authorities have a well-established purpose in the divine plan: they enable humans to realize their full nature. Disobedience of these laws, insofar as they are just, represents a disobedience of God. Divine law (*lex divina*) is divided between (4) old law and (5) new law. The Mosaic law was good, but imperfectly so, since it was not conducive to the ultimate end of human nature, namely, our clinging to God; the new law, or the law of Christ, represents the current determination of rights and obligations we have as Christians.

It is important to understand that all of these dimensions are called law analogically. In other words, they are what they are by analogical participation in the eternal law. Thus, the new law is not law in the same sense in which human positive law is law. It has different characteristics, just as it has different ends. We shall return to this point in due time.

53. Fortin, "Thomas Aquinas," 265.
54. McGrath, *Iustitia Dei*, 158.

We have to make two more points regarding this law. The first one has to do with the nature of the law—all dimensions of the law are included here. Aquinas calls law an "ordinance [or dictate] of reason."[55] Thus by its very nature it makes sense. It is not an arbitrary degree. One should not read too much of the intellectualist-voluntarist debate into this point. But Aquinas is convinced that God himself is a rational being, and that we ourselves participate in this divine rationality. We do not simply and blindly submit to an order we do not understand, but we can appropriate it, we can "own it." Brague reflects on the meaning of this "rationality," or better, "reasonableness," of the law: "Within the full extension of this term, one idea remains constant: that of a capacity to make something one's own, to appropriate what is given. One can become part of an order and not simply submit to it; one can understand a manner of acting and not merely imitate it in servile fashion."[56] This rational character of the law further signifies two things: on the one hand, the subjects to the law remain critically engaged with regard to law, being competent to discern its justice or injustice. On the other hand, a certain practical wisdom comes into play in the application of law to particular circumstances. Laws are not meant to be obeyed blindly, but they need to be understood in their very nature (i.e., their end).

The second consideration in regard to law has to do with its retributive function. Aquinas writes that "it is the fear of punishment that law makes use of in order to ensure obedience: in which respect punishment is an effect of the law."[57] The exact position of Aquinas in relation to theories of retributive justice is a matter of some controversy. On the one hand, he argues that temporal punishments are for the purposes of rehabilitation; they are corrective rather than retributive.[58] On the other hand, in some cases punishments ought to be preventive, as for example in the case of unrepentant heretics, who should be killed because they would otherwise jeopardize the health of the church.

Eleonore Stump argues against making Aquinas an Anselmian theologian concerned primarily with the righting of balances. She argues that punishment has the strict function of healing for sin. Punishment, in other words, is that part of penance (together with contrition and confession) that consists in the infliction of suffering for healing purposes. She holds that "the function of satisfaction for Aquinas, then, is not to placate a wrathful God but instead to

55. Aquinas, *ST* 1.2, Q 92, art. 1.
56. Brague, *Law of God*, 225.
57. Aquinas, *ST* I.II. Q 92; art. 2.
58. Ibid., II.II. Q 66; art. 6.

restore a sinner to a state of harmony with God."[59] Further, "any punishing, then, is strictly a means to an end."[60] God, she concludes, is not concerned with the balancing of the accounts, as in Anselm's satisfaction theory.

While the debate over the precise nature of Aquinas's theory of punishment remains open, Stump is surely too categorical about the functionalism of punishment. She is also wrong about the idea of divine wrath, as we shall see. While Stump's aim is not to argue against Aquinas's holding to a theory of retributive justice, the clear presence of retributive elements demonstrates that it is quite difficult to create too much distance between him and Anselm. While Anselm himself is not a clear retributivist, both writers share with retributivism at least one element, namely, that something (either punishment, as with Aquinas, or some other satisfaction, as with Anselm) must redress the balance of justice. This thought is as clear in Aquinas as it is in Anselm, for he explicitly argues that through punishment the "balance of justice is restored."[61]

Further, both writers share another principle of retributivism, namely, proportionalism. Aquinas argues that the punishment ought to fit the crime,[62] and when he gives different justification procedures for types of crimes, the first one is clearly retributivist: "A greater sin, all things being equal, deserves greater punishment."[63]

What the foregoing demonstrates beyond doubt is that, while other justification procedures for punishment are clearly present in Aquinas, the retributive dimension is unmistakable. What satisfies divine justice is not simply, as Stump wishes, "to present God with an instance of human nature which is marked by perfect obedience, humility, and charity, and which is at least as precious in God's eyes as the marring of humanity by sin is offensive,"[64] but clearly includes an element of punishment as a retribution. It is not necessarily, as we shall see, that it must include this element, but that it does include it, and fittingly so.

God's Fitting Reaction to Sin

In sinning, humans dent the honor of God. Aquinas has no fundamental disagreement with this Anselmian premise. The primacy of law comes again to the fore in his basically Augustinian definition of sin as "a word, deed, or action contrary to eternal law." Sin is also a disturbance of order. Thus, "a sinful act

59. Eleonore Stump, "The Problem of Evil: Analytic Philosophy and Narrative," in *Analytical Theology: New Essays in the Philosophy of Theology*, ed. Oliver D. Crisp and Michael D. Rea (Oxford: Oxford University Press, 2009), 271–72.

60. Ibid., 274.

61. Aquinas, *ST* 2.2, Q 108, art. 4.

62. Ibid., 2.2, Q 99, art. 4.

63. Ibid., *ST* 1.2, Q 105, art. 2, ad. 9.

64. Stump, "Problem of Evil," 276.

makes a person punishable in that he violates the order of divine justice. He returns to that order only by some punitive restitution that restores the balance of justice." This clearly operates along lines very similar to interpersonal satisfaction: "This restoration of the quality of justice by penal compensation is also to be observed in injuries done to one's fellow men. Consequently, it is evident that when the sinful or injurious act has ceased[,] there still remains the debt of punishment."[65]

Again, it is beyond any doubt that Aquinas retains a clearly retributive character to the proper amends for sin. However, what probably gives occasion to these contrary interpretations is that he refuses (1) to make punishment into a necessity obtaining on God, and (2) to cast it as the sole means of salvation, or as the only description of what goes on at the cross. Let us take the necessity issue first.

Despite stressing the overarching character of law, Aquinas is careful not to make God subject to law. He points out that "necessary things are not subject to the eternal law."[66] Even more explicitly, "Things pertaining to the divine nature or Essence are not subject to the eternal law, but are the eternal law itself."[67] This does not seem to clarify things a great deal, for what Thomas seems to be arguing is that God's very being is the eternal law. Thomas, in fact, holds to the position that God's being and God's existence are one and the same thing. We shall return to this debate in the next section of this chapter, which is the conclusion to our medieval discussion.

In the third part of the *Summa*, Aquinas turns to Anselm's argument about the necessity of divine justice. He first rehearses Anselm's negative answer to the question of God's gratuitous forgiveness: "He would deny himself were he to deny his justice, since He is justice itself. It seems impossible, then, for man to be delivered otherwise than by Christ's passion." To this Aquinas replies: "Even this justice depends on the divine will, requiring satisfaction for sin from the human race. . . . If He forgives sin, which has the formality of fault in that it is committed against Himself, He wrongs no one: just as anyone else, overlooking a personal trespass, without satisfaction, acts mercifully and not unjustly."[68] Aquinas here invokes some basic intuitions taken from human justice, but in doing this he seems to depart precisely from the Augustinian and specifically theological claim that God is not just another human being, and that therefore intuitions from the field of human justice do not necessarily obtain with respect to God.

65. Aquinas, *ST* 1.2, Q 87, art. 6.
66. Ibid., 1.2, Q 93, art. 4.
67. Ibid.
68. Ibid., 3, Q 46, art. 3.

On closer inspection, however, Anselm and Aquinas are not that far apart. What Aquinas is suggesting is that God could have determined his being (and therefore his law) in any other way. Nevertheless, he chose to make his justice essential in the order of his salvation. As Aquinas points out, "Christ willed to deliver the human race from sins not merely by his power," which he could have done without any impropriety, "but also according to justice."[69] In this, God demonstrates how much he values justice, choosing to abide by it in the process of salvation.

It was not necessary for God to draw on his conception of justice in the order of salvation. This raises some complications for Aquinas's doctrine of God, as the debate between intellectualism and voluntarism will show half a century later.

While it was not necessary for God to act according to justice, it was nevertheless "fitting." As Adam Johnson explains in his illuminating article,[70] fittingness for Aquinas is different from fittingness for Anselm, for whom it means appropriateness to the being of God. For Aquinas it means simply the way a particular act is preferable to another because it brings about more effects, which themselves contribute to the goal of the act. Anselm, Johnson shows, looks back from the act to the agent, while Aquinas looks forward from the act to the multiple effects it has. This "telic" fittingness "accounts for his exceptional readiness to incorporate seemingly disparate elements into his thought."[71]

To rehearse our point about the necessity of a particular means of atonement, while Aquinas does include a clear penal element in the manner of atonement, he refuses to say that God was under any necessity to act in such a way. The fact that God nevertheless did act in this manner can be demonstrated to be the most fitting. This brings us to the second point, about the specific manner of the atonement.

The Manner of Salvation

It would be best to state our conclusion from the outset: Aquinas's doctrine of the atonement includes clear elements of penal substitution, but he refuses to make this particular explanation the sole description of what goes on in the life and passion of Christ. Adolf von Harnack's conclusion is somewhat overstretched, but still captures some of the tension: "A vicarious penal suffering, in the strict sense of the terms, is not recognized even by Thomas, because on the whole question he allowed only a limited range to *iustitia dei*."[72] His later

---

69. Ibid., 3, Q 46, art. 6.

70. Adam Johnson, "A Fuller Account: The Role of 'Fittingness' in Thomas Aquinas' Doctrine of the Atonement," *International Journal of Systematic Theology* 12, no. 3 (2010): 302–18.

71. Ibid., 306.

72. Adolf von Harnack, *History of Dogma*, trans. Neil Buchanan (Boston: Little, Brown, 1907), 6:193.

comment is nonetheless right on the mark: Aquinas is "wavering between the
. . . objective and subjective redemption."[73] What Harnack means is that Aquinas is mixing and blending metaphors to such an extent that he incorporates
both Anselm and Abelard, in addition to anticipating later penal substitution.
He emphasizes both the objective satisfaction of the debt of punishment and
the subjective creation of love inside our hearts.

These are indeed the two essential components of Aquinas's doctrine of
the atonement. On the one hand, we have the objective work of Christ on the
cross. On the other hand, we have Aquinas's turn to the doctrine of merit,
which has to be subjectively appropriated through the sacraments. The presence of both of these elements is characteristic of Catholic doctrines of the
atonement and corresponds to the Catholic inclusion of sanctification (the
continuing acquisition of Christ's merit) in the process of justification. It is
as essential for Aquinas as it was for Anselm and Abelard that the work of
atonement include not only a legal dimension but also an ontological, transformative one. God cannot be ultimately justified in forgiving us and restoring
our relationship to him except on the basis of the creation in our souls of the
virtue of justice. Quite naturally, then, Aquinas too must provide his understanding of the objective and completed work of Christ with some linchpin
connecting the subjective appropriation in the human soul.

That there is a clear element of penal substitution in Aquinas is undeniable,
contra Harnack. Today, it is mostly critics of Aquinas, rather than his defenders,
who are prone to acknowledge it.[74] Although, on occasion, he seems to revert to
an Anselmian scheme, suggesting that what Christ offered to God was something
like an homage, as opposed to a penalty, talk of penalty is present as well. I shall
argue that Aquinas retains three fundamental elements of a penal substitution
theory, in the classic sense of the term. (1) Christ's death on the cross can be described as a punishment, even though other descriptions are also possible, most
notably sacrifice, but also example. (2) God the Father was indeed involved in
the sending of Jesus to the cross. In other words, God retains some agency in the
death of Jesus. (3) The event of the cross did have a causal effect on the wrath
of God, even as crude, anthropomorphic caricatures are avoided. After Aquinas
checks off all of these points, he turns to the doctrine of merit.

First, Christ's passion has the quality of a punishment that removes our
debt of sin. In book 3 of the *Summa theologiae*, Aquinas refers to Isa. 53:4,
arguing that as a result of his carrying our iniquities and sorrows, we were
freed from the punishment of sin. Aquinas's clear ontological vision of the

---

73. Ibid., 6:196.
74. See, for instance, Gorringe, *God's Just Vengeance*, 117.

believers' participation in and with Christ (Rom. 5) makes any such transfer, or imputation, of guilt/sin unproblematic. This is as clear an element of penal substitution as one could get: our sins are reckoned to Christ, who in turn dies for them. It is true that sometimes Aquinas quickly recoils into talk of a kind of nonpenal satisfaction. Although the great Anselmian scheme of *aut satisfactio aut poena* is well known, he makes no effort to distinguish himself from it. Thus it may be safe to infer that Aquinas in fact argues *both* that Christ pays the penalty *and* that he offers an infinitely valuable homage to God, far outweighing the debt of punishment deserved. Thus, in response to the question of how we were delivered from the debt of punishment, Aquinas answers: "Inasmuch as Christ's passion was sufficient and superabundant satisfaction for the sins of the whole human race: but when sufficient satisfaction has been paid, then the debt of punishment is abolished."[75] At times, Aquinas gives indication that there is no contradiction between these two manners: "It is a fitting way of satisfying for another to submit oneself to the penalty deserved by that other."[76] Other times, he indicates that it is precisely the penalty that is the satisfaction: "His goodness shines forth, since by no penalty endured could man pay enough satisfaction."[77]

Anselm's oscillation with regard to the quality of Jesus death is not mirrored in his determination of its agency: "In three respects God the Father did deliver up Christ to the passion. First, by ordaining that this passion would be the means of the deliverance of the human race; second, by infusing him with charity, and thus the will to suffer for us; third, by not shielding him and abandoning him to the prosecutors."[78] A penal substitution theorist might have liked Aquinas to add a fourth respect: in that God ordained death to be the penalty for sin (see Rom. 6:23); or perhaps even a fifth dimension: in that the human courts of justice, when legitimate, are executors of the divine will (see Rom. 13:4). But Aquinas does not stray so far. His main concern is not, however, to deny that God is a divine child abuser, although he does seem aware of this point. He argues that God did not simply deliver Christ to be killed: that would be a "wicked and cruel act." Rather, he "inspired him with the will to suffer for us."[79] Of course, such a disclaimer would be insufficient today, for it still has God demanding this sacrifice, and although Christ in his human nature and of his own free will goes to the cross, God can still be seen as delighting in it.

75. Aquinas, *ST* 3, Q 49, art. 3.
76. Ibid., 3, Q 50, art. 1.
77. Ibid., 3, Q 47, art. 3.
78. Ibid.
79. Ibid.

While Aquinas is far from the thought that God killed Jesus, he does affirm that it was the Father who equipped him with the desire to be obedient even to death. Thus Christ's death was indeed both ordained by God as the solution to human sin and something to which he "nudged" Jesus (in his human nature), as well as something in which he delighted.

This brings us to the third and final point in relation to the penal substitutionary elements of Jesus's death: by his death, Christ reconciles us to God. In book 3, Q 49, art. 3, Aquinas summarily dismisses caricatures of this idea: it is not "as if God had begun anew to love us," but that an objective determination of this love was accomplished by the removal of sin. There is no denying the fact that humanity had to be reconciled to God, but neither does the Doctor neglect the Godward dimension of the atonement: "Now it is the proper effect of sacrifice to appease God: just as man likewise overlooks an offense committed against him on account of some pleasing act of homage shown him."[80]

I have so far presented the positive contribution of Thomas in terms of his elaboration of a further, penal dimension in addition to the satisfaction and exemplarist ideas he borrows from Anselm and Abelard. The final component has to do with the transfer of the merit acquired by Christ. The foregoing has had to do with God's solution to the problem of past sin, including original sin. Now Aquinas attempts to explain the divine solution to future sin. His solution consists in the combination of a doctrine of merit with the doctrine of the sacraments.

Christ's charity merits grace for all people. This is consonant with Aquinas's theology of a grace that is merited. People have to make some work, in charity, that merits God's grace. The specification "in charity" goes back to the idea of law. Charity is the end of the law (Gal. 5:14; Rom. 13:8; 2 John 1:5). It is the virtue of love that springs naturally from our souls, not under any compulsion from the law, yet nevertheless being habituated into it by the law. It is impossible to have this charity apart from the prevenient grace of God. But one must assent to and cooperate with this prevenient grace. We have access to the superabundant merit of Christ through our sacramental incorporation into Christ, as his members. Nevertheless, and this is the crucial point, justification is a process whereby our souls, with the aid of and in cooperation with grace, continue to develop and acquire the virtue of charity. It is only insofar as our faith is demonstrated as love that we can be said to possess the virtue of justice. This love is nothing but the internalized law of Christ.

80. Ibid., 3, Q 49, art. 4.

John Duns Scotus (1265–1308)

God, Law, and Necessity

The thirteenth century was to witness an important theological conflict between two currents of thought on the relationship between divine intellect and will. On the one hand, Dominicans tended to be intellectualists in that they saw the divine mind as the chief spring of divine action. On the other hand, Franciscans were so-called voluntarists in that they regarded divine will as the primordial principle of divine action. The intellectualism of the Dominican school was of a piece with their Aristotelianism (and indeed Neoplatonism) and their general ontological orientation. Aquinas had insisted that although God was free to create differently than he did, the fact that he did create this present world is not entirely accidental. The Doctor did not quite argue that the world was necessary, but others perceived this conclusion as a risk, or even tendency, of his Aristotelian-inclined theology. The ontological participation of created reality in the divine being tended to imply the erasure of all distinctive individuality, as well as the destruction of the ontological distinction between God and humanity. Both of these claims were more or less explicitly held by Averroes, the Muslim interpreter of Aristotle through whose influence Thomas himself read the philosopher.

The Averroist theology that had taken root at the University of Paris was condemned in 1277. Duns Scotus's work is best understood as the defense of this condemnation. God's being had to be understood as absolutely different from the world. A consequence of this difference is that God's relationship to the world is that of a necessary being to contingent beings. It is not that Aquinas, or the Dominicans, denied the contingency of creation, but their Neoplatonism showed in their claim that God, in creating these natures, oriented himself according to his intellect. This seems to imply that the created essences somehow preexisted in the divine mind, ascribing a quasi-eternity to the world. Despite the fact that Thomas vehemently rejected this particular Aristotelian doctrine (of the eternity of the world), he nevertheless somehow held that God is still constrained by his intellect in the act of creation.

For Duns Scotus this amounts to a denial of God's freedom. The essences of things are not necessarily binding on God, because God simply wills them into being, rather than first contemplating them and then actualizing them as a result of his knowledge of them. While God knows all possibles, he is not compelled by anything intrinsic to them to actualize them. It is purely his will to create these particular beings that is the cause of their creation. There is nothing antecedent to this will. Thus Duns Scotus rejects the Thomistic ontological perspective, which sees the final end of things as their causes. God is not "caused" to create the things he does because he contemplates their final end, that is, their essences. He simply decrees their essences into being, and there is nothing that constrains his will to do so.

It follows that the relationship between God and the created world, including humanity, does not have a necessary framework other than the divine will. This resolute defense of God's freedom leads Duns Scotus to a much more restrained attitude toward the ability of law to mediate this divine-human relationship. We will briefly discuss his approach to law and then its consequences for his doctrine of the atonement.

The received opinion on Duns Scotus's voluntarism is that law, including natural law and moral law, is completely arbitrary since God could have enacted a wholly different law. Indeed, Duns Scotus does hint at something like this when he enunciates his important principle: things are good because God wills them and not vice versa. In other words, "the divine will is the cause of good, and so by the fact that He wills something it is good."[81] For example, God could have ordained a world in which it would be righteous to kill, or to steal, or to tell lies.

God is not bound to enact the particular law that he did in fact enact. Furthermore, as legislator, he is free to dispense with particular laws he has enacted, in order to achieve some other end. It would thus seem that law is a completely arbitrary interface between God and humanity. If that is the case, then we do not gain any knowledge about the nature of God by analyzing human nature and its laws. These laws might have been other, and this would not have been detrimental to either the goodness or the justice of God.

Despite the fact that, as we shall see, it is an exaggeration to claim that Duns Scotus has made law entirely arbitrary, one clear historical consequence of his views was to delineate between the kinds of things we can know by reason and the kinds of things we can know only by revelation. Human reason does not give us adequate insight into the natural law. Just as important from our perspective, we are not entitled to argue that human laws participate in any way, analogically or not, in eternal law. In fact, as Hannes Möhle points out, Aquinas's doctrine of eternal law has no importance in his system.[82] Although Paul Tillich somewhat overstates the case, as an interpretation of Duns Scotus, it adequately captures the significance of Duns Scotus for later thought: "The world is originally created by will and is for this reason irrational and to be

---

81. Quoted in Frederick Copleston, SJ, *A History of Philosophy*, vol. 2, *Medieval Philosophy: From Augustine to Duns Scotus* (1950; repr., New York: Image, 1993), 547.

82. Hannes Möhle, "Scotus's Theory of Natural Law," in *The Cambridge Companion to Duns Scotus*, ed. Thomas Williams (Cambridge: Cambridge University Press, 2003), 315.

taken empirically. On a secondary level it is intellectually ordered, but this order is never final and cannot be taken in by us in deductive terms."[83]

Pausing for a while, why might this be important for the atonement? From a historical perspective, I have argued that medieval atonement is centered on the newly discovered universality and eternity of law. This conception of law, of course, is taken in different ways by various theologians. Yet all of them, more or less, function within a framework of necessity. Anselm in particular has argued that if God is to save, then he *has to choose* between satisfaction or punishment. In other words, given that his primary aim is our eternal happiness, these are the only courses of action open to him, due to his justice. But if Duns Scotus is right, then the whole framework of law as setting the conditions for human-divine relations collapses. It therefore seems important to pay close attention to what Duns Scotus says about the law.

As an Augustinian, Duns Scotus agrees with Anselm's critique and rejection of Ciceronian justice. Their shared premise is the ontological difference between God and humanity: they are not equals, and therefore God does not owe any debt to anyone. That does not mean there are no constraints on divine justice, however, even for Duns Scotus. In his actions with regard to creation, God is bound by the goodness of his nature. The only principle that determines God's actions, and indeed the only practical principle of natural law, is the love of God. Writing about "legal justice"—namely, that justice which "has to do with another" and consists in the observance of a law that applies to all—Duns Scotus clarifies what this law that applies even to God may be: "Now, the first of these, namely, legal justice, could be postulated of God if there were some other law antecedent to any decision of his will, with which 'law and its legislator' as other his own will could rightly agree. Now, there is indeed this law, 'God should be loved'—if one ought to call it a 'law' rather than a practical principle of law; and in any case it is a practical truth that is prior to any decision on the part of the divine will."[84] Thus it isn't that God's actions toward the world are not constrained by any principle. But this principle of the love of God can be observed in a number of different ways, as we shall see.

With regard to another aspect of the law, namely, the justice of particular actions, or what Duns Scotus calls "uprightness in some specific aspect pertaining to law,"[85] he clarifies that there are two subdivisions: uprightness

83. Paul Tillich, *A History of Christian Thought: From Its Judaic and Hellenistic Origins to Existentialism*, ed. Carl Braaten (New York: Touchstone, 1972), 142.

84. John Duns Scotus, *Ordinatio* 4, dist. 46, as translated by Allan B. Wolter, OFM, *Duns Scotus on the Will and Morality* (Washington, DC: Catholic University of America Press, 1986). All other quotations from Duns Scotus refer to this translation.

85. Duns Scotus, *Ordinatio* 4, dist. 46.

toward another in an unqualified sense; and uprightness toward oneself as quasi-other. Only the second of these applies to God. This means that in his particular actions with respect to creatures, God is not bound by any obligation toward them, but only by the obligation to be upright with regard to himself as he deals with others.

We can illustrate this position with the help of a debate that captivated late medieval theologians. The debate concerned the so-called biblical scandals, namely, concrete instances of God's commanding people to do acts contrary to his law, such as Hosea's unchastity, the plundering of the Egyptians, or most flagrantly, the sacrifice of Isaac. The Dominicans, on the one hand, were accustomed to dismissing these as cases of insufficient information, lack of access to the divine intentions, or simply texts in need of better interpretation. Duns Scotus, on the other hand, takes them at their face value and "mak[es] the possibility of dispensation a basis for defining natural law itself."[86] He thus limits natural law to those principles of action that are logically deduced from the ultimate principle of God's love. The first table of the commandments given to Moses contain precisely such laws as can be directly derived from this principle. The second table of commands pertain to contingent creatures, and thus they cannot be held to obtain necessarily for God.

Again, it is important to point out that God is constrained by something after all: his goodness and self-love. This is one object, or one end, of his actions. Duns Scotus calls this the primary object. But this primary object may be accomplished in a number of different ways. These secondary objects of divine action are not binding on God, whereas the primary objects are. As Frederick Copleston explains, "God can, then, dispense in the case of the precepts of the second table, though he cannot dispense in the case of the commandments which belong strictly to the natural law."[87] The distinction between primary and secondary objects helps solve the tension between the seemingly cavalier divine approach to his own laws and the necessity of constancy of the divine action in the world.

To repeat, there are two possible kinds of justice, first, as rectitude of will as it pertains to divine goodness, and second, as "rectitude of will with respect to what the exigencies of creatures demand."[88] "However," Duns Scotus notes later, "the primary justice intrinsic to God does not determine him to be just in this second way in the same manner that it determines him in regard to his first act, because the primary act [of justice toward himself] does not look to any [created] object or secondary act, because insofar as it looks to such his

86. Möhle, "Scotus's Theory of Natural Law," 315.
87. Copleston, *Medieval Philosophy*, 549.
88. Duns Scotus, *Ordinatio* 4, dist. 46.

justice does not incline his will in any necessary manner, as was said."[89] And again, "In an unqualified sense where a creature is concerned, God is just only in relationship to the first justice, namely, because such a creature has been actually willed by the divine will."[90]

Merits and Atonement

We are now in a position to understand the immediate bearing of this analysis of justice and law on the doctrine of the atonement.

The distinctive character of medieval theology is the dual focus on the objective character of Jesus's atonement together with the subjective dimension of the appropriation of the merit earned by Christ. An Augustinian emphasis on divine grace is thus combined with a theology of merit that stresses human obligation to earn and participate in the merit of Christ. Anselm's chief contribution was to combine these two and to read the very cross of Christ in terms of merit. In addition, without exception, medieval thinkers affirmed the necessity of the infusion of divine love as the initial condition for the process of justification.

The theology of merit is severely weakened in the Scotist system of doctrine. The success of the medieval scheme depended on a possible equivalency between the value of the atoning work of Christ (the infinite value of his sacrifice) and the value of merit. God is thus placed under some obligation to dispense merit in response to the value of Christ's suffering. Similarly, with respect to the postbaptismal life, God dispenses merit in response to acts of charity. Buttressing this equivalence is the assumption that God acts under some legal necessity. Indeed, we identified this very advent of law as an important determination of medieval atonement theology. But Duns Scotus vehemently denies that God is under legal jurisdiction, or under any jurisdiction at all. There is no legal necessity pressing on God. But then in virtue of what does he reward the righteous and punish the wicked? With Duns Scotus, the reason for this "divine behavior" is not to be sought in the inherent quality of moral acts (righteousness or sin). Inasmuch as these qualities are outside of God's own being, they are merely contingent, and thus they cannot compel God in any way.

That God decides to act in this way depends exclusively on his will. The value of any human act before God depends solely on his estimation. Our moral actions are worthy only because God decides to accept them. But his acceptance (*acceptatio*) is in no way dependent on a prior divine evaluation

89. Ibid. (Wolter's clarifications.)
90. Ibid.

of the dignity of those acts. There is nothing inherent in them (as created, contingent acts) that can move God in and of itself.

Robert Mackintosh notes that both the concept of *acceptatio*, as well as the mirror (though not synonymous) concept of *acceptilatio* (the act of offering something that is eventually accepted as satisfactory), are to be found in Roman law.[91] Note how consonant this is with Duns Scotus's general voluntarist approach. There is only one principle that compels God's *absolute power*: divine self-love, including what derives from this, namely, the principle that creatures should love God. But in the wake of the fall, there are several possible economies of salvation, as it were. God decides to enact one of these. He decides to promulgate one of the many possible laws open to his wisdom. That God promulgated this law does not tell us anything about its inherent value against all the other possibles. Our grasp of the natural law, to which we are ordered, gives us no insight into the divine nature. For related reasons, God can dispense with the secondary laws without compromising his justice.

Thus, contra Louis Berkhof's estimation,[92] Duns Scotus is not suggesting that justice is irrelevant to the atonement. But he defines divine justice exclusively in relation to God's own self, refusing to extend it to his relationship to contingent creatures. What determines that realm is simply the divine will to enact a particular law. Yet any of the laws enacted by God that are not directly derived from the maxim of the love of God are not binding on God, though they remain binding on us. There is thus no contradiction in saying that God could have forgiven us without the cross. As Harnack notes, "Duns Scotus draws the true logical conclusion from the theory of satisfaction (as distinguished from the idea of vicarious penal suffering), by tracing everything to the 'acceptatio' of God. All satisfaction and all merit obtain their worth from the arbitrary estimation of the receiver."[93] This would be the logical conclusion since the very concept of satisfaction itself cannot appeal to any logic other than the divine will. Unless, that is, Anselm (primarily) and Thomas (less so) would succeed in demonstrating the binding character of the contingent laws of atonement/satisfaction on God himself. Duns Scotus does not argue, indeed it would be absurd to argue, that God does not operate according to justice, but his distinction between primary and secondary justice is compelling within an Augustinian framework. He places Anselm's whole argument within the realm of secondary justice, thus rendering it irrelevant to divine nature.

91. Robert Mackintosh, *Historic Theories of Atonement* (London: Hodder & Stoughton, 1920), 110.

92. Louis Berkhof, *Systematic Theology* (Grand Rapids: Eerdmans, 1996), 368.

93. Harnack, *History of Dogma*, 6:196.

Thus it is not simply that "omnipotence and divine will are more ultimate in the Divine nature than justice and truth are";[94] this dichotomy caricatures Scotist thought. Rather, divine omnipotence and freedom determine divine justice in a particular way.

The Death of Christ

To come back to the atonement as such, Duns Scotus holds that since God cannot be compelled by anything to make any kind of reward, it was not necessary for the Son of God to die. That there was nothing inherently equivalent to God's reward of merit is further shown by the fact that Christ suffered in his human nature. But a human death is of a finite value and therefore cannot accrue infinite merit. Nevertheless, God chose to regard this finite merit as having infinite value. There are overtones of the older notion of satisfaction here, for in Germanic as well as in Roman law the injured party has to *deem appropriate* (or satisfactory) a particular offer, in return for the injury. Indeed, for Anselm himself the notion of strict equivalency between infinite crime and infinite value of sacrifice is only demanded because he needs a quantitatively infinite treasury of merit to be made available to baptized sinners. Thus, it is Anselm's insistence on a theology of merit that brings him to the problematic issue of strict equivalency. In the objective terms of restoring the honor of God, no strict equivalency need obtain: God simply decides to accept the sacrifice of Christ, not as something necessarily equivalent, but as something fitting (*conveniens*).

God could have deemed some other measure as fitting. For instance, Duns Scotus points out, he might have rescued us by an angel, or by a man who should have remained free from original sin. Duns Scotus further flatly denies that the death of Christ had the quality of punishment, as something required by the justice of God. It is simply a sacrifice that God was moved to accept because of his love.

To conclude, in the words of Hastings Rashdall, "This attitude towards morality dispenses the Scotist from elaborate attempts to establish the justice of the atonement."[95] We might temper this statement just a bit, since Duns Scotus affirms that there is a justice proper to God's self-love and a justice God decrees for humanity but that is not absolutely binding on him. As we reflect on the mystery of Christ's death, we can only make rational sense of it up to a point, by drawing on the principle of God's love that we also find in our natural law. This much is binding on God. But the particular manner in which

94. William G. T. Shedd, *A History of Christian Doctrine* (New York: Charles Scribner's Sons, 1890), 2:316.
95. Rashdall, *Idea of Atonement*, 385.

God realizes his purposes for creation is something that we cannot infer from our study of nature, natural morality, justice, or any other contingent order.

Duns Scotus's Impact

Scholars have pointed out the numerous ramifications of the Scotist revolution. First, the Scotist weakening of natural theology led to the increased authority of the church. If human reason cannot probe nature and from it infer truths about the nature of God, then such information is available to us only by faith. For Duns Scotus, this faith becomes primarily acceptance of the doctrines and the authority of the Roman Catholic Church. Tillich comments on the consequence of the voluntarist and nominalist revolutions in late medieval theology: "The fact that at the end of the Middle Ages all universals were lost resulted in the imposition of the power of the church on individuals, making God himself into an individual who, as tyrant, gives laws to other individuals. This was the distortion that nominalism brought with itself, whereas the affirmation of the personal was its creative contribution."[96]

Second, here Tillich alludes to what can be taken as a more positive development. Duns Scotus stresses that, just as God is fundamentally will, human beings, bearing his image, are also possessed of free will. Together with his epistemological position between realism and nominalism (he argues that one can have knowledge of individuals), Duns Scotus's emphasis on free will led to an increased sense of the worth of the individual. While this tendency is taken to even further reaches in the full-fledged nominalism of William of Ockham and Gabriel Biel, it can be traced back to Duns Scotus, as well as Abelard. The trend in medieval theology was no longer leading in the direction of pantheism, which erases all individuality, but in the discovery of the power of human will.

Third, this turn toward free will has been shown to have had immediate consequences on the understanding of law and politics. Since the primary faculty is the will rather than the intellect, the nature of law is redefined accordingly. Thus the nature of human positive law consists not so much in dictates discovered in natural law by reason. That there are such maxims is not disputed. But their number is limited to those that can be directly traced to the principle of God's love. The limitation of the scope of natural law, however, opens up space for the free creation of human laws. The responsibility of human positive law before the tribunal of natural law is thus greatly weakened. But if there is no necessary structure of the world, it follows that

96. Tillich, *History of Christian Thought*, 144.

we are free to create our own legal, political, economic structures. Duns Scotus insists that the essence of human law consists in the idea of consent. A few years later, Marsilius of Padua will follow through Duns Scotus's thought in writing one of the most revolutionary political treatises of his time. He argues that all authority belongs to the people. Moreover, the people and their leaders have the authority to correct the church when necessary.[97] Heiko Oberman also notes how some scholars argue that, since Duns Scotus divorced "at least potentially" the realms of natural and divine law, he therefore can be described as a legal positivist.

Summary

1. The twelfth- and thirteenth-century legal revolution decisively affirms law from the ancient twilight as the universal context of social and religious relations. The Germanic and feudal ideals of peaceful arbitration, grounded in custom and social bonds, are replaced by the universality of law, including its retributive demands. Human justice and divine justice are once again thought to be transparent to each other.

2. While Anselm is not a legalist, his understanding of "corrective justice" holds that either punishment or satisfaction must follow a wrongdoing. An objective and universal law requires an objective righting of wrongs. Unless a satisfaction is offered from the human side, God can no longer bestow blessedness. Gratuitous divine forgiveness is impossible. Law and justice are now synonymous with the divine nature.

3. Abelard's nominalism dovetails with the same legal revolution, but it is less tied to legalism. While law remains important, it does not apply to God to the same extent as in Anselm. Nominalism also entails that there is no original sin and thus no infinite human debt. While actual sin does incur a liability to punishment, it does not transmit anything like a moral debt, only a disorientation of desire.

4. As a result, the task of the atonement is the mending of desire.

5. Aquinas views law as having a clearly positive role in relation to the natural ends of human beings. Nevertheless, he stays clear of ascribing necessity to this law in relation to God's being. While he clearly incorporates a retributive dimension in his theory, it is not regarded as necessary, but as fitting.

97. See William C. Placher, *A History of Christian Theology: An Introduction* (Louisville: Westminster John Knox, 1983), 167.

6. Duns Scotus decisively opens the way for modernity by securing the autonomy of the state in relation to the church. Human laws are fundamentally a matter of consent. There is no inherent rationality to them. The divine law in itself is not necessary but is a reflection of God's arbitrary will. It is not as if justice is unimportant for Duns Scotus, but his voluntarism forces him to define justice not in relation to God's own self (as in Anselm) but specifically in relation to his will.

7. Consequently, the death of Christ is not a punishment, such as would be necessitated by human trespass. God could have saved us in any other way consonant with his love.

The Reformation
Luther, Calvin, and the Tradition of Penal Substitution

Political and Legal Thought at the Time of the Reformation

The continuity between the legal philosophy of the sixteenth century and that of the Middle Ages is undeniable. The Reformers inherited many of the concepts and practices that were formed during the legal revolution of the eleventh and twelfth centuries. More immediately, they expressed an important legal and religious foment that was well underway even prior to 1517. John Witte is right to claim that "the Reformation . . . was the culmination of more than two centuries of dissent within the church against some of its sacramental theology, liturgical practice, canon law, and ecclesiastical administration."[1] Often that conflict pitted the church, with its all-encompassing claims for spiritual as well as temporal authority, against the princes, who desired emancipation from ecclesial authority. The struggle between the church and national rulers is going to prove to be one of the determinative contexts for the development of the legal and political philosophy of the Reformation.

1. John Witte Jr., *God's Joust, God's Justice: Law and Religion in the Western Tradition* (Grand Rapids: Eerdmans, 2006), 15.

As is well known, the seeds of this conflict lie in the late medieval trend toward voluntarism and nominalism, particularly in the work of John Duns Scotus and William of Ockham. Both Luther and Calvin stood under the influence of nominalism and voluntarism, although they were by no means slavish interpreters of these masters. For our theme it is significant to remember that Duns Scotus and Ockham had weakened the medieval theology of merit, even to the point of its destruction. There is nothing inherent in any moral act that can render it meritorious in the eyes of God. Whatever merit it might have depends on the manner in which God chooses to reckon it. This distancing of grace from nature also weakened the relationship between faith and reason. The ecclesial stock began to climb the minute reason was downgraded. At the same time, this deemphasizing of reason created a sphere of relative autonomy for the emerging state, which was then free to create its own laws as it saw fit. Thus, ironically, nominalism led both to increased ecclesial authority (the church being in possession of revelation), and to a clear demarcation and therefore increased autonomy of the state. Spiritual authority was clearly distinguished from temporal government, although it was still regarded as superior to it.

This compromise was inherently unstable. Revolution was in the air. Within the church, a growing dissatisfaction with the corruption of the hierarchy found its outlet in the Wittenberg theses. Outside the church, the German Revolution drove the first nail through the coffin of the ecclesial institution of the church.

Besides the growth of the nation-state, whose development likely constituted the salvation of a Protestantism that might otherwise have been crushed by the unified Catholic states,[2] there were other factors that influenced to some degree the theological shape of the Reformation. The late medieval critique of the doctrine of inherent merit coincided with the development of a money economy. The invention of money led to the relativization of the worth of goods. The fruit of one's work was only as valuable as what buyers were willing to pay for it.[3] Simultaneously, in the world of art, a transition had been taking place for quite some time, away from the honor-based feudalism, with its glorification of social bonds, to an emphasis on individuality and inwardness. The Renaissance portrait and Shakespeare's and Cervantes's parodies of the old honor society, among many other cultural shifts, indicated the onset of a new paradigm.

But while it is true that in many ways the Reformation only consolidated a trend away from feudalism toward a *Rechtsstaat*, and that perhaps every single

2. Timothy Gorringe, *God's Just Vengeance: Crime, Violence and the Rhetoric of Salvation*, Cambridge Studies in Ideology and Religion (Cambridge: Cambridge University Press, 1996), 127.

3. See Philip Goodchild, *Theology of Money* (Durham, NC: Duke University Press, 2009).

legal innovation it introduced had some sort of precedent either in Roman law or in the medieval legal revolution itself, the new legal culture was nevertheless new. This is true with regard to the legal philosophy of the Reformation, and Witte goes as far as to call it "the third watershed period in the Western legal tradition."[4]

The true originality of the Reformational legal philosophy consists in the particular arrangement of the temporal authority in relation to the spiritual authority of the church. I will argue that this distribution of legal power between the two spheres, or as Luther called them, the two kingdoms, can illuminate our understanding of the Reformation doctrines of the atonement. The argument of this book has been that theological descriptions and explanations of the divine salvific act inevitably draw on (and further shape) current understandings of justice and law. This is no less the case with respect to the sixteenth-century Reformation. Since the single most important legal contribution of the Reformation was the establishment and legitimation of the temporal (legal) authority of the prince in relation to the spiritual kingdom, their political theology and philosophy will be shown to contain insights relevant to the doctrine of the atonement.

Moreover, since Luther and Calvin differed in their political theologies and legal philosophies, it is to be expected that these divergences are also relevant for their divergent theories of the atonement.

There is an undeniable unity as well. Both Reformers were instrumental in emphasizing the necessity of a state that is ruled by law. Again, this had been anticipated in the legal revolution of the eleventh and twelfth centuries, but the medieval theologians and legal scholars had based temporal law on natural law. This in turn optimistically presupposed both the ability of natural reason to discern this law and the power of the will to abide by it (once illuminated). While the emphasis on natural law had conferred temporal law a welcome universality, it was a vague kind of universality. Increasingly complex economic situations required much more precise legislation, and this was difficult to establish on the basis of natural law alone. The trend toward nominalism can be seen in this light as well, as corresponding to the changing legal needs of the time. However, this reliance on nominalism also created a crisis in the grounding of law. If natural law is no longer entirely serviceable, what other basis might there be for positive law?

Luther's "breakthrough in the understanding of law"[5] was to find a new objective basis for positive law. F. W. Dillistone captures the historical necessity

---

4. Witte, *God's Joust*, 15.
5. Karl H. Hertz, "Luther and the Law," *Hastings Law Journal* 29 (1977–78): 1508.

for this objective basis: "For Europe the sixteenth, seventeenth and eighteenth centuries constituted a time of foment, wars, revolutionary tendencies, the struggle of minority groups for recognition and toleration. The one safeguard against complete anarchy was the existence of a system of law which was above individual caprice or even minority plots. Law could protect the few and the weak from the tyranny of the great: at the same time law could protect the ordered and the established from the wild upsurging of fanatics."[6]

To repeat the point: the legal originality of the Reformers consisted not simply in the establishment of the priority of law (this they inherited from tradition) but in the new basis they found for it, departing from the medieval basis of natural law. *The new basis also consisted in a reconfiguration of the relationship between God and law.* This new rearrangement determines, or at least influences to a large extent, the choices made by the Reformers in their respective understandings of the atonement.

Prior to an actual engagement with their doctrines of the atonement as such, I shall pursue three questions: What is the relationship between God and law? What are the uses of the law? What coherence is there between human justice and divine justice?

Law and the Nature of God

Sometimes it is useful to start from a generalization and then progressively refine it. The risk is that one only remembers the generalization, which is, after all, only mentioned to be quickly corrected. I will assume that risk and generalize on the distinction between Calvin and Luther with regard to this first question, the relationship between law and the nature of God: Luther tends to relegate the law to a secondary aspect of God's will, while for Calvin law is much more central to the very being of God. Broadly speaking, then, Calvin has a much more positive attitude with regard to law than Luther. This difference is not without consequences for their respective understandings of the atonement. Now, let us refine these statements, before it is too late.

It is not surprising to find both Reformers associated with voluntarism. Luther in particular, having studied with Gabriel Biel, stood under the influence of late medieval nominalism and voluntarism. Thus Alasdair MacIntyre, commenting on Luther's ethics, says: "The only true moral rules are the divine commandments; and the divine commandments are understood in an Occamist perspective—that is to say, they have no further rationale or justification than

6. F. W. Dillistone, *The Christian Understanding of Atonement* (Philadelphia: Westminster, 1968), 203.

that they are the injunctions of God."[7] This means, for MacIntyre, that they regarded the omnipotence of God as "an arbitrary omnipotence."[8] He lumps Calvin together with Luther on this point.

This evaluation is not without its critics, and with good reason. I. John Hesselink, whose monograph on Calvin's understanding of law makes a seminal contribution to our understanding of the Geneva Reformer, argues that although there is indeed a semblance of agreement between Calvin and late medieval nominalism, their theological outlook is nevertheless very different.[9] He is right not only with regard to the broader theological outlook but also with regard to Calvin's specific repudiation of the doctrine of the absolute power of God (*potentia dei absoluta*).

> Therefore, since God claims to himself the right of governing the world, a right unknown to us, let it be our law of modesty and soberness to acquiesce in his supreme authority regarding his will as our only rule of justice, and the most perfect cause of all things,—not as absolute will, indeed, of which sophists prate, when by a profane and impious divorce, they separate his justice from his power, but that universal overruling Providence from which nothing flows that is not right, though the reasons thereof may be concealed.[10]

Here Calvin explicitly rejects the Scotist doctrine of the absolute power of God, which may operate against justice. Nevertheless, in rejecting Duns Scotus, Calvin is not returning to Aquinas's intellectualism, according to which divine rationality is commensurable with human rationality, and human ends. *Calvin and Luther both resolutely reject any direct rational link between human ends, as apprehended by natural reason, and divine justice.* Divine justice and divine power form a unity, but their unity is not given, à la Aquinas, by God's knowledge of the end proper to human beings, and the end that we may also know through natural reason. Calvin insists that God has reasons for acting the way he does, even though those reasons are unknown to us. But it is never the case that he acts merely arbitrarily.

Calvin also rejects the idea that God may be without law: "Nevertheless, I do not suppose him to be without law (*ex lex*); for although his power is above all laws, still because his will is the most certain rule of perfect equity, whatever he does must be perfectly right; and therefore he is free from laws

---

7. Alasdair MacIntyre, *A Short History of Ethics: A History of Moral Philosophy from the Homeric Age to the Twentieth Century* (London: Routledge, 1998), 121.

8. Ibid., 123.

9. I. John Hesselink, *Calvin's Concept of Law*, Princeton Theological Monographs (Eugene, OR: Wipf & Stock, 1992).

10. John Calvin, *Institutes of the Christian Religion* 1.17.2.

(*legibus solutus*) because he is a law to himself and to all."[11] Law thus denotes "an inner necessity in accord with his own nature."[12] But Hesselink also notes that, for Calvin, God remains free to suspend the law and depart from it. He deviates from his own law for our own good. But, again according to Hesselink, Calvin insists that "to make God beyond law is to rob him of the greatest part of his glory, for it destroys his rectitude and his righteousness. Not that God is subject to law, except insofar as he himself is law."[13] The coherence of this position is not immediately clear. On the one hand, God is said to himself be law; on the other, he is free to depart from his own law. Indeed, Duns Scotus's position might appear the more intellectually solid in that he makes God to be essentially love, with God being able to work out this love in a number of possible just ways. Calvin, however, insists on making law itself central to God, but also (incoherently) insisting that God may depart from his own law. If indeed God can depart from his own law, it follows that law is not an essential attribute of the being of God. Calvin seems to want to have his cake and eat it too.

Luther is less determined to maintain the centrality of law to the nature of God. He regards law as belonging to the *alien work* of God, not to his proper work, represented by grace and love. Thus, as opposed to Calvin, God is *ex lex*. He relegates law to a secondary place, determined by the reality of sin and the necessity of dealing with it. Thus there are two wills, or two works, in God. God's proper work is grace. Still, for Luther, God wasn't quite free to do his proper work gratuitously, that is, without attending to his *opus alienum* (judgment and damnation). As Albrecht Ritschl has pointed out, although Luther relegates law to a secondary status, together with God's wrath, this aspect of law must still be dealt with. Thus Luther even talks about a "God against God." For Ritschl, this represents an inconsistency between, on the one hand, the idea that God is without law and, on the other, the idea that a sacrifice (demanded by law) is a requirement for salvation. Ritschl further notes, interestingly, that Luther applies this voluntarism only to the doctrine of predestination (Rom. 9:18), but when he comes to the atonement "he expressly describes the law as the eternal and immutable expression of God's will."[14] Ritschl is again right to claim that "on the whole, he makes love and wrath in God, notwithstanding his subordination of the latter to the former, to appear

11. Calvin, *Comm. Exod.* 3:22; see also Hesselink, *Calvin's Concept of Law*, 22.
12. Hesselink, *Calvin's Concept of Law*, 23.
13. Ibid.
14. Albrecht Ritschl, *The Christian Doctrine of Justification and Reconciliation: The Positive Development of the Doctrine*, ed. H. R. Mackintosh and Alexander Beith Macaulay (Clifton, NJ: Reference Book Publishers, 1966), 199.

as co-ordinate, and therefore as opposed and even (in certain circumstances) contradictory forces, for the harmonizing of which in God himself, endurance of punishment by the Mediator is necessary."[15]

We thus seem to be walking a very fine line between the freedom of God and his constancy. Luther and Calvin walk that line differently. Luther prefers to subordinate wrath to love, law to grace, but still talk about the necessity of law. This necessity, however, does not properly belong to the nature of God. But what external necessity might press on the being of God in such a manner? Calvin, for his part, equalizes divine love and divine law (which becomes wrath with the onset of sin) but insists on the possibility of God's deviating from his law. The question here is whether Calvin succeeds in distinguishing himself sufficiently from the abominable Scotism, whether indeed he has not fallen back to a doctrine of an arbitrary God. Furthermore, if this is the case, and there really is no "inner necessity," why insist on the punishment of Christ?

Clearly neither Luther nor Calvin has succeeded in addressing the question of the relationship between the attributes of God and his own nature. While it is unfair to portray them as simply practitioners without much interest in metaphysics, it remains the case that their primary interest was more soterio-logical than metaphysical. Calvin's *Institutes*, for instance, do not contain a full-fledged doctrine of God. This lack of systematic reflection does not mean that they did not have opinions on these matters, or that their theological positions were not ripe with metaphysical or ontological assumptions and implications. But they simply did not apply themselves singly to the project of clarifying these ontological relations. When they rejected Thomistic intellectualism, they ended up affirming a variant of Scotist voluntarism. The opposite is also true: whenever they denounced the "shocking, diabolical blasphemy" of Scotism, they did so in the name of a quasi-intellectualism, more broadly conceived than Thomas's, which they were ultimately unwilling to explicitly entertain.

This is not to say that there is no solution to what Ritschl calls "the highest of all theoretical questions."[16] Let us return then, briefly, to Calvin's descrip-tion of how law relates to God. As I pointed out, law occupies a much more central place in Calvin's ontology than in Luther's.[17] Law can be taken as a

15. Ibid., 202.
16. Ibid., 198–99.
17. I am aware that the two are working with slightly different conceptions of law: for Calvin, law can be described as more "conceptual," involving discursive distinctions. For Luther, law can be taken in a more "naturalist" sense, but also therefore more spiritualist, given his Platonism. Thus Luther values the law of Christ, the new law, but makes it entirely spiritual, inward. For Calvin, law retains an externality (its discursivity), but its true essence is also found in Christ.

shorthand for God's will for creation. As such, law is prior to sin (Gen. 2:16). Adam was created as an ordered being, abiding by the law of God. As Hesselink notes, "God's orderly will for creation takes on a normative character. Law in this sense is an essential ingredient of life and has nothing to do with disobedience or sin."[18] Law, in other words, is not dependent on the fall for its necessity, but it denotes the ordered will of God. Law is the very mode of relationship between humanity and God, even prior to the fall.

While there is nothing external about this law, it has to be said that this is still a "discursive" concept of law since it involves conceptual and logical relations and belongs, as it were, to the realm of reason. In other words, this initial (natural?) law does not simply denote a noncognitive, quasi-physicalist orientation of human nature, like animal instinct, but a divine order that can be understood and obeyed. Thus, while the law is not inscribed on tablets of stone, it is nevertheless discursively inscribed on the conscience (Rom. 2:15; 2 Cor. 3:3). As we shall see, Luther also affirms a concept of law, but he spiritualizes the concept to the point where he risks losing its epistemic content, and it becomes a merely instinctive movement of the soul.

For Calvin, there is no mutual exclusion between written (discursive) law and the ends for which the human being was designed (which we know through revelation). Calvin cherishes this form of law. As Hesselink notes, for Lutheran critics of Calvin, this amounts to a new form of legalism. But, as Edward Dowey observes, "For Calvin and Calvinism, Luther's view elevates the accidental, sin-caused function of the law into its all-inclusive role at the expense of what God meant to be the law's proper function both in creation and in redemption."[19] In other words, Luther forms his opinion about the nature of the law from one of its aspects that has been highlighted by the fall. Calvin argues that sin brought out the condemnatory dimension of law (2 Cor. 3:7), but that this is certainly not its essence. In its essence, law is the discursive, orderly will of God for creation, a will that in the presence of sin becomes wrath. This law is essentially tied to the character of God: "God reveals himself to us in the law and declares what kind of God he wishes to be towards us, lays down what he demands of us, and, in short, everything necessary to be known."[20]

Two further questions remain, one for each Reformer. Calvin has to face the question about the Pauline antithesis between law and grace: "The letter kills, but the spirit gives life" (2 Cor. 3:6). Luther, also like Paul, must wrestle with the fact that the "commandment is holy, just and good" (Rom. 7:12).

---

18. Hesselink, *Calvin's Concept of Law*, 54.
19. Edward A. Dowey, "Law in Luther and Calvin," *Theology Today* 41 (1984): 153.
20. John Calvin, *Comm. Isa.* 8:20.

Calvin's temptation is legalism; Luther's is antinomianism. Each will answer their respective questions by giving a rich description of the uses of the law, since as Paul says elsewhere, "We know that the law is good, if one uses it lawfully" (1 Tim. 1:8). This discussion will further highlight the distinctiveness of their respective theologies and prepare us for a better understanding of their theologies of the cross.

The Uses of the Law

Both Calvin and Luther agree on two uses of the law. Both of these initial functions have to do with its wrathful aspect.

The first use of the law is *civic*, or political. Law, through its threat of punishment, deters crime. In the first edition of the *Institutes*, Calvin referred to this as the second use of the law. This civil function is proper to both the natural law, as well as to the ceremonial, and civil law, although, as Witte notes, the focus of the three-uses doctrine is on natural law or moral law. All of these types are variants of God's orderly will for humanity.

Luther stresses the fact that this function of the law cannot redress human nature (Rom. 8:3). In fact, it only complicates the situation, for it leads humans to rebel against the law (Rom. 7:8, 13).

> For nature rebels at compulsion. No man likes to be a captive in chains. One does not voluntarily bow to the rod of punishment, or submit to the executioner's sword; rather, because of these things, his anger against the Law is but increased, and he ever thinks: "Would that I might unhindered steal, rob, hoard, gratify my lust, and so on!" And when restrained by force, he would there were no Law and no God.[21]

Although Calvin agrees with Luther on the soteriological inefficiency of the law, he does identify a positive purpose:

> Nay, this tuition is not without its use, even to the children of God, who, previous to their effectual calling, being destitute of the Spirit of holiness, freely indulge the lusts of the flesh. When, by the fear of Divine vengeance, they are deterred from open outbreakings, though, from not being subdued in mind, they profit little at present, still they are in some measure trained to bear the yoke of righteousness, so that when they are called, they are not like mere novices, studying a discipline of which previously they had no knowledge.[22]

21. Martin Luther, *Assorted Sermons* (Grand Rapids: Christian Classics Ethereal Library, 2000), 236.
22. Calvin, *Institutes* 2.7.10.

The second use of the law is *theological*. Law convinces humanity of sin and points to the need for a Savior (Gal. 3:23–24). In this capacity, law functions as a mirror, showing us our sin and inability to obey God. Luther and Calvin both stress this function of the law. They are both agreed that this law does not provide the cure, but only the diagnosis. Calvin picks up the medical metaphor: "The function of the law, then, is to uncover the disease; it gives no hope of its cure. It is the function of the gospel to bring healing to those who are without hope."[23]

Neither does this function of the law by itself provide the cure. For Luther, the inefficiency of the law is inherent to its character as a letter (Deut. 30:6; Jer. 9:25; John 6:63; Rom. 2:29; 7:6; 2 Cor. 3:6).

> To illustrate: A law promulgated by a prince or the authorities of a city, if not enforced, remains merely an open letter, which makes a demand indeed, but ineffectually. Similarly, God's law, although a teaching of supreme authority and the eternal will of God, must suffer itself to become a mere empty letter or husk. Without a quickening heart, and devoid of fruit, the Law is powerless to effect life and salvation. It may well be called a veritable table of omissions (*Lass-tafel*); that is, it is a written enumeration, not of duties performed but of duties cast aside. In the languages of the world, it is a royal edict which remains unobserved and unperformed.[24]

The law simply was not assigned to play a role in salvation (Gal. 3), despite what the scholastics argue. It only demonstrates the wrath of God (Rom. 4:15), as Luther puts it in *Table Talk*, "The law, with its righteousness, is like a cloud without rain, which promises rain but gives none; even so does the law promise salvation but gives it not, for the law was not assigned to that end, as St. Paul says, Gal. iii."[25]

It is when we come to Calvin's third use of the law that the divergence is most obvious. Calvin and Luther, I will show, had significantly different conceptions of the positive use of the law in the life of the Christian. For Luther, this translated into a radical distinction between earthly justice and heavenly justice, or righteousness.

Calvin's rendering of law as central to the divine nature naturally leads him to argue that the role of the law has not ceased with the coming of Christ. Indeed, the "third and most appropriate use of the law"[26] is toward the elect. While Calvin, no less than Luther, insists that the nature of the law

---

23. John Calvin, *Comm. 2 Cor. 3:7*.
24. Luther, *Assorted Sermons*, 237.
25. Martin Luther, *Table Talk*, 282.
26. Calvin, *Institutes* 2.7.12.

is discerned in Christ alone, the law, precisely as discursive, retains its positive role in the life of the Christian. The spiritual transformation of the individual does not render the law irrelevant. He writes, "Even if the Spirit engrafts the law on the heart, there are still two ways in which we profit from it."[27] The transformation of the mind, then, does not amount to a direct, unmediated knowledge of God,[28] but it requires the active participation of the human mind. The second way in which the believer continues to profit from the law is that "by frequently meditating upon it, he will be excited to obedience, and confirmed in it, and so drawn away from the slippery paths of sin."[29] The law thus becomes, as Hesselink puts it, "the peculiar organ of the Holy Spirit for renewing and reforming people in the image of God."[30]

The contrast between law and gospel is not as crisp in Calvin as it is in Luther: "But the Gospel has not succeeded the whole Law in such a sense as to introduce a different method of salvation. It rather confirms the Law, and proves that every thing which it promised is fulfilled. What was shadow, it has made substance."[31] There is thus much greater continuity in Calvin between the will of God as manifested in the law and the will of God as manifested in the gospel of grace. These are not two radically contrasting wills and actions, the *ratio* between them being unknown to us. Christ reveals himself as the true essence of the law. But once the revelation is made, the law does not thereby become redundant. Rather, by being oriented toward and anchored in Christ, it can finally fulfill its ultimate and most important task.

Grace abrogates law as a curse, not as a guide (Matt. 11:30). Law itself can be seen as part of God's gracious action in the world, even though sin has brought out its curse and its penal dimension. Once the legal curse is removed, however, the law can return to its original function as the divinely ordained means of divine-human relationship. Thus it is not law that stands between us and God, as the enemy, but the penal burden incurred by human sin.

Luther is very reluctant to accept this third use of the law. He continues to speak about "new law" (John 13:34; 1 John 2:8), "the law of Christ" (1 Cor. 9:21; Gal. 6:2), and "the law of grace"; but his use of "law" as pertaining to the new covenant is equivocal.

The essence of the law, for Luther, cannot be discerned through natural reason. Only the regenerate mind has the ability to discern the true essence

27. Ibid.
28. Luther does tend to speak in these terms sometimes.
29. Calvin, *Institutes* 2.7.12.
30. Hesselink, *Calvin's Concept of Law*, 251.
31. Calvin, *Institutes* 2.9.4.

of the law, because its will has been able to conform to it, not as an external rule, but by being transformed by God.

Once this transformation has been made, the law is of no continued use for the Christian (Rom. 6:14–15; Gal. 4:18). Law, however, remains the authority in the earthly domain. Sometimes Luther even slips into a position which denies that the faithful need any kind of law. His more guarded position, however, is that in the kingdom of Christ the valid law is the law of the gospel. The law remains in force in the earthly kingdom, and although God remains ruler of that world, we experience his lordship as wrath.

The contrast Luther seems to be drawing is between what I would like to call two competing governing authorities. On the one hand, in the secular kingdom, law functions as an external standard of conduct. It has a discursive quality. Its authority is epistemic, in the sense that a condition of obeying it is our *knowing that* we are obeying it, and what it might mean to obey it. It requires interpretation, and indeed Luther's theology promotes the role of the magistrates in upholding and clarifying the meaning of the law. But its function always inevitably comes short of the ultimate, heavenly end of human beings. Moreover, it does not lead to that end as a necessary step of a ladder. It is not continuous with grace. Its *only function* is that of condemning, threatening people with judgment, curbing crime.

Sometimes Luther seems to associate this impotence of the law with its quality as letter, or discourse. The law as letter cannot enter the human heart and thus transform it (2 Cor. 3:6). Thus the new man cannot be brought about by observance of the law. And people's observance of law, whether divine or positive, does not lead them any closer to God. Such a transformation can only take place as something utterly unanticipated.

> Therefore, God would have his Gospel message urged unceasingly as the means of awakening man's heart to discern his state and recall the great grace and loving-kindness of God, with the result that the power of the Holy Spirit is increased constantly. Note, no influence of the Law, no work of man is present here. *The force is a new and heavenly one*—the power of the Holy Spirit. He impresses upon the heart Christ and his works, making it a true book which does not consist in the tracery of mere letters and words, but in true life and action.[32]

This brings us to the second, competing governing authority, that of the Spirit. We enter under the authority of the Spirit through the wonderful exchange, represented by the atonement. But the principle of this authority is emphatically different from the discursive and epistemic authority of the law.

32. Luther, *Assorted Sermons*, 237, emphasis added.

Christ governs the souls of the disciples directly, in an unmediated fashion, as it were. This governance is indeed "law," but a spiritualized law. This "radical spiritualism," argues Johannes Heckel, is "the specific characteristic of Luther's legal doctrine."[33] Thus, Christ's authority over believers becomes spiritual, heavenly, inward, and hidden. Indeed, only by an equivocation can Luther continue to call this new authority "law."

Human and Divine Justice in the Two Kingdoms

What then is the purpose of the observance of law in the earthly kingdom, since it has no utility for the ultimate destiny of humanity? Luther's doctrine of the two kingdoms establishes the autonomy of the secular realm. There is a fundamental continuity between Luther's political theology and his broader theological outlook. I will attempt to draw out that continuity, even by risking some rather broad brushstrokes.

Remember the high medieval scholastic worldview. Theologians such as Thomas Aquinas had asserted a basic, though analogical, continuity between the human and divine realms. Part of what it means to fulfill human destiny consists in our living in the polis. There is no diremption between living as good citizens and being good Christians. What grace does, according to this framework, is to supplement the deficiencies of human nature. But in the *processus iustificationis* it necessarily draws on human faculties; it cooperates with human will as it aids it to achieve its ends. Grace perfects human nature with what is proper to it. In terms of the theology of the atonement, this yields the principle of *quod in se est*. One must do what is within oneself in order to fulfill one's obligations. While the sacrifice of Christ makes merit available to us, it remains up to us to earn it.

The effects of this framework on the political theology of the High Middle Ages consisted in promoting the supremacy of the church. Paul's argument about government in Romans 13 was taken as a defense of the ecclesiastical prerogative. While the papal revolution as such had beneficial effects, in particular the return to a reign of law, the spiritual "sword" was now regarded as being superior to the temporal sword. The church stands over and above the state, as its culmination. But ultimately God affirms human principles of justice (Roman or Ciceronian), for the application of which he supplies the willpower. As Hertz observes, "In a variety of ways, the corpus of natural law theory in connection with the interpretation of Romans 13 provided a fairly complete political theology for the middle ages."[34]

33. Johannes Heckel, *Lex Charitatis: A Juristic Disquisition on Law in the Theology of Martin Luther*, trans. and ed. Gottfried G. Krodel (Grand Rapids: Eerdmans, 2010), 45; see also 20.
34. Hertz, "Luther and the Law," 1512.

The Reformers shattered this medieval continuity. The framework was already in the process of disintegration through the attacks of nominalists on the optimism of natural theology. These attacks played, as we have seen, straight into the hands of philosophers like Marsilius of Padua and the budding tradition of secular autonomy and legal positivism. Luther not only supplied further theological rationale for the collapse of the medieval consensus but also succeeded in establishing the basis for a new model of cohabitation between the two "swords." His ultimate solution was to grant them relative autonomy in regard to each other. This was to have momentous consequences for the development of later legal and political thought.

One aspect of the Reformation's critique of the contemporary political theology was its critique of the continuity between human justice and divine justice. Natural reason cannot yield the principles of natural law, because of the corruption of human faculties. The essence of the law is only accessible through special revelation. Luther challenges the Augustinian understanding of *iustitia Dei* as being contiguous with *iustitia hominum* in that the former underlies concepts of human justice. Rather, *iustitia Dei* is revealed at the cross, and "it contradicts human conceptions of *iustitia*."[35] Human justice, the kind of justice that we see at work in the city, the kind of justice that is enforced by magistrates, has its own proper role in the government of the earthly kingdom. But it is no guide for the understanding the ultimate character of divine justice. The latter contradicts all understandings of human justice.

This is a point of seminal import, and it potentially clarifies Luther's theology of the atonement. If divine justice is contradictory to human justice, then we should not expect the salvific act of God to conform to human conceptions of what is just. Here I can only anticipate the discussion further below: God cannot be taken to be *justified* in forgiving us by the sacrifice of Christ. God does indeed remit our sins *in* the passion of Christ, but the logical link between that passion and the attendant divine forgiveness escapes us. This is the one major difference between Luther and Calvin. For Calvin, God is justified in forgiving us *because* Christ bears the penalty on our behalf. While for Calvin this is consonant with the reigning conception of criminal law (its retributive character), for Luther no such human conception of law can be taken as illuminating the ultimately mysterious divine justice. Christ does indeed bear the punishment for our sins, *but this is not what justifies God in forgiving us*. No human justice mechanism (retributive justice in this case) can be the linchpin to divine justice.

35. McGrath, *Iustitia Dei*, 232.

We have anticipated too much. Let us return to the specifically Lutheran contradiction between divine justice and human justice. The Wittenberg Reformer
saw the medieval continuity between the two realms as a confusion between law
and gospel. The church should not involve itself in the affairs of the world, as an
institution, although individual Christians are free to follow secular vocations.
Luther's attitude during the Swabian revolts of the 1520s is illustrative of this
separation. Upon being asked to support the peasants, who had invoked the
cause of the gospel, Luther replied: "The Gospel does not become involved in
the affairs of this world, but speaks of our life in the world in terms of suffering,
injustice, the cross, patience, and contempt for this life and temporal wealth."[36]

It is not hard to see how this kind of theology endeared Luther to the
secular princes. Despite this "intimate connection between Lutheran theology
and princely authority,"[37] however, Lutheran theology also places stringent
limitations on princely power.

The contradiction between the two realms, the two swords, is that one
is physical, material, "letteral," while the other is inward, spiritual, hidden.
But with Luther this almost becomes an antinomy between body and spirit,
whereby the Spirit does not supervene upon the body, as upon something that
it needs and with which it forms a unity. Indeed, Luther has not escaped accusations of Marcionism. While these accusations are far-fetched, it belongs
to the style and energy of Lutheran theology to argue away from the body,
from the law, from the letter, and toward the spiritual, the inward. For Luther,
the ultimate end of human beings is revealed in the cross. The ultimate end
of law is love. But once love arrives, no law is needed anymore. For Calvin,
on the other hand, although love is the essence of law, together with Christ,
justice (and thus law) remains a necessary instrument of love.

Luther and the Atonement

How do these different understandings of the theology and ontology of law
contribute to the Reformers' respective theories of the atonement? This section
will introduce Luther's view of the cross and its role in the economy of salvation.

Introduction: Luther and the Classic View

Despite the clear convergence between Lutheran and Reformed orthodoxy
on the question of the atonement, it is not immediately clear that Luther's own

36. Hertz, "Luther and the Law," 1520.
37. Harold J. Berman, *Law and Revolution: The Formation of the Western Legal Tradition*
(Cambridge, MA: Harvard University Press, 1983), 64.

theology falls within the lines of the so-called penal substitution theory. While Lutheran orthodoxy followed Philipp Melanchthon's view on the atonement, which was basically identical to that of Calvin, more recent work on Luther seeks to challenge too simplistic an assimilation of Luther to other Reformational views.

In short, Luther is invoked by two rival models, satisfaction and classic or dramatic. What is at stake between these two competing visions?

The traditional and, one might say, the consensus view among the historians of the Protestant Reformation is that Luther, together with Calvin, accepted the basic logic of the "Latin" view of the atonement, originating in Anselm's concept of satisfaction, though with some important adjustments. What is this basic logic? First, the model holds that God's action in the world is always determined in relation to his justice. Thus, this is a basically legal framework. This justice, furthermore, is analyzable and knowable by human reason. Sin consists in a disruption of this order of justice, both on the cosmic level and inwardly. As such, salvation has to consist in restoring the order of justice by some kind of operation on the human side. The emphasis on human agency in the work of the atonement is paramount for the Latin type of theology. But then the question becomes, How are the benefits of any particular human work, finite as they are, transferred to larger humanity? The specific approach of the Latin theory is to postulate an exchange between God and man. The man Jesus offers a work of supererogation, utterly undemanded of him; God chooses to regard that work as satisfactory, in view of its infinite merit (since this was also an infinite God); in return, God reckons Christ's infinite merit as applicable to humans. The great difficulty for the Latin view is that humans still had to earn this merit of Christ through works of penance and moral obedience. There is thus a double exchange: first, Christ's life and death are considered a sufficient satisfaction for the sins of many; and second, postbaptism human works of penance are considered a satisfaction for temporal sins. What governs this "exchange mechanism" is the distributive justice of God. There exists between God and humanity what the Lutheran theologian Gerhard O. Forde has called a "scheme of recompense," which apportions deserts and merits between God and humanity.

Described like this, the whole process sounds rather legalistic, cold, and calculated. There is an "arithmeticity" to sin, as many critics have pointed out, which makes possible an equivalence between the "quantity" of sins committed and the size of the restitution offered. This model also seems to oversatisfy the honor of God, to the point where divine salvation is no longer gracious forgiveness,[38] but a human right, necessitated by an equivalent

38. See, for instance, I. A. Dorner, *A System of Christian Doctrine* (Edinburgh: T&T Clark, 1890), 4:29.

recompense paid from the human side. I shall return to these critiques of the Latin legal type below.

The rival root metaphor is the dramatic image of a Christic victory over the powers. It was popular both before the medieval legal renaissance and, as we shall see, today, when we are witnessing a disintegration, fragmentation, and relativization of the very concept of law. The classic view does not share the assumption of an overarching legal scheme standing between God and humanity. It is not that God does not impose a (natural) law on humanity but that he himself is not forced to abide by it. The retributive principles of natural law need not apply to God. Moreover, this law can also be seen as the enemy blocking our access to God, with its impossible demands and failure to create just persons. The God who saves cannot be seen as somehow dependent on any such "law." His action must be seen as purely gratuitous, omnipotent, and swift. It cannot be conceived as being conditional on anything done from the human side, since there is no scheme for translating human action into divine merit. The dramatic view, as a result, described the action of God in atonement as a one-step action, requiring nothing from the human side as a condition. Salvation does not come in exchange for anything, but remains purely gratuitous. It consists in our being delivered from the forces that held us in bondage.

As we have already seen, while there is a narrative elegance to this view, while it caters to our intuitions about the power and freedom of God, and while it responds to a deep religious longing for liberation from the powers, it is plagued by its specific shortcomings. First, while God is free from the law, he does seem to owe something to the powers. The theory fails to explain what exactly empowers the powers. Another difficulty stems directly from the first one: it is difficult to understand how a death or indeed a resurrection can be seen as a defeat of the powers, all the more since the powers do not seem to have lost any of their power. Let me put it in the form of a question: What is the existential cash value of this defeat? How does it help with my current battle with the powers? Second, since we are not really illumined as to the *manner* of Christ's victory (What exactly was his "weapon"?), our own battle with the powers remains disconnected from Christ's. We may appeal to an abstract victory (though we do not know what it existentially means), but we are denied the use of the very thing that won us the victory. It is not accidental that the dramatic theory ultimately fails to account for the necessity of the death of Christ and therefore downplays and downgrades it in relation to the resurrection.

Luther's own ambivalence toward the law should be the first indication that he cannot be taken to support the Latin view without hesitation. Does this mean, however, that Luther can be described, as Gustaf Aulén describes him, as proposing a more advanced version of the classic view? It is clearly the case that Luther gives no systematic treatment of the atonement in his oeuvre. His main interest is pastoral, which is not to say that it is not theological, but it is a theology preoccupied less with crisp metaphysical distinctions and more with foundations for dealing with the existential experience of believers and theologians alike. The emphasis clearly falls on the doctrine of justification. The interpreter will have to work harder at reconstructing Luther's implicit theory from these adjacent topics. But the task is even more difficult; as Rashdall observes, "Far from wishing to rationalize or moralize the scheme of redemption, he exults in its irrationality."[39] We should not be surprised, therefore, to find apparently conflicting and contradictory images scattered throughout his work. The interpretive debate that has been raging now for quite some time in Luther studies at the very least shows that any view Luther might be shown to hold will be uniquely his.

Aulén's *Christus Victor: An Historical Study of Three Main Types of the Idea of the Atonement* challenges the traditional Lutheran interpretation of Luther as belonging to what he calls the Latin type. He points out Luther's use of "images and forms of expression which are regularly characteristic of the classic idea of the Atonement."[40] Luther also recovers the deception motif, problematic during its very own apogee, and thought by the scholastics to have been definitively abandoned. Luther shows how it was God himself, the Lord of glory, who was crucified, and this fact was concealed from the devil, or else he would not have dared kill him.

The use of such imagery, however, is not a sufficient demonstration. Aulén is aware of this and supplies "the decisive proof" in the following three points:

> First, in those places where it is altogether necessary for him [Luther] to express himself with the greatest possible care and the greatest possible exactness, as, for instance, in the Catechisms, he always returns to the dramatic idea. Second, he himself repeatedly assures us, with all possible clearness, that the statements of the meaning of the Atonement in dramatic terms give the very essence of the Christian faith; they are *capitalia nostrae theologiae*. Third, and chiefly, the dramatic view of the work of Christ stands in organic relation with his theological outlook as a whole.[41]

39. Hastings Rashdall, *The Idea of Atonement in Christian Theology* (New York: Macmillan, 1919), 398.
40. Gustaf Aulén, *Christus Victor: An Historical Study of the Three Main Types of the Idea of the Atonement*, trans. A. G. Hebert (New York: Macmillan, 1969), 103.
41. Ibid., 104.

Aulén picks up on these definite dramatic overtones in Luther's most elaborate discussion of the atonement, his *Commentary on Galatians*, at 3:13. I will let Luther speak for himself at some length here:

> For, by Himself to overcome the world's sin, death, and the curse, and God's wrath, this is not the work of any created being, but of almighty God. Therefore He who of Himself overcame these must actually in His nature be God. For against these so mighty powers, sin, death, and the curse, which of themselves have dominion in the world and in all creation, another and a higher power must appear, which can be none other than God. To destroy sin, to smite death, to take away the curse by Himself, to bestow righteousness, bring life to light, and give the blessing: to annihilate the former, and to create the latter: this is the work of God's omnipotence alone. But when the Scripture ascribes to Christ all this, then is He Himself the Life, and Righteousness, and Blessing—that is, in His nature and His essence He is God. Therefore those who deny Christ's Deity lose all Christianity and become mere heathens and Turks. Therefore the article of Justification must, as I am continually saying, be exactly understood. For in this all the other articles of our faith are included, and if this remains whole then all the others remain whole. When therefore we teach that men are justified through Christ, and Christ is the conqueror of sin, death, and the everlasting curse, then at the same time we testify that He is in his nature God.[42]

Aulén's point is that Luther describes justification in terms of our being redeemed by Christ from the powers. I will show that there are indeed reasons to believe that Luther has complicated his undoubtedly forensic picture with elements brought over from an entirely different, more mystical and ontological model. This will be shown to create an important tension in his doctrine of the atonement. As we shall see, Luther's doctrine of the "happy exchange" also seems to lend credence to Aulén's interpretation.

"Luther's interpretation of Christ's work," Aulén continues, "has all the typical characteristics of the classic idea of the Atonement."[43] First, there is here a continuity of divine operation. Aulén argues that "the power which is able to overcome the tyrants is God's omnipotence."[44] Luther, he implies, does not stress the atoning work done by the human Jesus, which God then recompenses with salvation. Aulén does indeed make an important point. Luther's doctrine of the *communicatio idiomatum*, or the transfer of properties between the divine and human natures of Christ, makes an important contribution to his understanding of the atonement. The second typical characteristic of such

42. Ibid., 106–7; for the original, see Luther's *Commentary on Galatians*, 3:13.
43. Aulén, *Christus Victor*, 107.
44. Ibid.

a model is that the atonement is again closely connected to the incarnation. As the longer quote above indicates, it all depends on a battle waged between the divine nature and the powers. Third, "the whole view is dualistic and dramatic."[45] This is again undeniable. An additional point, not mentioned by Aulén, is that Luther prefers to talk about sin as having been defeated rather than simply paid for. Luther stresses our bondage. However, for Luther, as for Calvin and the rest of Reformational theology, this bondage of the will does not exclude the reality of guilt before God.

Several questions immediately arise in regard to this interpretation. If Aulén is right, if the classic view is indeed the overarching scheme intended by Luther, then we will expect to find consistency in how Luther treats each of these questions. They are as follows.

First, if it was indeed divine omnipotence that overcame the powers, and "there is no thought of an offering made to God by Christ simply as man, in His human nature,"[46] what necessity can possibly attach to Christ's death? Any necessity that might characterize this death possibly conflicts with the idea that it is God's omnipotence alone that is the agent of the atonement.

Second, how does Luther treat the death of Christ? What kind of death is it? Under what aspect does this death defeat the powers? While Luther does indeed indulge in the fishhook metaphor, does this exhaust his range of descriptions when depicting the quality of Christ's death?

Third, it is a truism that, on the one hand, dramatic theories orient the atonement toward the powers. Humanity is in bondage to the devil. The work of Christ aims at achieving something in regard to these powers. On the other hand, the Latin type has a Godward orientation. God is the one who has to be satisfied, propitiated. If Luther is indeed a representative of the classic type, why do divine wrath and the curse play such a prominent role as the enemies that have to be defeated? There is "a real similarity of thought" between Luther and the Latin theory, as Aulén acknowledges:

> But the two solutions to the antinomy are poles apart. For the Latin theory, the satisfaction made by Christ is primarily a rationally conceived compromise between the demand for punishment and the remission of punishment; the demand of God's justice is satisfied by the compensation paid by Christ from man's side, from below. But in Luther every trace of this rationalism has disappeared; it disappears because the dualistic outlook is maintained, and because the victory over the Curse and the wrath is in the fullest sense God's victory.[47]

45. Ibid., 108.
46. Ibid.
47. Ibid., 115.

The question that remains, though, is how Luther's "God against God" motif coheres with the dramatic view. Doesn't Luther's absolutely novel notion of a conflicted God not explode the framework? Aulén is right, as I will show, that for Luther "the love of God breaks through the wrath."[48] But the sheer existence of such a conflict should be enough to warn us of any facile assimilation of this theology into the dramatic type.

Finally, how does Luther's description of Jesus's life cohere with the classic model, which normally tends to downplay both the passion and the life in favor of the resurrection? In what follows I do not intend to take up each of these questions in turn. I am merely flagging these as important concerns for a classic/dramatic reading of Luther's doctrine of the atonement. Ultimately I believe that Luther often answers these questions in ways that are incompatible with the dramatic view.

The Wondrous Exchange

Let us now turn to Luther's own thought on the matter and point out some of its salient features. One of the thoughts to which Luther returns again and again is that of the so-called great exchange (*admirabile commercium*). Aulén already alluded to this as the very definition of justification. There takes place an exchange whereby my sins are cast upon Christ and his righteousness becomes mine. In *The Freedom of the Christian*, Luther describes this exchange, which takes place by faith: "Christ is full of grace, life, and salvation while the soul is full of sins, death, and damnation. Now let faith enter the picture and sins, death, and damnation are Christ's while grace, life, and salvation will be the soul's. For if Christ is a bridegroom he must take upon himself that which are his bride's, and he in turn bestows on her all that is his."[49] Luther continues to render this exchange in dramatic terms:

> The result is a pleasing picture, not only of communion but of a blessed battle that leads to victory, salvation, and redemption. For Christ is God and man in one person. He has not sinned or died and he is not condemned. Nor can he sin, die, or be condemned. The righteousness, life, and salvation he possesses are unconquerable, for he is eternal and all powerful; however, by the wedding ring of faith, he shares in the sins, death and hell of his bride. In fact he makes them his own and acts as if they were his own. It is as if he sinned, suffered, died, and descended into hell in order to overcome them all; however, sin, death,

48. Ibid., 131.
49. Martin Luther, *The Freedom of a Christian*, 62.

and hell could not swallow him. In fact, they were swallowed by him in a mighty duel or battle. For his righteousness is greater than all sin, his life stronger than death, and his salvation more invincible than hell.[50]

This is an extraordinary picture. Luther seems to talk about a battle that rages in the very incarnation of Jesus. In the Galatians commentary, the victory seems to be ascribed to the sheer divinity of Jesus, thus supporting Aulén's thesis that the ultimate agent of redemption is the omnipotent God.

> Let us see how Christ was able to gain the victory over our enemies. The sins of the whole world, past, present, and future, fastened themselves upon Christ and condemned Him. But *because Christ is God* he had an everlasting and unconquerable righteousness. These two, the sin of the world and the righteousness of God, met in a death struggle. Furiously the sin of the world assailed the righteousness of God. Righteousness is immortal and invincible. On the other hand, sin is a mighty tyrant who subdues all men. This tyrant pounces on Christ. But Christ's righteousness is unconquerable. The result is inevitable. Sin is defeated and righteousness triumphs and reigns forever.[51]

Just judging from these texts alone, not only does Luther appear to be steeped within a clearly dramatic framework, but the victory seems to be won on the sheer basis of his unconquerable righteousness. This raises another set of questions: first, is the believer united to Christ's essential righteousness, that is, the righteousness he has by virtue of his divinity, or to his so-called acquired righteousness? The answer to this question determines whether the life of Jesus, his "active obedience," plays any part in the doctrine of the atonement, or whether atonement takes place by virtue of the incarnation alone.[52]

Here again, competing schools of interpretation suggest different solutions. It is useful to distinguish them at this point. I shall call the first one the mystical/ontological school. It draws much energy from Aulén's classic interpretation of Luther, but also from the new school of Finnish research on Luther's soteriology. The later school grew out of a Lutheran-Orthodox dialogue, and it quite naturally desires to weaken the forensic dimension of Luther's doctrine of salvation in favor of a theosis-oriented approach. Since the new Finnish school does not directly deal with the atonement, but more specifically with Luther's doctrine of justification, there is no need (or space)

---

50. Ibid., 62–63.

51. Luther, *Commentary on Galatians* 3:13.

52. I will show that, while Aulén is right to contend that Luther makes the incarnation again central to the atonement, it is not simply as incarnation, but as this particular incarnation whereby God takes on himself the human condition with all that it bears, including its penal sufferings.

to address it here. But both Aulén as well as the new Finnish school of Luther research argue that the fundamental soteriological thought in Luther is ontological rather than forensic. Thus in Lutheran circles they contribute to the rehabilitation of Osiander's teaching that the essence of justification consists in Christ's essential righteousness indwelling believers.

Other Lutheran theologians further weaken the forensic dimension. Gerhard O. Forde acknowledges that "the payment or satisfaction takes place, however, not by some machinery of compensatory reckoning vis-à-vis God, but rather in that the law and sin attack him and damn him but cannot succeed and are in turn conquered by his invincible righteousness."[53] Forde thus takes the *admirabile commercium* motif as central. He insists, however, that neither the classic nor the Latin type is an adequate representation of the unique thought of Luther. Somewhat controversially, he maintains that both the classic view and the Latin, satisfaction-based models are essentially pre-Reformation. Their basic structure is to escape, to ascend toward God, whether by law or moral improvement, or by victory over the tyrants. Atonement occurs, he argues, when the ascent toward God succeeds.[54]

Forde is most clear, however, in how he separates Luther from Anselm: "Satisfaction cannot be, as for Anselm, a substitution for punishment. Christ suffers the punishment and destruction of death in our place, our nature, in order to give us his. He must take our sins and destroy them, devour them."[55] But this sounds very forensic and penal, in that Christ suffers our punishment. Yet Forde will argue that, while Christ does indeed bear our punishment, this is not the condition on which God cancels our penal debt. There is thus a very important equivocation in recent Lutheran theology about the function of punishment in the atonement. While the penal dimension continues to be accepted, it is not given any wheels to turn, so to speak. It is rendered idle. What really makes the atonement work is the ontological transfer. The punishment is there as, one might say, a side effect of the incarnation.

We can already begin to glimpse how Luther's own ambivalence toward law and human schemes of justice informs this oscillation. For Forde, since there is no "scheme of recompense," no condition met on the human side can cause God to forgive us. That is the wrong way to put the matter. It remains stuck in the old "heavenward traffic" scheme, whereby humanity seeks to ascend to God on the basis of some law that holds between God and humanity. What the atonement does, however, is to make any such intermediary scheme

53. Gerhard O. Forde, "The Work of Christ," in *Christian Dogmatics*, ed. Carl E. Braaten and Robert W. Jenson (Philadelphia: Fortress, 1984), 54.
    54. Ibid., 47.
    55. Ibid., 52.

problematic. Yet since there is no such scheme, there can be no assured result. Forde does not shy from saying that the conflict in which Jesus engages is "not a foregone conclusion. Christ could and did die; he suffered the pangs of death and abandonment. Yet in the resurrection the divine power overcomes even death, and thus conquers, kills, devours, destroys, buries, and abolishes death, sin, the curse, the law, and all the tyrants."[56]

What Forde wishes to underscore is that the divine victory does not come as a response within an exchange. The resurrection was not guaranteed by anything else that preceded it. God was not forced to resurrect Jesus. Yet he did. This arguably represents an advance over the older classic theory. On the one hand, Luther and Forde intensify the conflict. They acknowledge not only the reality of the fight but also, and most importantly, the reality and importance of the Son's self-identification with human sin. Christ must actually become, not just be associated with, "Peter, the liar; Paul, the persecutor; David, the adulterer; Adam, the disobedient; the thief on the cross."[57] Luther also insists on the necessity of not making light of the real suffering of Jesus on the cross, but not only that. He must experience what we experience, our anxiety, our fear of God, everything that belongs to the human condition. This indeed is the punishment Jesus underwent.

But the key difference from penal substitution is that Christ underwent all of these things not as something demanded by God as a requirement for our absolution but as what is entailed in his assuming our condition and wrestling with it. The absolution that ultimately comes, the divine victory, is not a foregone conclusion. Christ does not satisfy a law that mediates between God and humanity, but defeats a law that incurs divine wrath. The real strength of this interpretation is that it does not shy away from the horror of the cross and it refuses to portray the Son as somehow aloof in his divinity from the suffering of his human nature. This is not a sanitized punishment, where God is not at risk, but God himself is stepping into our messy condition and overcoming it, redeeming it. Again, the key difference is that the victory is entirely gracious. On the other hand, is the "God against God" idea comprehensible? Moreover, can Luther succeed in making the law itself a tyrant?

Relegalizing Luther

I will now turn to some of the recalcitrant evidence that stands in the way of a delegalized Luther. What I hope to show is not that Luther can be drafted into the service of a pure theory of penal substitution. I do not think that is the

56. Ibid., 56.
57. Luther, *Commentary on Galatians* 3:13.

case. However, there are clear penal and substitutionary dimensions in Luther. These, however, are cast as part of a narrative structure that presents us with its own set of challenges. Minimally, one could say that Luther incorporates into his system aspects of the penal substitutionary logic. Maximally, one might even say that Luther tells the story of penal substitution in a unique and richly stimulating way.[58]

That Luther could be interpreted as a Latin theologian of the atonement used to be the normative view in Luther research. Thus Dorner mentions that Luther, just like Anselm and Thomas, "also takes God's justice into account."[59] He then concedes that the emphasis on justice and the law is much stronger in Melanchthon. Nevertheless, God's justice remains very much in the foreground for Luther, according to Dorner. Laurence William Grensted is even more convinced, suggesting that Luther appeals to "blind justice," which is utterly objective and external.[60] The death of Christ is clearly viewed as a legal penalty for sin. Rashdall, perhaps predictably, pronounces that there is no doubt about the substitutionary character of sacrifice in either Luther or Calvin.[61]

It is not only critics of Luther that point out this legal scaffolding, but also Lutheran scholars like Paul Althaus, who scathingly critiques Aulén's dismissal of the juridical dimension of Luther's thought: "The powers with which Christ struggled had their power and authority only through God's wrath" (1 Cor. 5:5).[62] Moreover, they are instruments of God's wrath against the sinner. The freedom from these powers is consequent on our freedom from God's wrath. Thus the work of Christ is clearly forensic, in the sense that his death is our punishment borne on our behalf. The powers had their hold on humanity in view of sin and its guilt. Thus, Althaus argues, atonement is oriented toward God, within a framework of justice.

I will focus on two legal notions that retain their centrality in Luther: propitiation and satisfaction. These are but two sides of the same legal coin. The first of these refers to the effect on God of the work of Christ; the second, to the quality of Jesus's action. Since the same act could be presented under a variety of descriptions, including descriptions of its effects, it is understandable that there will be a tremendous amount of overlap between these two notions.

58. As I hope to show, there is no single doctrine or theory of penal substitution, but a number of central notions that can be cast in different relations, some better than others. See N. T. Wright, "The Cross and the Caricatures," *Fulcrum: Renewing the Evangelical Centre*, http://www.fulcrum-anglican.org.uk/news/2007/20070423wright.cfm?doc=205.

59. Dorner, *A System of Christian Doctrine*, 4:22.

60. Laurence William Grensted, *A Short History of the Doctrine of the Atonement* (Manchester: Manchester University Press, 1920), 201.

61. Rashdall, *Idea of Atonement*, 399.

62. Paul Althaus, *The Theology of Martin Luther* (Philadelphia: Fortress, 1966), 220.

Althaus demonstrates that "God cannot simply forget about his wrath and show his mercy to sinners if his righteousness is not satisfied."[63] There is a condition internal to God that must be met in order to experience God's grace. The Abelardian-exemplarist idea of a God who is exclusively described as love is unacceptable. Divine wrath cannot be dismissed, and it has to be appeased. While salvation is free, it is not offered without cost. Althaus quotes Luther: "All this does not take place for nothing or without the satisfaction of God's righteousness; for mercy and grace cannot be thought of as being effective over us and in us or as helping us to eternal blessings and salvation unless God's righteousness has previously been completely satisfied, . . . for no one can come to God's rich grace unless he has absolutely and completely satisfied God's commandments."[64] This immediately raises a question about Aulén's confident remark that there is no thought of an offering made from the human side in Luther's doctrine of the atonement. Moreover, the reason why something like this must take place has to do with a requirement internal to God's own nature.

The question is how to spell out that requirement and, more importantly, how to relate it to God's essential attribute of love. Luther's choice is to talk about a "God against God." As already pointed out, Ritschl identifies an inconsistency in Luther regarding the idea that God is *ex lex*, on the one hand, and the inherent necessity that a sacrifice is to be paid for salvation, on the other.[65] While Luther does indeed elevate love over wrath, "on the whole, he makes love and wrath in God, notwithstanding his subordination of the latter to the former, to appear as co-ordinate, and therefore as opposed and even (in certain circumstances) contradictory forces, for the harmonizing of which in God himself, endurance of punishment by the mediator is necessary."[66]

However we construe this admittedly difficult aspect of Lutheran theology, Aulén's proposal that God's grace is not conditional on something offered from the human side cannot stand. There is a conflict between God's love and God's wrath precisely because what his love wants to save cannot enter into the presence of God because of sin. God's grace, therefore, remains conditional, but not therefore less gracious, since it is a condition that God himself will meet.[67]

63. See his discussion in ibid., 202.
64. Ibid., 202n4.
65. Ritschl, *Christian Doctrine*, 199–200.
66. Ibid., 202.
67. According to Forde ("Work of Christ," 56), while God meets this condition, its satisfaction does not guarantee the ultimate victory, which is established not by the death but by the resurrection.

How is God propitiated? Althaus argues that there are two ways in which Christ makes satisfaction: "He fulfills the will of God expressed in the law; he suffers the punishment of sin, the wrath of God. Both are done in our place and for our benefit."[68] Luther rejects the Anselmian alternative between satisfaction and punishment. He takes the Thomistic view that satisfaction and punishment are one and the same thing. Christ satisfies God's justice by bearing our penalty on our behalf.

Wherever Luther critiques the medieval concept of satisfaction, he does it on the grounds that it does not go deep enough, for the medievals had succeeded, Luther thought, in separating Christ from our sins. They had concentrated on the supererogatory works of Christ, losing from sight the utmost identification with sin. Christ was made to be sin, as Paul notes in 2 Cor. 5:21. This should be taken literally. Of course, what Luther is concerned with is that a soteriology emphasizing Christ's obedience as merit results in a doctrine of Christian life that stresses the continued need for meritorious action. But that is precisely what drives humanity to the depths of despair. Once one realizes that Christ identified himself with human despair and that he conquered it by removing the guilt, then his death can indeed be existentially relevant and comforting.

Thus the problem with the medieval concept of satisfaction and the attendant doctrine of merits, with its own attendant practices of penance, besides the fact that it had proved useless against Luther's *Anfechtungen*, was that it failed to grasp the extent and significance of Jesus's identification with our sins. For Luther, it was precisely this identification, captured by the concept of the great exchange, that soothed his fears, for the victory of Christ consisted precisely in this, that sin and death are defeated.

Thus Althaus is right to note that Luther extends the concept of satisfaction beyond anything that Anselm had imagined. Rashdall also makes a similar point with regard to the notion of substitution, which Luther, he argues, pushed further than it had ever been, even up to the point of Christ's descent into hell—as sufferer first. Christ experiences the full extent of God's wrath in his passion. By making this experience of divine wrath a component of the satisfaction required by God, he bends the language of satisfaction to a new purpose, as Gorringe also observes, thus moving beyond the medieval paradigm.[69]

Christ really was made a sinner, as Luther argues in his Galatians commentary, so that our sins would not be thrown back at us. This is nothing but the nonimputation of guilt, since Christ had our guilt imputed to himself.

68. Althaus, *Theology of Martin Luther*, 205.
69. Gorringe, *God's Just Vengeance*, 135.

Conclusion and Critical Remarks

I have tried to demonstrate that, for all the complexity and uniqueness of Luther's larger soteriology, there are concepts that properly belong to the penal substitutionary framework. God is turned from wrath to love, to put it very crudely, by an offer made from the human side. The death of Christ is also clearly penal and substitutionary at the same time. The presence of these elements does not entail that Luther is simply advancing and expanding the Latin model. But it is also a mistake to discount the presence of these notions.

A remaining question has to do with the overall coherence of this position. Can Luther weave these multiple threads into a single unified conception? Timothy George argues that we should not distinguish too sharply between Christus Victor and satisfaction. Indeed, "this may well be Luther's major contribution to atonement theology." Luther "saw that the cross of Christ was at once the scene of Satan's definitive defeat and the objective basis of justification by faith alone."[70] I believe we can be a little more confident than that. The correlation between the cross as the basis of justification and the cross as the scene of cosmic victory is more than just occasional. Althaus is right to claim that the two are logically related: Christ has defeated the powers *in that* he removed our guilt.

It is the connection between the forensic and the ontological aspects that is more troublesome. I will spell out the problem in simple terms. There are two possible strands in Luther's thinking on the atonement. On the one hand, what I have called the forensic track traverses concepts like propitiation, satisfaction, punishment—all of which are legal concepts and presuppose the establishment of a legal framework. This track is very much part of the Latin inheritance. The presence of the above-mentioned legal concepts seems to suggest that we are definitely in this tradition. Althaus, Eckhardt, and others have no doubts that we are. On this logic, God rewards the satisfaction that Christ makes by extending his forgiveness. This is still very much a logic of exchange, presupposing the applicability of a legal framework between God and humanity.

The trouble is that Luther seems to push against that framework every time he is presented with the opportunity. His theology of law in particular makes any such interpretation problematic. As we have seen, there is a tremendous ambivalence about the law in Luther. One might call this a "dialectic," together with George, as long as the term retains the idea of a serious tension and even

---

70. Timothy George, "The Atonement in Martin Luther's Theology," in *The Glory of the Atonement: Biblical, Theological and Practical Perspectives*, ed. Charles E. Hill and Frank A. James III (Downers Grove, IL: InterVarsity, 2004), 275.

conflict. Moreover, the wrath of God itself is an enemy. Thus the law and the wrath of God are not simply benign or neutral factors in the human predicament but are positively regarded as the enemies that must be destroyed. We are clearly not within the normal Latin theory once we understand how starkly Luther presents these elements as negative.

The other possible track is the mystical/ontological one. Here divine salvation is offered without any constraints having to be met. God unilaterally and out of his love unites himself with our condition and defeats the powers. This interpretation also runs into trouble, for Luther presents God as being conflicted and thus not the unitary subject of the classic theory. Moreover, Luther also emphasized the two dimensions of Christ's obedience, active and passive. These suggest that salvation does not take place through the sheer force of the incarnation, as in *some* Eastern patristic models.

Is there any thread that might combine these tracks? Luther's position on the atonement is best captured by the idea that the death of Christ has a clear penal and substitutionary quality, and that such a death is a necessary though not sufficient condition of atonement. It is a necessary condition in that God did not forgive gratuitously, without any sort of satisfaction. In Luther, there is no speculation on whether God could have done so. His theology starts from the historical reality of the cross, and at the cross we see what it cost God to save us. But the condition is not therefore also sufficient: while the death as such eliminates our guilt, it does not account for the novelty of the new dimension of grace inaugurated by the resurrection. One might argue that the penal substitutionary death of Christ stands for the forensic dimension of the atonement, while the resurrection represents the ontological dimension of the work of Christ. The atonement is much broader than the mere legal dimension of absolution of guilt. It involves a new reality in which death, the powers, sin, and the law have been defeated. However, to understand this new dimension in Luther's terms, one must understand that it is not anticipated in terms of the law.

God acts in Christ's passion according to law because law belongs to the human condition. Christ identifies himself with this human condition and everything it entails, including suffering and death. But he does it not merely to pay its just penalty (though he does not do less than that), but to rescue it, to heal its nature. This is the thoroughly ontological level signified by the happy-exchange metaphor. But this ontological dimension *supervenes* on and yet is *underdetermined by* the forensic dimension of Christ's passion. Thus the punishment of Christ on the cross is what is entailed by his identifying himself with our full humanity. This punishment is the condition of the ultimate victory, yet the ultimate victory is not achieved in this penalty alone.

Here Luther's ambivalence with regard to the law influences his understanding of the atonement. Since there is no congruity between divine justice
and human systems of justice, including the new retributive justice system in
full ascendancy at that time, God's salvific action does not depend entirely
on such systems. Yet, since it is a historic action deployed in the midst of the
human condition, it must face this legal divine wrath straight on and satisfy
it. That is the conflict for which the crucifixion of Jesus is the high point.
But the resurrection and exaltation are entirely incomprehensible from the
standpoint of the old framework. Oswald Bayer best captures this dialectic:

> God's mercy stands opposite God's wrath. Luther gives full weight to what
> makes this brand-new start so incomprehensible. He does not use the way the
> law operates and what it declares, attributing sin to a person and driving that
> person into destruction, into the hell of damnation, to convey the way the gospel
> operates and what it declares; he lets the rupture stand. On the other side of
> that rupture, the Gospel begins afresh with a second, new and final message
> from God.[71]

Thus, while there is a clear legal element, in Luther's thought it is ultimately
subsumed under, though not transcended by, the ontological victory represented by the resurrection.

Divine Wrath and Love in Calvin's Doctrine of Penal Substitution

Introduction

With Calvin we reach the doctrine of penal substitution as such. Neither
Anselm nor Luther represents the full logic of penal substitution as Calvin
endorses it. While both of them recover or retain the importance of law and
justice, neither elevates divine justice to quite the level it reaches in Calvin's
thought.

Berkhof summarizes four points of departure from Anselm's thought. First,
the satisfaction theory focuses on the honor and dignity of God rather than his
justice. The context is that of private rather than public law. The restoration
of the divine-human relationship depends on the free decision of a sovereign
and private Lord. The decision as to what is ultimately a *satisfactory* atonement belongs entirely to him and can indeed alter from case to case. Second,
there is no place in Anselm's thought for the biblical idea of Christ's bearing

---

71. Oswald Bayer, *Martin Luther's Theology: A Contemporary Interpretation*, trans. Thomas
H. Trapp (Grand Rapids: Eerdmans, 2008), 228.

of our punishment on our behalf. Rather, Christ offers himself as a sacrifice deemed acceptable in lieu of our being punished (Isa. 53:10). While Calvin retains the central idea of *satisfactio*, the specific act required will no longer be a life freely offered, but a penal death. Third, Berkhof argues that there is no place for the active obedience of Christ. This might seem puzzling,[72] yet it is not the death that effectively procures atonement for Anselm, but the infinitely valuable offer of Christ's life. Berkhof does not underline this fact, but there is a decidedly ahistorical attitude in Anselm's rationalized doctrine of the atonement. Christ's purity—as a condition of the perfect sacrifice—is construed abstractly as a will ordered to God, rather than specifically within a covenantal, legal context. Calvin, and especially later Reformed theologians, will give redemptive significance to Christ's life of obedience to God, not as abstract purity of will, but as concrete obedience to the law. Finally, the fourth weakness sensed by the Reformers is that the Latin satisfaction model turns on a purely external transfer of merits. The believer is left to his or her own devices to continue to earn the surplus merit of Christ. The Reformation doctrine of justification by faith made this aspect of the satisfaction theory completely untenable, emphasizing instead faith as the acceptance of Christ's righteousness (Rom. 3:22; 4:24; 5:1; Gal. 2:16; 3:24; Phil. 3:9). The Latin theory was thought to construe the work of Christ in such a way that it remained compatible with a continued human effort to earn its benefits (2 Cor. 7:15). While, as we shall see, an economy of exchange will continue to characterize the Reformed understanding of the atonement, the satisfaction of God is construed in such a way that it can only be accomplished by the Redeemer, and it cannot be replicated by believers seeking to earn their salvation. Christ's work is final (Heb. 7:27; 9:28; 1 Pet. 3:18) and unrepeatable.

Luther and Calvin share in their critique of these doctrinal points. Their common doctrine of justification by faith, ruling as it does their understanding of the atonement, leads them to positions that construe the work of Christ as final, and as something that can be appropriated by faith, with no need of further works of penance. But they differ as to what makes Christ's work final. The difference is not immediately visible. Indeed, it may be easier to glimpse from the competing interpretations of their theology. This is especially true for Luther. As I have shown, there are competing construals of his doctrine of the atonement, and in particular the significance of its forensic element. I concluded that while the forensic element is clearly present, the divine redemption somehow *supervenes* it. Luther does not construe the relationship between divine and human justice as one of continuity. Divine justice is not established

72. Louis Berkhof, *Systematic Theology* (Edinburgh: Banner of Truth, 1958), 385–86.

by the human legal apparatus. While there is a place for retribution in Luther, it is not the *cause* of the redemption. Grace remains central for Luther in the sense that the ultimate victory is not guaranteed or even anticipated by the retributive conflict. That Christ suffers the punishment is not the fundamental screw in the atonement mechanism, but what precedes the redemptive victory. God is ultimately victorious *despite* the death of Christ, not so much *because* of his death (Acts 2:23–24). It is much less clear that, for Luther, Christ *merited* salvation. In this sense Aulén is to be commended for drawing our attention to the dramatic and even mystical atmosphere of Luther's thought: redemption consists in the defeat of death, sin, wrath, and the law.

Calvin makes the legal dimension much more central to, and indeed effective in, the divine plan of salvation. Rather than construing law as the enemy that must be defeated, it is rather the means by which the ultimate victory is won. The centrality of law in Calvin's theology has already been outlined in a previous section. The question, then, is whether this creates a tension with the love of God.

Divine Wrath and Love

Two observations need to be made about Calvin's use of the legal framework in his atonement theory. The reader will already be familiar with these points, but it is useful to reiterate them. The first point to be made is that Calvin inherits a shift that was already in motion during the early sixteenth century, a shift to a retributive understanding of justice. The necessity of punishment was regarded as a necessary component in the transition from a private to a public law. Retribution belonged to the very essence of the law, as the necessary consequence of its trespass. Dillistone comments on the different legal atmosphere:

> The general atmosphere of Calvin's writings is also strikingly different: . . . the key-terms in Anselm (and the later scholastic theologians) were those belonging to Roman civil law and to medieval feudal law—debt, liability, compensation, satisfaction, honour, price, payment, merit; . . . [but] in Calvin we find constant reference to punishment, death, the curse, wrath, substitution, surety, merit, imputation—in other words to criminal law reinterpreted in the light of the Biblical teaching on the law, sin, and death.[73]

Calvin finds an important continuity between the criminal law of his day, codified, for example, by Schwarzenberg, and the biblical principle that "without

---

73. Dillistone, *Christian Understanding of Atonement*, 195.

the shedding of blood there is no remission [of sins]" (Heb. 9:22, my trans.). This is not to reduce justice to its retributive dimension, but to insist on its necessity.

The second observation is related to the first. If justice consists at least partly in punishment, and this is not merely a principle of human justice (such as one that Luther might be inclined to mistrust), but a positive principle of eternal divine justice, then the same continuity will be demonstrated at the level of the institutions through which this justice is carried out. It will follow that human courts of justice are continuous with and representatives of the divine justice court (Rom. 13:4). Calvin does not hesitate to draw this conclusion. For this reason, it was imperative that the death Christ would die would be a consequence of his condemnation in a human court of justice, "by the formal sentence of a judge, ranked among criminals"[74] (Isa. 53:12; Luke 22:37). Human courts of law carry divine justice. With the thought of this continuity, Calvin ensures that the wheels and screws of a human justice mechanism can efficaciously influence divine redemption. God saves not despite this mechanism *but in and through it*.

How does the free and gratuitous love of God, emphasized so clearly by Calvin elsewhere, cohere with the apparent necessity of his retributive justice? Has Calvin succeeded in making God's love the prisoner of his justice? To be sure, the relationship between God's wrath/justice and his mercy/love has established itself as the major hurdle for any Latin type of atonement theory. Calvin no less than Luther has to wrestle with it. The question is whether he succeeds to offer a satisfactory solution to this problem.

Unperceptive critics have been quick to caricature the Calvinist doctrine as suggesting a tension between a loving and forgiving Son and a vengeful, wrathful Father, who awaits to be appeased by the Son. A related caricature has God turning from his wrath to love upon the accomplishment of the sacrifice of his Son. Neither of these pictures is true to the facts of Calvin's exposition.

Despite giving such a central place to law and justice, Calvin is emphatic that salvation begins with the love of God. Echoing Ephesians 1:3–4, he points out that God chose us in Christ before the foundation of the world.[75] A spate of recent scholars has been emphasizing the priority of divine love in the order of salvation.[76] Indeed, it could only be love, since there was nothing in us that

74. Calvin, *Institutes* 2.16.5.
75. Ibid., 2.16.4.
76. Robert A. Peterson, *Calvin and the Atonement* (Fearn, UK: Mentor, 1999); Paul Helm, *John Calvin's Ideas* (New York: Oxford University Press, 2006); idem, *Calvin at the Centre* (Oxford: Oxford University Press, 2010); Charles Partee, *The Theology of John Calvin* (Grand Rapids: Eerdmans, 2008).

made us likeable to God. God's election is from eternity, and it is grounded in his free will (2 Tim. 1:9).

Calvin does not accept that God could have been "moved" from wrath to mercy. While he does not explicitly determine this on the basis of a doctrine of divine immutability, he does hold to such a doctrine. He draws the conclusion on the basis of the incarnation: why would God have sent his Son to die for us if he hadn't already been lovingly disposed toward us? In his commentary on Romans, Calvin writes, "We were enemies when Christ interposed for the purpose of propitiating the Father: through this reconciliation we are now friends. . . . But the apostle seems here to be inconsistent with himself, for if the death of Christ was a pledge of divine love towards us, it follows that we were already acceptable to him, but he says now that we were his enemies."[77] It is thus apparent that later modern critiques of penal substitution misconstrue the theory as holding that the temporal, historical death of Christ had a temporal and historical effect on God's disposition. Calvin never held such a position.

But the problem of the scriptural language still has to be reckoned with. Why do the Scriptures present God to us as being moved from wrath to love by the sacrifice of his Son (Col. 1:20)? Why is God portrayed as having been our enemy (Rom. 5:10)? Calvin's solution is to turn to the doctrine of accommodation. God presents himself as being moved from wrath to love because the ultimate purpose is that of moving the sinner to repentance. He asks, "Will not these considerations move him the more deeply, the more strikingly they represent the greatness of the calamity from which he was delivered?"[78] Before we might have the chance to reply that such a principle risks destroying the reliability of the revelation, Calvin adds, "Though this is said in accommodation of the weakness of our capacity, it is not said falsely."[79] Here Calvin makes a distinction between a "mere gratuitous love [that] prompts him to receive us into favor" and what we might call "final love." The former love is conceivable, Calvin writes, because of our creatureliness. We still bear the image of God, and there is still something in us that God can love. But such a love cannot be final, due to our sin: "If there is a perpetual and irreconcilable repugnance between righteousness and iniquity, so long as we remain sinners we cannot be completely received."[80]

This indeed is a surprising position,[81] for it grounds God's love for sinners on something that is in them, namely, that they bear the image of God. This

77. Calvin, *Comm. Rom.* 5:10
78. Calvin, *Institutes* 2.16.2.
79. Ibid., 2.16.3.
80. Ibid.
81. See Helm, *John Calvin's Ideas.*

is significant, for Calvin is typically more deprecative of the inherent worth of human beings. If God could have found something in us worth his love, why is a further step necessary? Moreover, even in this case there seems to be a movement within the divine disposition, between two kinds of love. Calvin does not elaborate this position in any detail, but it seems to burst open his position by introducing an element of gratuity (at least for a time), a logic of love unrestrained by justice.[82]

Robert Peterson points out the risk of appealing to the doctrine of accommodation: "Accommodation can be overemphasized to the place where God's wrath loses all reality."[83] Calvin certainly does not wish to do that. But above all, his doctrine of divine immutability will not allow for such a change in dispositional states in God.

Paul Helm invokes precisely this doctrine to argue that the accommodation principle helps Calvin demonstrate that it is divine love that is the very source of redemption. God has always loved us, and he hasn't been moved from wrath to love. The change from wrath to love is one that characterizes *our experience* of redemption. Thus, while Peterson argues that accommodation can only be a part of the answer to this dialectic, Helm insists that it is a sufficient solution. Helm quotes François Wendel approvingly:

> The sacrifice offered in time by the Christ modifies, at least considered from the human point of view, the attitude of God himself towards men. In reality, that attitude is unchanged and immutable; it cannot therefore be influenced a posteriori by the work of Christ. That work is limited to the removal of the obstacle that prevents the divine love from making its way to men. The initiative remains moreover with God, and it is his love for men which has removed the barrier constituted by sin, and the divine wrath that was the consequence of it, by deciding to accept the satisfaction to be offered by Jesus Christ.[84]

Helm clearly wishes to underscore the priority of God's love. A tension, or dialectic, between wrath and love is out of the question. God has always loved us. But, as we have seen, Calvin hesitates at this crucial point. Something objective with regard to the divine disposition still had to happen: God's love could not be final unless the iniquity, which offended righteousness, was removed. Now, this is not something that has to do merely with our attitude

---

82. Ritschl points out another inconsistency, between Calvin's doctrine of election, which is entirely gratuitous, and his doctrine of providence, which operates under the constraints of justice. See Albrecht Ritsch, *A Critical History of the Christian Doctrine of Justification and Reconciliation*, trans. John S. Black (Edinburgh: Edmonston and Douglas, 1872), 208.

83. Peterson, *Calvin and the Atonement*, 22.

84. Helm, *John Calvin's Ideas*, chap. 13.

to God, but with his acceptance of us in his presence. Thus either Calvin's immutability doctrine is challenged (by the shift from gratuitous to final love), or he risks turning atonement into a subjective doctrine, a risk Helm seems to run even more.

The real question, therefore, is how God's wrath and love are related to each other in God's own being. At this point, Bruce McCormack blows the whistle: "Calvin's difficulty in this area was due in no small measure to the very scant attention he gave to the classical problem of the attributes of God. His treatment of the being and attributes of God was thin, to say the least."[85] McCormack also points out that the final outcome of Calvin's theory is that he makes God's mercy the prisoner of his righteousness. We can best explain this by returning to the dialectic of the two loves: while God gratuitously loves us, he cannot finally love us unless his righteousness has been satisfied. The wrath of God has to be appeased. Although this necessity still springs out of free divine love, it has to follow the course constrained by his justice. Thus the tension between gratuitousness and necessity returns. McCormack is not content with the position of Peterson, among others, who sees the love of God as being at the origin of the atonement: "It is not enough to affirm that the reconciling activity of the Son of God has its ground in the divine love if we are not then able to affirm in a coherent way that that love is operative at every step along the way in the accomplishment of our redemption."[86] To understand why McCormack thinks Calvin makes this mistake, we need to turn our attention to the redemptive significance of Christ's life.

Christ's Active Obedience

Critics of the Calvinist doctrine of penal substitution sometimes argue that the whole force of the theory falls on the death of Christ. Paul Fiddes, for instance, laments the fact that Christ's active obedience, for both Luther and Calvin, does not function within atonement, but it merely "inspired a moral life which follows atonement: the act of atonement itself is founded only upon the 'passive obedience' of Christ, or his enduring of penalty."[87] He further notes that "Protestant theologians who followed Calvin were intrigued by the place which Christ's active obedience had within the scheme of salvation, but as long as they held to a theory of penal substitution they remained perplexed

---

85. Bruce McCormack, "For Us and Our Salvation: Incarnation and Atonement in the Reformed Tradition," *Greek Orthodox Theological Review* 43 (1998): 281–316 (here 303).

86. Ibid., 302.

87. Paul S. Fiddes, *Past Event and Present Salvation: The Christian Idea of the Atonement* (Louisville: Westminster John Knox, 1989), 100.

and confused about it."[88] Fiddes makes several points here: First, Christ's active obedience had no place in Calvin's doctrine of the atonement. Second, emphasis on Christ's active obedience would lead atonement theory into a more subjective direction, somehow incompatible with penal substitution.

Fiddes's position does not represent the consensus opinion of Calvin scholarship. Even Ritschl points out that Christ's active and his passive obedience do not function independently of one another. These "ought to be regarded in light of one another; the active obedience and the perfect holiness of life as the general ground that gives value to the suffering, the graduated suffering as the constant manifestation of the sinless life."[89] The penal death of Christ is worthless, in Calvin's thought, without his active obedience. An unwilling sacrifice would have been of no avail. There are indeed, as a number of authors have recently pointed out, significant elements of a *recapitulatio* theory of the atonement in Calvin. Christ's obedience to the law is precisely what satisfies God, as a representative of a reconstituted humanity, replacing Adam.

What, then, is the redemptive significance of Jesus's life? McCormack argues that the problem does not so much lie in the fact that his active obedience is idle in atonement as much as in the fact that it is given an entirely legal(istic?) reading in Calvin. His fundamental failure is to have construed the significance of the Savior's life in terms of the law, and thus in terms of merit, as opposed to grace.

Calvin is indeed very explicit about Christ's submission to the law (Gal. 4:4) in its most minute details. Furthermore, his obedience to the law constitutes the basis for our justification, in that it is precisely his acquired righteousness that is imputed to us.

Moreover, Calvin stresses the unity of this active obedience as one component of the satisfaction offered to God, along with his passive obedience, that is, his death. Commenting on Romans 5:19, he points out that "from the moment he assumed the form of a servant he began, in order to redeem us, to pay the price of deliverance."[90] While this position elegantly ties the life of Christ to his death under the rubric of obedience (Phil. 2:8), it construes that obedience in strictly legal terms. Christ, then, fulfills the conditions of God's righteousness to the letter.

The reason why such a position appears suspicious to McCormack is that, again, it makes God's love conditional on the fulfillment of legal conditions.

88. Ibid.
89. Albrecht Ritschl, *A Critical History of the Christian Doctrine of Justification and Reconciliation*, trans. John S. Black (Edinburgh: Edmonston & Douglas, 1872), 214.
90. Calvin, *Institutes* 2.16.5. See also John Stott, *The Cross of Christ* (Leicester, UK: InterVarsity, 1986).

This means that, while redemption does indeed originate in divine love, it is made conditional on the satisfaction of conditions imposed by divine justice. For McCormack, this makes it impossible to maintain the idea of the priority of divine love. One might add that Calvin is de facto forced back into Luther's "God against God" theology, whose tension is solved mathematically, by strict equivalence, within an economy of exchange. I shall return to these critiques after a discussion of the redemptive significance of Jesus's death.

The Death of Christ

Here I will address two rubrics. The first one concerns the quality of Jesus's death. On this matter, Calvin's position is clear: this was a penal death, a death in God-abandonment (Matt. 27:46; Mark 15:34), the kind of death we were supposed to experience but Christ experienced on our behalf (Rom. 5:8–9; 8:34; 1 Thess. 5:10). The second rubric asks about the efficacy of this death: why is a penal death of any redemptive significance? Calvin's position will be to show that Christ's death is the equivalent of our death in God-abandonment, and that it is efficient because it pays the price for our guilt, propitiating God, and thus *meriting* our salvation.

The concept of guilt is the missing link in the Latin theory of the atonement. It is thus a prominent theme in the Reformational understanding of the cross of Christ. "God's wrath and curse," writes Calvin, "always lie upon sinners until they are absolved of guilt. Since he is a righteous Judge, he does not allow his law to be broken without punishment, but is equipped to avenge it."[91] It is this guilt that, as Brunner has put it, stays with us forever, determining our condition and standing between us and God, as a curse. Indeed, Calvin says, "Our acquittal is in this that the guilt which made us liable to punishment was transferred to the head of the Son of God (Isa. 53:12). We must especially remember this substitution in order that we may not be all our lives in trepidation and anxiety, as if the just vengeance which the Son of God transferred to himself, were still impending over us."[92] The Latin theory failed to relieve the deep anxiety (1 Kings 8:46; Eccles. 7:20; Rom. 3:9) and in fact further intensified it. The Reformational stress on the substitutionary death of Christ relieves the anxiety by removing the legal basis for guilt (Rom. 8:1).

The reason guilt is removed is that the penalty for sin has been paid in the body of Christ. Calvin talks about a twofold satisfaction offered by Christ. First, through his active obedience, he positively fulfilled the law (Phil. 2:8).

91. Calvin, *Institutes* 2.16.1.
92. Ibid., 2.16.5.

Second, in his death, he bears the punishment incumbent upon us (Gal. 3:13), the trespassers of the law.

A mere bodily death would not have sufficed, argues Calvin. Christ had to feel the full weight of divine vengeance. His soul had to experience the anguish of separation from God and the pangs of hell.[93] "And certainly had not his soul shared in the punishment, he would have been a redeemer of bodies only."[94]

The penal quality of his death is further reinforced by the fact that he was sentenced and executed by a criminal court. It is not accidental that he was thus condemned: "For in order to remove our condemnation, it was not sufficient to endure any kind of death."[95]

To summarize, Christ saved us by the whole course of his obedience, from cradle to grave, although Scripture assigns the mode of salvation "peculiarly and specially to the death of Christ."[96] Thus his death is "the effectual completion of salvation because by it we are reconciled to God, satisfaction is given to his justice, the curse is removed, and the penalty paid; still it is not by his death but by his resurrection that we are said to be begotten again to a living hope (1 Pet. 1:3)."[97] While the death of Christ is the culmination of Christ's obedience and of legal satisfaction, it clearly isn't the only thing going in atonement: "by the former [death] sin was abolished and death annihilated; by the latter [resurrection] righteousness was restored and life revived."[98] It is therefore somewhat disingenuous to claim, as Grensted does, that "Calvin's discussion depends upon the equation of sin with guilt, an equation which is not even consistent with his own conception of sin as an inherent corruption."[99] There is a lot more going on in Calvin's doctrine of the atonement, though not less, than his emphasis on guilt and the legal means of doing away with it.[100]

Turning to the second rubric, that of the efficacy of Christ's death, I have already stressed that it removes the guilt of sinners. But by virtue of what is it able to do that?

As a condition of exploring these questions, some thought must be given to the necessity of the atonement. Could God not forgive gratuitously? The preponderant opinion is that Calvin does not think such questions are appropriate.

93. Ibid., 2.16.8–10.
94. Ibid., 2.16.2.
95. Ibid., 2.16.5.
96. Ibid.
97. Ibid., 2.16.13.
98. Ibid.
99. Grensted, *Short History*, 216.
100. See, for instance, Peterson on all the other metaphors of the atonement, although he is much too hesitant when he claims that it is "difficult to determine which of the three atonement themes plays the greatest role in Calvin's thought" (*Calvin and the Atonement*, 79).

He considers Socinus's speculation about God's freedom apart from the historical revelation of God's will in the Mediator to be dangerous. Based on revelation, we only know that this is how much it has cost God to procure our salvation. Thus the consensus opinion has been that Calvin makes the justice of God the necessary framework for the accomplishment of his salvation.

However, it is possible to read this necessity in more than one way, as Paul Helm helpfully clarifies. He distinguishes between the fact of the reconciliation and its mode. An absolute view holds that "necessarily, given the fact of sin, there is to be reconciliation via the God-man."[101] This is Anselm and Augustine's view, who make the incarnation necessary. The "necessary view" is that "necessarily, given the fact of sin, *if there is to be reconciliation*, then it will be via the God-man."[102] Once the decree of God to save has been made, there is one and only one way in which this decree can be carried out. There is only one mode of the fact of reconciliation. Finally, the "hypothetical view" stipulates that "given the fact of sin, if there is to be reconciliation, then possibly it will be via the God-man."[103] Helm goes on to argue that Calvin endorses a version of the third view, the hypothetical view, although from the *Institutes* alone it would seem that Calvin endorses the second, necessary view. Helm, however, produces some quotations from Calvin's commentaries and sermons that certainly give us pause: "God might have redeemed us by a single word, or by a mere act of his will, if he had not thought it better to do otherwise for our benefit, that, by not sparing his own well-beloved son, he might testify in his person how much he cares for our salvation."[104] Or in a sermon on Matt. 26:36–39, he says, "He could, indeed, have rescued us from the abyss of death in another way, but he desired to display the treasures of his infinite goodness when he did not spare his own son. By this means our Lord Jesus Christ chose to give us a splendid token of his care for us, in willingly offering himself up to death."[105] Paradoxically, later in the same sermon, Calvin seems to reverse his position: "That is why he yielded himself up to death, since we cannot be reconciled in any other way, nor appease God's wrath provoked by sin, except through his obedience."[106] This alone suggests that this isn't some later view of Calvin's but that it is integrated into his overall conception.

But does it not clash with the apparent demand for God to redeem according to his justice? Helm does not think so, because Calvin is not considering

101. Helm, *Calvin at the Centre*, 166.
102. Ibid.
103. Ibid.
104. Ibid., 172, from Calvin, *Comm. John* 15:13.
105. Helm, *Calvin at the Centre*, 172.
106. Ibid., 173.

atonement in the abstract. He writes, "For him there are not two equivalent alternative means to the same end, salvation, but alternative means to alternative ends. If we consider the end in optimal terms, in terms that maximize the love and grace of God to sinners by best displaying it, then for Calvin there is only one possible means to that end, namely, atonement by the incarnate logos and satisfaction by the God-man."[107] Helm, moreover, goes against the great majority of Calvin scholarship in saying that "it is not that the atonement is necessary given divine justice. As far as I can see Calvin never or seldom suggests this in the *Institutes*. It is rather that the atonement is necessary, or is required, if (and only if) God wants, in pardoning us, to show his great love for us."[108]

According to Helm, then, the necessity attaching to the mode of reconciliation is consequent on the particular end sought, *which is not simple pardon.* For that a "simple word" might have sufficed, as Calvin argues. Rather, besides pardoning, God is after a "pardon that is to be optimally beneficial,"[109] which involves moving believers to action. This brings Calvin's theory noticeably closer to the moral example theory. Helm seems to reinforce this notion when he elsewhere says that Christ's work "is limited to the removal of the obstacle that prevents the divine love from making its way to men." A purebred moral example theory will insist that the block stands in the way of humanity's discovering this love of God. But the difference is only at the surface since a doctrine of divine immutability is brought in to deny any dispositional change in God, thus rendering the block entirely subjective.

It may be that Helm claims too much for Calvin. While the latter certainly does not have in mind mere pardon, but a much richer concept of reconciliation, and while the death of Christ does seem to play a great many interlocking roles, it nevertheless seems clear to me that the key role it plays is that of bearing our punishment. Helm's version of the doctrine of immutability forces him to tether atonement to subjectivity, to the point where a Godward dimension is basically denied.

I do not wish to discard this position altogether, however. On the one hand, if the position denies that the atonement can be Godward in the sense of temporally affecting God's disposition toward humanity, there is nothing wrong with it. On the other hand, if the position suggests that sin makes no difference, that it is not a real block standing between us and God, that it does not have to be positively removed—then it has clearly abandoned orthodoxy. I very much doubt that this is what Helm wishes to say. But the fact remains that the death of Christ cannot be simply given the function of revealing to us the extent of

107. Ibid., 178.
108. Ibid., 180.
109. Ibid.

God's love, to the exclusion of a more "objective" effect. While Helm is right to resist construing that objective effect in terms of affecting the divine attitude, he might be more explicit about the objectivity of guilt and its removal. And this is certainly more than the quasi-exemplarist picture that he paints.

To summarize my position on the necessity of the atonement by the God-man, I would hold that Calvin does after all make the mode of reconciliation necessary by virtue of God's justice, conceived (necessarily, though not sufficiently) in retributive terms.

Turning our attention, finally, to the question of efficacy: How does this substitutionary penalty succeed in obtaining our salvation? Often post-Reformation theologians, on both the Lutheran and Reformed sides, argue that the penal sufferings of Christ are equivalent to the penalty incumbent upon humanity as a whole. The problem is very simple: how might the temporally limited suffering of one man be equivalent to the eternal damnation and suffering of the whole of humanity? The Lutheran and the Reformed solution has been to appeal to the union of the divine with the human nature. It is in virtue of the union with the divine nature that the suffering of the Son in his human nature is given infinite value.

McCormack, however, argues that this is not a solution, since there is no real exchange of properties between the human and the divine natures in Christ. If the suffering, in the good tradition of impassibility, is confined to the human nature of Christ, and there is no traffic from the human to the divine (only from the divine to the human, for the Lutherans), then there is no way in which this suffering can acquire infinite value. This is no solution.

As a result, for McCormack, the whole framework of merit has to be abandoned as well. Not only can it not be made to work (no strict equivalency is possible), but it also makes grace redundant. If Christ, as a human being, experiences a suffering that somehow compels God to grant us salvation, there is nothing left to be gracious about. Salvation and forgiveness are strictly merited.

McCormack does not deny that the framework of merit is home to Calvin's doctrine of the atonement. He is right. Calvin adds a whole section (*Institutes* 2.17) in which he discusses the relationship between merit and grace. He denies that the fact of Christ's having earned redemption for us renders the idea of a gracious God empty. God's grace remains the first cause of redemption, but Christ's merit remains the instrumental cause. There is no contradiction involved here, for "there is nothing . . . to prevent the merit of Christ from intervening in subordination to this mercy."[110] Calvin does stress that no human deed is inherently meritorious, including Christ's, were it not for the grace of

110. Calvin, *Institutes* 2.17.1.

God. "I admit," he writes, "that were Christ opposed simply, and by himself, to the justice of God, there could be no room for merit, because there cannot be found in man a worth which could make God a debtor."[111]

Does the idea of Christ's having merited our salvation clash with the priority of grace? Calvin does not seem to think so. He treats divine grace as following a prescribed course of operation, within which it can be properly said that Christ merits salvation. His grounding is again scriptural, and he identifies passages in Scripture which show that Christ merited our salvation for us. "By his obedience, however, Christ truly acquired and merited grace for us with his Father. Many passages of Scripture surely and firmly attest to this. I take it to be commonplace that if Christ made satisfaction for our sins, if he paid the penalty owed by us, if he appeased God by his obedience—in short, if as a righteous man he suffered for unrighteous men—then he acquired salvation for us by his righteousness, which is tantamount to deserving it."[112]

Thus Calvin remains steeped within an economy of exchange: "Christ bestows on us something of what he has acquired. For otherwise it would not be fitting for his credit to be given to him as distinct from the Father, namely, that grace is his and proceeds from Him."[113]

Further problems remain for the theory of penal substitution, either in its Calvinist version or in other post-Reformation versions. I will address many such critiques in the final chapter. What is essential to remember about Calvin is that redemption takes place precisely through (although it is not exhausted by) the penal death of Christ, which satisfies and propitiates God and thus remits our guilt. All of this takes place within a legal framework with its deserts, merits, and rights. While this legal medium has its origin in the grace of God, it is at the same time identical with his very being and character. Nevertheless, since being and existence are identical in God, this does not create an unbearable tension, at least not for Calvin.[114]

Summary

1. The Reformation affirmed the authority of the secular princes against the overreaching ecclesial power. Temporal autonomy and positive law are thus given more autonomy in the wake of nominalism.

111. Ibid.
112. Ibid., 2.17.3.
113. Ibid., 2.17.2.
114. Chapter 6 (below) explores in greater detail how the concept of simplicity is significant for the doctrine of the atonement.

2. Luther and Calvin differ in their valuations of the function of law and its place in the divine economy. This in turn affects their understanding of the logic of the atonement.

3. Luther ties the law to sin and restricts its function to leading people to Christ and to curbing sinful behavior under the threat of death. The Christian, however, has stepped out from the realm of the letter of the law into the kingdom of the spirit of the law. The victory of Christ does not take place through enacting a provision within the law, but rather transcends the law. While Luther at times comes close to the theory of penal substitution, his reservations about the law ultimately prevent him from fully embracing that logic.

4. For Calvin, grace abrogates law as a curse, not law as a guide. Law is not a divine reaction to sin, but it is anterior to the fall. Law continues to inform Christian living. Christ saves us precisely according to the law, bearing our penalty on our behalf.

Modernity

Atonement and the Cure of the Soul

Modernity, Law, and Justice

Rémi Brague regards modernity as having brought about a separation of the two poles of the law, which up to that point had been united. The two poles represent the distinction between counsel and commandment. Counsel stands for the law of nature, for the very direction and constitution of human nature. Commandment represents the externality of a law, which stands over against nature. We witnessed some of this dialectic through our discussion of medieval law. Brague insists that in premodern times there was a dialectic between the two. Positive law, or commandment, was based on an understanding of natural law. Although not entirely identical with it, positive law required its foundation in natural law for its legitimacy. "Counsel," Brague writes, "preceded the law that was based upon it, but it also surpassed the law by adding a further stage to it. On the one hand, the law was what had to be observed in order to assure the full deployment of a nature that, by that fact, realized what counsel wanted. On the other hand, counsel, in the form of evangelical advice, led to reaching beyond the minimal demands stated in the law and to striving for perfection."[1] In true Aristotelian fashion, the task of positive law was to be an aid in the perfection of our nature. Human beings are political animals, and the perfection of our human nature can only take place within the *polis*, or the community; hence the law, as the regulatory form of community life, is directly connected to our highest good. Although positive law could never be identified as such with this highest good, it was not unconnected to it. The link between law (positive and divine) and justice was strongly asserted. While medieval juristic and theological scholars brought about a clearer distinction between universal law and local custom, the law was never sundered from nature.

However, the voluntaristic and nominalistic undercurrents will eventually reach their climax in the foundation of modernity. Law comes to be defined more and more on the basis of *the will* of the people, regardless of the legitimacy of the content of that will. Clearly, the seeds of modernity had been planted in the European consciousness long before the French Revolution. These particular genealogical issues aside, the particularly modern approach to law consists in the extrication of law as commandment from counsel. Brague again puts it well: "Thus the law manifests itself in its full purity when it takes the opposite course from counsel."[2] In modernity there is an implicit assumption, derived in particular from Hobbes, that the function of law is that of restraining human nature rather than allowing it to arrive at its own perfection. Thus the function of law begins to be purely negative, a restraint imposed on an otherwise self-destructive nature.

Kant can be understood as the culmination of this diremption between counsel and commandment, or between nature and spirit. He both autonomizes law, substituting a purely human and rational legitimation for the former divine authority of the law, and at the same time he formalizes it. In its pure formality, the law must repress any impulse coming from nature, from our affections, interests, passions, or indeed from natural and social bonds.

In this chapter Kant will be discussed in depth, not because he is the only important intellectual figure in the development of modern jurisprudence, but in particular because of the formative influence he has had on two seminal theologians of the atonement, Friedrich Schleiermacher and Albrecht Ritschl. It will be my contention that their complex views of the atoning work of Christ can best be understood against the background of their ethical and legal theories. These, in turn, are deeply anchored in a specifically modern project of law, in the development of which Kant's influence is decisive. This

1. Rémi Brague, *The Law of God: The Philosophical History of an Idea* (Chicago: University of Chicago Press, 2007), 232.
2. Ibid., 234.

chapter will thus give a description of a unified, modern approach to law and its direct and even explicit consequences for atonement theology.

"Legal" modernity makes two significant, related contributions to the study of the atonement. First, changes in the understanding of the very nature of law have discouraged theologians from appealing to a legal, forensic framework in their atonement theories. To abbreviate this, law becomes positivized in modernity. Its authority becomes purely human, pragmatic, and political. It loses its ties with either divine sanction or human nature. It simply represents human will, for better or for worse. As a consequence, the link between positive law and morality (and justice) is weakened. Theologians like Schleiermacher and Ritschl will thus start from the premise of the inferiority of any legal framework and will reconstruct theology along moral and personal lines.

The second contribution consists in a changing understanding of the nature of punishment. The late eighteenth and early nineteenth centuries bring about a series of penal reforms throughout Europe. These will affect the perception of punishment and the role this might play in a divine economy of salvation. I will discuss these contributions before turning to Kant.

The Diremption of Spirit from Nature

Although there could be many other representative shorthand expressions for the essence of modernity, for reasons that will become clearer when I discuss Schleiermacher and Ritschl, the "diremption" between nature and spirit is especially poignant. A more, though not sufficiently precise, description would be to say that while "nature" becomes the object of the study of the natural sciences, the modern project consists (partly, of course) in carving out a space for the specifically human, in the realm of spirit. Human beings are partly physical and partly spiritual, with an always-mysterious relationship between these two aspects of their nature. The extraordinary advance of the natural sciences constituted a threat to what some thought to be the specifically human spirit, namely, reason. Kant accomplished this task of identifying the specifically human by defining the human as the realm of freedom. Freedom from natural constraints is what constitutes our particular human identity. So much hangs on this exercise of freedom, Kant thought in his earlier moral writing, that a failure to exercise this freedom in the proper way leads to bondage, and therefore to a loss of complete humanity. The distinction becomes clear: on the one hand, nature is the domain of cause and effect, of natural laws; on the other, spirit is the realm of freedom, and indeed for that very reason spirit is the realm of a moral law that is rational and autonomous rather than determined by what is "natural."

Whereas feudal law was steeped in local custom and the social bonds that unite a community, modern law manifests itself as such precisely in redefining those bonds as merely conventional and not natural. Sociologists of law have made the case that this dissolution of social bonds and the turn to subjectivity was determined by increasing urbanization and changing relations of work. Roberto Unger, for instance, writes that "the loosening of the ties of community fosters a particular mode of consciousness and is fostered by it. This outlook begins with the insight that conventions of behavior are shaped by history; it goes on to the denial of their intrinsic goodness; and it ends in the conviction that they are based upon the naked acts of will by which people choose among conflicting ultimate values."[3] Thus a budding historical consciousness erodes a previous consensus regarding the highest good. This highest good becomes a matter to be decided democratically and without necessary regard for its connection to what is natural.

The naked will, in turn, becomes the ultimate good, the only proper seat of goodness. The modern project is also, in part, the isolation of a universal morality. The task of modern ethics, Alasdair MacIntyre argues, is the isolation of the a priori and unchanging elements of morality. But this will result, as we shall see, in a purely formal, almost contentless morality. One may argue that this result is inevitable given the self-imposed restrictions of this project: the isolation of the a priori conditions of morality. The end result is the further reassertion of the will as being alone the seat of goodness.

Thus the "legality of the law" is determined by its being the proper manifestation of a common will of the people. Our duty to obey the law does not derive from any intrinsic goodness of the law, but merely from its being consented to as authoritative. We do not obey the law because the law is right and moral, but simply because it was appointed as such by a sovereign who has the power to impose its will. The value of the law is strictly connected to the will of the sovereign. Although both medieval nominalists and modern philosophers of the Enlightenment define positive law in the same way, for the medievals the sovereign is a historical figure, but for the moderns it is the sovereign self that gives itself its own law through the democratic process. For the moderns, the medieval historical lord is replaced by the useful fiction of the state, which represents the ideal consensus of sovereign selves.

To go back to the idea of a diremption of spirit from nature, the modern person thinks of the spirit side of the equation as the unencumbered and free

3. Roberto Unger, *Law in Modern Society: Toward a Criticism of Social Theory* (New York: Simon & Schuster, 1977), 169.

will. But the will is free in the sense that it is not bound by anything external to it, such as natural ties, affections, desires, social bonds, and so on.

Thus is modern law positivized. One feature of this type of law is that it is gradually distinguished from society. Brendan Edgeworth makes the astute observation that "traditional or customary law, which represented a significant element in the fabric of feudal law, was secreted in the interstices of society. It followed that [premodern] law could never be seen to change society; rather, law changed imperceptibly, as society changed."[4] Modern sovereignty, on the other hand, entails that the process of social change is something that can be willed, that it can be imposed on society from the outside, as it were, given the externality of the law.

The consequences of this shift are numerous and far-reaching. The detachment of law from morality prompts three types of question. The first has to do with the proper course of action in response to immoral laws. Is one's duty to obey the law conditional on its morality? A second set of questions has to do with the possible overestimation of the freedom of the will. Does not a putatively free and democratic will really conceal a set of interests? If the law is positive, what kind of arguments ought to determine the exercise of the democratic will of the people? Third, can the law ever be formal enough to be distinguished from concrete moral schemes and traditions? As the discussion of punishment will ask, what ought the state do with inmates? Should it sanction a process of the moral reformation of the criminal? If so, as most everyone agrees it should, which administrative body of the state should determine its activity, once the body of magistrates (the law) is supposedly independent of morality?

On the one hand, these questions reveal, at the very least, the complications inherent in any such detachment of law from morality, and in its reattachment to a democratic will that is supposedly free. On the other hand, the new stress on the positive nature of the law brought with it a renewed realism about the extent of human wisdom and justice. Our laws are human, and we ought to be well aware of their inherent limitations. This fresh understanding of both the glory and the perils of our common humanity was instrumental in the penal reforms of the eighteenth and nineteenth centuries.

Penal Reform and the "Relaxation of Penalty"

The emphasis on the humanity of the laws and their purposes, together with the legal positivism that sometimes undergirded them, led to a different

4. Brendan Edgeworth, *Law, Modernity, and Postmodernity: Legal Change in the Contracting State* (Aldershot: Ashgate, 2003), 71–72.

valuation of punishment generally. To put it in condensed form, punishment shifts from retribution to either deterrence or rehabilitation. In many ways, this is the natural outcome of the diremption between the natural and the spiritual. In retributive justice, punishment is seen as a way of rectifying the broken balance of nature. Wrongdoing disrupts the distributive order of nature, an order that is just. Punishment is justified as a response to that wrongdoing in that it redresses that order. But once modernity has denied any link between nature and spirit (including the legal systems that are devised by it), the function of punishment has to be conceived in terms internal to spirit, as opposed to nature. Punishment, in short, can no longer have any bearing on nature, including restoring an order of nature.

The chastening of punishment, motivated as it was by positivism, was further supported by theological assumptions. William Blackstone, one of the champions of British penal reform, demonstrates this renewed penal realism: "As to the end, or final cause of human punishments. This is not by way of atonement or expiation for the crime committed; for that must be left to the just determination of the supreme being."[5] Similarly, writing in 1785, William Paley names deterrence as the end of punishment, for only God is in a position to make the punishment fit the crime.[6] Retributive justice is predicated on a human ability to understand the disruption caused by the crime. But this understanding is no longer thought to be possible. A new function for punishment had thus to be found. Paley also insists on the difference our humanity makes to the success of our laws: The God "whose knowledge penetrates every concealment can create a law that proportions punishment to crime. But when the care of the public safety is entrusted to men, whose authority over their fellow creatures is limited by defects of power and knowledge, . . . a new rule of proceeding results from the very imperfection of their faculties."[7]

Not only was the function of punishment revised, but the severity of punishment also came in for intense scrutiny. In particular, the very common capital penalty was thought to be an overextension of human competence. Blackstone sees this as a theological matter: "To shed the blood of our fellow creatures is a matter that requires greatest deliberation, and the fullest conviction of our own authority; for life is the immediate gift of God to

5. William Blackstone, *Commentaries on the Laws of England: A Facsimile of the First Edition of 1765–1769* (Chicago: University of Chicago Press, 1979), 4:11.
6. See Timothy Gorringe, *God's Just Vengeance: Crime, Violence and the Rhetoric of Salvation*, Cambridge Studies in Ideology and Religion (Cambridge: Cambridge University Press, 1996), 164.
7. Ibid.

man; which neither can he resign, nor can it be taken from him, unless by the command and permission of him who gave it; either expressly revealed, or collected from the laws of nature or society by clear and indisputable demonstration."[8] In Italy, the great penal reformer Cesare Beccaria bases his rejection of the death penalty on the deterrent function of punishment. Thus "the death penalty is not authorized by any right." As long as the laws of a state are in force and obeyed, "a punishment, to be just, should have only that degree of severity, which is sufficient to deter others."[9] However, the death penalty remains an option "only in times of anarchy," when the rule of law is no longer respected.[10] Reaction against capital punishment spilled over into the United States, where William Bradford settled for an exclusively deterring function of punishment: "The only object of human punishments is the prevention of crimes."[11] Moreover, Bradford becomes one of the pioneers of an alternative to capital punishment, which was to become the norm throughout the Western world in only a span of forty years, between 1780 and 1820, namely, incarceration. Among the possible advantages of "perpetual imprisonment," he lists the following: "Reparation may sometimes be made to the party injured. . . . If, in a course of years, the offender becomes humbled and reformed, society, instead of losing, gains a citizen."[12]

On a very large scale, therefore, we find the following characteristics: (1) The retributive function of punishment is bracketed as belonging to a different, divine jurisdiction. (2) The predominant functions of punishment become either deterrence or the reformation of the criminal. Finally, (3) capital punishment is universally condemned and rejected in normal circumstances.

This theoretical approach is mirrored in actual penal reforms throughout Europe. Prior to this "revolution," capital punishment was the rather indiscriminate response to a wide variety of offenses. One might be hanged for all kinds of crimes, from stealing to sodomy to witchcraft. Neither was capital punishment applied only to mature offenders. The minimal age at which one was liable to such a punishment was seven, and Timothy Gorringe reports that children as young as fourteen were actually executed. In the American colonies the situation was no different. People of all ages were executed for all kinds of crimes.

8. Blackstone, *Commentaries*, 4:11.
9. Basil Montagu, ed., *The Opinions of Different Authors upon the Punishment of Death* (London: Longman, Hurst, Rees, Orme & Brown, 1812), 13.
10. Ibid.
11. Ibid., 252.
12. Ibid., 253.

The reform also included criminal procedures: These procedures should no longer be held in public. Due process should not be biased against the accused. Torture should be abolished as a means to confession. Sentences should be given in accordance with a precisely framed penal code and should no longer be dependent on judicial whim. Moreover, cruel punishments should no longer be regarded as effective deterrence.

As we have seen, many of these reforms were actually initiated in the twelfth-century legal revolution. Yet while the medieval revolution succeeded in establishing the universal character of law, and indeed the rule of law, one might say that justice remained clearly retributive, given the strong link with natural law. Once that link was severed, or at least weakened, retribution gave room to deterrence and rehabilitation.

An optimistic reading will explain this development as the transition from a barbaric and judgmental culture to a "humanistic" modernity. If, however, our historical study has some truth in it, the humanistic turn was not without theological motivation. For instance, the humane treatment of prisoners was as much the result of the Christian doctrine of the *imago Dei* as it was of a "humanistic modernity." Nevertheless, it is clearly the case that modernity coupled that respect for our common humanity with a pronounced reservation about human ability in regard to justice. Thus not only are criminals treated with respect before being led to the podium; they also are no longer terminated. This is indeed a salutary development.

Criminals are no longer executed, but the dominant response to crime is incarceration. Michel Foucault canvasses the "prompt substitution" that occurred around 1810. What he calls the "relaxation of penalty in the eighteenth century" consists in a gradual transition from punishment as retribution, to punishment as example (deterrence), and finally, in a very short span, to punishment as rehabilitation, or treatment. Foucault focuses his critical gaze on the motivation of this transition, taking issue with the usual optimistic humanistic narrative. The reform was not the result of an idealistic movement from outside the system but was the self-tuning of the system itself, aiming for greater efficiency, eradication of loopholes, and more sustainability and profit. He summarizes this process as follows: "not to punish less, but to punish better; to punish with an attenuated severity perhaps, but in order to punish with more universality and necessity; to insert the power to punish more deeply into the social body."[13]

I believe Foucault is making an indirect comment precisely on some of the contradictions I have indicated above. Let me explain. Foucault's point is that

---

13. Michel Foucault, *Discipline and Punish: The Birth of the Prison*, trans. Alan Sheridan, 2nd ed. (New York: Vintage, 1995), 82.

punishment quickly became "treatment," a method of moral transformation and moral progress applied to criminals. But witness the contradiction to the new legal philosophy, which had just sundered legality from morality. If it is not within the purview of law to repair or redress nature (retribution), how could it be within its purview to treat a human nature? William Paley, as we saw above, understood that the only possible function of punishment is deterrence precisely because it is not within the power of humanity to rehabilitate itself. No matter how much and how severely we punish, we cannot create moral progress in other people, much less criminals. But with the onset of the prisons, a whole industry of moral rehabilitation was created, against the fundamental principle of the separation of law and morality. Foucault understands that the regime of prisons presupposes a morality. Of course, Foucault also decries any attempt to prescribe a morality, but he senses the contradiction with empirical precision. Rather than judges deciding what form this process of rehabilitation must have, a whole new class of technocrats associated with prisons arose who were put in charge of the moral development of inmates. A law, which has nothing to do with what is "natural," is now involved in the process of altering human nature and shaping it according to a particular moral vision. The service Foucault renders to this study is to expose the empirical difficulty of a purely formal system of law. At some point, morality will be smuggled back into the system, under a guise. Nevertheless, it is precisely this diremption on which the modern legal project has been based.

Let me rehearse the conclusions thus far, before moving on to Kant's contribution. (1) The modern legal project consists in emphasizing the positivity of law, namely, law's being a human creation. (2) As a result, law is loosened from a concrete morality and associated more with the unbound freedom of the will. (3) The law, being positive, has a much more restricted scope. It aims not so much at doing complete justice as aiming at the protection of the interests of the sovereign selves, which legitimize the law itself. (4) The relaxation of punishment, which encapsulates the penal reforms of the late eighteenth and early nineteenth centuries, led to incarceration as the primary response to wrongdoing. (5) Nevertheless, incarceration was justified not only as deterrence but also as rehabilitation and treatment, which—ironically—is precisely a moral concept. Thus the ideal separation of law and morality is fraught with contradictions.

Immanuel Kant on the Moral Law (1724–1804)

Kant is significant for our discussion for the following reasons. (1) While Kant provides much of the justification for the modern concept of sovereignty by grounding it in the idea of freedom, his particular notion of freedom is a "demanding" one, as Michael Sandel notes.[14] Kant does not take freedom to mean the ability to do whatever one wants, but he ties it to the *moral law*, and thus to responsibility (James 1:25; 2:12), as we shall observe. (2) Going against the current of Enlightenment optimism, Kant conceptualizes the notion of *radical evil*, thus coming near (but only near) to an Augustinian conception of self and sin. (3) Also against current trends, Kant defends the notion of *retributive justice*. (4) He maintains and reinforces the *diremption between nature and spirit*. And finally, (5) he strongly emphasizes the reality of human *guilt* and the necessity of *atonement*.

Let's begin by reflecting on Kant's rejection of eudaemonism, which suggests that the highest good consists in my ability to act according to my inclinations and pleasures. Kant rejects this option because it consists in a heteronomous use of the will. Whenever I act according to my inclinations, I act according to an end I have not chosen for myself. True freedom, however, entails the ability to choose freely. But I have not chosen my inclinations. They belong to my nature. As such the highest good cannot consist in my acting according to my inclinations.

Witness how the modern diremption between nature and spirit plays out in Kant's ethics. To act according to my natural impulses is to act in a manner that is not free. Whenever I do that, I sabotage my own freedom, Kant argues. And whenever I sabotage my own freedom, that is, whenever I choose to act according to ends and maxims that I have not chosen, or that I have not chosen for the right reasons, my "personality wanes," as John Silber puts it.[15]

But what am I supposed to act in accordance with if I am to be free? Kant's famous response is that a person is acting autonomously when she acts according to a law she gives to herself. Kant calls this the moral law. I am autonomous when I choose to act out of duty (to the moral law) and not in response to my inclinations.

The content of this law is a set of precepts that are able to be discerned by reason and also applied universally. To act autonomously, therefore, is to act according to a categorical imperative, as opposed to a hypothetical imperative. (*If* I wish to become a concert pianist, I should practice eight hours a day.) The hypothetical imperative, on the one hand, stipulates a manner of action that is consistent with a particular end. But that particular end is left without a justification and is thus not universalizable. (Not all people ought

14. Michael J. Sandel, *Justice: What's the Right Thing to Do?* (New York: Macmillan, 2009), 108.

15. John R. Silber, "The Ethical Significance of Kant's *Religion*," in Immanuel Kant, *Religion within the Limits of Reason Alone*, trans. T. M. Greene and H. H. Hudson (New York: Harper & Row, 1960), xciv.

to become concert pianists.) The categorical imperative, on the other hand, is universal. It denotes an absolute, universal requirement that imposes itself simply in virtue of my being a rational person.

The authority of the moral law resides simply in its reasonableness. It is transparent to reason. As Julius Stone puts it, "Kant's 'natural law' is discovered by his transcendental method, without reference to experience, and not by way of intuition of values deemed immanent in experience."[16] Its authority does not rely in its being authored by God himself. This is a crucial distinction. Kant thus delineates the idea of human sovereignty according to a law, given in reason, that is distinct from any heteronomous source of authority, and also from natural inclinations.

The law functions as a command, but a command that I give to myself. Kant distinguishes between *pathological love* and the *love that can be commanded*. The first one is the spontaneous, natural affection that we feel for particular persons. My loving my daughter or wife is not a morally worthy action, because I am acting out of my natural inclination. On the other hand, my loving my enemy or my neighbor out of duty is morally worthy (Matt. 5:43–44). Now Jesus himself commanded me to love my neighbor (Luke 6:27; see also Rom. 12:20). However, if I were to love my neighbor out of obedience to Jesus, I would be acting heteronomously. My act would not be moral, even though it conformed to the contents of the moral law ("Love your neighbor"), because I would be obeying the moral law for the wrong reason.

Thus, for Kant, it is not enough that an act be conformed to the moral law, or to be done with an interest (Luke 6:35) in its being counted as morally worthy. One must also obey the moral law for its own sake, or as Kant likes to put it, out of duty.

This explains why Kant's concept of freedom is so demanding. One is free, paradoxically, when one acts according to a law. True, this is a law that we give to ourselves, but it nevertheless remains law.

While Kant insists that the highest good does not consist in happiness, still, because of the kind of being that we are, it has to somehow incorporate this happiness. It would be intolerable, Kant argues, if duty were not crowned eventually with happiness.[17] Yet it is empirically clear that virtue is not rewarded with happiness in this life (Eccles. 7:15; Matt. 5:45). This leads Kant to the postulate of immortality: personal existence must extend beyond death, such that happiness can finally accompany virtue. Kant even argues that God has

16. Julius Stone, *Human Law and Human Justice* (Stanford, CA: Stanford University Press, 1965), 84.
17. Alasdair MacIntyre, *A Short History of Ethics: A History of Moral Philosophy from the Homeric Age to the Twentieth Century* (London: Routledge, 1998), 196.

created the world in such a way that this will happen. This does not happen naturally, as if happiness becomes a natural consequence of virtue, since it was already argued that the links between spirit (virtue) and nature (sensuous happiness) are much weakened. Rather, God ordains happiness as an *external reward* for a virtuous life.

While a complete association is controversial, there is some affinity between this conception and legal positivism, as Jeremy Waldron suggests. In particular, it is Kant's dim view of nature that suggests such an association. Waldron writes that "the biggest problem in the state of nature is people trying to figure out rights and justice for themselves . . . and that, in fact, one's primary duty is to leave the state of nature as soon as possible and embrace what appear to be the decidedly heteronomous obligations of civil law."[18] Waldron also points out that Kant, like Hobbes, thinks of the state of nature, the situation "before external legislation endowed with power appears,"[19] as a condition of violence.

Kant on Radical Evil, Guilt, and Punishment

For Kant, morality is a matter of doing one's duty for duty's sake. The moral law is not a heteronomous standard but is internal to the very moral structure of the self. However, this self is not the "phenomenal" self that is empirically visible to other selves, but an ideal, "noumenal" self. Moral progress consists in the gradual transition from the phenomenal, sensuous self to the noumenal self, guided by duty. This transition is always difficult, since we are always under the influence of our desires and inclinations. Morality consists in overcoming these heteronomous impulses and choosing duty for duty's sake.

The moral law, on the one hand, is external without being heteronomous. Civil law, on the other hand is heteronomous, since the considerations that go into its creation are not always purely moral and rational, but may include pragmatic (and thus contextual as opposed to universal) considerations.

Kant is quite confident that, despite our natural inclinations, we can still choose duty for duty's sake. In other words, we can still deny who we are most naturally, our passions and desires, and will to obey the moral law for its own sake. The self is free to exercise its own will in the direction of duty. In this the self is much like God, as Jean Bethke Elshtain comments: "Noumenal, autonomous will puts us as close to God as we are going to get, for God created

---

18. Jeremy Waldron, "Kant's Legal Positivism," *Harvard Law Review* 109, no. 7 (1996): 1535–66 (here 1544).

19. Ibid., 1546 (the quotation is Kant's).

morality in the first instance as an act of will. The Augustinian emphasis on love disappears as the rational moral law is followed by autonomous sovereign selves who work like clockwork: there are no caveats, exceptions, no allowances to be made for human weakness."[20]

Elshtain's comment nevertheless may convey the wrong impression about Kant to the uncareful reader. While it is true that Kant was a moral optimist in claiming that the free will can choose duty for duty's sake despite the centripetal pull of one's nature, Kant went against the current of his age in affirming a strong notion of radical evil and indeed guilt. I will briefly expound this aspect of his thought, as it will be picked up by both Schleiermacher and Ritschl a few decades later.

The moral law imposes a universal duty on free and rational selves. However, the flip side of any strong libertarianism is an equally strong rigorism, for failure to act in accordance with the maxim of duty incurs a debt. Kant is not advocating an unbound freedom, but a freedom that only preserves itself in choosing the moral law for its own sake. In his earlier philosophy, mainly in the second critique, Kant insists that such a misuse of freedom is self-destructive. John Silber explains the Kantian position:

> A transcendentally free human being, if tempted to abnegate his freedom in the expression of it, is categorically obligated to actualize its free nature. He is obligated to be autonomous, to be the spontaneous individual that he is, and to avoid self-rejection in heteronomy. And because his personality wanes as the law of his nature and the condition of its fulfillment is denied, the law has an inescapable jurisdiction over him. He has the freedom to reject the law, but he cannot escape its condemnation and its punishment in the destruction of his personality.[21]

Kant, like no other philosopher of his age, sees the inescapability of incurred guilt. Not only is guilt inevitable, but it is also the kind of debt that cannot be shaken off. This is not because of some religious, and thus heteronomous, stipulation of law, but because of the very moral law, which is constitutive of our free selves. The very idea of a self is possible only if continuity across time and across a variety of actions can be affirmed. As Kant puts it in *Groundwork for the Metaphysic of Morals*, a self is the subject whose actions are capable of imputation. There must be thus a direct link between myself and my actions, including my past actions. That is why guilt cannot be simply shaken off, for I would be undermining the very continuity of my own self across time if I were to sever the link between my self and my own actions.

20. Jean Bethke Elshtain, *Sovereignty: God, State, and Self* (New York: Basic Books, 2008), 177.
21. Silber, "Ethical Significance," xciv.

R. R. Reno argues that two fundamental principles represent the driving force behind what he calls Kant's "we-matter-most humanism." One is the principle of "personal potency," according to which moral change must be possible. Although we are innately evil, we by nature retain a potency toward goodness.[22] The second principle is that of "personal continuity," according to which the story of our souls must explain how the evil person is connected to the good person he or she seeks to become.[23] Kant articulates the issue of guilt on the basis of these two principles. Reno explains how Kant succeeds in making guilt palatable in a post-theological, rationalist framework: "We should be clear, then, that Kant's use of the concepts of debt and punishment are not 'legalistic' in any narrow sense. 'Debt' and 'payment,' 'punishment' and 'satisfaction' express the humanistic conviction that our lives are consequential. They are abstractions that help bring to the fore our existential anxieties about the disjunctive dangers of moral change, worries that who we are now (as those seeking moral change) may have no role in a hoped-for reign of righteousness."[24] These words may sound somewhat cryptic, but they will be clarified soon by Kant's doctrine of atonement.

The guilt I incur is infinite. But its infinity is not due to the status of the offended party, whether God or another human being or oneself. Here one can easily recognize a jab in the direction of Anselm's construal of sin as an infinite offense against God. Kant, however, wants to affirm the pervasiveness and decisiveness of guilt, but without appealing to such theological and heteronomous notions. Guilt has to be defined strictly in terms of the free personality. But it is precisely here that Kant thinks he has located a universal ground for the infinity of guilt. Guilt is infinite because of "the fact that this moral evil lies in the disposition and the maxims in general, in universal basic principles rather than in particular transgressions."[25] What this means is that the infinity of guilt derives from the fact that evil is a characteristic of our very dispositions and maxims.

Kant continues to argue that "because of this infinite guilt, all mankind must look forward to endless punishment and the exclusion from the Kingdom of God."[26] Thus, not only is the pervasiveness and deep-seatedness of sin acknowledged, together with the infinite debt it incurs, but so is the necessity

22. R. R. Reno, *Redemptive Change: Atonement and the Christian Cure of the Soul* (New York: Continuum, 2002), 161.
23. Ibid., 169.
24. Ibid., 174.
25. Kant, *Religion*, 66.
26. Ibid.

of retribution. Such is this necessity that even God cannot forego punishment. Atonement has to be made in some fashion.

Kant defines punishment as physical harm. Such harm is demanded by the nature of the offense, namely, a trespass against moral law. In *Groundwork of the Metaphysics of Morals*, he argues that "the law of punishment is a categorical imperative." Punishment must be applied universally, and God does apply it universally. Such was Kant's confidence in this principle that it brought him to make the well-known claim that

> even if a civil society were to be dissolved by the consent of all its members (e.g., if a people inhabiting an island decided to separate and disperse throughout the world), the last murderer remaining in prison would first have to be executed, so that each has done to him what his needs deserve and blood guilt does not cling to the people for not having insisted upon this punishment; for otherwise the people can be regarded as collaborators in this public violation of justice.[27]

Interestingly, Kant also accepts a consequentialist view of punishment, as Thom Brooks further notes. Seeing why there is no contradiction between this position and his retributivism can shed further light on our discussion. Kant argues that the state has the ability to dispense punishment as deterrence. But that is only because states are concerned primarily with pragmatic matters rather than matters of justice. There is a dichotomy, therefore, as we have already noticed, between the moral law and the civil law. The moral law exists even though it may never be applied anywhere historically. It exists as a transcendental dimension of our free natures. Civil law, being positive, is always in the process of catching up to this moral law. Here Kant shows himself as a realist in that he understands the limited scope of government in achieving justice, as his letter to Johann Benjamin Erhard shows: "In a world of moral principles governed by God, punishments would be categorically necessary (insofar as transgressions occur). But in a world of moral principles governed by men, the necessity of punishments is only hypothetical, and that direct union of the concept of transgression with the idea of deserving punishment serves the ruler only as a prescription for what to do."[28]

This rigorism with regard to the moral law, guilt, and punishment would seem to render divine forgiveness an impossibility. As the great historian of dogma Isaak Dorner points out, Kant's thought was indeed developed in this direction. Kantians like Flatt and Elder drew the conclusion that forgiveness

27. Quoted in Thom Brooks, "Kant's Theory of Punishment," *Utilitas* 15, no. 2 (2003): 206–24 (here 210–11).
28. Quoted in ibid., 217.

of sin is impossible. But they held that it was nevertheless not necessary for amendment. Others, like Süskind, argued that the execution of punishment may have injurious moral effects and thus there is a practical necessity of remission, since without such remission no true amendment is possible (i.e., without inner joy and cheerfulness).[29] Dorner thus argues that the antinomy Kant seeks to escape is that, on the one hand, punishment is morally necessary, but on the other it is morally injurious. Such a contradiction is the motivation behind the question of the atonement. Moreover, how is atonement possible without violating both human autonomy and the moral law, which demands punishment?

Kant on the Atonement

Let me rehearse the main points that we have seen Kant make thus far: (1) The moral law is universally binding, and it is a condition of our moral personality (rather than a heteronomous source). (2) The highest good consists in the proportioning of happiness to virtue. (3) Virtue, however, does not consist in seeking happiness for its own sake but in doing one's duty for duty's sake; in other words, the whole thrust of ethics is that of overcoming one's phenomenal nature and reaching for one's ultimate human nature, as free spirit. (4) Failure to conform to the moral law, which is evil, amounts to a failure to achieve virtue, and incurs a necessary and untransferable debt. (5) Justice demands an eternal punishment in response to radical evil. (6) But of course, such eternal punishment would be detrimental to achieving our highest good, to making moral progress.

It follows that atonement must somehow be possible. Several other salient points can be made as a preparation for this discussion. First, Kant admits the pervasiveness of sin. Not only is radical evil present in actual transgressions of the law, but it is also infinite in that it resides in corrupted maxims and drives (Rom. 7:15, 19). However, second, Kant assumes that moral progress, if possible, must be possible on the basis of autonomy alone. In other words, if there is to be moral progress, then the process itself must be able to be imputed to me, which means that it must spring from the free exercise of my will. This means that it cannot be *caused* by any other principle outside of myself. If that were the case, it would no longer be recognizable as *my own* moral development, but as somebody else's. Such is the strength of Kant's principle of "personal potency" that it seems to preclude any divine assistance. We are therefore facing an antinomy, or more precisely what Reno calls an "anthropodicy": "Whereas classical theism must square evil with the presumptive power

---

29. I. A. Dorner, *A System of Christian Doctrine* (Edinburgh: T&T Clark, 1890), 4:43.

and goodness of God, modern humanism must coordinate an affirmation of the sufficient power of personal identity for the highest good with the reality of evil."[30] To put it more simply: if we are so evil, down to our very motive principles, whence can we draw the strength for moral improvement, and how might we be able to cleanse our heart (Jer. 4:14)?

Kant simply assumes that we have such a power, that moral progress and something like moral conversion are possible. The reasons for this may lie in the fact that he has construed the will as a formal ability, as free in the absolute sense, in such a way that neither the maxims of nature nor those of duty press on it irresistibly.

But even assuming that moral progress and change are possible, some problems still remain. First, what is one to do about the continuing reality of guilt? Second, how might God be justified in forgiving us? The force of these questions derives precisely from the manner in which Kant construes moral law, guilt, and punishment. But first, let us look at Kant's account of moral change.

Moral change is described in terms of the presence in humanity of a superior disposition. This disposition is "supersensible in its nature."[31] This means that the disposition is not itself actual, but is in the process of becoming actual. Thus Kant can make a distinction between a change in personal identity, represented by a sudden revolution, and a change in character, which is empirical conformity to moral law, and which is naturally gradual. Moral change therefore amounts to a change in personal identity. The changed person is a morally different person, brought about by a "revolution in disposition."[32] One passes from the old self to the new self (2 Cor. 5:17; Gal. 6:15; Eph. 4:24).

Kant also talks about this moral change in terms of the "new man undertak[ing] the disposition of the Son of God"[33] (Gal. 2:20). Under no circumstances is this to be construed heteronomously. Kant portrays Christ as an archetype, a symbol of new humanity. It is not important for salvation that this archetype also exists historically and empirically. It is enough that it exists as an idea (1 Cor. 2:16; Phil. 2:5), which we make our own. Christ is the archetype of moral perfection, an *Urbild* we aim to embody. The existence of the moral law and the attendant duty to obey it for its own sake implies that moral progress is possible. For Kant, *ought* implies *can*.

But there is a problem: guilt. Even if I have become a morally different person, there remains the objective reality of guilt, which undermines moral

30. Reno, *Redemptive Change*, 155.
31. Kant, *Religion*, 60.
32. Ibid., 68.
33. Ibid.

progress itself. Virtue cannot be crowned with happiness while guilt persists (Rom. 8:34, 39). Kant puts it thus: "Whatever a man may have done in the way of adopting a good disposition, and, indeed, however steadfastly he may have persevered in conduct conformable to such a disposition, he nevertheless started from evil, and this debt he can by no possibility wipe out."[34]

Kant's solution builds on the moral distinction between the old self and the new self. The penalties deserved by the old self are in fact undertaken by the new self. But this in itself seems unjust.

> After his change of heart, however, the penalty cannot be considered appropriate to his new quality (of a man well pleasing to God), for he is now leading a new life and is morally another person; and yet satisfaction must be rendered to Supreme Justice, in whose sight no one who is blameworthy can ever be guiltless. Since therefore the infliction of punishment can, consistently with the divine wisdom, take place neither before nor after the change of heart, and is yet necessary, we must think of it as carried out during the change of heart itself, and adapted hereto.

Thus we can discover "in this very act of reformation such ills as the new man, whose disposition is now good, may regard as incurred by himself (in another state) and, therefore, as constituting punishments whereby satisfaction is rendered to divine justice."[35] It seems that the penalty deserved for the trespass is undertaken in the transformation itself, which represents a sacrifice: "The coming forth from the corrupted into the new disposition is, in itself (as 'the death of the old man,' 'the crucifying of the flesh'), a sacrifice and an entrance upon a long train of life's ills. These the new man undertakes in the disposition of the Son of God (Rom. 6:8; 2 Cor. 5:14), that is, merely for the sake of the good, though really they are due as punishments to another, namely, to the old man (for the old man is indeed morally another)."[36]

Guilt is thus discharged in the very process of one's transformation. The ills of life that the new self continues to endure is nothing but vicarious suffering. God is thus justified in forgiving me because he counts the new disposition, though incompletely actualized in this life, as fully obtaining. God treats humanity's becoming well pleasing to God as if humanity were already in full possession of moral perfection. This is Kant's idea of grace, that we should be credited with something that is only anticipated in our lives.

34. Ibid., 66.
35. Ibid., 67.
36. Ibid., 68.

Kant nevertheless remains adamant that this grace has to be merited: "We can certainly hope to partake in the appropriation of another's atoning merit, and so of salvation, only by qualifying for it through our own efforts to fulfill every human duty—and this obedience must be the effect of our own action and not, once again, of a foreign influence in the presence of which we are passive."[37] That we need this grace is undeniable since it is patently impossible to attain such moral perfection in this life. If we are ever to reach the highest good (which we must think possible, or else the whole idea of the moral law would implode), then we find ourselves in need of this divine grace. To repeat, the highest good consists in the proportioning of happiness to virtue, which is clearly not a reality in this life, but only in the next. Thus our inevitably insufficient moral effort and progress must be supplemented by divine grace if we are ever to merit the final happiness.

Alister McGrath nicely sums up the coherence between the doctrine of reconciliation and Kant's moral theory:

> The importance of the doctrine of reconciliation to Kant is that it provides a means for the morally renewed man to avoid total despair over the guilt attached to his former evil way of life. The inevitable moral consequence of such permanent guilt would be moral indifference or quietism, in that the individual in question would argue that, since guilt was so great that it could not be wiped out, there would appear to be little reason for his attempting to lead a moral life. It is therefore essential for Kant to develop a moral equivalent of absolution, so that the individual's moral guilt may be set behind him, in order that his new way of life may proceed unimpeded.[38]

I will defer a much-needed critique of this position until the end of the chapter, restricting myself to a brief summary of Kant's position on the atonement: (1) Atonement is a moral necessity in virtue of the possibility of achieving the highest good, which undergirds the very notion of the moral law. (2) The new self undertakes the sufferings of life, which were incurred as punishments by the old self, under the disposition of the Son of God. Finally, (3) God is justified in acting gracefully toward us because of the worthiness of the new self, who has altered his or her disposition in such a way as to merit divine grace.

In both Schleiermacher and Ritschl we shall observe the influence of Kant. This influence is aptly summarized by J. K. Mozley: "Kant's influence on

---

37. Ibid., 108–9.
38. Alister McGrath, "The Moral Theory of the Atonement: An Historical and Theological Critique," *Scottish Journal of Theology* 38 (1985): 216.

soteriology, which, as Baur most truly says, could not fail to be immense, sprang inevitably from the primacy which he assigned to the ethical over the speculative interest."[39] Kant's undeniable achievement is to conserve the preeminence of the moral law, together with its attending concepts of guilt and penalty, in an age utterly averse to consciousness of sin, moral evil, and divine grace.

Schleiermacher's Doctrine of the Atonement in the Context of His Ethical System (1768–1834)

Schleiermacher's Ethics

Jacqueline Marina, whose penetrating discussion of Friedrich Schleiermacher's ethics and theology is one of the most compelling analyses of his thought, argues that his ethics stands "in the closest possible unity to his theology." It is, she says, "in the end, a description of how divine causality expresses itself in the natural world through individuals."[40] My argument will be that Schleiermacher's doctrine of the atonement derives its particular contour from his ethical system. In particular, Schleiermacher's rejection of Kant's deontologism, his different view as to the relationship between spirit and nature, and the resulting conception of punishment—all contribute to a unique vision of the atonement. It is much beyond the scope of this book to give an exhaustive description of all the factors that feed his theory of the atonement. In emphasizing the ethical sources of his position, I am not denying that relevant factors may be found in other quarters of his intellectual system, from his particular theological methodology, to his doctrine of God, to his understanding of Christology. This goes without saying. My interest, however, is to understand the ways in which the particular conception and function of law may itself determine one's options in atonement.

Let's begin by situating Schleiermacher's ethics among the options of the day. First, Schleiermacher rejects eudaemonism for much the same reason invoked by Kant. It collapses reason into nature, and it confuses what we are to become with what we are at present. But Schleiermacher reserves his most biting critique for Kant. The attention given to Kant above will thus assist in our understanding of Schleiermacher.

The fundamental problem of deontologism is that it isolates and separates the moral self from the empirical and historical world. Indeed, as we observed,

---

39. John Kenneth Mozley, *The Doctrine of the Atonement* (New York: Charles Scribner's Sons, 1916), 161.

40. Jacqueline Marina, *Transformation of Self in the Thought of Schleiermacher* (Oxford: Oxford University Press, 2008), 147.

Kant construes the categorical imperative as arising from a duty that is not located in concrete nature but, as it were, in the noumenal self, as its moral constitution. But the will that aims at the moral law is itself completely neutral. It is not compelled by anything from within. Kant's notion of libertarian freedom precludes any such irresistible attractions on the will. Schleiermacher points out, contra Kant, the fundamental juridical, "negative" function of reason in relation to nature, constraining impulses without producing positive ethical realities of its own. In other words, as long as the will remains "unattached" to desire, to one's moral constitution as such, its always unconstrained choices leave this moral nature unchanged. Thus moral transformation can never happen as long as freedom of the will is upheld in this precise Kantian sense. In response, Schleiermacher's compatibilism suggests that we can only impute an action to an agent if some version of determinism holds. Unless my actions spring ineluctably from my own self, that is, unless they are determined by who I am, they do not belong to me. On this basis alone, Schleiermacher thinks, are punishment and legal responsibility possible.

Schleiermacher is right to identify a problem in Kant's account of moral change. It is unclear, if one accepts Kant's version of libertarianism, why one should ever consider an agent to have undergone moral transformation. If the will remains free, one can always revert to the old self. Kant himself is forced to admit that this moral transformation is not an empirical reality and can thus only be hypothesized. We can never be sure of our own moral transformation. But the problem is not only that we cannot be sure we have been transformed, but also that the very notion of transformation does not make sense, as long as the will is denied any inertia stemming from prior choices. The will is not determined in its nature by the choices one makes. It remains a purely formal capacity. Transformation, as such, does not fit the libertarian logic.

Schleiermacher senses this problem in Kant's thought. The moral law is all about the duty to make choices "away from nature." It consists in the refusal to obey our impulses and strive for independent and universal duty. But in the will's taking leave of nature, nature is thus left unchanged. This is Kant's fundamental problem. For Schleiermacher, on the other hand, there are impulses present within our own nature that compel us either to obey our natural and basest inclinations or to obey the moral law. The will is not neutral but is affected by desire. The ethical task, therefore, is not the rationalistic one of clearing the vision so that one may adequately perceive the moral law. That would never be enough, for even if we knew the moral law, what would compel us to obey it? For Kant, the answer to this question is that the moral law resides in the very nature of our noumenal selves, that by choosing the law we maintain our personality rather than abnegate it. Schleiermacher is not convinced. For him, what causes the will to choose the moral law is the desire for the law. Thus, "As soon as we see that the moral law cannot affect our will and determine it in any other way than by means of the moral feeling that relates to that law, it becomes an increasingly urgent task for us to increase the practical influence of this feeling."[41]

Marina comments that "Schleiermacher seems to have put his finger on a fundamental problem in Kantian ethics, and that is that it cannot explain how the material of willing, that is, the given desires and their attendant maxims supplying the content of Kant's ethical formalism could themselves be transformed."[42]

This provides the opening for Schleiermacher's own ethical system. Understanding this contains the key to understanding his atonement theory as well. I will briefly summarize his position before elaborating on it in more detail. First, Schleiermacher holds that the key to moral improvement is that "our structure of affect" has to be changed. Second, this change cannot come through any sensuous means, for that would involve a retreat into eudaemonism. This, as we shall see, rules out punishment as a means of moral improvement. Third, this change can only be accomplished by an influence on our God-consciousness, and this influence takes the historical form of Jesus Christ.

Neither eudaemonism nor deontologism being an adequate ethical system, Schleiermacher proposes the alternative of, in John Wallhauser's words, an "ethics of the indwelling of reason in nature, transforming and elevating nature into new being."[43] Jacqueline Marina calls this third principle the principle of godlikeness.[44] The needed transformation takes place at the level of our very affections. But, contra the Aristotelianism of Thomas Aquinas, for instance, this transformation of the moral self cannot take place through the education of the senses, either through punishment or through acts of penance. Schleiermacher denies any such direct link between nature and spirit. That is because Schleiermacher himself does not see the task of ethics in the encouragement of the natural state of humanity. This, as we shall see, is to speak euphemistically. In fact, Schleiermacher will prove himself quite the Manichaean. But I am anticipating.

Moral progress entails the elevation of God-consciousness, or the spiritual consciousness of human nature. God-consciousness does not happen

41. Friedrich Schleiermacher, *On the Highest Good*, trans. H. Victor Froese (Lewiston, NY: Edwin Mellen, 1992), 53.

42. Marina, *Transformation*, 158.

43. John Wallhauser, "Schleiermacher's Critique of Ethical Reason: Toward a Systematic Ethics," *Journal of Religious Ethics* 17, no. 2 (1989): 25–39 (here 30).

44. Marina, *Transformation*, 161.

deontologically, through a neutral and disinterested choice of duty, or through the stimulation of the senses in the direction of sanctification. Rather, if ever such a change is to take place, it will bypass both of these channels. It can only happen because of the saving efficacy of God. As Marina puts it, "Contra Kant, Schleiermacher's fundamental ethical insight springs from the confidence that the highest good, which he understood as 'the ensouling of human nature by reason,' will occur, for it is, after all, the working of God's efficacy in the world."[45]

In an unfashionable way, Schleiermacher makes a turn away from the pre-scriptive toward the descriptive. Ethics is not quite about a simple description of basic human nature but about the nature in the process of becoming ensouled with reason, through the influence of the God-consciousness of Jesus. Ethics is not about making disinterested choices guided by reason, but about listening to, nay, being influenced by, a consciousness shaped by historical forces not of our own making. The departure from Kant's libertarianism could not be more complete.

Kant's problem is to have made happiness a component of the highest good. But since such empirical happiness is not available in this world, the only option left is to speak about a transcending of human nature altogether. For only in such transcendence can we hope (practically) for our virtue to be crowned with happiness. But this type of ethical system abandons the world. "For Schleiermacher, on the other hand, the natural world itself is to become the arena in which each being harmonizes his or her being with all other be-ings. The whole of nature itself is in the process of transformation, that is, of becoming the arena of the ethical."[46]

The highest good, contrary to Kant, has to be something possible and concrete in itself. As Wallhauser comments, "The good refers not only to the obedient will of the subject of some supreme good beyond this life but precisely to those products of willing deposited into the objective moral world."[47] We may anticipate a little at this point, to see what this yields for theology. The consequence, theologically speaking, is that, in faith, morals derive from the gifts of the Spirit, not from some external, objective duty that is nevertheless supposed to be compelling.

For Kant, on the one hand, happiness is a matter of hope, requiring the postulate of immortality. Schleiermacher argues, on the other hand, that happi-ness has no place in rational ethics. Kant's ethics, although rational, mistakenly incorporates or correlates happiness with the highest good.[48] For Kant, the

45. Ibid., 148.
46. Ibid., 160.
47. Wallhauser, "Schleiermacher's Critique," 35.
48. Schleiermacher, *Highest Good*, 86.

highest good is the complete fitness of intentions to the moral law, together with happiness in perfect proportion to such fitness. Such a highest good is unattainable in this life, since Kant seems to have in mind an empirical, sensuous sort of happiness.[49] Yet the moral law obligates us to achieve happiness as the necessary object of pure practical reason. Hence Kant is forced to turn to the logic of worthiness and reward and the concepts of immortality and God. For Schleiermacher, as we have seen, this abandons concrete human nature and leaves it untransformed.

Instead of happiness, Schleiermacher argues, correcting Kant, one should talk about blessedness. Kant, according to him, has confused "well-being" with "happiness." Blessedness is the harmony of desires. This is what Schleiermacher means by the "ensoulment of nature." What he has in mind is the necessity of human nature itself being repaired. Yet this repair is not some "happiness" that is externally bestowed as a reward, but something that is concretely possible in this life. As we shall see, it is this mending of our desires that Christ understood as his mission.

What about the law? Clearly, there is much less room in Schleiermacher's system for the law. Kant's moral law is external to nature, though internal to pure reason. Schleiermacher is skeptical that such an externalized correlation can be of any service in the mending of nature. Neither is the divine law, or the law of Moses, of any use in the process. In his church history lectures, he approvingly outlines Agricola's view that the Mosaic law, itself only a civil law, is of no use in Christian piety, in which everything comes from the Spirit.[50] Brague helpfully captures the contrast with Kant, who tipped the legislative to the moral side. Schleiermacher, however, prohibits the legislative dimension from religion. Later, Ritschl will call Schleiermacher's understanding of moral progress "mechanical," lamenting his diminution of the place of the law. The point is that, very much unlike Kant, *moral change happens through divine intervention in the ordering of our desires*. This change is not incompatible with human freedom or with human responsibility.

One question remains, though. What happens to guilt? We have shown that Kant's seminal contribution, in his context, was to provide a moral justification and explanation of the reality of guilt, as well as a justification of God's dealing with it. Schleiermacher, having denied the importance of the law, is hesitant to describe sin as fundamentally a transgression of the law

---

49. See Marina, *Transformation*, 149.

50. Hermann Peiter, *Christliche Ethik bei Schleiermacher: Gesammelte Aufsätze und Besprechungen / Christian Ethics according to Schleiermacher: Collected Essays and Reviews*, ed. Terrence Tice, trans. Edwina Lawler (Eugene, OR: Pickwick, 2010), 335.

(1 John 3:4; 5:17). But how does he account for the feeling of guilt, which is an undeniable component of human experience?

What about the reality of punishment? Schleiermacher objects to Kant's retributive justice. For Kant, the relation of happiness and virtue is what justifies physical punishment for an evil deed because it joins awareness of culpability (*Strafwürdigkeit*) to that deed. In this way, Kant justifies his retributive conception of justice. Every evil deed deserves a physical evil in response. It is my physical, empirical suffering that connects my own self to the culpability for this particular action. Pain, which is sensuous, is an appropriate response to evil. One might say that happiness or pain is Kant's way of reconnecting nature and spirit.

Kant had also argued that every punishment must first be justified as harm before it can be regarded as beneficial. In other words, before we think of any further consequences of punishment, it must first be demonstrated that it is linked to this particular evil act, in response to which it effects harm on the agent. Schleiermacher disagrees with this conception. The only true thing about this conception is that punishment is justified if we are punished by the appropriate authority. In other words, Kant's principle should be taken to mean that punishment should not be undertaken by just anybody who loves someone and who thinks that such a punishment will be beneficial to that person. Kant's principle can only be taken as far as to say that, even if a punishment will be beneficial to a person, it can only be administered by someone in authority. If this is what is correct about this maxim, then one (who is in authority) must only demonstrate the benefit of the action to justify the exercise of that authority. No further correlation between penalty and crime is required—if, again, one already has this authority.

Schleiermacher therefore undermines the logic of retributive justice. Divine punishments do not have to be justified by any correlation between individual evil and the act of punishment. Since God is in authority over us, it is sufficient that these punishments can be proved to be beneficial. Through this discussion, Schleiermacher also erodes the basis of Kant's atomism in relation to individual guilt. He treats humanity as a lump, as a collective body, with God as a causal force that molds it. Guilt is, as a consequence, collective. Sin is similarly collective (Rom. 5:12, 15; Gal. 3:22). Thus the object of divine justice is not the individual. "We degrade that attribute to the status of a mere counterpart of civil justice, which we so often feel as injustice"[51] when we take the individual to be the object of divine justice. The penalty is similarly collective, or corporate

51. Friedrich Schleiermacher, *Christian Faith* [hereafter *CF*],], ed. H. R. Mackintosh and J. S. Stewart (Edinburgh: T&T Clark, 1989), 84.2.

(1 Pet. 4:6): "We reach a complete vindication of the principle that all sin is reflected in evil, and that all evil can be explained by sin."[52]

Thus the totality of evil encountered in the world is the result of divine penalties, which spring out of divine love (Prov. 3:12; Rev. 3:19). These penalties, however, are not retributive, but have a different function. The only role of punishment, he argues, is deterrence. It is necessary as long as the sensuous consciousness dominates humanity. But once this consciousness is replaced with a divine consciousness, punishment will no longer be necessary. Civil law is similarly consigned to such a restrictive role.

Schleiermacher is very specific that punishment cannot be reformatory: "If the God-consciousness could be strengthened by punishment, a system of divine penalties as perfect as possible could have been made to serve instead of redemption."[53] Neither are punishments retributive, since the Deity cannot be susceptible to irritation. The only possible purpose for these, again, is deterrence: "Insofar as the power of the God-consciousness is as yet inactive in the sinner, its object . . . [is] to prevent the dominant sensuous tendencies from meanwhile attaining complete mastery through unchecked habit."[54]

Schleiermacher on the Atonement

Schleiermacher's ethical system of his doctrine of the atonement might be summarized as follows: (1) Salvation cannot be understood according to a logic of reward. Kant mistakenly incorporates happiness into the highest good, at the cost of making salvation supranatural. (2) The highest good consists in the harmony of desires, awakened by the God-consciousness. (3) Given the force of evil and sin, such a transformation needs to be effected from the outside. (4) Punishment, as physical harm, does not serve any soteriological purpose, being oriented toward the sensuous nature.

Schleiermacher reacts no less vigorously against Kant's "empirical heresy," by which he means Kant's exemplarism. Christ cannot be conceived as simply an archetype of the new self. Such an external example is of no use to us, whose desires are disoriented and need refocusing. Christ, as a historical individual, is absolutely crucial for the awakening of this God-consciousness in his followers. Thus the fundamental role of Christ is to instill in us the perfect God-consciousness of which he was possessed. This, however, happens through historical channels and mainly through the formation of the church.

52. Ibid.
53. Ibid., 84.3.
54. Ibid.

Not only does Schleiermacher reject Kant's atomism—the individual faced with the universal ideals of humanity—but he also helpfully emphasizes the collective nature of sin. Exemplarism does not work precisely because of the pervasiveness of sin. While Kant understood radical evil, his optimism in regard to moral progress was unwarranted in light of the extent of sin. This criticism of Kant's exemplarism does not entail a return to the doctrine of original sin, however, which to Schleiermacher is offensive and incredible. Nevertheless, he argues that sin can be both universal and inevitable without its being an inheritance from a particular act that changed human nature.[55]

According to Schleiermacher's specific Kantian starting point, theology is a reflection on the contents of religious consciousness, and the specifically Christian religious consciousness derives from the historical person of Jesus. Hence it is not surprising that he asserts, "We have the consciousness of sin whenever the God-consciousness which forms part of an inner state, or is in some way added to it, determines our self-consciousness as pain; and therefore we conceive of sin as a positive antagonism of the flesh against the Spirit."[56] Thus the consciousness of sin itself only arises "as the effect of the Redeemer's self-revelation, as indeed it certainly does come to full clarity only as we contemplate His sinless perfection."[57]

Therefore sin is fundamentally a matter of consciousness. Sin is also inherited socially, rather than naturally, as an inherited predisposition to sinfulness, or what he also calls "a growth in congenital sinfulness." This yields an incapacity for the good, which directly falsifies Kant's moral optimism.

Such an incapacity can only be overcome through Christ's influence. His perfect God-consciousness, the "mind of Christ" (Phil. 2:5), is capable of being imparted to his followers. Marina argues that this impartation of the mind of Christ is not mere exemplarism, but that Christ is the one who actively produces a new human personality. Let's try to understand this in relation to Kant. Christ imparts to his followers his blessedness. This flies in the face of what Schleiermacher calls "magical" views of the atonement. According to these, atonement consists in the erasure of a debt (Col. 2:14). Kant indeed comes close to this, although he views the substitute not as the historic Christ but as the new self, continuous with the old self. At any rate, magical views are seriously flawed. On the one hand, they do not account for the importance of the community and the historical mediation of salvation (2 Cor. 5:18). The transfer from the merit of Christ to the salvation of the individual is

55. See Walter E. Wyman Jr., "Sin and Redemption," in *The Cambridge Companion to Schleiermacher*, ed. Jacqueline Marina (Cambridge: Cambridge University Press, 2005), 134.
56. Schleiermacher, *CF* 66.
57. Ibid., 100.2.

therefore "magic." On the other hand, such views overlook what Marina calls the "person-forming character of Christ's work."[58]

This is absolutely essential for Schleiermacher's conception of the highest good. What Christ does is to impart blessedness, by which Schleiermacher means the ordering of desires, whereby the God-consciousness predominates and the sensuous consciousness subsides. This blessedness is different from Kant's happiness precisely in that the latter functions on the framework of the senses: it is empirical happiness. But Schleiermacher eludes the empirical and the sensuous altogether. Blessedness consists in a kind of a blissful orientation toward the divine, despite the disruption that may come from the senses. Such an impartation of blessedness comes through Christ's person-forming activity. This activity consists in the reorientation of the consciousness away from pleasure and pain and toward God.

There is something clearly "mystical" about this view. The person-forming activity of Christ does not operate along "ethical" channels, whereby his followers listen to his teaching and attempt to emulate it. Schleiermacher seems to avoid the "ought" implied in the idea of such a body of teachings and counsels altogether, since he locates the problem at a "deeper" level, the affective. Thus, as John Crossley helpfully points out, Christ brings about a new motivation, not so much a new morality.[59] The fundamental influence of Christ is to "mystically" alter the structure of our will, so that it is oriented toward the God-consciousness. The reorientation is never complete, but God nevertheless regards it as complete, on the basis of faith: "Our union with Him, accordingly, although it never attains more than relative manifestation, is yet recognized by God as absolute and eternal, and is affirmed as such in our faith."[60]

In God's eternal plan and decree, such a transformation of human nature was ordained to occur through the influence of Christ. It is only because of the person and work of Christ that redemption and reconciliation are possible. Schleiermacher is thus bound to give an account of the person and work of Christ that avoids the magical view, while at the same time doing justice to the historical reality of his suffering. What must be true about his life for this kind of influence to be possible?

Schleiermacher argues that Christ did take on the sin of humanity: "He had a sympathetic feeling of the world's sin and thus carried that sin."[61] However,

---

58. Marina, *Transformation*, 207.

59. John Crossley, "Schleiermacher's Christian Ethics in Relation to His Philosophical Ethics," *The Annual of the Society of Christian Ethics* 18 (1998): 93–117 (here 109).

60. Schleiermacher, *CF* 104.3.

61. Ibid., 104.2.

this "sympathy" does not amount to an actual possession of the burden of guilt incurred by sin. As a result, his death cannot have been a case of divine punishment on account of sin. Neither did Christ feel the divine wrath on account of that sin. That idea "deprives the human consciousness of Christ of all human truth, by regarding as his own personal consciousness what from the nature of the case could in him be only sympathy."[62]

It may nevertheless be said that Christ suffered on account of our sin (Rom. 4:25; 1 Pet. 2:24). Schleiermacher regards this suffering as an inevitable part of his humanity and includes it under the idea of "passivity": "There is never any activity without some definite occasion—which always presupposes a passive state; and just as little is there ever any activity without limits to what is effected by it—and these limitations also are felt as suffering."[63] He rejects the strict demarcation of Christ's active and passive obedience. These are always active and present together. Christ's suffering "accompanied him throughout his life," as a condition of it, given the nature of human existence. The necessity of the suffering does not stem from his having to bear the retributive pain for our sins but was a necessity of the incarnation: "The action of Christ without the suffering could not have been redemptive, nor the suffering without the action reconciling."[64]

Christ's distinctive identity consists in the way in which he embodied the highest good of humanity. His sensuous consciousness was purely passive, giving room to his God-consciousness. Thus Schleiermacher can argue in *The Life of Jesus*, "Not only was his moral development progress without struggle, but also his intellectual development progress [was] without error."[65] Marina also points out Schleiermacher's suspicious conclusion that Jesus could not have been genuinely tempted (see Heb. 4:15), for, as she explains, "to think that the sensuous self-consciousness in Jesus was able, of itself, to determine something as attractive or repulsive in such a way that he had to struggle with it, is to posit the origins of sin, even if infinitely small, in Jesus."[66] The sensuous consciousness, which regards pleasure and pain as incentives to action (thus giving rise to temptation), was simply absent, or utterly passive, in Jesus.

Yet evil can be regarded as punishment only if the pain inflicted can act as an incentive to action. But Jesus's consciousness was such that he could not have regarded the pain in such a way. It is therefore problematic to argue that Christ experienced the evil of the cross as punishment. Nevertheless, precisely

62. Ibid., 104.3.
63. Ibid., 104.2.
64. Ibid.
65. Quoted in Marina, *Transformation*, 202.
66. Ibid., 203.

in this it may be said that Christ acts as our "satisfying representative": Christ abolishes our punishment. He does not do it in the sense of bearing it, but in the sense of altering our self-consciousness after his own image, so that, just as he did not perceive the evil of the cross as punishment, neither shall we react to the evils of life under the influence of our sensuous self-consciousness (1 Thess. 1:6; 1 Pet. 2:19; 3:14). "We may say that through the suffering of Christ punishment is abolished because in the fellowship of his blessed life even the evil which is in the process of disappearing is no longer at least regarded as punishment."[67]

Schleiermacher is here dealing with the fundamental problem in his system—that of consciousness. The problem with the magical view of the atonement is that it confuses guilt, which is the most intensely personal feeling, with liability to punishment. It falsely assumes that the transfer of the latter onto Christ coincides with our being healed of personal guilt. Christ did not die in our place in the sense that we shall no longer have to experience suffering, but so that we might be able to experience it like he did.

These benefits of Christ's activity, however, are only available to us if we are united to his God-consciousness (Eph. 2:12). It was not Christ's active obedience to the law and his passive obedience to the point of the cross that earned him a kind of merit that could then be transferred to us. Such a view misunderstands the fundamental problem of humanity, which is a disorientation of the will. The idea of punishment (of Christ) functions in a framework that is itself problematic and has to be replaced, because punishment can only be experienced as such if the sensuous consciousness is allowed primacy. This is not the solution, but the very problem. Christ alters our consciousness in such a way that our consciousness is transformed from one of sin, whereby we perceive God as being against us, to one of grace, whereby we treat the evils of life with the detachment befitting the Son of God.

Schleiermacher's doctrine of the atonement, as Dorner puts it, "almost entirely ignores the divine justice in relation to the work of the atonement . . . [and] strictly excludes all influence upon God."[68] Unlike Kant, who considered God to be under obligation to act justly, in conformity to the moral law, which demands punishment, Schleiermacher treats the very idea of law as somehow missing the point. One might say that Schleiermacher interiorizes the law: goodness and moral uprightness are matters of the right ordering of desires rather than rational and free conformity to the law for the sake of duty. While this account seems more personal and hu-

67. Schleiermacher, CF 104.4.
68. Dorner, System of Christian Doctrine, 4:51.

mane than Kant's, it is adopted at the cost of regarding sin as a natural and unfortunate occurrence.

Albrecht Ritschl (1822–89)

Ritschl on Schleiermacher, Kant, and Law

Kantian and neo-Kantian influences are strongly felt throughout Ritschl's theological system. While there is not enough room to detail Kantian influence in terms of his theological method, it suffices to point out that Ritschl objects to Schleiermacher's relegation of religion to the realm of "feeling" (*Gefühl*), this being of a piece with his preference for Kant's ethical emphasis. Thus Ritschl regards religious judgments as value judgments. Metaphysics makes the mistake of lumping together matter and spirit, when these should be distinguished. Since we cannot conceive the thing apart from its relationship to observers, it follows that God himself cannot be perceived in his actions, but known only in revelation, through the consciousness of the church. Much like Schleiermacher, Ritschl insists on the methodological and epistemological priority of Christian consciousness. We have no access to God, no knowledge of sin, except through the influence of Christ, present in the church.

Unlike Schleiermacher, however, Ritschl understands this influence not as mystical, acting on the preethical level of our desires, but in terms of the kingdom, which is a moral principle. In other words, the influence of Jesus extends through history not by what is, after all, despite Schleiermacher's claim to the contrary, a magical method of transmission. Rather, Jesus affects the course of human history through the foundation of an ethical and historical body, his kingdom.

Ritschl praises Schleiermacher for characterizing Christianity as a monotheistic religion of the teleological type, in which everything is related to the kingdom of God. However, Schleiermacher fails to apply this definition consistently, falling back into a preethical, mechanistic mode of thinking and thus leaving behind the *ought* of Kant's ethics.

There is yet another aspect of Schleiermacher's thought that he rejects, namely, its determinism. For Ritschl, the religious question is one of freedom over nature. James Brandt helpfully points out the different contexts in which the two modern masters wrote. He argues that this difference of context puts in perspective Ritschl's vigorous reaction to Schleiermacher, since he does not pay attention to the latter's historical context. Schleiermacher was mainly opposing the moralistic reduction of religion and the rationalism of his day. As a response, Schleiermacher affirmed the sui generis nature of Christian piety (feeling). For Ritschl, this blurs the line between nature and spirit. But Ritschl has his own ax to grind. He represents a reaction against the scientism and materialism of his day, which threatened to reduce religion to an aspect of nature.[69]

It will help to keep this difference in mind, particularly in terms of the nature-spirit relation. Schleiermacher conceived the ultimate soteriological task as that of mending nature through the influence of God-consciousness in history. He conceived the highest good as the ensoulment of nature by reason. Ultimate freedom does not consist in being free from natural constraints but in the harmony of these irrepressible and inescapable influences. There is no contradiction between authentic personal freedom and a determinism of this kind. For Ritschl, on the other hand, the task is (again) the liberation of spirit from nature, the elevation of spirit, in the exercise of its freedom, from the constraints of nature. Thus Schleiermacher's emphasis on divine causality in creation (which is the force that mends nature) has to give way to a renewed emphasis on the intrinsic value of the individual.

While Ritschl was by no means an individualist and was making appropriate corrections to Kant's atomism, nevertheless for him the ethical implies individual freedom. In choosing a naturalist and determinist perspective, and thus dropping the individual from sight, Schleiermacher also—as we have seen—failed to appreciate the significance of individual guilt. Salvation is not mediated through the ethical stance of the individual but is simply divine causality at work in history, repairing the "lump" of humanity. As Claude Welch has put it, Schleiermacher's starting point in feeling "represents an aesthetic rather than an ethical view. It diminishes the moral feature of the community of believers and precludes a true appreciation of mercy and pardon."[70] Mercy is not really required since sin, as an inevitable condition of our development in the natural world, is not really a trespass of the law.

Thus Ritschl returns to Kant's *ought* as the condition for the realization of God's kingdom. Kant was the first to have realized the importance of ethics for the kingdom of God, as an association of persons bound together by laws of virtue. Schleiermacher simply lost this from sight, despite his correct understanding of Christianity's teleological character. But morally good action is necessary because Christianity has the supramundane kingdom of God as its ultimate purpose. Moreover, Luther's and other Reformers' failure to recognize God's kingdom prevented them from solving the problem of good works.

69. See James M. Brandt, "Ritschl's Critique of Schleiermacher's Theological Ethics," *Journal of Religious Ethics* 17 (1989): 51–72.

70. Claude Welch, *Protestant Thought in the Nineteenth Century*, vol. 1, *1799–1870* (New Haven: Yale University Press, 1972), 10.

Whereas Schleiermacher could not conceive of the completion of the atonement without some interiorization to the realm of feeling at the preethical level of the natural conditions of our actions, Ritschl similarly leaves the atonement as incomplete apart from its realization at the level of the actions of individuals bound together in a community of love. In typical modern fashion, both of these theories of the atonement understand the essence of Christ's work in the creation of a new condition for human subjectivity (Schleiermacher in feeling, Ritschl in ethical action). Thus they can both be labeled "moral influence" theories—as long as this does not obscure the important differences remaining between them. Both of them participate in a larger reaction against orthodoxy, especially its forensicism. Schleiermacher, on the one hand, rejected both the legal framework of orthodoxy and the Kantian moral law. Ritschl, on the other hand, rejects forensicism on account of its failure to lead to the development of moral personality above the constraints of nature.

It is essential to understand Ritschl's ethical starting point in the formation of the kingdom. The task of this kingdom is the achievement of a unity "through mutual and social action prompted by love" and not limited to the characteristics of family, class, nation, and so on. "It consists," as Welch renders it, "in achieving independent moral personality, in which spirit dominates over nature." As we shall see, Ritschl tends to conflate the "legal" with the positive, civil law. He contrasts it with the moral: "We must keep moral law and civil law altogether distinct."[71] The relations of family, class, and nation are constituted either by laws of nature (as in the case of family) or positive laws (the state, class). The unity to be achieved under such laws either is a natural unity, determined by compulsive love or what Kant calls "pathological love," or is maintained through the force of the powerful (or through a social, democratic unity, established through consensus and maintained through force). Both of these are exclusive unities, failing to reach universal status. The unity of the family is dominated by love—love between parent and child, husband and wife—but therefore also by the exclusion of those who do not belong to this family. Similarly, the unity of the state is maintained by force against possible threats from the outside. All of these unities, whether natural or consensual, are exclusionary of other social formations. They thus fail to represent the universal end of the kingdom of love, which envisions a unity maintained through the laws of virtue.

Kant's categorical imperative helps to clarify this position. The unity of the kingdom is the unity of a group of individuals who command themselves to

71. Albrecht Ritschl, *A Critical History of the Christian Doctrine of Justification and Reconciliation*, trans. John S. Black (Edinburgh: Edmonston & Douglas, 1872), 269.

love one another out of the sake of duty (1 Cor. 12:13; Eph. 2:14). Their love is not pathological and is therefore not determined by extraneous conditions. It is simply a love for its own sake. This love is also universal, since the duty to love is a universal duty. It extends beyond the confines of one's class, race, family, and state.

Thus the purpose of Christ, in the establishment of this kingdom, is to draw all people in this community of love. Whereas for Schleiermacher salvation is about the mending of nature, for Ritschl it is precisely about departing from nature, for nature can only compel me to love a restricted number of people. The Spirit does not work at the preethical level, which is itself natural, but its role is that of lifting one's personality above the requirements of nature and incorporating him or her into the kingdom of virtue.

Let me rehearse Ritschl's reaction against a number of theological options: (1) First, orthodoxy is rejected for its failure to understand the distinction between the legal and the moral. This rejection is much in line with Schleiermacher's own rejection of the same tradition. Orthodoxy confuses guilt, which is intensely personal, with liability to punishment, which is a question of legislation and does not bear on our moral nature. However, (2) Ritschl also rejects Schleiermacher's mystical approach for its failure to appreciate the centrality of the kingdom to salvation and the importance of individual ethical action in constituting this kingdom. The ethical standpoint, lost to Schleiermacher's romanticism, has to be recovered.

I would like to clarify Ritschl's approach to the law. I have already pointed out that modern philosophy of law betrays a tendency to emphasize positive law. This is not to say that there are no traditions of modern natural law. Indeed, Kant, as Stone points out, was quickly drafted in the service of just such a tradition. But despite this emphasis on positive law, modernity does weaken the links between civil law—which is positive, created through the sheer *will* of the people, and legitimated independently of its links with morality—and moral law, which, at least for Kant and Ritschl, is universal, transparent to reason, and applicable.

Ritschl without question accepts this separation of jurisdiction. He treats all external legality as being of a positive nature and therefore having a very restricted function, if any, in the development of moral personality. As Dorner has clarified, legal right refers merely to *outward order*, to the system of actions that subserve the ends of a *particular* state. Notice again the contrast between universal and particular. Legal order is particular. Moral law is universal. The moral framework, in conclusion, is much wider than the legal framework.

Here from another vantage point we can observe Ritschl's rejection of forensicism. First, we can only appreciate divine action from the perspective of its results among us in the kingdom of God. But—second—this kingdom is one of virtue and moral action, of universal love (Col. 1:13), not of legalistic justice (Matt. 23:13; Luke 16:16). Thus our doctrine of God should not be based on independent speculation about conceptions of justice. All our conceptions of divine justice are derived from our moral experience of the kingdom, not independently of it. As Leonhard Stählin puts it: "Nothing, however, can be more incompatible with Ritschl's empirical point of view than the idea of an essential right or essential necessity."[72] All of these are merely abstractions.

Ritschl on Sin and Punishment

Having defined Ritschl's relation to Kant and Schleiermacher, we are now in a position to move deeper into Ritschl's theological system as such, as we seek to clarify other relevant conditions to his atonement doctrine. His stance on sin and his philosophy of punishment are particularly relevant.

It is perhaps not surprising, judging from his appreciation of Kant's moral standpoint, that Ritschl also affirms a strong doctrine of personal guilt. He inveighs against the Enlightenment theologians, who have weakened guilt too much and thus denied the need for divine pardon and grace.[73] Ritschl does find some extenuating circumstances, however. Orthodoxy had tied the concept of guilt so closely to original sin, and a particular account of the transmission of this original sin, that skepticism with regard to the latter concept was bound to affect the credibility of the former. But the idea of guilt does not depend on the idea of original sin. The idea of guilt, as for Kant, is sufficiently buttressed by the notion of the moral law. That the Reformers derive this moral law from God, while Kant derives it from the principle of freedom, makes no difference to theology.[74] There exists such a moral law, and failure to comply with it places a burden of guilt on the individual. Kant's theory of transcendental freedom proves the universality and objectivity of guilt in a way not accomplished by the orthodox treatment of the notion.

Ritschl also argues that original sin needs the idea of a moral law in order to be known as guilt (Rom. 5:13). I must understand that this sin is my own sin. Needless to say, Ritschl, together with nominalism, rejects the idea of generic sin. All sin is actual. But with Kant, he also retains the notion of radical evil, namely, the deeply pervasive and insidious character of sin. Against

---

72. Leonhard Stählin, *Kant, Lotze and Ritschl*, trans. David Worthington Simon (Edinburgh: T&T Clark, 1889), 211.

73. For an excellent discussion of this, see Ritschl, *Critical History*, 387; also see Alister McGrath, "The Moral Theory of the Atonement: An Historical and Theological Critique," *Scottish Journal of Theology* 38, no. 2 (1985): 205–20.

74. Ritschl, *Critical History*, 390.

Kant, however, he does not believe we can choose the good without divine help. Thus Ritschl firmly rejects Kant's moral optimism.

However, Ritschl's methodological starting point constrains him to define sin as ignorance. Much like Schleiermacher, he affirms that we can approach sin only from the perspective of our consciousness of Christ. Only through the lens of God's revelation in Christ do we arrive at an awareness of sin. This leads him to affirm that, since sin is fundamentally ignorance, there is no difficulty of forgiveness on the part of God.

Furthermore, it makes no sense to speak of sin as infinite in an objective sense; this is "the result of a purely rational inference."[75] Instead, a "graduated" conception of sin fits much better with our intuitions and consciousness of guilt. There are degrees of sin, depending on our ignorance and limited ability. We can allow Ritschl to speak for himself, at some length:

> For either the "infinity of sin" is to be understood objectively, in which case we land ourselves in Manichaeism; or the idea is a subjective impression, in which case it means only that we cannot with all our efforts of imagination arrive at, nor with all possible intensification of our own consciousness of guilt represent exhaustively, the extent of sin in space and time, and its power to disturb the orderly course of human history. But for that reason sin, as a *product of the limited powers of all men*, is yet limited, finite, and quite transparent for God's judgment.[76]

But Ritschl also affirms that there is a kind of sin (Eph. 4:17–19) that cannot receive divine forgiveness: "There also exists a degree of sin which can only expect to be expelled from the divine world order."[77] This is the sin of the finally obdurate, those who finally and decisively reject the faith. Such sins cannot be forgiven even by God. The fate of these can only be that of an eternal exclusion from the kingdom of God.

This graduated view of sin, together with Ritschl's conviction that the finally obdurate will not be forgiven, suggests a peculiar understanding of divine love and forgiveness. According to Ritschl, God can only love those people still capable of redemption: "Therefore the love of God can be conceived in relation only to such sinners as have not fallen into that degree of sin which excludes conversion of the will."[78] The existence of such a definitively evil will

---

75. Albrecht Ritschl, *The Christian Doctrine of Justification and Reconciliation: The Positive Development of the Doctrine* [hereafter *JR*], ed. H. R. Mackintosh and Alexander Beith Macaulay (Clifton, NJ: Reference Book Publishers, 1966), 368. This is a translation of vol. 3 of the German work.

76. Ibid., 369.

77. Ibid., 379.

78. Ibid., 383.

means that there remains nothing left in that person that might be lovable, by which Ritschl means no trace of the image of God.

Ritschl remains ambiguous in regard to the fate that awaits these finally obdurate. To be sure, he does not suppose that we could discover who these people might be, if any. This is merely a judgment from the perspective of God (Matt. 25:32; Rom. 12:19; Heb. 10:30). But in all this, Ritschl's intention is to point out that divine forgiveness is possible because humanity's rejection of God is based on ignorance (Luke 23:34; Acts 3:17; 7:60). It is a weakness of the will (Rom. 6:19), as opposed to a will resolute in its refusal, based on full knowledge of everything that is required and entailed.

What, then, of punishment? In the first volume of *The Christian Doctrine of Justification and Reconciliation*, Ritschl praises Kant's retributivism[79] as a necessary entailment of the moral law. In every punishment, he echoes the Königsberg sage, there must be justice, namely, a physical evil. All trespass is punishable, and it merits the loss of happiness. Ritschl critiques Schleiermacher for failing to regard sin as a transgression of the law (1 John 3:4), and thus meriting punishment. Moreover, guilt deserves eternal punishment. Guilt is not transferable like monetary debt. It is "personal in the highest degree and can only be borne by the culprit itself."[80] This is clearly retributive justice of the most intensely personal kind, which denies that the penalty could be borne by another. While liability might be transferred, this does not in any way deal with the aspect of guilt.

By the time he wrote *The Positive Development of the Doctrine*, Ritschl seems to have been vacillating on the topic of retribution. There he argues that retribution is a Hellenic idea,[81] supported by the assumption of a legal relation between God and humanity. The church, he argues, has imported the idea of retribution by applying the conception of public and state law to the relation between God and humanity. He then argues, in departure from Kant's physical harm requirement, that the essence of punishment is separation from God. Guilt itself is the punishment: the consciousness of guilt is "itself already the initial manifestation of punishment as the forfeiture of the privilege of divine sonship."[82]

James Orr agrees that there is a clear inconsistency here: "It is difficult to reconcile these positions of the first volume [of *The Christian Doctrine of Justification and Reconciliation*] with Ritschl's later dogmatic positions and especially with his rejection of the idea of 'retribution,' which he came to

79. Ritschl, *Critical History*, 396.
80. Ibid., 411.
81. Ritschl, *JR*, 478.
82. Ibid., 384.

regard as a 'Hellenic' notion."[83] In the second volume, as Orr further notes, there is no exercise of the properly punitive will of God. "For the mechanical relation between character and reward, good and evil, there is substituted the organic relation of ground and consequence—of seed and fruit."[84] Guilt is the organic consequence of the trespass of the law.

Yet against Schleiermacher, Ritschl insists on the importance of this individual guilt. In §42 of the second volume, Ritschl takes up the question of the relationship between sin and evil. He takes issue with Schleiermacher for regarding all evils as punishments for sin. Naturally, as we have seen with Schleiermacher, the function of these evils is to deter humanity from entering deeper into the way of sin. They are not retributive. Ritschl, on the other hand, wants to maintain a distinction between evil, which is not a religious concept, and sin, which is a concept deriving directly from the consciousness of guilt, which itself derives from the consciousness of reconciliation.

The link that Schleiermacher himself makes between sin and all evils, as deterrent punishments, derives from a legal logic that Ritschl contends is foreign to the God of the Bible. "Now, punishment in its legal sense is a deprivation, entailed by the authority of civil society, upon one who has acted contrary to his legal obligations, in order that the absolute claims of civil society may be affirmed. But the Christian religion is not a legal federation between God and man."[85] Ritschl will always insist that the legal framework— any legal framework—is inadequate for the moral relation between God and humankind.

The notion of evil, on the contrary, is a religiously neutral notion. It is defined by the notion of the freedom of the individual since "evil signifies the whole compass of possible restrictions to our purposive activity."[86] Considering this, it is problematic to consider all of these restrictions as being somehow bound up with divine punishment. It is only on a legalistic basis that we can make such a pronouncement. On the contrary, "Christ's express declarations warn us against taking the degree of evil, in legal fashion, as an indication of the degree of transgression on the part of those afflicted."[87]

Now, it might be appropriate to perceive some such evils—though never all of them—as an instance of divine punishment. However, and this is the key point, such a correlation depends on a preexisting notion of guilt. "The

83. Ibid., 478.
84. James Orr, *The Ritschlian Theology and the Evangelical Faith* (London: Hodder & Stoughton, 1897), 147.
85. Ritschl, *JR*, 362.
86. Ibid., 351.
87. Ibid., 362.

view of evils as punishments is conditioned, rather, by the specifically religious consciousness of guilt; not merely by the judgment that we have incurred a restriction of our freedom by our own act, but by the judgment that the act in question has contradicted the divine moral law."[88]

Schleiermacher's (and orthodoxy's) identification of all evil with punishment can lead to restricting the doctrine of reconciliation to our liberation from sin and guilt. But for Ritschl, reconciliation also entails—in true Kantian fashion—our liberation from the world. Reconciliation, Ritschl argues, is "also the ground of deliverance from the world and the ground of spiritual and moral lordship over the world."[89] The orthodox forensic framework views evil as a punishment mechanistically applied in response to a transgression. This cannot be appropriate, for our relationship to God does not take place in terms of civil law. Schleiermacher views all evil as deterrent punishment, but without any sense of individual guilt correlating the trespass to the punishment. Ritschl, however, suggests that all evil is not divine punishment, but the result of friction between our free actions and the world, which acts as a limit. When these actions represent breaches of the law, guilt ensues. But, just as in Kant, guilt does not ensue as an objective reality in a legalistic fashion, as determined mechanistically by a stipulation of the law. Rather, guilt occurs organically, as the natural consequences of breach of the moral law. In that sense, "the unrelieved feeling of guilt is not so much one penal state among others, but is itself actually that of which all external penal evils are but the concomitant circumstances."[90]

However, as long as this trespass is not final, divine forgiveness is possible. Since the response to the trespass is not a strict stipulation of the law, God responds to the crime in all kinds of ways.

Ritschl on the Atonement

A summary of our findings so far would be helpful at this point. (1) Ritschl understands the ethical task as the development of personality such that free persons elevate themselves above the constraints of nature. (2) Christ accomplishes this in the founding of a community of love, which is the kingdom of God. (3) The way in which Christ draws people into this community of love is not through some preethical, mystical influence at the level of a person's desires but by fully drawing on the freedom of individuals as they engage in properly moral action. (4) Failure to act according to the moral law does

88. Ibid., 355.
89. Ibid., 357.
90. Ibid., 365.

not incur an obligation on the part of God to obliterate that person. Such a view betrays a legalistic, not a moral, way of thinking. Rather (5) the guilt the individual feels amounts to his or her estrangement from God, which is the essence of God's punishment. All of these points lead to Ritschl's specific doctrine of the atonement.

First, it should be clear by now that Ritschl rejects Kant's exemplarism, together with the Socinian position on forgiveness, which denied any relationship between the forgiveness offered by God and the historical position of Jesus Christ.[91] "The Socinians derive the forgiveness of sins merely from Christ's spoken word, which they represent as independent of his personal virtue."[92] This rationalist reduction of the positivity of Jesus Christ obscures the fact that Christ as a historical being makes possible something entirely new in humankind's moral experience. "For beyond all doubt Jesus was conscious of a new and hitherto unknown relation to God and said so to his disciples; and His aim was to bring His disciples into the same attitude toward the world as His own, and to the same estimate of themselves, that under these conditions He might enlist them in the world-wide mission of the Kingdom of God, which He knew to be not only His own business, but theirs."[93] Thus, "only through the impulse and direction we received from Him, is it possible for us to enter into His relation to God and to the world."[94] Alfred Garvie sums up Ritschl's position: "The forgiveness of sin is inseparable from the Person of Christ, for He puts men into the same relation to God as he holds. His priesthood consists in his maintenance of that relation throughout His life. His submission in death is the clearest expression and most convincing evidence of his maintenance of that relation. Hence the forgiveness of sin especially attaches to his death."[95]

We shall come back to the idea of the special significance of Christ's death. Ritschl insists that the new dimension he brings, which is not simply a new motivation, although it includes it as well, does not bypass the freedom of his followers. In that, it is eminently ethical and *followable*: "Inasmuch as Jesus desired His own attitude to God to be shared by the rest of mankind, He laid upon his disciples, as their aim also, the union of mankind through love, or, in other words, the realization of the Kingdom of God; and through His own personal freedom in relation to the world, He led His disciples, in accepting

91. Ibid., 538.
92. Ibid., 536.
93. Ibid., 386.
94. Ibid., 387.
95. Alfred E. Garvie, *The Ritschlian Theology, Critical and Constructive: An Exposition and an Estimate* (Edinburgh: T&T Clark, 1899), 319.

their view of the world from Him, to the assured conviction that human life is of more worth than all the world."[96]

Freedom is paramount here. Christ's influence, if any, has to be conceived in human, historical—as opposed to either magical or mystical—terms. Christ does not legislate a particular course of action, but his example of love may be embodied in a variety of different concrete, historical ways. The purpose of Christ's mission is the kingdom of God, "but since this end is served by setting up the universal principle of brotherly love, it is not any defect of the moral code of Jesus as such that the ordering of the separate provinces of moral life is left to the free application of this supreme principle."[97] This amounts to something like a sapiential imperative: Christ did not come to lay down another law, except the law of love. It is up to us to figure out the concrete ways in which this love can be embodied in human existence.

Christ's mission is to demonstrate for us the nearness of God. Christ's Godward activity has the purpose of making a change possible, not in God, but in human beings. He does this by fulfilling in himself that which is also to be fulfilled in others. In him "the individual impulses of self-preservation, avoidance of pain, and the keeping inviolate of personal honor" were "subordinate to the consciousness of his vocation." The saving efficacy of his death consists precisely in this "consciousness of his vocation," as we shall see below. The point of his vocation was to once again make ethical life possible for us. A condition for this possibility is the removal of our estrangement from God, in the form of the consciousness of guilt. Only by once again accepting ourselves can we turn toward others in love. But this is done only by transcending the logic of law. "The multitude of spirits, who, for all their natural and generic affinity, may yet, in the practical expression they give to their will, be utterly at variance, attain a supernatural unity through mutual and social action prompted by love, action which is no longer limited by considerations of family, class, or nationality—and this without abrogating the multiplicity given in experience."[98]

The transcending of law makes genuine love possible (1 John 4:18). This amounts to nothing less than the reconstituting of humanity around the principle of love. The church, therefore, is not an addendum to the primary work of individual salvation, but is its final end. Salvation cannot be conceived independently of ecclesiology.

> For even the Evangelical Christian's right relation to Christ is both historically and logically conditioned by the fellowship of believers; historically, because a

96. Ritschl, *JR*, 414.
97. Ibid., 414–15.
98. Ibid., 280–81.

man always finds the community already existing when he arrives at faith, nor does he attain this end without the action of the community upon him; logically, because no action of Christ upon men can be conceived except in accordance with the standard of Christ's antecedent purpose to found a community.[99]

Christ is both the head (1 Cor. 11:3; Eph. 4:15; 5:23) and the representative (Heb. 3:1) of this community. For that reason, our always-inadequate embodiment of divine love does not represent an impediment to God's love. God regards humanity as reconstituted in the person of Jesus Christ. Here again, Ritschl takes leave of Kant's "atomistic independence," which finds the idea of a representative to be unthinkable.[100]

Representation is not substitution. Christ did not stand in our place in such a way that we don't have to obey, but precisely so that he might liberate us in order to obey (Rom. 6:8; 2 Cor. 5:14–15). Such a representation is inclusive rather than exclusive or substitutive. What he has done, and shown that it can be done, we must do as well. "This use of representation," Ritschl argues, "is inclusive, not, as it generally is, exclusive. The meaning of the idea is not that what Christ does as a priest, the community does not require to do; but rather that what Christ as a priest does first in the place and as the representative of the community, there the community itself has accordingly to take up this position."[101] The difference from the traditional Reformed position is clear, as Garvie notes: "While for the orthodox, the sinner is forgiven for the sake of what Christ has done, according to Ritschl, he is forgiven with a view to what he may become as a citizen of the Kingdom."[102]

For Ritschl, the death of Christ is to be seen in continuity with his life. For "we should not conceive the purpose of Christ's death under any principle which would be opposed to the purpose of his life."[103] The purpose of Christ's life was clearly obedience. His death is therefore nothing else than his continued obedience to God's will, even in the face of death (Phil. 2:6–11). The fact that the Gospels place special stress on his death as crucial for salvation is not to be dismissed. Indeed, Ritschl concedes that a special significance attaches to his death. However, it is "not the 'occurrence' of the death of Christ [that] conditions its sacrificial value; but His submission to this decree of His opponents as an appointment of God and highest proof of His fidelity in His vocation makes this decease significant for others." One might say that

99. Ibid., 549.
100. Ritschl, *Critical History,* 411.
101. Ritschl, *JR,* 546.
102. Garvie, *Ritschlian Theology,* 317.
103. Ritschl, *JR,* 543.

his death makes most fully clear Christ's obedience to his vocation and his determination to bring it about in others.

Ritschl also denies the punitive value of Christ's death. This follows directly from our discussion of the philosophy of punishment. In order for an evil to be experienced as punishment, it must be accompanied by a feeling of guilt. But since Christ was not possessed of such a feeling, he could not have regarded his death as punishment. Rather, the essence of Christ's sacrifice consists precisely in liberating us from fear of God's judgment.

Christ's death does not turn any screws to catalyze divine forgiveness. Ritschl considers the fact that Jesus freely forgives sins even before his death (Mark 2:9; Luke 7:48) quite significant. Although a strong connection remains between his death and forgiveness, it is not the death as such, as an occurrence, that makes this forgiveness possible. "The fact that He pronounced the forgiveness of sins in those cases really refutes all those theories which are designed to show that Christ, by his death as a satisfaction for human sins, succeeded in making God willing to forgive, while they either view his morally normal life as being the expression of his duty, or regard it as enhancing the effect of his voluntary death."[104] Such cases have to be either dismissed or reinterpreted as being made beforehand in the light of his future vicarious suffering. "This, however, would be no exposition, but a violent importation, which theological caprice cannot allow itself without pronouncing its own condemnation."[105]

Forgiveness is, in most cases, unconditional. As long as something lovable remains within us, God will love us and forgive us, even though he sometimes may punish us in order to correct us. Yet God does not vindicate his righteousness by punishing sin. That would only make sense within a legalistic framework. Rather, he vindicates it by establishing his kingdom. Thus God's forgiveness depends on the ministry of Jesus. Forgiveness was necessary in order to establish the kingdom. Even more precisely, forgiveness is the equivalent of acceptance into this community. But this forgiveness depends precisely on the ministry of Jesus. As Garvie puts it, "That he may be encouraged and enabled to keep the law, his breaches of the law are not reckoned any more against him."[106]

Summary

1. Modernity severs morality from legality. Secular law is defined as primarily the will of the people. For Kant, the moral law should still be

104. Ibid., 537.
105. Ibid., 543.
106. Garvie, *Ritschlian Theology*, 317.

universal, but no attempt should be made to ground it in nature. In fact, nature is precisely what needs to be transcended, as humanity embraces free and universal reason.

2. Modernity also witnesses a so-called relaxation of penalty. Retributive justice falls on hard times in the collective consciousness of modern states. Punishment retains only the function of deterrence and rehabilitation.

3. Kant is somewhat atypical in regard to some of these trends. He retains a strong version of retributive justice and opposes legal instrumentalism. He also retains a strong sense of radical evil and guilt.

4. Nevertheless, Kant's libertarianism forecloses some options in atonement. Kantian salvation cannot happen from outside of us, but must preserve the so-called personal potency principle. It has to lie within our power to reform ourselves. This provides an analysis of the very concept of moral formation and the ultimate good assumed by Kant. We bear our own guilt and atone for our own sins, as different persons, when we adopt the attitude of Christ.

5. Schleiermacher rejects Kant's libertarianism as ethically irrelevant. If our will is not bound to our nature, then our natures will never be healed of their brokenness.

6. Yet the reformation of our natures cannot come through sensuous means, for it is precisely the chaining of our natures to sensuality (either as pleasure or pain) that disorients them. Thus punishment is ruled out as a means of moral improvement. Only by God's influence on our consciousness through the historic activity of Christ can our natures be mended.

7. Finally, Ritschl in turn objects to Schleiermacher's mysticism and his circumvention of the ethical moment. The moral transformation cannot happen except through Christ's moral teaching (something Schleiermacher neglects) and in the community founded by Christ himself.

8. All of these writers place an important stress on the subjective understanding of the atonement. They deny an economy of exchange that makes salvation into a good that is either merited or unmerited. They perceive the necessity of understanding salvation in relation to moral transformation.

5

Atonement and the Postmodern Critique of Law

Questioning Agency

This last chapter of our historical survey approaches a variety of atonement theories formulated in the last fifty years or so and inspired by the development of what has been called "postmodernity," but which I prefer to call "late modernity." Older theories of the atonement have certainly not passed away. Nor has their influence waned. In fact, it can be confidently put forward that the most influential late modern theologies of the cross revive the classic, Christus Victor model. Yet they do so by employing an explanatory—or I should say a narrative—framework that is resonant, as one should expect, with contemporary culture and that departs in some significant ways from the details of the classic model.

The story of the transition from modernity to late modernity, even if only in terms of agency, can only be sketched out rather impressionistically here. I am hoping that painting with such broad strokes has the advantage of capturing the larger ideological trends, even if it will lack some of the crispness of detail. I suggest that the overarching theme of late modern atonement theories is nonviolence. All of the theories that I will be discussing here accept the maxim that violence is inherently reprehensible, that God cannot be entangled in it, and that as a result the atonement cannot be the demonstration of a violent justice. Late modern theories of atonement renounce violence, including the violence of law, as an ingredient of the divine logic of salvation. The supreme relationship between humanity and God must transcend law.

Clearly, outrage at the association of God with violence is not new. The claim that God forgives gratuitously, without demanding anything in return, has been forcefully made both by Greek church fathers and by medieval as well as modern theologians. Yet the reader will notice significant changes in the late modern reaction. I will focus on a particular reaction to modernity and show how it results in a modification of modern atonement theories.

The undisputed historical turning point between modernity and late modernity is the two World Wars and in particular the Holocaust. Such has been the enormity of these events that significant theologians have argued that every theology worth its salt must be done self-consciously in the wake of the Holocaust, or Shoah. In what concerns this discussion, *the experience of the Holocaust problematizes for a late modern mind the relationship between legality and justice.* As the cases of Eichmann and Demjanjuk demonstrate (see discussion below), strict adherence to law does not replace one's duty to live and act justly, even if this means going against the law. For postmodern jurisprudence, the Holocaust definitively demonstrates that the justice system cannot evade questions of morality and justice by taking refuge in the pure formality of law. Legal positivism, so the argument goes, is bankrupt.

In the next section I will return to precisely these debates about the duty to obey the law, and examine the very nature of law, since I believe these issues are crucial for understanding the criminal (or sinful) act and its atonement. Not only does Shoah problematize legal theory (positivism), but if Heidegger is right, we must understand the Holocaust in terms of the technical essence of Western metaphysics coming into its own, an indictment that postmodern philosophers accept—indeed, one should understand postmodernity as the rejection of the modern metaphysical project.

But how, one might ask, is this in any way relevant to the atonement? To understand the connection, we have to come to the question of agency. Emmanuel Lévinas was a Ukrainian-born Jewish philosopher who might be regarded as one of the most influential late modern thinkers. For Lévinas, the entire metaphysical project is an attempt to render the world intelligible to the self. Metaphysics attempts to give a neutral description of the world, to dig up the very structure of reality. From Plato to Hegel, it is a project that translates the *Other* (world, other persons, God) into the language of the *same*, by projecting universal categories and concepts onto the particulars. Such a project, Lévinas argues, is essentially idolatrous (it makes the world, others, God into the self's image) and violent (it overpowers particular beings with thought). Metaphysics colonizes being with thought; it is *logocentric*.

The modern self is a self emptied of its most cherished ideals and desires.[1] It is a neutral self, a human being among other human beings who live together on the basis of law. The justice of that law consists in (1) respecting the universal human rights of fellow human beings and (2) respecting the free contractual agreements into which persons enter. The self of modernity is fundamentally libertarian, its particular passions and desires being accidental to its fundamental human nature. Modernity is thus predicated on the notion of the free individual. Justice is based on this freedom. Law cannot concern itself with questions of morality (understood as natural law), but with a *fair* distribution of goods, where fairness is described independently of the particular ends and wants of individuals.

The consequence of this has been the formation of an abstract "legal person." Constas Douzinas poignantly observes that "if the legal person is an isolated and narcissistic subject who perceives the world as a hostile place to be either used or defended against through the medium of rights and contracts, he or she is also disembodied, genderless, a strangely mutilated person."[2] The modern self is thus constituted through exclusion of demarcation. In other words, it is a repressive and a repressed self.

In modern jurisprudence, if an agent is fully in possession of his or her rational faculties, then his or her responsibility for the crime is to be calculated coldly and dispassionately. As Douzinas comments: "Legal rules ensure equality before the law and guarantee the freedom of the parties. But this equality is only formal; it necessarily ignores the specific history, motive, and need that the litigant brings to the law in order to administer the calculation of the rule and the application of the measure."[3] In order for this system to work, however, it has to be based on a whole architecture of knowledge, a complete repertoire of crimes, circumstances, criminals, motives, and so on. In other words, it has to be based on an ontology.

Michel Foucault, whose analyses of power/knowledge will concern us in the next section, highlights the centrality for modern jurisprudence of the so-called juridical person, or legal person. The architecture of knowledge required for the functioning of the legal system pretends to operate on the basis of a neutral, universal ontology of "the human." For Foucault, on the

1. For a wonderful exploration of these themes, see Robert Musil's work of fiction, *The Man without Qualities* (New York: Alfred A. Knopf, 1995).
2. Constas Douzinas, "Law and Justice in Postmodernity," in *Cambridge Companion to Postmodernism*, ed. Steven Connor (Cambridge: Cambridge University Press, 2004), 212.
3. Ibid., 213.

contrary, this body of knowledge is anything but neutral, a machinery for the construction of "docile subjects" of law. The legal person is the end result of a process that places individuals under surveillance and situates them in a whole network of writing (documentation). As Jean Cohen and Andrew Arato point out: "The modern legal person endowed with rights is a dimension of modern individuality that, far from indicating autonomy, is functional to, even the product of, disciplinary control. Through observation, continual surveillance, sorting, partitioning, ranking, examining, training, and judging, discipline creates the material counterpart of the juridical subject by investing the body with power relations."[4]

Thus Foucault attempts to dispel the myth of autonomy. Human identity is neither a given (natural law), nor is it something we choose for ourselves (libertarianism), but the result of dispersed power. This process operates fundamentally by demarcation and exclusion: sane/insane, normal/abnormal, male/female, gay/straight, master/slave, rich/poor, educated/analphabet, black/white, and so on. Foucault's point is that the creation of these dichotomies is part of a structure of "disciplinary power," which fixes identity. To the sovereign, free individual, master of her own destiny, Foucault opposes a constructed self, caught between transpersonal and systemic forces of discipline. The interesting thing is that this discipline, which Foucault regards as violent, does not spring from ignorance but precisely from knowledge. This brings us back to Heidegger's point about the complicity between (1) absolute evil and violence (as in the Shoah) and (2) culture/knowledge. Nowhere is the contrast between modernity and postmodernity clearer than here: whereas the former dreamed that knowledge spells the end of factions, a Foucauldian postmodernity fears that knowledge is itself exclusion.

The trouble with the Other is that, as psychologists tell us, it cannot really be repressed. Postmodernism excels at demonstrating that our seemingly unitary identities are fragmented, that our apparently homogeneous cultures are plural, that our identities and selves are no more unified than our deconstructable texts. The border between sane and insane, between free and slave, runs through the middle of each of us. Feminist and postcolonial scholars, to mention but two of the many groups, argue against all kinds of essentialism: against human nature and against feminine nature, for example. All binary oppositions are unmasked as enforcing power by projecting a normalcy, a this-is-just-how-things-are resignation.

Late modernity takes precisely this systemic "plausibility structure" as the culprit. Metanarratives (to use Jean François Lyotard's term), which pretend to give a description of reality untainted by one's interests and perspective, are

4. Jean L. Cohen and Andrew Arato, *Civil Society and Political Theory* (Cambridge, MA: MIT Press, 1994), 287.

inherently violent. But this also reflects the notion of agency and responsibility: although I am indeed responsible for my actions, this does not exhaust my responsibility. My actions, together with my identity, aren't the result of a free exercise of my will, but are partly the result of the influence of the forces that bear upon my being, and to a certain extent they are inescapable and irresistible.

We are thus well on the way to a recovery of the notion of humanity as standing between cosmic and systemic forces. These forces are no longer described as demonic (that would be Platonic, a failure of nerve resulting in evacuating us of responsibility and excusing us from exercising justice), but as transpersonal, symbolic, systemic. In the next section we shall return to these forces. The point here is that their reality, functioning under the pretense of objectivity, metaphysics, and representation, complicates the picture of agency and responsibility. In terms of atonement, it is these forces that become the real culprit.

The fundamental character of these disciplinary practices, what Foucault relevantly calls "pastoral power," is violence toward the Other. They culminated in the Holocaust, but they are also evident in racial and gender discrimination, in denial of access to education, in treatment of refugees and immigrants, in processes of globalization. The twentieth century, more than any other century, brought these acts of exclusion before our eyes with a paralyzing violence.

Postmodern jurisprudence, in reacting to this failure of the modern project, turns toward the Other as both constitutive of the self and transcendent and untamable. But once knowledge has been indicted and representation accused of betrayal, what possible ways do we have to "know" or understand the Other? Remember that Foucault accused the whole system of knowledge as being complicit with power. What means do we then have to "tend to" the Other? Or is postmodernism content with simply affirming a generic, empty, and featureless Other?

Lévinas argues that knowledge of the Other cannot mediate my relationship with the Other. To define the Other is to inscribe him or her within a conceptual framework that neutralizes his or her uniqueness. Instead of knowledge, the proper mode of relation to the Other is desire. This is a "metaphysical desire" that "tends toward *something else entirely*, toward the *absolutely other*."[5] Such a desire is not based on a need, which would originate in the self and would again read the Other in terms of my interests. It is a relationship nourished by the Desired, but a relationship that is not the "disappearance of distance,

---

5. Emmanuel Lévinas, *Totality and Infinity: An Essay on Exteriority*, trans. Alphonso Lingis (Dordrecht, NL: Kluwer Academic, 1979), 33.

not a bringing together."[6] It is "a relationship whose positivity comes from remoteness, from separation, for it nourishes itself, one might say, with its hunger."[7] As I will point out, this means that justice is never done in the sheer application of the *logocentric* law. Justice has to attend to the Other as Other, not as the legal subject of this particular legal structure.

Lévinas's is not the only late modern option for the rendering of identity. The Christian social and moral philosopher Alasdair MacIntyre has revived an Aristotelian understanding of justice as teleological and coupled it with an account of narrative as the best way of rendering identity. He critiques what he calls the "genealogical" moral theory of Nietzsche and his followers. (Foucault and Derrida are his targets, although with some disclaimers I would include Lévinas here as well.) The genealogist notion of a fragmented and dissipated self cannot sustain the very project of genealogy (Nietzsche), archaeology (Foucault), or deconstruction (Derrida). MacIntyre writes that

> in making his or her sequence of strategies or masking and unmasking intelligible to him or herself, the genealogist has to ascribe to the genealogical self a continuity of deliberate purpose and a commitment to that purpose which can only be ascribed to a self not to be dissolved into masks and moments, a self which cannot but be conceived as more and other than its disguises and concealments and negotiations, a self which just insofar as it can adopt alternative perspectives is itself not perspectival, but persistent and substantial.[8]

By this, MacIntyre certainly does not wish to return to an essentialist notion of human identity. But human identity can nevertheless be rendered within a teleological structure, which is more than the fragmented self of postmodernity. Such a structure is narrative. In *After Virtue*, MacIntyre makes the point that "we are never more (and sometimes less) than the co-authors of our own narratives."[9]

MacIntyre obviously makes more of both rationality and the common telos of a community than Lévinas seems to make. This is not to say that, for Lévinas, law is useless. It remains important because any relationship to an Other involves a Third: "The other is from the first the brother of all the other men."[10] This requires law as a calculation of equality and symmetry of rights, since

6. Ibid., 34.

7. Ibid.

8. Alasdair MacIntyre, *Three Rival Versions of Moral Inquiry: Encyclopaedia, Genealogy, and Tradition; Being Gifford Lectures Delivered in the University of Edinburgh in 1988* (London: Duckworth, 1990), 54.

9. Alasdair MacIntyre, *After Virtue: A Study in Moral Theory* (Notre Dame, IN: University of Notre Dame Press, 1984), 213.

10. Emmanuel Lévinas, *Otherwise than Being*, trans. Alphonso Lingis (Dordrecht, NL: Kluwer Academic, 1981), 158.

my responsibility before the Other is tempered by my responsibility to Others. But the point remains for him that justice is not based on *knowledge* of the Other, who remains transcendent, but simply on proximity to the Other. Law is secondary to justice and can never fully approximate it. Constas Douzinas adequately captures the "aporia" of postmodern justice: "To act justly one must treat the other both as equal and as entitled to the symmetrical treatment of norms, and as a totally unique person who commands the response of ethical asymmetry."[11] I will return to this aporia when discussing the "act" in the context of postmodernity.

Sinners into Victims

It is not difficult to understand the consequences of this revisioning of agency for the doctrine of sin. Risking an overgeneralization, hopefully it is useful to say that for late modernity, responsibility shifts in the direction of victimization. If selves are no longer unitary and sovereign, their wrongs are no longer simply attributable to them, but to larger structures standing above them and holding them in bondage. This is the fundamental upshot of the previous discussion. These systems are both prior to the exercise of agency and condition it significantly. They serve to repress both the particularity of the self and the uniqueness of the Other facing the self. Thus my colonial attitudes and actions toward the Other make me guilty before the Other, but they are also the outcome of a structure of plausibility, not of my making or choosing, which conditions me to behave in such a way.

This is another tension running through the middle of postmodern culture: the question of whether the recognition of the power and control of these transpersonal forces evacuates me of responsibility altogether. This is relevant for the atonement question. If my responsibility for crime can be deflected to these structures, then I am neither under an obligation to pay a penalty for my (nonexistent) guilt nor able to extricate myself from this bondage without the aid of an external liberating force. On the other hand, if I retain responsibility, I incur a duty to liberate myself from these structures. The former (external liberation) is the path of certain types of modern Christus Victor theories; the latter (self-liberation) is the path of feminism. We shall analyze both of these below.

Whether or not sin understood as systemic domination annuls my responsibility for wrongdoing, it is a distinctive contribution of late modernity to bring to our attention again this transpersonal and transintentional dimension of sin. There is no space to probe the roots of this understanding, though it is an

11. Douzinas, "Law and Justice in Postmodernity," 214.

interesting question whether and how this understanding of sin is connected to the theological shift away from personal conceptions of divinity toward more immanent and impersonal symbols of divinity associated with generic "spirituality."[12] Alan Mann speculates that such a shift to a spirituality without a personal God makes the concept of sin, as responsibility before a personal Being, unpalatable. The attending notion of guilt is also meaningless for a society that no longer anchors standards of moral conduct in a personal, transcendent God but in variously constructed and justified immanent human standards. Mann notices that in such a regime, "the only rewards and consequences for our actions are self-generating."[13] This is significant because it means that the logic of sin-punishment is nothing but a human construct, intended perhaps to control the escalation of crime, or (cynically) to form docile subjects. The point is that if we suffer, it is not because we have triggered a divine logic of wrath and punishment but because we are victims of cultural mechanisms of control. In other words, we are no longer sinners, but *sinned-against* victims. Thus Mann comments, "As the victim we are helpless, the casualty of social structures, institutions and corporate bodies. It is with these that responsibility lies, not with the 'innocent victim' of their distorted practices."[14]

Although it might seem that we are back to familiar notions of bondage to the devil or to personal powers and principalities, this is not the case. There has been no return to the pre-Enlightenment world of spirits and demons. There are indeed evangelical theologians of the cross, whom I call "evangelical Christus Victor" theologians, who retain belief in such personal powers and principalities. I discuss their work elsewhere.

The late British theologian Colin Gunton is typical (one might say the godfather) of a generation of hermeneutically inclined theologians who take the biblical language of the demonic to be metaphorical. By this he does not mean merely figurative or ornamental, but the only possible way to talk about a reality of bondage that has a dual dimension: personal and extrapersonal. The language of the demonic, he argues, is "an attempt to express the objectivity and irrationality of evil in the only way in which it can be adequately expressed: as a reality generating its own momentum and sweeping up human beings into its power."[15] Further, the language of demonic possession is used

12. See the religious turn of someone like Derrida, for example, not in the direction of an impersonal theism but in the direction of an apophatic God beyond being.

13. Alan Mann, *Atonement for a Sinless Society: Engaging with an Emerging Culture* (Milton Keynes, UK: Paternoster, 2005), 20.

14. Ibid., 25.

15. Colin Gunton, *The Actuality of Atonement: A Study of Metaphor, Rationality, and the Christian Tradition* (New York: Continuum, 2005), 69.

to express the helplessness of human agents, as demonic forces prevent people from distinguishing between good and evil.

It is doubtful that Gunton can legitimize his revisionist interpretation as an exegesis of the thought of the biblical writers. He is symptomatic of a whole trend of "depth hermeneutics," which probes beneath the conscious intentions of biblical authors. It may have been more elegant, though less religiously and theologically useful, to say that Luke, Paul, and Peter were simply wrong to hold such primitive beliefs. Gunton wants to hold on to the language without keeping the metaphysics and ontology that comes with it. He obviously does not think that we need to reify those powers as personal forces, and that an immanent description of their reality and manifestation will do.

Whether the procedure of immanently reifying "forces" is ontologically more acceptable and elegant is another matter. I do not wish to enter this discussion of ontological parsimony here. For now it is important to understand that, whatever these extra- or transpersonal "things" are, they manipulate, control, and influence human agents to such an extent that their intentionality is misdirected, or as Alistair McFadyen puts it, it is "disoriented."[16] This disorientation has to do with a blindness, a clouding of vision, a failure to understand and appreciate the good and the desirable. One might say that its roots are epistemological. This is yet another difference from the more ancient understanding of our bondage to Satan, which tends to be construed in terms of a "fallen nature." For Gunton, McFadyen, and almost all other theologians I will discuss, the bondage is epistemologically mediated, one might say gnostically mediated. What enslaves us is a failure of vision. Consequently, what would liberate us is a removal of the cataract, a defogging of our vision of the good. If this is the case, it would seem that we are not that far removed from so-called moral example or moral influence theories. Some differences, however, will become obvious in due time.

The concept of clouded vision (John 12:40; 2 Cor. 4:4) brings us back to our discussion of Foucault. We fail to desire the good because we have been educated, trained, disciplined in such a way that we simply do not see the good. Our epistemological impairment is thus determined by the "plausibility structures" we have inherited, with their binary oppositions, conceptual schemes, prepackaged understandings of justice, and other conceptual constructions determinative of action. For instance, we constantly find ourselves excluding the strange, the foreigner, the different. We do so because we have

16. Alistair McFadyen, *Bound to Sin: Abuse, Holocaust, and the Christian Doctrine of Sin* (Cambridge: Cambridge University Press, 2000).

been preconditioned to see the strange as "outside" of us, as "gentile" (Acts 10:28). We defined ourselves as unitary and normal over against the abnormal, the strange. These binary oppositions, which structuralism makes so much of, operate at a subconscious level and effectively lead to the exclusion of the Other.

It is not only the binary oppositions that prepare an ontology for us but also entrenched ways of dealing with conflict that prescribe courses of action for us. So it is, Foucault would argue, with the logic of sin-punishment. The fact that crime or wrongdoing incurs guilt (John 16:8), which demands an objective righting of the wrong through punishment (Rom. 5:16), is a cultural construction. It turns us into avengers. It promotes violence. It thus contributes to, enforces, and consolidates exclusionary violence. Similarly, practices of scapegoating, thought to be an ancient and medieval relic, are actually entrenched in legal and political systems. As Mark Heim illustrates: "To take some examples (not all of similar scope and scale), we may consider the Stalinist terror in the Soviet Union; the National-Socialist terror in Germany; and in the United States, the Red Scare after World War I, the practice of racial segregation, and the daycare child abuse hysteria of the 1990s. One feature of interest in all these cases is that the legal and political systems themselves, in principle curbs against sacrificial crisis, were in various measures consumed by it."[17] We are thus back to the point where the real culprit is the system, structural evil, the powers and principalities—not in heavenly places but of our own making. More important, perhaps, these are not just obscure forces, the stuff of conspiracy theories, but positive legal and political systems, real systems of justice, real educational, medical, and penal systems, even certain theologies of the atonement, as some will argue. As Jennings argues, it is the very idea of law that is the problem, the very idea that God would be angry at sin and sinners.

Let us now look at several concrete theologies of the atonement. Since understanding moral culpability is the first step toward understanding why the atonement is even required, I will focus on these theologians' understanding of responsibility for sin. I have selected several who are indicative of this understanding.

Andrew Sung Park (1952–)

In *The Triune Atonement: Christ's Healing for Sinners, Victims, and the Whole Creation*, the increasingly visible and respected Asian American theologian Andrew Sung Park expands the scope of the object of the atonement. Traditional

---

17. S. Mark Heim, *Saved from Sacrifice: A Theology of the Cross* (Grand Rapids: Eerdmans, 2006), 60.

atonement theories cater almost exclusively, he argues, to the sinners. However, while there are indeed sinners, guilt from sin is not the universal experience of humanity. On the contrary, there are significant segments of the human population for whom it is another experience that is fundamental to their being and that determines every aspect of their existence: the experience of being sinned against. Not only has the traditional preoccupation with sinners neglected a whole category of people, but it has in fact aggravated their misery. *The idea that improper theologies of the atonement become part of the oppressive structures that serve to exclude and marginalize is a major aspect of postmodern thinking about the cross.* Treating everybody as sinful promotes the impression that the suffering of the victims is somehow their desert (Lam. 3:39). This discourages any attempt to liberate themselves from their situation. Further, it glorifies their own suffering as somehow redemptive. It also legitimizes the aggressor as the representative of God, and thus as quasi-divine, further disorienting the intentionality of the victim. Against this mythology, "Jesus' cross restores victims' integrity and dignity by repudiating the idea of a sin-punishment formula"[18] (John 9:2).

Park invokes the Korean concept of *han* to illustrate the effects of wrongdoing on victims. Arguing that it is a specifically Korean concept, not translatable into Western categories, he nevertheless provides an approximation of its meaning:

> In Korean, *han* is a deep, unhealed wound of a victim that festers in her or him. It can be a social, economic, political, physical, mental, or spiritual wound generated by political oppression, economic exploitation, social alienation, cultural contempt, injustice, poverty, or war. It may be a deep ache, an intense bitterness, or the sense of helplessness, hopelessness, or resignation at the individual and collective levels. *Han* can be seen in the survivors of the Nazi Holocaust, the Palestinians in the occupied lands, the hungry, the racially discriminated-against, unemployed workers, battered wives, the molested, the abused, the exploited, the despised, or the dehumanized. *Han* is frustrated hope.[19]

Han is an open wound, a mark left on the victim, a negative creation that itself breeds further *han*. Park shows the dialectic between *han* and sin: victims of *han* become themselves sinners. From the homeless who become drug addicts or alcoholics to the experience of terrorism, retaliation, and vengeance, sin produces a vicious cycle of violence. "Sin or injustice causes *han*, and *han*

---

18. Andrew Sung Park, *Triune Atonement: Christ's Healing for Sinners, Victims, and the Whole Creation* (Louisville: Westminster John Knox, 2009), 69.
    19. Ibid., 39

produces sin or injustice. The sin of the oppressors may cause a chain reaction via the *han* of the oppressed. Sometimes *han* causes *han*. Furthermore, unattended or unhealed *han* gives rise to evil. This evil can regenerate *han* and sin. Also, sin and *han* collaborate to engender evil. They overlap in many tragic areas of life."[20]

Park does not exclude the reality of sin and responsibility for it. However, he does not think this responsibility requires a "sin-punishment formula." He never explicitly argues why, once he accepts the notion of sin, he can nevertheless deny the "legal" consequences of that notion. We may infer that it is this complicated picture of agency and responsibility that explains it. We remain responsible, but we can invoke many attenuating circumstances. As MacIntyre put it: "We are never more (and sometimes less) than the co-authors of our own narratives." We sin and commit injustice because of *han*, because of the structures of exclusion and oppression.

One may nevertheless wonder why Park should insist on retaining the concept of "sin" to describe our remaining responsibility. The very concept of sin makes sense as part of a family of concepts that include divine holiness, divine wrath, punishment, guilt, and so on. Park's rejection of the idea that God would punish sinners upsets the whole network of concepts. At the same time, it would be difficult for any thinker concerned with justice, as Park is, to label an act as a wrongdoing or as a crime without also calling the agent a criminal, or a sinner. It remains the case, nevertheless, that the sin is against humanity, not so much against divinity. The problem is that Park cannot and should not make this distinction. And once he accepts that humans sin against God, besides or through sinning against their fellow humans, the attendant notion of guilt and due divine punishment, whether relinquished or executed, is unavoidable.

The vertical dimension of sin (1 Kings 8:46; Rom. 3:23) has been almost completely obfuscated by its horizontal dimension. Park is to be commended for bringing to the foreground this neglected dimension of human corruption, but unless its ties with the vertical dimension remain clear, the concept of sin is meaningless. Park thus fails to provide a rich description of the scope of atonement unless the guilt that human beings incur before God is also definitively dealt with.

Feminist Critique of Sin

While Park is reluctant to completely abandon the concept of sin, a number of feminist theologians have no such qualms. Rosemary Radford Ruether argues

20. Ibid., 41.

that the very idea of the fall, of original sin, turns women into scapegoats. Rita Nakashima Brock comments that the concept "takes personal responsibility for behavior out of people's hands and turns it over to some power that commands you." To the astute reader this signals a noteworthy departure from the idea of the self's being under the control of higher powers. As we shall see, many feminists reject the Christus Victor theory precisely because it promotes the idea that we need salvation from an external force. This, they argue, stifles revolutionary action and liberation.

Nevertheless, feminists agree with the likes of Park on the structure of domination, specifically the culture of patriarchy. But this is a hegemony that can be opposed by regular human beings. What, then, is the salvific point of the cross?, one may ask. None whatsoever. The cross is to be understood as a tragic miscarriage of justice. It plays no role at all in the economy of salvation. There is nothing salvific or redemptive about suffering and death. These are tragic realities—and that is the end of the story. I will allow Brock to speak for herself:

> I think this sense of helplessness keeps us fundamentally in a victimized state. It's telling people that you don't have a right to protest when terrible things happen to you. It short-circuits the legitimate expression of tragedy and grief that is fundamental to our psychological health. We ought to be outraged that the Roman Empire crucified Jesus, not grateful, not happy that he died for us, but outraged at this travesty of justice.[21]

I will return to the feminist positive construal of atonement in a later section, but for now I will continue to explore their understanding of agency, responsibility, and sin.

Commenting on the wrongheadedness of the moral influence theory, which describes Jesus as providing for us an example of self-sacrificial love, Brock spares no words: it is "sick, . . . manipulative and evasive. This strategy assumes there is no power available to me other than the power to elicit guilt from another and put him in my debt. This binds the other through pain. This is not a strategy of freedom, but a rearrangement of bondage."[22] Echoing the same sentiments, Slavoj Žižek writes that "it is more satisfying to sacrifice oneself for the poor victim than to enable the other to lose the status of a victim and

21. Rita Nakashima Brock, "Can We Talk?," *Re-Imagining: Quarterly Newsletter of the Re-Imagining Community* 1 (November 1994): 5, quoted in Inna Jane Ray, "The Atonement Muddle: An Historical Analysis and Clarification of a Salvation Theory," *Journal of Women and Religion* 15 (1999): 105.

22. Rita Nakashima Brock and Rebecca Ann Parker, *Proverbs of Ashes: Violence, Redemptive Suffering, and the Search for What Saves Us* (Boston: Beacon, 2002), 48.

maybe even to become more successful than ourselves." This strategy only reinforces the status of the victim, even as it binds the victim to God, her bene-factor. In the name of erotic love, feminists resent all such hierarchies, even the divine-human one. Ruether argues that the concept of divine parenthood must be abandoned since it places God over us in some kind of patriarchal relation-ship—even when we speak of him as Mother. Sallie McFague encourages us to think of God as Friend, one who exists in a relation of mutuality to humanity.[23]

Sin, then, is not an attitude that sets oneself up as equal to God, but precisely that which does not promote this mutuality and equality between humans. In *Sexism and God-Talk*, Ruether asserts:

> The critical principle of feminist theology is the promotion of the full human-ity of women. Theologically speaking, whatever diminishes or denies the full humanity of women must be presumed not to reflect the divine or an authentic relationship to the divine, to reflect the authentic nature of things, or to be the message or work of an authentic redeemer or a community of redemption. This negative principle also implies the positive principle: what does promote the full humanity of women is of the Holy, it does reflect a true relation to the divine, it is the true nature of things, the authentic message of redemption and the mission of the redemptive community.[24]

Thus the quintessential sin is that which reinforces women as subalterns.

A theology that enforces such hierarchical structures is itself sinful. This in-cludes hamartiologies, such as Reinhold Niebuhr's, that view sin as fundamentally rebellion and pride. As Anthony Thiselton notes,[25] Niebuhr was instrumental in bringing to the consciousness of Western theology the structural dimension of sin, particularly in *Moral Man and Immoral Society*.[26] This brings with it guilt, blame, and self-hate, and it encourages powerlessness, since self-assertion is seen as problematic. Yet Niebuhr's analysis of structures of domination, control, and violence turned on the notion, developed in *The Nature and Destiny of Man* (1941), that the quintessential sin is "man's pride and will to power."

Feminist scholars, however, perceive Niebuhr's to be a male-dominated understanding of sin that should not be applied to women, whose fundamental

23. Sallie McFague, *Models of God: Theology for an Ecological, Nuclear Age* (Minneapolis: Fortress, 1987), 61.

24. Rosemary Radford Ruether, *Sexism and God-Talk: Toward a Feminist Theology* (Boston: Beacon, 1993), 19.

25. Anthony Thiselton, *The Hermeneutics of Doctrine* (Grand Rapids: Eerdmans, 2007), 301. Thiselton also mentions Paul Ricoeur, John Macquarrie, and Alistair McFadyen as contributing good discussions of this dimension of sin.

26. Reinhold Niebuhr, *Moral Man and Immoral Society: A Study in Ethics and Politics* (New York: Scribner, 1932).

"sins" are of a different nature. Valerie Saiving argues that among specifically feminine sins are "triviality, distractability, and diffuseness, lack of organizing center and focus, dependence on others for one's own self-definition," negation of self. The qualities related to and distorted by pride, such as self-worth, assertiveness, courage, determination, self-assurance, are precisely the qualities women need in order to attain their fullest humanity. Portraying the fundamental predicament of humanity as pride smothers the development of these qualities.

A traditional understanding of sin objectifies binaries: sovereign/subaltern, divinity/humanity, father/children. Brock argues that patriarchal ideologies produce splits: a self-righteous split divides self and world so that psychological self-examination and personal responsibility are set against the political realities of institutionalized oppression. As long as my personal relationship with God is secure, these systems are outside of my area of concern. The grace of the Father allows a select group to occupy a favored position with the Father, while the overall destructiveness of the oppressive systems of the patriarchal family remain intact. To this "power of hierarchy," Brock opposes "erotic power." The former is all about dominance, status, authority, control over the people, what Julia Kristeva calls the "Law of the Father," while the latter restores and nurtures relationships and is all about vulnerability, openness, caring.

What may we conclude about the feminist take on agency, responsibility, and sin? Feminists agree with Park that the powers are there. But they disagree with Park that we need to be liberated from these powers from the outside. Theologies that promote notions of original sin quench the authentic spirit of rebellion against the powers of patriarchy. It stands within our power to oppose these. Christ did not die on the cross to demonstrate his solidarity with the exploited. If he did, there is nothing salvific as such about this gesture. Christ's death is yet another example of how justice is miscarried in human affairs.

Postcolonial Contributions

The emerging discipline of postcolonial theology presents the theology of atonement with a new set of challenges. Wonhee Ann Joh, along with Park, writes as a Korean American theologian. Her 2006 book, *Heart of the Cross: A Postcolonial Christology*, further complicates the notion of agency, particularly in light of the realization that identities are never unitary and are always fragmented.

Drawing on Hommi Bhabha's notion of "hybridity," she argues that our identity is always composed at the intersection of multiple conflicting discourses, such as those of the colonizer and the colonized. But Joh, following the work of Bhabha, Gayatri Spivak, and Julia Kristeva, challenges the "politics of identity" and "politics of gender" that has dominated the feminist agenda for quite some time. I have noted some of the claims by, for example, Saiving that there are specifically feminine, as opposed to masculine, sins. To a new wave of feminist writers, this amounts to resurrecting an "essentialism," this time descriptive of a "feminine nature." Joh argues that identity of all sorts is "neither fixed nor simplifiable." In this she joins the social constructivist tradition of feminist scholars.[27] While essentialism may sometimes be strategically useful,[28] it should never obscure the fragmentation of identity. We should remain cautious about constructing an identity simply on the basis of race or gender. This caution does not signal a return to Susan Frank Parsons's "appropriate universalism,"[29] but Joh is aware that "one of the dangers of constructing an identity solely based on one subject, such as race, is that we tend to overlook the 'epistemic violence' that takes place within the complex web that constructs identity."[30] Gender ought to be replaced with "relationality" more generally, not simply difference, to capture the larger variety of interactions and interstitials. Thus the critique of early feminism on the basis of a philosophy of difference can backfire in that it "has created deep chasms that stand in the way of coalitional politics."[31] It would seem that Joh desires both to have both a philosophy of difference and to temper it with an understanding of a profound relationality that unites all these different identities. Apart from such a common relationality, true liberation would be impossible since we would all be frozen into our parochial selves. She approvingly quotes Susan Friedman: "The exclusivity of difference-talk fosters politically dangerous balkanization and suppresses both the utopic longing for connection and the visibility of the everyday realities of intercultural mixing. . . . The exclusivity of hybridity-talk can in turn slip into a romantization that elides the existence of collective identities on the one hand and the structures of power that construct them, on the other."[32]

The opposite of this relationality is precisely *han*. Joh contrasts *han* with *jeong*, which she defines as

27. The distinction between the liberal and the social constructivist trajectories in feminism is made by Susan Frank Parsons in her wonderful book, *Feminism and Christian Ethics* (Cambridge: Cambridge University Press, 1996).

28. See Gayatri Spivak's notion of "strategic essentialism," described by Wonhee Anne Joh, *Heart of the Cross: A Postcolonial Christology* (Louisville: Westminster John Knox, 2006), 2.

29. Parsons, *Feminism and Christian Ethics*, 180.

30. Joh, *Heart of the Cross*, 14.

31. Ibid., 16.

32. Ibid., 18.

a Korean way of conceiving an often complex constellation of relationality of the self with the other that is deeply associated with compassion, love, vulnerability, and acceptance of heterogeneity as essential to life. It not only smooths harsh feelings, such as dislike or even hate, but has a way of making relationships richly complex by moving away from a binary, oppositional perception of reality, such as oppressor and oppressed. I will argue that *jeong* is the power embodied in redemptive relationships. It can even be argued that redemption emerges within relationality that recognizes the power and presence of *jeong* to move us toward life.[33]

If *han* is the festering wound opened by sin and injustice, *jeong* is the power to heal that wound in mutuality and all-embracing relationality.

Again, there is no place for a concept of sin against divinity in this model. In fact, the fundamental goodness and relationality of humanity continues to exist as a repressed "bond." "The mother-child relationship is not something that the mother has to struggle to recognize, for here the subject-object is of one flesh; the other is within, and the gap with the other is not absolute."[34] Joh immediately goes on to draw an inference immensely important for her take on the atonement: "The social bond, not force, is what threatens the symbolic order."[35] The implication is double. First, sin does not disrupt our humanity irretrievably, such that we can only be rescued by a *force* outside of us. This is very much in line with feminist abhorrence of "spectacles" of salvation that do not involve humanity. Second, salvation is not the irruption of something completely new; it is not the opening up of a previously unknown possibility but the living according to *jeong*, namely, according to a repressed relationality that has been there all along. Jesus went to the cross because his life in accordance with this bond (*jeong*) was intolerable to the "Law of the Father," to the symbolic order that is predicated precisely on the maintenance of oppositions and exclusions.

To conclude this introduction to Wonhee Anne Joh's perspective on agency and responsibility, we notice a further weakening of direct responsibility for sin.

Deconstructing Law and Justice

Having looked at the late modern fate of agency and responsibility, it is now time to turn our attention to the current discussions of justice and law. It is the thesis of this book that since atonement theories are historical and cultural

33. Ibid., xxi.
34. Ibid., xxi.
35. Ibid., 103.

constructions, they will inevitably draw on regnant conceptions of justice and law. Exegeting the demonstration of divine justice tacitly appeals to normative ideas of law and its relationship to justice.

My intention is, again, not to provide a comprehensive analysis of the state of jurisprudence and thinking about justice. Rather, I wish to capture some broad attitudes to law. Although these attitudes have certainly influenced the legal field, it cannot yet be said that their influence has been decisive. The active infrastructure and conceptual framework in jurisprudence remains largely unaffected. Nevertheless, these attitudes cohere with larger cultural forces, and they have been affecting intellectuals worldwide. In our case, I will argue that atonement theologians have been decisively influenced by skepticism about the ability of law to dispense justice. Law itself is, if not undermined, then certainly disenchanted. Pretensions to fairness in law are unmasked as covert politics. This deterioration of trust in law is, I argue, one of the ways in which we can understand what is common to the bulk of postmodern approaches to the atonement. If God is to be considered just, then this need not involve "legality," because in its very essence, law is unfit for God's love and his ultimate relationship to humanity. If anything, law is that which must be transcended.

How have we come to this place? I could start my narrative in several places, but I will begin with two cases of justice in relation to the Holocaust. The first one is, or should be, quite well known. It is the case of Adolf Eichmann, the chief logistical "officer" of the Nazi Final Solution, entrusted with the organization of transporting Jews to the Nazi concentration camps. Captured in Argentina, Eichmann was then tried in Jerusalem, in a trial that was to become emblematic for the very nature of law and our duty to obey it. The second case is much more recent. It involves John Demjanjuk, a former Ukrainian member of the Soviet Army, captured and imprisoned by the Germans. Demjanjuk was then offered the opportunity to become a concentration camp guard, which he duly accepted. After a failed trial in Jerusalem (he was accused of being the famed guard Ivan the Terrible), he was extradited from the United States to Germany, where he was put on trial for being an accessory to the murder of some 28,000 Jews at Sobibor.

Eichmann was a chief bureaucrat, not a lawmaker, nor a leader. Demjanjuk, it might be said, was at the other end of the extermination apparatus. Both of them, as they strenuously argued, were only carrying out orders, obeying the law, as it were. In her detailed report and reflection on Eichmann's trial, Hannah Arendt comments, "As he told the police and the court over and over again; he not only obeyed orders, he also obeyed the law."[36] Demjanjuk's de-

---

36. Hannah Arendt, *Eichmann in Jerusalem: A Report on the Banality of Evil* (New York: Penguin, 2006), 135.

fense was, predictably, similar. He had no choice. He was a prisoner of war, and he took a course of action that would make his life easier. His choices were constrained to such a degree that this was the only open option.

Neither of these defenses was ultimately successful. But what is so interesting about these cases is that they were not only trials of two individuals but also an indictment of a whole system of law as well, moreover an indictment of a whole legal philosophy (legal positivism). Both of these cases, Eichmann's in particular, bring out the way in which law bends desire. As Foucault would say, they both demonstrate the way in which law is part of a disciplinary structure of biopower. Arendt reflects that "the sad and very uncomfortable truth of the matter probably was that it was not his fanaticism but his very conscience that prompted Eichmann to adopt his uncompromising attitude."[37] He saw himself as being bound by duty to obey the law of the land, which is the law of the führer. Arendt reflects on this situation, where law can create a moral obligation that reverses the natural inclinations of law-abiding citizens:

> And just as the law in civilized countries assumes that the voice of conscience tells everybody "Thou shalt not kill," even though men's natural desires and inclinations may at times be murderous, so the law of Hitler's land demanded that the voice of conscience tell everybody "Thou shalt kill," although the organizers of the massacres knew full well that murder is against the normal desires and inclinations of most people. Evil in the Third Reich had lost the quality by which most people recognize it—the quality of temptation. Many Germans and many Nazis, probably an overwhelming majority of them, must have been tempted *not* to murder, not to rob, not to let their neighbors go off to their doom (for that the Jews were transported to their doom they knew, of course, even though many of them may not have known the gruesome details), and not to become accomplices in all these crimes by benefitting from them. But, God knows, they had learned how to resist temptation.[38]

The point is not that Eichmann was not responsible for his crimes. But to understand the nature of his responsibility, one needs also to understand the nature of his "predicament." Also noteworthy is the fact that it was the whole legality of a system of government that was put into question. Eichmann was, after all, conducting his business according to the laws of the country. In the name of what was he now being sentenced? Some will argue that it is in the name of a new legality, the law of the victor.

37. Ibid., 146.
38. Ibid., 150.

At least with respect to the Demjanjuk case, several commentators heralded the sentence as a victory and return of natural law. According to these, what plays out in trials such as these is the conflict between "natural law" and "legal positivism." Indeed, another writer pointed out that Demjanjuk's conviction was possible precisely at the time when a new generation of German judges finally replaced an older generation standing under the influence of legal positivism.

But what is legal positivism? According to John Austin's definition, "A law is a command which obliges a person or persons. But, as contradistinguished or opposed to an occasional or particular command, a law is a command which obliges a person or persons, and obliges generally to acts of forbearance of a class. In language more popular but less distinct and precise, a law is a command which obliges a person or persons to a course of conduct. Laws and other commands are said to proceed from superiors, and to bind and oblige inferiors."[39] The distinguishing mark of positivism is that it defines law as that set of rules which proceeds from superiors, under certain conditions, and which as a sheer result of this fact incur a duty to obey upon the inferiors.

As we saw in the last chapter, legal positivism distinguishes law from morality. It is the quintessential legal philosophy of modernity and condemns natural law theory for failing to distinguish between law as it ought to be from law as it is. It is not that legal positivists like Jeremy Bentham and John Austin disregarded the relation between the two types of laws, but they were essentially pragmatists who wanted to clearly establish the very nature of law. Thus they were also essentialists to a certain extent. They argued that law has an essence, that there are some things that are improperly called laws.[40] As we saw with Austin, there are certain *formal* conditions for a command to become a law. These conditions have nothing to do with the morality of the particular statute. As H. L. A. Hart points out, "What both Bentham and Austin were anxious to assert were the following two simple things: first, in the absence of an expressed constitutional or legal provision, it could not follow from the mere fact that a rule violated standards of morality that it was not a rule of law; and, conversely, it could not follow from the mere fact that a rule was morally desirable that it was a rule of law."[41]

The upshot of this formalism was that law became dissociated from morality and thus from its roots in social and historical life. It became a putatively objective formality, neutral between ends and desires. The modern illusion is that the sheer application of this form ensures overall fairness. However, what

39. Austin, "A Positivist Conception of Law," in *Philosophy of Law*, 5th ed., ed. Joel Feinberg and Hyman Gross (Belmont: Wadsworth, 1995), 36.
40. See Austin's examples in ibid., 37–38.
41. H. L. A. Hart, "Positivism and the Separation of Law and Morals," *Harvard Law Review* 71 (1958): 593–629 (here 599).

the Second World War demonstrated was that law is not necessarily neutral between ends. The Nazi legal system actively promoted the Holocaust. On the one hand, one might argue that this is an exception that should not reflect negatively on all legal systems. On the other hand, the thinkers we are discussing as central to postmodern thought argue that, even though the violence of other legal systems may not be as blatant as the Shoah, these systems are still predicated on exclusion, and it is precisely this exclusion that constitutes a wrong in itself. It should not be thought, however, that postmodern philosophers advocate anything like a return to natural law when they critique legal positivism. The sheer formality of law is not to be replaced with a natural, theological vision of the good, but with a philosophy of alterity.

As Hart observes, as early as 1958 the tide was rapidly turning away from legal positivism:

> At the present time in this country [USA] and to a lesser extent in England, this separation between law and morals is held to be superficial and wrong. Some critics have thought that it blinds men to the true nature of law and its roots in social life. Others have thought it not only intellectually misleading but corrupting in practice, at its worst apt to weaken resistance to state tyranny or absolutism, and at its best apt to bring law into disrespect.[42]

Unknown to Hart at the time, he was noticing the first signs of a shift in legal thinking toward postmodernity.

Gustav Radbruch was one of the most influential legal scholars in both prewar and postwar Germany. Initially a legal positivist and a relativist, Radbruch became utterly disenchanted with positivism in light of his experience of the war. In his earlier positivist phase, he would say, "I would rather commit injustice than stand disorder." Yet he came to affirm that "where justice is not even striven for, where equality, which is the core of justice, is constantly denied in the enactment of positive law, there the law is not only 'unjust law,' but [also] lacks the nature of law altogether."[43] The first statement is positivist in that he considers one to have a duty to law irrespective of the morality of the law. The second reinserts morality into the very nature of law, as one of its conditions of legality.

Let us briefly return to the Eichmann and Demjanjuk cases. These were not, by far, the only such trials.[44] Questions appear: In the name of which law

---

42. Ibid., 594–95.

43. Quoted in Julius Stone, *Human Law and Human Justice* (Stanford, CA: Stanford University Press, 1965), 249.

44. Lon L. Fuller gives further such post-war examples in "Positivism and Fidelity to Law—A Reply to Professor Hart," in Feinberg and Gross, *Philosophy of Law*, 80–84.

was Eichmann sentenced? In the name of a natural law? In the name of the law of the victor? If we are agreed on the failure of legal positivism, what is the way forward? Is there a positive, constructive way forward?

Disenchantment with the modern legal system is not restricted to these cases. Helen M. Stacy points out that modern jurisprudence was predicated on the idea of the law as being autonomous alongside society and its values. It was also dependent on the idea of the autonomous individual. We have already discussed the postmodern critique of both these ideas. Stacy describes the new direction of law in postmodernity: "Under the rubric of sociological jurisprudence, legal institutions were criticized for their hierarchy, their arcane terminology and their alienating effects."[45] She further summarizes the new critical direction:

> Thus law has commenced its turn into postmodernism. Deconstruction and the social construction analysis revealed that the dominant modes of thought in the English-speaking Western jurisdictions are based upon a hierarchy that subordinates women to men, that places the colonial population over the indigenous population and/or the white over the coloured population, the affluent over the poor, the employed over the unemployed. In legal institutions, it emphasizes the effect of the hierarchy of judges and lawyers over plaintiffs and defendants.[46]

Commenting on the seminal work of James Boyd White, the authors Joseph Dellapena and Kathleen Farrell point out what appears to be a consensus with regard to the sorry state of the judiciary:

> In discussing law, many people have complained that lawyers do not mediate relationships in order to build or maintain community, but rather have complicated even the most basic human transactions for personal gain. Many have also expressed amazement at the inability of courts to employ common sense solutions to fairly straightforward problems. Many have also been dismayed at what they see as the judicial perpetuation of injustice to blind adherence to questionable readings of legal text or context.[47]

To summarize these points so far: there seems to be a prevailing cultural attitude of distrust regarding the justice of law, in particular its ability to mediate relationships between particular individuals in a fragmented world. In what

---

45. Helen Stacy, *Postmodernism and Law: Jurisprudence in a Fragmenting World* (Aldershot: Ashgate, 2001), 51.

46. Ibid., 57.

47. Joseph W. Dellapena and Kathleen Farrell, "Law and the Language of Community: On the Contributions of James Boyd White," *Rhetoric Society Quarterly* 21, no. 3 (1991): 38–58 (here 42).

follows I introduce Foucault's, Lévinas's, and Derrida's thinking about law and justice in particular.

Michel Foucault (1926–84)

Law, according to Foucault, is quite clearly a form of power that forms legal subjects. As pointed out, Foucault no longer treats sovereignty as localized or identified with a sovereign king. Rather, power is dissipated, diffused throughout society and culture. This power is also always linked with knowledge. There is no such thing as disinterested knowledge. According to Foucault, law is precisely the instrument that mediates the activity of power on its subjects. As Stacy comments, "Foucault argued that law is pivotal in aiding 'disciplinary technologies' to suppress discourses (i.e., collections of statements, practices, classificatory scheme and objects of analysis) that are at variance with the larger 'juridico-discursive' discourse that police individuals' behavior by turning them into docile subjects."[48]

Law, in colluding with power in this way, has no way of legitimizing itself by appeal to an object (nature, for instance) that is outside its discipline. Indeed, as Joseph Rouse points out, Foucault is characterized by a "strong nominalism in the human sciences: the types of objects in their domains were not already demarcated, but came into existence only contemporaneous with the discursive formations that made it possible to talk about them."[49] This is the same claim we will hear from Derrida: there is nothing outside of the text. Law is pure power.

In relation to the Eichmann and Demjanjuk cases, this equation of law with power would seem to support the cynical conclusion that what justifies the sentence in these cases is another power, just as arbitrary. Foucault's pessimism and cynicism is indicative of at least one of the trajectories of postmodern ethical reflection. Once the metanarrative of a natural end, a common good, has been abandoned, one alternative is to retreat into a "politics of difference," where truths are local and untranslatable. The difficulty in this scenario is to understand how community and relationships can still be sustained if there is no truth independent of its regime. Foucault's position is by no means normative for everything that might be called postmodern, but it is certainly one influential proposal, even though it succeeds in its critique more than in its positive reconstruction. As a deconstruction, it certainly illustrates the contemporary disenchantment with the legal system as oppressive rather than

48. Stacy, *Postmodernism and Law*, 63.
49. Joseph Rouse, "Power/Knowledge," in *The Cambridge Companion to Foucault*, 2nd ed. (Cambridge: Cambridge University Press, 2005), 96.

liberating. As Foucault notes, the free spaces the law is supposed to protect have already been filled by other forms of power. Thus laws are no longer predominantly applied to prevent harmful transgressions but to dispose more efficiently the relations between members of the population.[50]

To summarize Foucault's largely negative stance: law is neither a representation of nature nor a pure and neutral formality, but is itself a form of power, enforcing distinctions, oppositions, and hierarchies that are ultimately violent.

Emmanuel Lévinas (1906–95)

Where Foucault is more inclined to unmask the false pretenses of the law, Lévinas is concerned with a positive discussion of justice. Yet Lévinas accepts the fundamental premise that knowledge, representation, and metaphysics constitute a discourse that is inimical to justice as such. He untangles justice from law: "Justice . . . is not a natural and anonymous legality governing the human masses, from which is derived a technique of social equilibrium, placing in harmony the antagonistic and blind forces through transitory cruelties and violence, a state delivered over to its own necessities that it is impossible to justify."[51] The application of such a blind calculus is always injurious to the Other's otherness.

Sometimes Lévinas contrasts the justice of law, of lex talionis for instance, with ethics. On the one hand, the demands of justice are rational, ordered, and always cruel. They admit of no interruption. On the other hand, there is something that rises above this logic of retribution, which Lévinas calls the ethical. Forgiveness and mercy are its manifestations. The ethical is that which arises from the encounter with the Other. Prior to this encounter, there is no knowledge, no representation, on which the ethical might be dependent. The ethical is a spontaneous interruption of the logic of exchange that characterizes lawful relationships between persons. What we see here in Lévinas is an attempt to describe a moment that, by its definition, is entirely spontaneous; it does not rest on a calculation, and it is impossible to capture by concepts.

Yet Lévinas does not stop here. He does not see justice and the ethical as being simple opposites. On the contrary, he argues, justice itself originates in the proximity of the Other. It is in the ethical encounter that I am summoned, exposed, made uncomfortable by the presence of the Other. Out of this pure

50. See Victor Tadros, "Between Governance and Discipline: The Law and Michel Foucault," *Oxford Journal of Legal Studies* 18, no. 1 (1998): 75–103.
51. Emmanuel Lévinas, "Peace and Proximity," in *Emmanuel Lévinas: Basic Philosophical Writings*, ed. Adriaan Theodoor Peperzak, Simon Critchley, and Roberto Bernasconi (Bloomington: Indiana University Press, 1996), 169.

proximity, mercy and forgiveness spring. As I am faced with the Other, I desire to forgive and accept. But this desire does not spring from any "reason." It is a pure gift.

However, since my encounter with the Other always involves a third, as I pointed out in my discussion of agency above, this forgiveness and mercy needs to be tempered. A calculation will have to intervene. Thus justice as embodied in law becomes inescapable. But for Lévinas, justice as embodied in law does not precede the encounter with the transcendence of the Other, defining it, constructing this encounter; thus justice is secondary and instrumental to ethics. While Lévinas does not engage the debate about the duty to obey the law, it is not hard to imagine him taking Radbruch's line: should this law do violence to the Other, it loses its character as law.

For Lévinas, then, justice requires the law. Yet ideal justice is always distinct from the partial justice the law administers. Since the law is necessarily abstract, legal judgment requires the consideration of particular circumstances. As Marty Slaughter comments, "Law therefore compares what ethically speaking is incomparable—the singular, absolute otherness that is found in the ethical encounter—and in so doing the juridical order 'negates mercy.' It does not bring the singular, unique individual before it, but rather an abstraction. The singular individual is outside of the time of narrative, category, and representation. Justice never has the 'now' of the Other before it."[52]

Despite this realism with regard to law, Lévinas makes two important claims about law and justice. First, he does not share Foucault's cynicism with regard to the ability of law to dispense justice. Second, he denies the opposition between justice and forgiveness and mercy. Both justice and forgiveness and mercy spring from the ethical situation of encounter with the Other. They both respond before the tribunal of the Other, or rather the community of Others, not any universal and abstract law.

Jacques Derrida (1930–2004)

Stacy notes that "Derrida's critique of subject-centered reason aroused great suspicion in Anglo-American law schools during the 1980s."[53] His affirmation of the ubiquity of texts, that there is no reality outside of texts, has been greatly misinterpreted. His work is still regarded with much suspicion in departments of analytic philosophy, to say nothing of theological seminaries. One does not have to agree with Derrida to be appalled at the caricatures of his work.

52. Marty Slaughter, "Lévinas, Mercy, and the Middle Ages," in *Lévinas, Law, Politics*, ed. Marinos Diamantides (London: Routledge, 2007), 57.
53. Stacy, *Postmodernism and Law*, 89.

Derrida makes several contributions to postmodern jurisprudence. Like Foucault, and to a certain extent like Lévinas, his contributions are largely negative.

First, Derrida rehearses Foucault's point about the violent origins of law. In his essay "The Force of Law: The 'Mystical Foundations of Authority,'" he scathingly critiques modern legal thought. He concludes that (1) "the ultimate founding moment or origin of law" is only a *coup de force*, neither just nor unjust; (2) more positively, there is no justice without the experience of the aporia. The second point in fact echoes Lévinas's dialectic between law and justice:

> To address oneself to the other in the language of the other is, it seems, the condition of all possible justice, but apparently, in all rigor, it is not only impossible (since I cannot speak the language of the other except to the extent that I appropriate it and assimilate it according to the law of an implicit third) but even excluded by justice as law (droit), inasmuch as justice as right seems to imply an element of universality, the appeal to a third party, who suspends the unilaterality or singularity of the idioms.[54]

Justice is "infinite, incalculable, rebellious to rule and foreign to symmetry, heterogeneous, heterotrophic," while law is "legitimacy or legality, stabilizable and statutory, calculable, a system of regulated and coded prescriptions."[55] Derrida follows Lévinas in extricating ideal justice from any calculation. He speaks of it in terms of gift: "This 'idea of justice' seems to me to be irreducible in its affirmative character, in its demand of gift without exchange, without circulation, without recognition or gratitude, without economic circularity, without calculation and without rules, without reason and without rationality." One might as well speak about it as "madness." Elsewhere he speaks about this ideal of justice in terms of unconditional hospitality, a hospitality not conditional on the foreigner first identifying himself or herself. This thought continues Lévinas's idea that ethics does not require metaphysics, but transcends it. For Derrida, this "implies that you don't ask the other, the newcomer, the guest, to give anything back, or even to identify himself or herself. Even if the other deprives you of your mastery of your home, you have to accept this."[56]

Law, in its essence, colonizes the other with the garrison of thought. It inscribes the Other within a language. Therefore it deprives the other of his or

---

54. Jacques Derrida, "Force of Law: The 'Mystical Foundation of Authority,'" *Cardozo Law Review* 11, no. 5 (1990): 919–1045 (here 949).

55. Ibid., 959.

56. Jacques Derrida, "Hospitality, Justice, and Responsibility: A Dialogue with Jacques Derrida," in *Questioning Ethics: Contemporary Debates in Philosophy*, ed. Richard Kearney and Mark Dooley (New York: Routledge, 1999), 70.

her alterity. Authentic ethical and just relationships between selves, according to Derrida, transcend law. In fact, the transcendence of law is precisely deconstruction. Derrida identifies justice with deconstruction: the deconstruction of law and legal concepts occurs "in the name of justice: justice requires the law. So justice is not simply outside the law, it is something which transcends the law, but which at the same time requires the law."[57] In identifying deconstruction with justice, Derrida does not claim that this particular deconstructive practice is just but that the very project and direction of deconstruction coincides with justice. Deconstruction aims at justice, in exposing the limitations of law.

What are the consequences of deconstruction for jurisprudence? Stacy is quite optimistic: "The aim in legal philosophy now is to develop a jurisprudence that does not have the potentially disastrous political consequences that a crude reading of postmodernism might suggest, and which also avoids the universalizing assumptions of traditional modern thought."[58] While critics are unanimous that Derrida begins to move in a more constructive direction, there is still a consensus that the actual legal consequences of this kind of philosophy have not yet been implemented. It is undeniable that there is a general feeling of dissatisfaction (in theory) with the blind formalism of the judicial process. Law and legal process are widely perceived as alienating, fragmenting, corrupt. Law has indeed lost its aura and credibility. This is not to say that centripetal forces of legal conservatism are not there. I have not attempted to paint a comprehensive picture of the legal field, but only to illustrate a significant reaction that I think captures a broad cultural sentiment. I will argue that this sentiment is also very much at work in contemporary theologies of the atonement.

Charles Taylor expresses worry with regard to Foucault's program, which applies to our discussion of what justifies the sentencing of Eichmann and Demjanjuk. Taylor fears that, according to Foucault, "liberation in the name of 'truth' could only be the substitution of another system of power for this one."[59] By denying the adequacy of representation, as mediating relationships between selves, are we not resigning ourselves to a universal will to power after all? Can an ontology of violence, to use John Milbank's term, sustain the concept of justice? As we saw, some postcolonial writers express similar reservations: can we make sense of the bonds that unite us into communities apart from a set of general concepts? Does law, after all, retain a place? The best place to enter this discussion is with the apostle Paul.

57. Ibid., 72–73.
58. Stacy, *Postmodernism and Law*, 89.
59. Charles Taylor, "Foucault on Freedom and Truth," in *Foucault: A Critical Reader*, ed. David C. Hoy (Oxford: Blackwell, 1991).

Postmodern Visions of the Cross

René Girard (1923–)

The work of French anthropologist and sociologist René Girard provides a novel interpretation of the atonement with substantial appeal to theologians wishing to disentangle God from the patent violence of the cross, but more importantly, from the divine violence implied in the Jewish sacrificial system. Like other atonement theories we are discussing in this chapter, one of its fundamental premises is that the law cannot serve as the final metaphysical background for God's dealings with humanity. Girard's particular critique of the law is actually a critique of culture in general, with the law as an inevitable aspect of all cultures. His thesis, which we shall unpack in this section, is that law, the judicial system, is an inherently but covertly violent attempt to hold in check a more generalized and self-destructive violence of all against all.

Girard does not ground his theory in something like Foucault's social and political critique of "power," although there is much similarity between the two Frenchmen on that level. His starting point is what one may call a "paleontology of desire." He asks, How do humans arrive at violence? What do they do to prevent it? This will be a purely anthropological and sociological account conducted at the level of immanence, without any account for transcendence. There are no personal malevolent forces to explain (and solve) the human predicament. Any account of it has to make sense in purely immanent terms.

Desire, according to Girard, is *mimetic*. We desire certain objects because we see others desiring the same objects and wish to imitate them. A child suddenly desires to play with a neglected toy when he or she sees a sibling or friend playing with it. But this mimesis works at higher levels of culture as well. Fashion is one such example. Although originality is prized to some extent, it is only fashionably acceptable if it respects certain rules, a certain uniformity. We like to imitate people whom we admire. This desire for imitation is precisely what makes society possible.

Notice how this account of desire is antitheological: we do not desire things because they may be inherently desirable. Beauty and value may be taken as compliments we pay to things because we first see them as pursued by people we admire. There must really be something worthwhile in *that* object if *this* person desires it. Therefore I will desire it as well. This brings us to the realization that mimetic desire inevitably leads to competition and thus to violence. Given the scarcity of goods that people desire, competition ensues, threatening what Girard has called the "violence of all against all."

Since there are no inherently desirable things, neither are there inherently repugnant objects. People imitate each other equally in their perversions. It is not only desire-for but also desire-against that we copy from our models.

Girard does not probe beyond this observation of the mimetic character of desire. There is no metaphysical account of human nature, or an attempt to give an explanation of our being "wired" in this particular way. He simply takes it as an element of our human nature, independently of any evaluation. From a theological standpoint, one could therefore ask whether it might be precisely this indiscriminate desire, this fundamentally animalic conditioning, that is "sin." Not on Girard's account. "Sin" is a valuation that can only characterize a cultured human nature. Sin cannot be a description of a "natural" human condition, such as a fallen human nature. Instead, sin refers to a problematic cultural response to violence, as we shall see.

As this violence generated by mimetic competition threatens to engulf the whole community, ways of curbing it have to be found. One of Girard's important contributions to anthropology is his analysis of the scapegoating mechanism. He scoffs at Hobbes's solution of social contract. As Michael Kirwan comments, "Girard is scornful of the idea that a group of people who are at each other's throats would have the capacity, *precisely at the moment when the conflict is at its most intense*, to cease hostilities and recognize that they need to work out a social contract."[60] Rather, what prevents a community from self-destruction is its ability to channel violence toward a single victim, or a limited number of victims. The selected victim is usually the stranger, the foreigner, the weird, someone who generates sufficient antipathy to galvanize the community against her. She is certainly not blameless, though the crime she is charged with (the attempted destruction of the community) is too sinister to be credible. Many victims throughout history have suffered this fate: the Christians blamed for the burning of Rome, Jews accused of undermining the German interwar economy, illegal immigrants for the state of the American job market and even economy, and so on.

Once the (typically voiceless) victim is finally murdered, the community discovers a renewed sense of unity. The trouble with scapegoating, Girard notes, is that it actually works. Communities turn away from their internecine anger and find ways to continue their common habitation. Moreover, they will now treat the murdered and voiceless victim as quasi-divine: the victim is the savior of the community. This move obviously stems from a desire not only to find a "utility" for the crime but also to attenuate the guilt from it (after all, the victim was divinized and will forever be remembered by the community).

60. Michael Kirwan, *Discovering Girard* (London: Darton, Longman & Todd, 2004), 45.

Myths are also invented to dress up the barbaric crime and reinterpret it as a soteriological event.

Girard's important point is that it is precisely such a response to the threat of violence, in the form of sacrificing a scapegoat, that is the very foundation of culture. Religion is a cultural method used to reassure the people of the efficacy of scapegoating. It disguises the murder so that it will appear as a salvific, messianic event.

Clearly, what we have in Girard so far is a "depth hermeneutics," namely, an attempt to go beyond the letter of the founding myths of society and understand what it is that they are in fact concealing. The "things hidden since the foundation of the world" are sinister indeed. Culture itself is founded on horrific acts. Moreover, it reenacts such events with a certain regularity, since the "peace" obtained through the scapegoating does not last. More and more sacrifices are needed in order to maintain this costly and fragile peace.

It is important to realize that, for Girard, this scapegoating mechanism does not simply refer to ancient, primitive cultures, but characterizes our modern societies just as much, although in a slightly different way. Girard scathingly attacks the presumption that modernity has arrived at a "rational" way of dealing with conflict, in strict opposition to the "rule of vengeance" practiced by antiquity. Precisely where Hobbes understood legality as a free, unencumbered rational solution and check against violence, Girard sees in legality only a more sophisticated and efficient, but nonetheless violent, way of responding to violence. The myth that violence is the way to combat violence is still maintained even in modernity.

Let me unpack that a bit. The modern line was that primitive cultures were irrational in that they sought their victims arbitrarily. They were thus unjust because they did not correctly apportion blame. Modern systems of justice, however, assign blame where it is due, neutrally and correctly, and then administer the punishment. Modernity sees justice precisely in the abstractness, neatness, calculability, and impartiality of this system.

For Girard, the idea that the law, the legal system, is impartial and just is nothing but a myth covering another kind of violence. Just as in the case of primitive scapegoating, concealment is a necessary condition of the operation of the legal system. The law must be thought to be just, the system to be reliable. Unless that happens, anarchy threatens. Thus for Girard, there is a fundamental identity between violence, primitive vengeance, and modern legal punishment. Modern societies may appear to be more rational, but that is only because the institution of the law has been depersonalized, or transcendentalized. Law denotes an abstract institution uncorrupted by our drives and desires and thus able to administer justice: "Only the transcendental quality of the system, acknowledged by all, can assure the prevention or cure of violence."[61] The increasing "rationalization" of justice (as response to crime) entails less rather than more transparency as to its nature:

> The "curative" measures, ostensibly designed to temper the impulse toward vengeance, become increasingly mysterious in their workings as they progress in efficiency. As the focal point of the system shifts away from religion and the preventive approach is translated into judicial retribution, the aura of misunderstanding that has always formed a protective veil around the institution of sacrifice shifts as well, and becomes associated with the machinery of law.[62]

Thus the law becomes transcendent, mysterious, while the judicial system, retaining its autonomy from the political and "transcend[ing] all antagonists,"[63] is able to mete out punishment proportionately to the crime: "Modern man has long since lost his fear of reciprocal violence, which after all provides our judicial system with its structure. Because the overwhelming authority of the judiciary prevents its sentence from becoming the first step in an endless series of reprisals, we can no longer appreciate primitive man's deep-seated fear of pure, unadulterated violence."[64]

In an interesting twist, we are brought back to Aeschylus's tragedy the *Oresteia*. In many ways postmodernism returns to ancient conceptions of justice. This is also true for atonement theories, as we are currently observing. Girard notes that the primitive person was quite willing not to punish the guilty. The foundation of the legal system, which Aeschylus portrays in his tragedy, is predicated precisely on the necessity of breaking the cycle of violence. While to us turning to an innocent victim seems "perverse and idiotic," to the primitive person it was a mechanism of self-preservation. Yet, if Girard is right, it is a mistake to overstate the differences between primitive and modern people. If anything, modern humanity acquired a more sophisticated means of covering up violence. Ironically, one may quip, modernity is much more gullible with regard to its own legal myths than primitive persons ever were about their sacrificial myths.

More so, but not completely. For the "injustice of justice" is still unmasked from time to time. Moreover, "our penetration and demystification of the system necessarily coincides with the disintegration of the system."[65] This

---

61. René Girard, *Violence and the Sacred* (London: Continuum, 2005), 24.

62. Ibid., 22.

63. René Girard, *Things Hidden since the Foundation of the World* (London: Continuum, 2004), 12.

64. Girard, *Violence and the Sacred*, 28.

65. Ibid., 24–25.

brings us closer to the theology of the cross, because, according to Girard, it is precisely the Judeo-Christian tradition, and primarily the cross, that produced this exposure. In fact, our very ability to conduct such a "depth hermeneutics" of our culture and its founding myths is made possible by the revelatory event of the cross.

It would seem that Girard's generalized critique of law and sacrifice sets him squarely against the Scriptures. Nevertheless, his hermeneutics does not prioritize the apparent authorial intention of the texts that seemingly legitimize sacrifice. Rather, as S. Mark Heim argues in his thoroughly Girardian *Saved from Sacrifice*, "The Bible is engaged in a struggle over the sacred. It is a struggle waged in the substance of the texts themselves."[66] The myths surrounding sacrifice invoke the divinity in an attempt to legitimize these practices. The same appeal to a divine justification is both made and resisted in the Bible. Hermeneutically, "what is needed is an interpretive path through the problematic texts and not around them."[67]

Girard indicates that the Old Testament was already well on its way to undermining the logic of sacrifice. The victim is not voiceless, as we can see from the stories about Isaac, Job, and Joseph, and in the Psalms. (One might also add the daughter of Jephthah.) In all of these cases, the victim protests, challenges, asks, and confesses his or her innocence. There is a temporal distance between the decision to kill and its carrying out, in which the case of the victim is allowed to be made. This undermines the very logic of scapegoating because it risks upsetting the hallucinating confidence of the mob that they have the right person.

The Scriptures also graphically depict the sacrifices. Opposed to other ancient Near Eastern myths, which involved a turning away from sacrifice, "the Bible is riddled with dangerous honesty about sacrifice."[68] This makes these stories bad myths, which speak too directly and concretely, failing to sanitize the story.

Finally, the prophets critique the sacrificial system. Hosea has God saying, "For I desire mercy, not sacrifice, and acknowledgment of God rather than burnt offerings" (Hos. 6:6). The message of the prophets, in essence, is that to know God is to know the cause of the victim (Mic. 6:8). "Implicitly and explicitly they saw a direct connection between the social victim and the ritual victim." Thus, Heim continues, "if Girard is right that ritual sacrifice largely comes from our social conflicts to begin with, then the prophets are only following it back to its roots."[69]

66. Heim, *Saved from Sacrifice*, 68.
67. Ibid., 7.
68. Ibid., 65.
69. Ibid., 95.

Reading the Bible between the lines instead of privileging one implied authorial voice brings out this battle waged in the substance of the texts, a struggle over the very nature of God and the practices he condones, encourages, or legislates. If this hermeneutics is right, then Girard's skepticism with regard to law is consonant with at least a strand of biblical witness. The lex talionis (Exod. 21:24) is after all not a divine principle but the glorification of a mistaken human response to violence. In their depths, subtly, the Old Testament texts undermine these very practices, together with the idea that the best way to respond to violence is with more violence.

The culmination of this Old Testament deconstruction of sacrifice is in the passion of Jesus Christ. The cross must not be interpreted within the framework of the law, because it is that very framework that the cross implodes. It is true, the Scriptures appear to explain the cross in those very terms, but it is important to understand exactly how the cross is related to the framework. Both Girard and Heim argue that it is crucial to distinguish the will of God (in sending Jesus to the cross) from the will of the human agents of the crucifixion (Acts 3:13; 5:30). Heim argues that there is a superimposition of the divine will on the will of human agents, not in such a way as to validate their logic but so as to indict it. "Jesus didn't volunteer to get into God's justice machine. God volunteered to get into ours. God used our own sin to save us."[70]

Girard and Heim, like other postmodern writers on the atonement, really struggle with the blatant biblical language about the cross, which is quite clearly sacrificial, penal, and indeed paternalist. Those theologians who still want to claim some sort of biblical responsibility have to find ways to explain that language. Heim and Girard turn to the concepts of unmasking, revelation, exposure. Postcolonial writers will later turn to the concept of mimicry. In their own ways both attempt to find precisely what Heim calls "a way through the problematic texts."

Heim argues that such language was inevitable since our condition can only be understood in those terms. While there was nothing sacrificial about the cross,

> without the language of sacrifice, innocence, guilt, punishment, substitution, and blood, we can't tell the truth about our situation and what God does to liberate us, a truth that the cross makes available to us in a new way. With it we always run the risk of taking the diagnosis for a prescription. Sacrifice is the disease we have. Christ's death is the test result we can't ignore and at the same time an inoculation that sets loose a healing resistance. The cure is not more of the same.[71]

70. Ibid., xi.
71. Ibid., xii.

By now it should be clear that for both Girard and Heim, violence seems to be the fundamental human malady. Perhaps not violence as such, but the particular myth that the proper response to violence is "more of the same," more violence. Jesus exposes that myth by appearing as the undoubtedly innocent victim.

Girard seems to incline more closely toward something resembling a moral example theory. Jesus's seminal achievement was to *reveal* the violent nature of our culture. Girard seems to assume that it is sufficient for humans to be made aware of this, and then to follow Jesus's example. On this account, Jesus uses the very same mimetic mechanisms in order to inspire a different, nonviolent, mimesis. However, since there is nothing inherently desirable, what will ensure that we won't change our model, reverting to imitation of, say, Bonnie and Clyde? On Girard's account, Jesus leaves the fundamental mimetic structure of our "human nature" unaffected, unchanged. It would seem that the only substantially attractive thing about Jesus would be our impulse for self-preservation, which might calculate that it is more profitable (because more peaceable) for society as a whole to follow Jesus. Desiring Christ, then, would be an instance of the categorical imperative.

Heim understands, better than Girard, that Christ's example cannot be just another offer on the shelf of products. There must be something objectively compelling about this Christ. We have seen moral example theorists struggling to account for this surplus. What is this magnetic pull? James Alison, in *The Joy of Being Wrong*, writes about the "pull" of Christ's "non-reciprocation": "This surprising non-reciprocation is what pulls the other person experiencing it out of the reciprocating mode of being and enables that person to begin to receive and then transmit love as something simply given."[72] Alison also talks in terms of the "new intelligence" that Christ makes available to us through his resurrection.

Heim prefers to talk about this surplus in terms of Christ's creating a new community. Nevertheless, neither Heim nor Alison nor Girard escapes a purely immanentist logic. God simply helps us understand a long-standing delusion, that violence heals violence. He does this by demonstrating that the mechanism leads to the murder of innocent victims. But from a theological standpoint, Girard's account of desire is utterly inadequate. While it is impossible to fully engage in this complicated discussion, I will make a couple of points.

First, the scapegoat theory of the atonement does not seem to solve the more fundamental problem that seems to me to be the indiscriminate and

72. James Alison, *The Joy of Being Wrong: Original Sin through Easter Eyes* (New York: Crossroad, 1998), 76.

disoriented nature of human desire. What compels us to desire utterly worthless things and enter into raging conflicts over minutiae? Perhaps Girard does not think it important to answer this question because for him desire seems to be precultural or prevalue. In other words, desire as such is morally neutral. But even if desire were morally neutral, it stems from a problematic inclination in human nature. Girard's variant of the moral example theory provides no solution to this problem. It may well be that law, culture, and the whole symbolic order do merely provide one possible actualization of this first nature. The law demonstrates the sinful orientation of human beings. It is not so much the law that is corrupt, or the culture, but the symbolic order that is problematic because it instantiates a primary human nature, which is fallen.

Second, what about the desire for justice? Admittedly, Girard is tentative when it comes to his positive vision for culture and society. Can we positively live together without some kind of law, unjust as it may be? What shall we do about wrongdoing? Gratuitous love and consistent nonreciprocation, together with Derrida's unlimited hospitality, not only seem like imprudent courses of action in a world still riddled with evil, but also fail to account for our desire for retribution. It may be that this desire is purely mimetic and can therefore be "unlearned." Nevertheless, while sometimes just retribution masks vengeance, one ought not lump them together, as Girard does. The legal system's occasional scapegoating, miscarriages of justice, and corruption ought not to be taken as an incrimination of the system as a whole. Just as the law brings out our basest desires, so it often embodies our most noble inclinations.

In other words, it may well be that our desire for retribution is not simply mimetic but is one of those "valuable desires" that cannot and ought not be tamed.

John Milbank (1952–)

The late modern critiques of law and of the morality of punishment find a consistent echo in Milbank's work. Milbank portrays the law, whether human or Mosaic, as one of the powers that must be overcome. Echoing the work of G. B. Caird (as well as Alain Badiou), he writes that "laws are many and (Gal. 4:9) derive, not from God but from diverse (and *weak*) powers of the air, although their operation is permitted by God (Gal. 3:19)."[73] Law is thus one of the enemies that has to be abolished (Eph. 2:15). Milbank associates this particular enemy with the quintessential sin, which is violence, enmity,

---

73. John Milbank, "Can Morality Be Christian?," in *The Word Made Strange: Theology, Language, and Culture* (Oxford: Blackwell, 1997), 227.

exclusion, again falling in line with the postmodern diagnostic of the human predicament.

One of the fundamental failures of the law is that it deals at a very high level of generality and abstraction. This fundamentally postmodern critique of law, tied as it is to a critique of metaphysics and epistemology in general, ought to be familiar to the reader by now. As will be noted, Milbank does not reject metaphysics wholesale, only its pretentions at giving an objective and neutral description of the structure of reality. Nevertheless, he agrees with the critique of all law as violent. He makes at least two points about this generality, both of which are grounded in theological imagination, not simply in philosophical critique of "law."

First, there is a link between the generality of law and death (Ezra 7:26). He argues that "such generality is only required because of the prior assumption of external threat, internal weakness, death and scarcity. The eternal demand for uniformity is paradoxically an emergency measure to sustain a unity of a thoroughly abstract kind."[74] Law is predicated on the assumption of a prior (and ontological) violence. It assumes that the individuals who form society are in necessary relations of rivalry and competition, which risk degenerating into an all-out conflict of all against all. Law as such is required as an external-ity to this conflict, as a way of preventing it or managing it (Gal. 3:19). Law proposes to restrain the natural animality of human beings.

This restraint, however, can only operate by making stringent demands of the individuals it attempts to manage. In effect, if desire sets individuals against each other, it is precisely desire that has to be quenched. But this would amount to the destruction of the individual as such. It is precisely for this reason that the demands of the law are impossible to meet. "The abstractness of the law ensures that we will never have sufficiently accorded to its demand which can always be more perfectly embodied. We are here to *give up* to a degree our concrete desires for possessions, other people, self-expression and so forth, and this giving up being defined as running against the grain, and as for the sake of an abstract principle, not a concrete benefit, can never, in the nature of things, be complete."[75] The law is predicated on, and leads to, death. Death is the very nature of the law.

A picture is beginning to emerge according to which law is the very prob-lem. "The letters always threaten us, they require the death of ourselves, and abstract impersonal justice must always have its real truth in concrete revenge carried out by the threatened, established interests. In consequence, as Paul

---

74. Ibid., 226. This does not seem to fit with Paul's logic. For Paul, law is prior to sin. See Rom. 7:13; but also 5:13.

75. Ibid., 227.

puts it in Galatians (3:10–13), to be under the law is to be under a curse; to remain in the place of curse impurity, and to have the threat of further slander hanging over our heads." Such are the requirements of the law. God cannot and does not act according to these requirements, but moves to destroy them.

The threat of natural, animal violence is precisely the myth that law requires in order to sustain itself: "Every legality has always claimed validity by virtue of its keeping at bay an essentially imaginary chaos."[76] Against Girard, sacrifices need not be the founding order but precisely the "mechanisms by which a hierarchy sustains itself."[77] Thus law is a massive deception complicit with death and the destruction of self. The implacable logic of exchange that it demands is itself destructive of life, demanding more than anyone could ever offer.

Milbank makes a second point about the generality of law. He continues the idea that laws, as manifold, derive from the diverse powers of the air and concludes that "legality therefore, even Jewish, is *polytheist* and not monotheist, because *not diverse enough*—not absolutely divine and so absolutely many-in-one."[78] The Trinity founds Christian universality, which preserves the particularity of identity without subsuming it under the category of law. Legality is polytheistic in that it presupposes an ontology of mutually competing gods, values, and individuals that needs to be restrained. Christianity, however, transcends even morality, if by morality we understand obedience to general principles. Any such generality is deathly. The resurrection "restores no moral order, but absolutely ruins the possibility of any moral order whatsoever, . . . any reactive moral order, which presupposes the absoluteness of death." Christianity is another city, whose civility is mediated through a different logic from that of compulsion, restraint, and exclusion.

Girard gets some of this right, but Milbank suggests two fundamental problems in his theory. The first has to do with his theory of religion, which Milbank labels as positivist. Religion "secures" society; it makes possible its cohesiveness. In other words, religion has a purely social function. It masks the founding societal violence. Girard can only argue the social function of religion, however, by assuming that all desire is mimetic. Milbank points out that this is a distinctly modern idea. Thus Girard invokes a modern concept to legitimize the notion of an egalitarian primeval society that only at a later point invented religion to masks its conflicts. But why should a state of original equality be more "natural" than a "primordial hierarchical society, in which

---

76. John Milbank, *Theology and Social Theory: Beyond Secular Reason* [hereafter *TST*] (Oxford: Blackwell, 1993), 398.
77. Ibid., 397.
78. Milbank, "Can Morality Be Christian?," 227–28.

certain positions and values were regarded as objectively more important and desirable than others"?[79] Milbank's larger religious point seems to be that "legality" is not a secondary, cultural, as opposed to natural, phenomenon but that it is part of the very structure of the primeval social world. If the very foundation of culture is violent, Girard has denied himself any possible alternative culture of nonviolence. His theory of religion and culture is largely negative, providing no political alternative.

This brings us to the Milbank's second critique of Girard, which is christological. We also, therefore, come to Milbank's positive contribution to atonement theology. Girard's pessimism with regard to culture also translates into a failure to do justice to the "kingdom"' component of Jesus's identity. The reader will hopefully forgive me for indulging in a longer (and typically dense) quote from Milbank:

> In fact, given Girard's identification of culture with a mimetic desire, and denial of the possibility of an objective desire or a benign eros, it is difficult to see what "the kingdom" could really amount to, other than the negative gesture of refusal of desire, along with all cultural difference. Girard does not, in fact, really present us with a theology of two cities, but instead with a story of one city, and its final rejection by a unique individual. This means that while his metanarrative does, indeed, have politically critical implications, these are too undiscriminating, because every culture is automatically sacrificial and "bad."[80]

Let me try to translate some of that. According to Milbank's ultimate proposal, Christianity is the foundation of a city, a kingdom, in which some things are inherently desirable (God, for example). These desires, however, although constituting a hierarchy, and thus a culture, need not lead to violence. Violence is bred precisely by the "mythos," which suggests that difference must be held in check. On the contrary, under an ontology of peace, differences peacefully coexist in a harmony where the individual is neither swallowed up into "totality" nor has to aggressively defend himself or herself against others. Such a society was inaugurated by Jesus. This is precisely what the idea of kingdom refers to. And it is precisely what Girard fails to notice. This new society is not predicated on death. Ethical coexistence does not require the denial of the self (à la Lévinas) but is sustained by a love that overflows from the self toward the other, as gift.

---

79. Milbank, *TST*, 394. Milbank critiques Girard for too readily mixing exclusion with sacrifice. Milbank is more inclined to accept a certain kind of exclusion, as exteriority to the new city of God, but deny the cult of sacrifice. He thinks that primordial hierarchical societies are structurally exclusionary, though not necessarily sacrificial.

80. Ibid., 395.

How are we to understand Christ's ministry and identity? In what follows I will set out the main elements of Milbank's theology of the atonement.

First, Milbank rejects the "cultic" interpretation of Christ's death. Since law is not the creation of God, but precisely that which obstructs the conviviality of a community of peace, the cross must not be understood against that background. It is precisely the law that needed to be undone. This is not to be taken in the antinomian sense that Paul himself rejects. Rather, the Christ moment inaugurates the practice of desire for God, what Frederick Christian Bauerschmidt calls "discipleship." To put it in rather pedestrian terms: the cross inaugurates an age where our relationship to God, and to each other, is mediated not by law (which kills) but by an overabundance of desire, wrought in us by Christ. Sometimes Milbank describes this as "new law," just as Badiou talks about a "law beyond law," and as Paul speaks about the "law of Christ." "Whereas 'Moses' is just the name of the mediator of the law, 'Jesus' is the name of the new law itself, because now the word of God is found to be located, not in the dead letter of the law over against the power of bodies [an allusion to Girard's mistaken idea that law is required to keep self-assertive people in check], but in true, strong, peaceful relationships, beginning with the practice of Jesus."[81] The advent of Jesus gives the lie to the idea that our sins inflict the direct punishment of God. That is the pretense of the law. It is the law that has "the threat of further slander hanging over our heads." "Whereas, if we fail to receive divine *grace* and to be simultaneously gracious to others, still no judgment, no punishment from God follows: simply we do not receive anything any more, we are self-judged, alone, in hell."[82]

This is the familiar idea, elaborated so well by C. H. Dodd and others,[83] that divine wrath is in fact the withdrawing of the grace of God, leaving people to suffer the inertial consequences of their own sins. There is no place for violence in God, no punishment, only the stubborn offer of grace.

This brings us to the second point: if the cross is not a divine application of the law, what is its significance? While Milbank does not inscribe the cross within a divine logic of sin-punishment, neither does he simply echo the feminist evaluation of the cross as simply a tragic case of a miscarriage of justice. There is something intentional about Jesus going to the cross. I agree with some writers who associate Milbank with a moral influence theory, specifically on account of his desire to symbolize something through Jesus's death. Yet we should not think of the significance of this death as being independent

81. John Milbank, "The Name of Jesus," in *Word Made Strange*, 157.
82. Milbank, "Can Morality Be Christian?," 227.
83. C. H. Dodd, *The Epistle of Paul to the Romans* (London: Hodder and Stoughton, 1944), 22–23.

of the *practice* of forgiveness that it inaugurates: "If Christ's death is necessary in addition to the practice of forgiveness, then monstrous consequences ensue," for it would make the perpetrators of violence "the necessary agents of redemption."[84] It is hard to pin Milbank down on this question because of his reflections on the significance of historical facts. He claims that it is impossible to objectively describe historical facts apart from their unfolding consequences. This is consonant with the ecclesiological orientation of his thinking: we cannot identify Jesus apart from describing the church, the practice he founded. "Jesus figures in the New Testament primarily as a new Moses, the founder of a new or renewed law and community. It is for this reason that he cannot be given any particular content: for the founder of a new practice cannot be described in terms of that practice, unless that practice is already in existence, which is contradictory."[85]

In effect, Milbank here is almost "remythologizing" the cross, stripping it of its historical facticity and uniqueness in order to evacuate its meaning into symbol and metaphor. There is a certain recoil from the positivity of the historical event of the cross, which seems to be motivated by Milbank's desire to enlarge the scope of the atonement. He asks, "What difference does the mere *fact*—however astounding—of God's identifying with us through incarnation make to our lives, or even to our pictures of what God is like, what he wants of us? How can mere belief in the event of the atonement be uniquely transformative for the individual? . . . How can incarnation and atonement be communicated to us *not* as mere facts, but as characterizable modes of being which *intrinsically* demand these appellations?"[86]

The point is that atonement, or even the cross, does not (simply?) name a discrete historical event, but it is a cipher, a symbol for the ongoing practice of the church. Does this somehow imperil the uniqueness of Jesus? Milbank in fact argues that Girard's position effectively undermines the necessity of Jesus's atonement, since a process of disenchantment with sacrifice was already unfolding in Old Testament history. If sin is constructed as mimetic desire, then it is sufficient to be given another example (Pelagius). In Girard, sin is utterly naturalized, domesticated. There is nothing ineffable about it. If that is the case, "it becomes unclear why . . . only God incarnate can 'expose' the futile and sinful social structure of fallen humanity."[87] Milbank still believes that something like an exposure inherently compelling and transforming is necessary. But a God-man is the only one who can do the job because sin,

84. Milbank, "Name of Jesus," 159.
85. Ibid., 152.
86. Ibid., 148.
87. Ibid., 160.

as such, is "ineffable," beyond definition, except from the vantage point of Christ's new practice. We should note, though, that while Milbank does account for the "subconscious" aspect of original sin, he still remains stuck in a quasi-gnostic account whereby sin is fundamentally a problem of ignorance and blindness, and not so much of a corruption of nature.

Christ's death was the inevitable consequence of his opposition to empire. Milbank, however, goes to great lengths to minimize the logical place of the death of Christ in the Gospel narratives. He places all the emphasis on the resurrection, which founds the church and the practice of forgiveness, such that the death becomes almost an anomaly, quickly to be overtaken: "Fully to die, for St. Paul, means already and automatically to be resurrected." The death in itself turns no screws in the mechanism of the atonement. "Already, in dying, because he is God, Christ is not truly abandoned, but through apparent abandonment is finally and inexorably returned to us." And again, "Christ's earthly self-giving is but a shadow of the true eternal peaceful process in the heavenly tabernacle, and redemption consists in Christ's transition from shadow to reality."[88] Christ submits himself to the powers, who are the true object of his "sacrifice," "but only in a comical sense." "Christ is delivered over to the corrupt (or semi-corrupt?) angelic forces who are the guardians of laws and nations; yet Paul's point is that these powers are nothing, are impotent, outside the divine power which they refuse: hence such a sacrifice becomes, in Christian terms, absurd."[89]

To conclude, first, Milbank argues that the cross undoes mimetic rivalry by (1) offering an enabling sign, and (2) by the inauguration of a practice. The identity of Jesus, according to Milbank, is a collection of stories, symbols, and metaphors, which are truly compelling and enabling. Christ is not a mere example toward whom we remain neutral and whom we freely choose. No: Christ presents himself before us as truly desirable. It is essential for Milbank to suppose that human beings retain their ability to perceive that which is truly desirable. Second, Milbank confuses Christ with the community he establishes. Atonement is not an event in the past, in which we have to believe, but an ongoing practice, in which the church participates with God.

Feminist Atonement

Stephen Finlan points out a "potentially fatal contradiction in what Girard says about the cross."[90] In unmasking the human practice of scapegoating, God

88. John Milbank, *Being Reconciled: Ontology and Pardon* (London: Routledge, 2003), 100.
89. Ibid.
90. Stephen Finlan, *Problems with Atonement: The Origins of, and Controversy about, the Atonement Doctrine* (Collegeville, MN: Liturgical Press, 2005), 93.

himself seems to be making use of it. "But this may re-ensconce the scapegoat mechanism on the divine level if it implies that God did order *one* scapegoat event."[91] God in fact wills the sacrifice of Jesus as the only method by which the folly of our practices can be revealed.

Feminist theologians argue strongly that the cross cannot form any part of the divine plan. It cannot be willed by God. If God were to will the cross and the suffering of the innocent Jesus, it would make suffering in some way redemptive. But feminist writers insist that theology should not be taken to underwrite suffering of any kind. The key difficulty, then, is to understand the significance of the cross and, indeed, the possible saving significance of the cross of Christ. Here feminists diverge: some argue that the cross is devoid of saving significance, being just a tragic event, while others continue to insist that the cross as such does achieve something in terms of the atonement.

Feminists have raised several objections with respect to all the three major atonement models, sometimes indicting the whole Christian tradition with much virulence. Most feminist critiques of the atonement could be labeled "consequentialist." That is, if a particular theory can be shown to have certain "bad consequences," then the theory in itself is wrong. Traditional doctrines of the cross are seen to be misguided in that their central symbols support ideologies of manipulation, coercion, and domination. Some feminists would possibly suggest that such a formulation, which utilizes a conception of objective truth and falsity, is not appropriate and that it misconstrues their argument. Truth, the argument goes, is a matter of use, utility, application. It is not the name of a relationship that obtains between a static world awaiting representation and a language reflective of the structure of that world. Truth, in other words, is not correspondence to reality. Truthfulness, more appropriately, is a matter of conforming our language and beliefs not so much to a static world but to the ultimate divine intentions for creation.[92]

If it is the case that certain atonement theories promote images of suffering that ultimately frustrate those divine plans (which are not to be achieved in isolation from humanity at all, as I will show below), they are not truthful and should be rejected.

Joanne Carlson Brown and Rebecca Parker argue that the image of divinely sanctioned violence appears in each of the three metaphor families. In Christus Victor, suffering seems to be a necessary and even illusory prelude to the triumph of the resurrection. Christ has to appear in a lowly form so that he might suffer at the hands of Satan, who thereby oversteps his authority. For

91. Ibid.
92. See Ruether, *Sexism and God-Talk*, 19.

feminists, this upholds a model of submission to victimization. Girard himself, for all his insistence against the divine sanctioning of violence, does describe God as willing the suffering of Jesus. For feminists, one such instance of divinely sanctioned suffering and violence is too much. The ransom theory is also problematic from the perspective of the divine-human relationship. It employs images of a passive humanity and an active divinity, thus perpetuating and enforcing feelings of helplessness and lack of self-worth in women. Salvation is achieved by a force that stands over against us. Moreover, it seems to be won in a battle that does not involve us. As Brock argues, it makes Christ's victory something otherworldly and spiritual, leaving the structures of oppression intact. Together with the divine sanctioning of suffering, the underwriting of passivity and dependence are equally guilty for the current condition of women.

The moral example theory of Abelard (and modernity) is equally problematic from the standpoint of feminist critique. It builds on the assumption that only an innocent suffering victim can move us out of our condition of sin. Thus, as Brown and Parker point out,[93] victims are used for someone else's edification. One innocent individual has to suffer in order to provide an example of authentic living. This only promotes self-sacrificial lives, and it further supports the perpetrator's actions by encouraging the victim to accept the suffering because it is divine, and it may serve for the benefit of others (children, abusive husband, et al.).

From the standpoint of feminism, by far the most repugnant atonement theory is the satisfaction/penal substitution family. Whereas the two theories just mentioned simply glorify the necessary suffering or the saintly victim, penal substitution also glorifies the perpetrator. Not only does penal substitution teach that Christians become Christlike by enduring suffering like Christ, thus encouraging women to accept their condition of subjugation; but it also justifies domestic violence and abusive relationships because it teaches that the supreme example of divine love includes an element of violence. It undercuts the opposition between violence and love. If God's salvific love is conditioned by the punishment of an innocent human being, then it may well be that one's abusive husband is still loving in a way that reflects divine love. Male oppressors thus bear the image of the powerful Father. Abused women enjoy and are thankful for those moments of grace when they are spared.

Rita Nakashima Brock sees traditional atonement theology as instantiating patriarchal ideology, which produces splits. She contrasts patriarchal ideology with "erotic power," which produces creative synthesis. "Patriarchal systems

93. Joanne Carlson Brown and Rebecca Parker, "For God so Loved the World?," in *Christianity, Patriarchy, and Abuse: A Feminist Critique*, ed. Joanne Carlson Brown and Carole R. Bohn (Cleveland: Pilgrim, 1989).

split off parts of oneself: a self-righteous split divides self and world so that psychological self-examination and personal responsibility are set against the political realities of an institutionalized oppression."[94]

Feminists note several ways in which the patriarchal ideology of penal substitution underwrites domestic abuse. First, it tells women that suffering is worthy and Christlike. Moral example theories can also be seen to support this idea. Second, it tells victims that they are sinners and deserve to suffer anyway. Some feminists suggest (mistakenly) that penal substitution means their suffering at the hands of abusive husbands is a way to atone for their own sins. Third, as Brock notes, it portrays salvation as involving a spiritual realm distinct from the material realm, where the struggle for dismantling the powers of oppression takes place. In this it continues to provide an opiate for the victims, by shifting their attention in hopeful expectation of a "Platonic" salvation that does not involve the liberation of their tortured bodies. Finally, it whispers that you can do nothing for your salvation. Your worthlessness and sinfulness is, however, counterbalanced by Christ's sinlessness and power to save. With this, any remaining spark of rebellion is drowned by the tears of repentance.

The cross has become what Ruether calls "an exquisite tool for justifying domestic violence."[95] Rebecca Parker adds to the above elements the following propositions, which support the victimization of women: Love suffers; silent obedience is virtuous; suffering love is redemptive; God is closer to those who suffer; the oppressor becomes holy.

While Darby Kathleen Ray is more appreciative of traditional atonement theory, she argues that there are three issues in need of fixing. The first issue is the traditional view of sin as rebellion and pride, which brings with it guilt, blame, and self-hate. It also induces powerlessness, since self-assertion is seen as problematic. Ray suggests an enlarged notion of sin as rebellion against God's care for the world. The second problem has to do with the concept of God, which has traditionally valorized divine sovereignty at the cost of condoning human infantilism. Ray argues that, coupled with God as Father, the abusive potential of these ideas become incontrovertible. And third, it romanticizes death. The notion of self-sacrifice is hardly appropriate for victims of violence, who are never able to live up to the requirement that they be as innocent as Christ was. Here Ray makes an interesting affirmation: the requirement to forgive, she writes, often undermines true justice. One might ask, Why would sacrificial forgiveness be unjust? Because it would leave the abuser unpunished?

94. Rita Nakashima Brock, *Journeys by Heart: A Christology of Erotic Power* (Eugene, OR: Wipf & Stock, 2008), 42.

95. Rosemary Radford Ruether, *Introducing Redemption in Christian Feminism* (Sheffield: Sheffield Academic Press, 1998), 99–100.

Or because it would keep the victim within the influence of the abuser? It is unlikely that Ray understands justice as the necessary application of punishment. But is the other option (the victim leaving the relationship) clearly not a punishment? It certainly is not inflicting a physical punishment in that the wife does not physically retaliate. In many cases, though, feminist scholars lament precisely the failure of these victims to call the police, to appeal to the law, in other words, to appeal to a retributive mechanism. Yet even in cases where criminal law will not be invoked, leaving the husband can be understood as inflicting a kind of violence, perhaps even punishment, to the husband. For leaving home does indeed subject the abuser to a form of nonphysical, emotional stress.

The point of all this is that, unless we are willing to make Weaver's quite problematic distinction between a nonphysical coercion (nonviolent) and physical coercion (violent), feminists themselves seem to invoke some violent, just response to the abuse, either in the form of getting the law involved or in the form of leaving the domicile. To our question, What is the just response to crime?, it does not seem that the stakes are between violent and nonviolent responses. Any response to crime, given the nature of fallen reality, will be violent to someone.

I shall return to these matters in the final chapter. Let us now turn our attention to positive feminist proposals for the atonement. We may summarize the majority of feminist theories of the atonement in the following way: the suffering and death of Jesus have no salvific value whatsoever. It is the ministry of Jesus, conceived not independently but mutually and ecclesially, that forms the focus of his redemptive work. The cross is the predictable yet tragic response of his opponents. Not all feminist scholars affirm this view about the significance of the cross. Most, however, do.

Ruether argues that the death and resurrection of Jesus can only be seen as redemptive in the context of his struggle for life against unjust suffering and death. She insists that Jesus's death does not "effect" redemption. It is simply "paradigmatic" and exemplifies a way of life. In fact, Ruether will take up another important feminist theme on the atonement when she argues that "Christ, as redemptive person and word of God, is not to be encapsulated 'once for all' in the historical Jesus. The redemption signified by Christ is both carried on and communicated through redemptive community; this means that Christ can take on the face of every person and group and their diverse liberation strategies." This is the theme of mutuality: neither God nor Christ should be portrayed as achieving something on our behalf, or in our stead, independently of us. Precisely this binary opposition creates the "splits" that encourage submissiveness, dependence, self-loathing, and so on. The ministry of Jesus was revolutionary, and it depends on our imitation for its success. But it is not our imitation of the suffering and death that is intended. Rather, it is our imitation of Jesus's rebellion against the powers.

Brock echoes the same theme of mutuality: when Jesus suffers in our place, what is missing is "interdependence and mutuality. We are not called to embrace our own suffering." She opposes "erotic power," demonstrated in the ministry of Jesus, to "the power of hierarchy," to which Jesus himself was opposed. Erotic power, on the one hand, nurtures, restores relationships, and is characterized by vulnerability, openness, and caring. The power of hierarchy, on the other hand, demonstrates dominance, status, authority, and control over people, nature, and things.

The penal substitutionary image of the cross depicts the relationship between the Father and the Son in such a way that they "became a mirror of validation for violently dysfunctional patriarchal families, including the patriarchal 'family' of the church."[96] Feminists display a wide range of understandings of trinitarian theology. Ruether even argues that the concept of the parenthood of God has to go, since it places God over us in some kind of patriarchal relationship, even if we would speak of God as Mother. God is no longer omnipotent, according to Ruether.

This interdependence between God and the world also applies to the intratrinitarian relationships. It is inconceivable that the Father, as a self-contained subject, can act on the Son, as a self-contained subject. Mutuality entails that the Father is present in and with the Son in everything the Son does. A particular understanding of an intratrinitarian transaction is thus ruled out by this notion of mutuality. As I will show, there are many valuable elements in this reconfiguration of trinitarian theology, which, in less outlandish elements, is not unique to feminism. Yet feminists, in dispensing with all hierarchies, in particular between God and the world, stray a long way from classic orthodoxy.

Before I move on to two feminist proposals that are more appreciative of traditional models, I want to summarize our findings so far. Feminist scholars hold the following major distinctive positions.

1. Traditional thinking about the atonement promotes the myth that suffering is redemptive.

2. Penal substitution in particular supports an ideology that frustrates the divine intention and care for creation.

3. The cross is devoid of saving significance.

96. Inna J. Ray, "The Atonement Muddle: An Historical Analysis and Clarification of a Salvation Theory," *Journal of Women and Religion* 15 (1997): 100.

4. It is the ministry of Jesus as an exemplification of a revolutionary and egalitarian way of life that is redemptive.

5. Yet Jesus's redemption ought not to be conceived as a completed and "heroic" event, but one that requires our participation as the "redemptive community."

As I have alluded, not all feminist scholars dismiss the saving significance of the cross. In the remainder of this section, I will point to the work of Kathryn Tanner as a more hopeful feminist appropriation of the atonement tradition.

In her essay "Incarnation, Cross, and Sacrifice: A Feminist-Inspired Reappraisal," Tanner makes a sustained argument that the cross retains some saving significance. Although Tanner is appreciative of the feminist critiques of the cross (for all the reasons we have already discussed), she points out that they have a tendency to throw the baby out with the bathwater. While "the usual recourse of feminist and womanist theologians is to dismiss the idea that there is anything saving going on in the crucifixion," this dismissal "can eclipse any further theological accounting of how Jesus saves in and through the extreme opposition that his mission faced and in contradiction to it."[97] Tanner does well to underline the centrality of the cross for the Gospel accounts. Feminists, she fears, fail to do justice to this centrality and have no account of the positive place of the cross. But the trick is to provide a logic of the cross that does not cast God in the role of supreme punisher. The task is to find a positive function of the cross that does not end up glorifying suffering.

Tanner attempts to do precisely that by a return to the Christus Victor model combined with a much more prominent role for the notion of "incarnation." "Incarnation," she argues, "becomes the primary mechanism of the atonement, replacing, I will suggest, the vicarious satisfaction or penal substitution models with their obvious problems from both feminist and non-feminist points of view." In fact, Tanner affirms the centrality of humanity's union with God through Christ. It is through the incarnation that the battle with the powers is engaged, and it is through the "happy exchange" of properties that humanity fully benefits from the saving power of God. Clearly Tanner departs from the panentheist feminism of someone like Ruether or McFague. God remains the sovereign Lord, and humanity is still in desperate need of divine salvation.

However, the incarnation could not have been completely successful without the cross. It is presumably not specifically a cross that was required, but death as such, as the last enemy that had to be defeated (1 Cor. 15:26). "If

---

97. Kathryn Tanner, "Incarnation, Cross, and Sacrifice: A Feminist-Inspired Reappraisal," *Anglican Theological Review* 86, no. 1 (2004): 39.

the powers of the Word are to reach humanity suffering under the forces of sin and death, the Word must assume a life like that, become one with it, as Jesus goes to suffering and abjection on the cross."[98]

Let me try to be more exact about the role of the cross in Tanner's thought. Christ's passion is not the legal requirement, demanded by God, in order to forgive. Tanner believes that, in light of the union of humanity with God in the incarnation, there is not a "sufficient externality" for forensicism to work. The passion is not the condition of forgiveness. Instead, the passion is one aspect of the human condition that requires healing. Tanner puts it nicely: "Jesus had to be humiliated on the cross for the sake of salvation the way one has to be sick to go to the doctor, not the way one has to swallow one's pride and make amends in order to be forgiven, let back into another's good graces."[99] The legal framework is not applicable here: "This incarnational identification rather than Jesus' standing before the law is what makes him our substitute in the prosecution of our case."[100] Like Irving, Tanner points out that Christ assumes a fallen human nature in order to progressively lead it "from corruption to incorruption."[101]

There is much in Tanner that I wholeheartedly affirm. In my constructive chapter (chap. 6) I will be making a similar claim about the death of Christ as being a condition of his mortality, something he would have assumed at the incarnation. Nevertheless, Tanner does not say anything about this mortality being a curse. Although she mentions Athanasius in relation to Christ's assuming all the horrors of humanity, she fails to point out that for Athanasius, as for other fathers, these horrors have a penal dimension. As legal consequences, death and mortality are tied to sin. That Christ assumes our mortality from the very moment of the incarnation, only on the cross to defeat it as the last enemy, does not exclude a penal dimension to the cross. Nevertheless, it significantly recasts our understanding of the actual punishment on the cross in ways that should provide satisfactory answers to many legitimate concerns voiced by feminist theology. However, a fuller discussion of these matters must wait until the next chapter.

Postcolonial Atonement

There is substantial continuity between postcolonial and feminist approaches to the atonement. This is not surprising since both may be classified

98. Ibid., 44.
99. Ibid.
100. Ibid.
101. Ibid., 46.

as "liberationist" schools of thought. But there are also important discrepancies. While feminism is currently undergoing something of an internecine war, coming under the increasing influence of deconstruction, which pushes against its traditional liberal image, postcolonialism has defined itself from the beginning against the Western liberal project and, under the influence of thinkers like Spivak and Bhabha, made a decisive postmodern turn. It is safe to argue, though, that poststructuralist notions are much more at home within this latter discourse than they are within feminism.

One of these notions, as we have already discovered, is hybridity. The idea that selves are not unitary has repercussions for Christology and atonement. But it is important to understand that the notion of hybridity makes the most sense against the background of the postmodern deconstruction of binary oppositions. At times this plays directly against the feminist "politics of identity," which assumes that there is a well-defined "femininity" over against "masculinity." Postcolonial writers have of late been suspicious of such "essentialism," although they sometimes recognize that it is politically expedient. By and large, however, postcolonial thought, under the influence of Spivak and Bhabha, has moved beyond the strict binary oppositions between the colonizer and the colonized, powerful/powerless, master/slave, exploiter/exploited. Such strict distinctions overlook the many-faceted ways, historically documented, in which oppressors themselves are influenced and affected by the oppressed. Thus, unlike much feminist thought, the criminal is not clearly circumscribed, nor are the victims neatly localized. Human reality is tragic; the good are mixed with the bad. It is conceivable that to some feminists this inclination toward political realism only serves the status quo, doping the masses into thinking that they are also powerful in some sufficient way and thus removing the motivation to revolt.

The deconstruction of binary oppositions also erodes law. Postcolonial writer Wonhee Anne Joh invokes the work of Julia Kristeva and her contrast between the symbolic and the semiotic. The symbolic indicates what she calls "the law of the Father," the order imposed on relationships, the conceptual distinctions, prohibitions, rituals, and practices that form one's identity. The semiotic denotes the pre-Oedipal, prelinguistic bonds that are repressed and managed by the symbolic but that nevertheless manage to reemerge. Law, as a field that works precisely by creating such binary oppositions, represses the natural bonds that link human beings and that Brock's "erotic power" seeks to reestablish. When it comes to atonement, then, law again cannot be the ultimate framework that makes the cross intelligible. Joh writes:

> Every attempt to view suffering as caused directly or indirectly by God is in danger of linking God with sadism. Given the traditional masculinist constructions of

the divine and the attending doctrines, it is hardly surprising that sadism has become part of the imagined divine. The symbolic maintains its orderliness and order not only through the repression of the semiotic but [also] through the discipline of punishment and retribution. According to this logic, atonement is only possible as a result of suffering.[102]

This is consonant with everything I have been arguing about the common approaches to law to be found in current atonement theories. Law is repressive. The punishment the law administers has the function of promoting the sovereignty of law. It does not make due retribution, for the very catalog of crimes is an invention, a superimposition of an alien order.

Not only is hybridity an aspect of the human condition, but it also aptly describes Christ and God. This notion is also continuous with feminist critiques of all hierarchies and of masculinist, heroic conceptions of the atonement. With Christ or God portrayed as hero, human beings are infantilized and rendered passive. Kwok Pui-lan argues that traditional Christology has imposed on Christ a forced unity, serving a political purpose. In contrast, we should be willing to accept the basic indeterminacy of Christ's own self. "The space between Jesus and Christ is unsettling and fluid, resisting easy categorization and closure. It is the 'contact zone' or 'borderland' between the human and the divine, the one and the many, the historical and the cosmological, the Jewish and the Hellenistic, the prophetic and the sacramental, the God of the conquerors and the God of the meek and lowly."[103]

This hybridity of Jesus, existing between humanity and divinity, resonates with the hybridity of dislocated people, of immigrants, and indeed of multicultural people. Sang Hyun Lee calls this space "liminality."[104] He contrasts "marginalization," which is sinful, with liminality, which is descriptive of God's own intratrinitarian life. In fact, the concept denotes the very life of the Trinity, Lee claims:

> As the Father's love moves him to give himself (while also remaining himself) to the Son, the Father moves into a liminal place by letting go of his divinity and his divine status (while also retaining them). As the Father withdraws from the Son (while also remaining in the Son), he allows an "action room" (*Spiel-Raum*) or a space of possibilities for the sake of the Son's being a genuine Other to the Father, that is, One who can exercise absolute freedom.[105]

102. Joh, *Heart of the Cross*, 84–85.
103. Kwok Pui-lan, *Postcolonial Imagination and Feminist Theology* (Louisville: Westminster John Knox, 2005), 171.
104. Sang Hyun Lee, *From a Liminal Place: An Asian American Theology* (Minneapolis: Fortress, 2010), esp. 63–89.
105. Ibid., 59.

Although Lee does not specifically tie "law" to marginalization, the implication is inescapable. Reflecting on the fallen condition of humanity, Lee interprets the fall as a failure to embrace liminality:

> Instead of being open to the new ideas, human beings absolutized certain finite principles and condemned different ideas as false. Instead of forming community and solidarity through liminality, human beings clung to the human-made borders, living in alienation from each other. Instead of providing the absolutized centers of societies a prophetic criticism from the liminal space, human beings joined with those at the dominant centers and became oppressive to those at the periphery.[106]

Thus the condition of liminality can be described as absolute openness to the other, without any hierarchical constraints. It is precisely out of this condition that *communitas* emerges. When people leave the comfort of their homes, freed from their social orders, they are open to create free bonds with other displaced individuals. "*Communitas* is an egalitarian and intimate communion between two or more human beings who completely respect and accept each other in all their otherness."[107]

Joh also understands the fundamental human problematic as violence, domination, marginalization. Jesus's redemptive ministry has to be understood as a deconstruction of these symbolic systems of domination. In the remainder of this section, I will present her specific contribution to atonement theology.

Joh describes Jesus's hybridity as a combination of *han* and *jeong*. That is to say, his personality is both an image of abjection, *han*, and the embodiment of *jeong*. The cross in particular "embodies and continues to function as an embodiment of abjection and love, both *han* and *jeong*."[108] The symbol of the cross "performs a double gesture and requires a double reading."[109] The cross must be understood to represent divine redemptive transformation of relationships (*jeong*), but not more so than the cross also reflects, not simply a surgical and sanitized victory, but the worst abjection.

Joh is trying to make a path between feminists and liberation theologies. Feminists, as we have seen, lament the cross as utter abjection, as having nothing salvific about it. Liberation theologians, however, draw much strength from the symbol of the cross.[110] Thus Joh is among several postcolonial writers who think it "necessary to ask why the cross, with all the suffering it signifies,

---

106. Ibid., 60.
107. Ibid., 70.
108. Joh, *Heart of the Cross*, 83.
109. Ibid., 104.
110. Joh is only one of several postcolonial scholars.

continues to empower and perform as emancipatory symbol for many who are suffering and oppressed throughout the world."[111] In this, postcolonial theologians depart from the feminist argument that the cross should not serve as a religious symbol at all. I will show below in what way the cross still serves a redemptive function.

Even as Joh critiques feminists for completely disregarding the saving function of the cross, she also takes Jürgen Moltmann to task for his understanding of the role of the passion in the scheme of redemption. She argues that Moltmann's position, by making suffering an intratrinitarian event, contains the abjection within the Trinity. Thus the cross "is kept untainted," "it seems tidy."[112] Instead of recognizing that "the cross means human beings rejecting other human beings,"[113] "Moltmann lets the work of redemption be done within the divine Trinitarian relationality."[114] But this means that we are back to a heroic framework, which does not include human participation in salvation. Moreover, the violence of the cross appears again as divine violence, thus working against Moltmann's best insights.

This "logic of inner-Trinitarian containment" also reverts to an insufficiently mutual relationship between the Father and the Son. For Moltmann, their relationship is unilateral: "What comes across is not a mutual relationship but a unilateral relationship in which the Father takes the initiative. The Son remains passive and remains the abject." Joh then wonders, "Would not the inner-Trinitarian relationality be strengthened if the Father would take on and become as abject as the Son?"[115] Joh suggests that Moltmann does not sufficiently "fuse" the Father and the Son. She argues that the whole logic is detrimental to what Moltmann aims to accomplish. If we retain an active Father and a passive Son, the idea of domination is reensconced into the very project that aims to deconstruct it. Joh provocatively follows up: "*It is my contention that what is transformative and menacing is not the Son who is rescued by his Father but the Son who is the abject.* He is the abject who stares back and mimics and mocks the powers that have rendered him abject. That is what is transgressive and transformative about the cross."[116]

For Joh, a heroic atonement entails a divine power that saves without being actively involved in suffering. The suffering of Jesus is sanitized by being absorbed into the life of the Trinity, yet without really affecting the Trinity.

111. Ibid., 79.
112. Ibid., 77.
113. Ibid.
114. Ibid., 78.
115. Ibid., 81.
116. Ibid., italics original.

Salvation is obtained by the Father, who absorbs suffering without really participating in it, without being himself abjected on the cross.

To sum up, on the one hand, the problem with feminist atonement is that it ascribes no saving significance to the cross. On the other hand, the problem with the liberationist type of atonement theology represented by Moltmann is that it unintentionally sanctifies and sanitizes suffering. But can we ascribe a religious function to the cross without at the same time domesticating the abjection? The difficulty of this question is precisely the difficulty stemming from hybridity and liminality. The identity of Jesus involves multiple discourses: that of law, that of empire, that of the abject, and so on. As Marion Grau points out, it is always a difficult task to sense the disruptive voice of God from underneath the discourses it necessarily inhabits: "The resemblance to known forms of power remains, and it remains with a vengeance. While images of divine economy do threaten and challenge certain forms of patronage, gender, and class hierarchies, they retain (ideologically loaded) certain power and knowledge formations."[117] The consistent message we are getting from postmodern writers is that we should be aware of the complex use God may be making of these various discourses. Heim and Girard have explicated this in relation to the language of sacrifice: Jesus gets into this mechanism and exposes it from within, as it were. The inherent risk is to conflate the divine intention with the mechanism itself. Similarly, postcolonial writers like Joh argue that Jesus's ministry performs this "double gesture": he enters the mechanism of sin-punishment, hierarchy, and social domination, but at the same time he deconstructs it.

Moltmann himself appears to acknowledge this: Jesus did not passively accept his death. His cry of dereliction was both a recognition of a reality and a cry of protest against it. Yet Moltmann does not see in that cry itself anything liberating. The liberation comes from God, who absorbs and therefore heals the suffering in an intratrinitarian logic of exchange. Joh, on the contrary, wants to locate the saving significance of the cross precisely in this abjection. She turns to the concept of mimicry, a notion developed within postcolonial literature by Hommi Bhabha. I will indulge a lengthier quote from Joh at this point:

> The rulers of the Roman Empire deployed the cross in order to terrorize people into submission. The fact that early Christianity used the same symbol to mimic and mock the empire attests to the subversive understanding of the cross that was part of the early church movement. Hence, postcolonial notion of mimicry

117. Marion Grau, *Of Divine Economy: Refinancing Redemption* (New York: T&T Clark, 2004), 214.

sheds light on our understanding of the cross as a menace when it mimics and so mirrors back a powerful counterinterpretation to the oppressive order and law of the imperial power. The act of execution on the cross by the Roman Empire was by no means a glorious form of punishment. Execution on the cross was always a veiled threat that terrorized the oppressed into staying properly subjected. However, through the power of mimicry, this very sign of abjection becomes a sign of love/*jeong* that is inclusive of the perpetrators. The double-crossing on the cross is this: even as the cross embodies abjection, it works simultaneously against abjection through Jesus' embodiment of *jeong*.[118]

In his abjection, Jesus embodies through his mimicry a critique of the powers. He makes "a public spectacle" (Col. 2:15) of their tools of domination. The cross is not part of the divine tool of redemption, but a human tool of oppression, not simply passively and depressingly accepted by Jesus, but turned against itself, ridiculed. What is salvific about the cross is not that this human suffering is swallowed up into the divine life and somehow mended independently of human agency, but it is precisely Jesus's human agency, as desolate and abject, that is the means through which these structures of domination are mocked and resisted.

Yet the postcolonial sensitivity to the political situation leads to the counsel that complete justice and utter reversal of domination remain impossible dreams. God himself, as an abject human being, seems to be limited in what he can do with regard to these structures of power. As human beings, "we can never completely reverse but only mimetically inhabit present structures and inhabit them to subvert them from the inside, as well as create new structures that reinscribe those present."[119] Since God himself does not act in isolation, but in mutuality and equality with human beings, the consequences for atonement are clear: "A postcolonial reading of divine commerce describes then an exchange in which a tricksterlike Christ mimics and mocks the boundaries of ownership and slavery."[120]

Indeed, unlike feminist thought (with the exception of Ray and Tanner), postcolonial atonement makes unapologetic use of the themes of divine deception. Joh's notion of mimicry is present in Grau's concept of the "sacred trickster":

Like a sacred trickster, he shows forth the shocking; performs perfidy; hails the hysterical; provides a hermeneutics of hyperbole, a syntax of sarcasm; and invents idioms of irony. Tricksters are performers of mimicry and incarnate ambivalence.

118. Joh, *Heart of the Cross*, 76.
119. Grau, *Of Divine Economy*, 214.
120. Ibid.

> This scandalously different Christ, a rather suspect and marginal "persona" or mask for divine agency, appears, then, as holy fool, divine trickster. Deceiving the devil, counterfeiting the counterfeiters, Christ the Counterfeit might help us invent ways to unveil and resist the con men of our times.[121]

This amounts to a renunciation of a heroic atonement, in that "Christ would not appear as the messenger of divine omnipotence and all-possessiveness, but of a measured, wise, and just power that works—trickster-like—in and through situations of oppression. The divine economist is always already invested (clothed), embodied, incarnate in the economy of creation."[122]

Mimicry, deceit, and trickery are the only open courses of action if we are to uphold the imperative of nonviolence, as Darby Kathleen Ray points out: "[Divine deceit] points to the reality that any struggle against oppression and injustice that seeks to avoid violent means or that emerges from a context of relative powerlessness must rely on cunning and ingenuity rather than ascribed authority and power."[123]

What may we say in response to such creative proposals? First, postcolonial theology is to be commended for drawing our attention to the problematic character of human identity. Theologians of the atonement can certainly learn from its unmasking of the illusion of a self-possessive identity. The "turn to relationality" is a welcome new direction in theology.

Second, the concept of mimicry points to an important and highly neglected element in Christian soteriology. While God does indeed make use of the human practices of sacrifice, these practices need not be the final word about God, nor do they seamlessly embody God's intentions for creation. There is indeed a place for a depth hermeneutic, if that project remains under the constraints of the redemptive-historical divine intention as scripturally embodied. Nevertheless, these mechanisms and practices are not altogether human and wrong. A theology of creation suggests that there is something worthwhile about them even if they may be exclusively relative to the reality of sin. Law and its logic of sin-punishment are not God's final world about reality, but it is nevertheless God's designed method of dealing with a broken world. I shall return to these ideas in the next chapter.

Several directions of critique may also be identified. While I think the christological and trinitarian proposals are most deficient, a fuller discussion belongs

121. Marion Grau, "Divine Commerce: A Postcolonial Christology for Times of Neocolonial Empire," in *Postcolonial Theologies: Divinity and Empire*, ed. Catherine Keller, Michael Nausner, and Mayra Rivera (St. Louis: Chalice, 2004), 177.

122. Ibid., 183.

123. Darby Kathleen Ray, *Deceiving the Devil: Atonement, Abuse, and Ransom* (Cleveland: Pilgrim, 1998), 138–39.

to the next chapter. Here I will only point out that Joh and Kwok Pui-lan simply dismiss the patristic christological consensus as political, despite the vigorous theological and textual discussions that lead to the eventual consensus, precarious though it was. Both theologians are right, though, to point to the instrumentality of christological categories. Nevertheless, they fail to account for the intuitions and rules of faith that these (instrumental) concepts of orthodoxy preserve.

Joh's critique of Moltmann also betrays a deficient trinitarian theology, as she suggests a fusion between the person of the Father and the Son. She does not explain in what way she intends to preserve the uniqueness and particularity of each divine person, and her concept of mutuality and hybridity, if left unchecked, threatens to degenerate into modalism.

I shall return to these elements of dogmatic critique below, but not before mentioning some extratheological concerns, as it were. Postcolonials, like feminists and all postmodern theologians presented here, dogmatically condemn any positive evaluation of "violence." Short of a violent response to violence, mimicry and mockery seem to be the only alternatives. Real power resides in this mimicry, as it does in *jeong*. These are not "weak" alternatives. However, while oppressors might indeed find themselves challenged when faced with the abject, I have little doubt that they would prefer the peaceful response of mimicry rather than the violent response of revolution. Dictators are fully aware of and often tolerate the occasional joke about the regime. It provides the masses with outlets for their frustration. Thus the repressed returns in a space that does not threaten the stability of the regime. Its disruption is minor and dampened. So such outlets for venting frustration are important components of the very regime of oppression. The implications for atonement are rather bleak: Jesus is no longer the human being who mocks and disrupts the system, but is utterly and completely another piece of its machinery, tolerated by the system. The *communitas* he creates, moreover, is a conglomerate of "weak" humans, content to mock the system but devoid of any real power. Does this hopeless and pessimistic message really resonate with people seeking liberation from the powers? I suspect that the reason why the oppressed find motivation in the symbol of the cross is not because of its ultimately impotent theatrics but because a definitive and ontological victory has indeed been (violently) won.

Summary

1. Postmodernity laments the modern diremption between law and morality for two reasons. First, modernity misunderstood morality for a

universalized calculation (Kant's categorical imperative, for example), a discourse that abstracts from individuality. Second, it deconstructs all law as being immoral in that law masks the interests of the powerful.

2. The modern emphasis on libertarian freedom gives way to a recognition of the social construction of selves and of a deconstruction of agency. Guilt thus disappears, perhaps to be replaced with shame. The fundamental condition is no longer that of sinners but of sinned-against victims.

3. Law is regarded as inherently violent. Its institutions are based on hierarchies, they employ arcane language, and they have alienating effects. Justice is to be described independently of jurisprudence or morality, as proximity to the Other (Lévinas).

4. Since any legal system is necessarily violent, God cannot be thought as being complicit with law. The fundamental drive of postmodern atonement theories is that of critiquing the mechanism of law. Atonement is now understood as the very unmasking of violence of all kinds.

5. Girard's work extends this critique to the divine law itself, now regarded as a human projection and self-validation. Christ strips away the curtain, revealing the delusion. God does not need a victim. Humans need scapegoats.

6. For Milbank, Christ undoes mimetic rivalry by offering an enabling sign and by inaugurating a practice. God does not need to punish Jesus: the law of retribution is a human invention.

7. Feminist theories of the atonement typically portray the death of Christ as a tragic occurrence, not willed by God. The logic of penal substitution only justifies abusive relationships and fails to challenge the status quo.

8. Finally, postcolonial critiques of the atonement focus on the hybridity of Christ, whose life and ministry is a commentary on the fate of dislocated people, of exiles. Christ is not a heroic figure who either enacts a provision of the law (penal substitution) or transcends the law, but primarily a victim himself.

6

Atonement and the Perfection of Divine Agency

Introduction: On the Uniqueness of Divine Agency

In the preceding pages I have sought to engage in a critical reading of the atonement tradition. Any story is told from an angle, and this one is no different. I have expounded on a variety of atonement theories from the perspective of their interaction with theories of justice and with attitudes toward law. I have made no claim, however, to offer an exhaustive causal explanation, and I am not suggesting that one historical trajectory *explains* the other. Cultural discourses such as theology and law are deeply enmeshed with each other. Nonetheless, the exercise has been, I hope, illuminating in a variety of ways, of which I shall mention only a few.

First, the doctrine of the atonement has been deeply affected by historical developments in the arena of politics and law. Theories of the cross are thus deeply political. They assume visions of the just society, of right responses to wrongdoing, of the place and rule of law in relation to the telos of a given community. This particular theological conversation is therefore intensely practical.

A second, related advantage of this angle is that we can now more clearly understand the relationship between atonement and ethics. Reflection on the just is coterminous with reflection on the good, as we have seen. Questions having to do with whether God's action in Christ is moral and how the cross actually contributes to moral transformation have always been central to this history.

Third, perhaps to a lesser extent, one can also discern that political configurations and systems of justice are themselves deeply theological. That is, they make assumptions that are theological in nature: about the ends of humanity, about human nature, about human ability to do good, about guilt and forgiveness. Claims to *explain* atonement in light of changing conceptions of justice tend to forget that legal and political development itself is shaped partly by religious assumptions. Interdisciplinary traffic flows both ways between these crisscrossing histories.

Finally, but perhaps most importantly, it has emerged that the history of atonement theories is really a debate about the nature of God. This is the fundamental issue at stake in this ongoing conversation. But again, the convictions one has about the nature of God do not run free of the assumptions one makes about theories of justice. Let me briefly rehearse this story by highlighting this relationship.

The first period we encountered, the so-called patristic paradigm, shows, like each of the other periods, a concern to preserve the justice of God. Yet here the justice of God tends not to be construed in relation to the law of God, a law that norms the divine-human relation itself. God's primary interest, as far as his justice is concerned, is to preserve the order he has decreed in human relations. Divine justice is not accomplished by strict observation of law; indeed, sometimes it meant transcending this very law. Thus, when theologians like Gregory of Nyssa and Augustine sought to interpret the action of God in the crucified and risen Christ, they did not start with the assumption that God is the kind of agent whose justice demands strict observation of the law. While they were singularly concerned to preserve the justice of God, their concern did not involve a "legalistic" economy of exchange. God's justice is preserved in that he rescues humanity from bondage (Gregory), thus restoring an order and indeed reordering human nature to its proper end (Augustine).

The second, medieval period witnessed a debate between competing conceptions of God. The conflict occurred against the background of the emergence of law as a fundamental aspect of justice, including divine justice. Not all theologians we have discussed agreed that law is something that applies to God himself. While Anselm predates the legal revolution of the twelfth and thirteenth centuries, he nonetheless shared in the growing enthusiasm about a universal justice that characterized the High Middle Ages. God's justice restricts his options in dealing with sin. Either God punishes humanity, or he accepts a satisfaction on behalf of humanity. In Anselm, God's justice appears to nicely fit feudal expectations. Abelard's reaction to Anselm reveals a starkly different conception of the divine nature. There is nothing that constrains divine love. Abelard prioritizes the divine attribute of love in relation to God's justice. Aquinas's position is more akin to Anselm's in that God's response to sin has to be "fitting" to his nature. Further, given his doctrine of divine simplicity, prioritizing one attribute such as love to the detriment of another one, such as justice, is simply bad theology. With Aquinas the continuity between a human sense of justice and eternal law is reinforced. Human laws, it might be said, analogically participate in God's eternal law. Thus law (eternal) is both the framework for divine-human relationship and one of the means toward the human telos (divine and human law). Duns Scotus shattered this continuity between the divine and human realms. Duns Scotus's God is a God of pure will, who creates and orders however he wishes to, without being in any way constrained by his vision of the ends of what he creates (contra Aquinas). The ordering of human justice (the principle of retribution, for example) does not reveal anything about divine justice. Thus God cannot be compelled to act in a particular way by anything external to his will. Duns Scotus does not disregard divine justice but explains it in terms of what he calls divine self-love. Again, one divine attribute (love, self-love) seems to be elevated above other divine attributes (holiness, for example). God's "secondary justice," namely, his uprightness toward another in a qualified sense, is determined only by God's self-love.

During the Reformation, Luther and Calvin generally maintained law as the framework of divine-human relation, but with very different attitudes. Luther, on the one hand, tends to think of the law as being God's alien work in the wake of sin, thus raising questions about a conflict between love and justice in the very nature of God. Calvin, on the other hand, places law much closer to the essence of God and further argues for a third use of the law. Neither of these theologians, however, gave much thought to the coherence between the divine attributes of love and justice. While Luther tends to speak in terms of a God against God, Calvin resorts to metaphorical expressions like "God loved us even when he hated us."

Modernity is the fourth paradigm we looked at, by focusing on two theologians: Schleiermacher and Ritschl. Both theologians reduce the nature of God primarily to love. No divine law obtains between God and humanity, as this would destroy the moral personality of humans. The moral law is dissociated from positive law as well as from nature. Kant locates human freedom and morality in the realm suspended between nature and the polis. Schleiermacher and Ritschl both perpetuate and rebel against the Kantian legacy. Schleiermacher argues that Kant's imperatives are insufficiently related to nature and thus cannot lead to a transformation and reordering of desire. Ritschl sides with Kant against Schleiermacher, but faults the former for his mere exemplarism: the transformation of humanity cannot take place by sheer example, in autonomy, but involves the particular heteronomy of the kingdom of God, which Jesus came to inaugurate. Both Schleiermacher and Ritschl object to Kant's exemplarism and stress the centrality of the historical person of Jesus Christ for atonement. Yet both deny that Jesus mends something between us and God. Neither conceives of any obstacle in the way of divine forgiveness. The problem is squarely on our side.

The fifth and final period, that of "postmodernity" (or "late modernity," as I suggested), takes the critique of law even further. While the Kantian Enlightenment critiqued positive law in the name of a self-legislated moral law to be established by universal sovereign selves, we are now witnessing the very erasure of the notion of a universal moral law. Neither positive law nor moral law is an apt framework for justice. The modern turn to a rehabilitative conception of justice (as opposed to a retributive one) only proved to mask another sort of violence (social engineering). If there is to be justice, it must evade and deconstruct all forms of law. The just aims of the God of postmodernity seem to consist in the very destruction of law. We are thus returning to the Christus Victor pattern of a God who rescues us from bondage. Only this time it is not an extraneous bondage but the self-inflicted bondage of presumed-divine-but-really-human systems of coercion: sacrifice and retribution.

Several questions arise from this historical journey. First, What is the relationship between justice as humanly understood *and administered* and divine justice? If law, as I argue, does indeed constitute the framework of divine-human relation, to what extent are we to think of human courts of justice as carriers of divine justice? Are state authorities the powers and principalities from which we ought to be rescued, or are they "established by God" (Rom. 13:1), "God's servants, agents of wrath to bring punishment on the wrongdoer" (cf. 13:4)? Does the Christian theology of atonement rightly sanction state violence, or is it called to offer resistance to forms of state injustice? The more immediate question has to do with the Roman court that sentenced Jesus. Was Pilate doing the will of God, serving as God's executioner? Or, as Peter charges his audience in Acts, "You killed the author of life, but God raised him from the dead" (3:15)?

A second, related question is, What is the relationship between the justice of God and positive Mosaic law? This is a clearly complex issue, given that the New Testament seems to both exalt Mosaic law and transcend it. Have we been redeemed according to law (1 Cor. 15:3; Heb. 5), or apart from the law (Rom. 3:21)? A powerful objection to both penal substitution and satisfaction models is that Christ seems to be deconstructing rather than confirming the law. This question will need to be tackled later.

Finally, What justifies God in forgiving us? Does God need any justification in order to forgive us gratuitously, as many theologians assume that he does? This, I argue, is precisely the question of the relation between the divine attributes. It has cropped up again and again throughout this history. Even Aeschylus records this complaint against the gratuitous forgiveness of the gods. If the gods forgive, there must be something that justifies this forgiveness. Otherwise they would be unjust to leave the guilty go unpunished.

In many ways the history we have recounted can be told from the perspective of two divine attributes: justice and love. As I have argued, this is only to be expected. *Atonement theory is an attempt to ascribe a particular action to God.* Just as it happens in human courts of law, an argument is made that assigns responsibility for an action to a person. But the situation in the case of atonement is slightly different. In human jurisprudence we are attempting to assign responsibility for *an action we have already understood and interpreted.* Certainly this knowledge is only partial, and it might be more exact to say that we have a description of an event (e.g., a killing). Certainly we cannot suppose we have given a full account of that event until we also describe it as an intentional action of a particular agent, to whose intentions and reasons the act itself would be correlated. The case of Christ's death bears both similarities and dissimilarities to this pattern. As for similarity, we have a partial description of the action in this case: an execution commanded by a Roman tribunal, incited by Jewish priests, and carried out by Roman soldiers. But this hardly gets at the religious significance of the action. Insofar as God was an agent in this act, as most Christians have affirmed, what was his particular agency? In what way is God to be held responsible for the action we have just described as a Roman execution? And there is dissimilarity: in the case of the atonement, we have to ascribe a yet-to-be-described action to God.

The history of the doctrine, though, shows that the manner in which responsibility is assigned in both cases (human courts and atonement theories) bears another important similarity. In both cases ascriptions of responsibility and agency are made on the basis of assumptions about the character of the presumed agent. Is the alleged criminal actually capable of this kind of crime? Do the ascriptions fit with what other witnesses bear out about his moral standing? In the "atonement court," divine attributes are just as important a basis for the ascription of action to God. Does God's moral character allow us to make certain kinds of predications about his actions? Thus the ascription of atoning agency always presupposes a particular description of divine attributes. Surely descriptions of divine action and of divine attributes go together. We do not first establish the divine attributes independently of ascribing particular actions to him. Rather, the doctrine of the atonement is inextricably entangled with the doctrine of God.

There is further dissimilarity, which hasn't often been identified in these debates, but which I believe makes a huge difference. Human agents possess moral attributes in addition to physical ones. Their agency is conditioned by these attributes and the relationship to their physical limitations, as I will explain. The Christian tradition has always thought of God as also possessing certain metaphysical attributes. These are the kind of attributes that distinguish God from any other created being. The suggestion I want to make is that these attributes—particularly simplicity—qualify divine agency in a distinct way and differentiate it from any human agency. If this is the case, these qualifications are relevant to our discussion since atonement theory seeks to ascribe agency to God.

In this final chapter, I make the following argument. The Christian tradition, by and large, has always affirmed that, unlike human attributes, divine attributes attach in a unique way to the being of God. We have called this the attribute of "divine simplicity." While this attribute has taken a recent beating in certain philosophical and theological circles, it is an important staple of doctrinal orthodoxy, as I will show. But if ascribing actions to God depends on our understanding of his moral character, and if the doctrine of simplicity describes a particular relation that obtains between divine attributes, then it is quite possible that this doctrine will make a difference in the way we describe divine action. I suggest that this concept is immensely fertile for atonement theology, not only because it restricts certain kinds of affirmations about God's actions, but also because it makes possible a particular kind of description of these actions.

To put it simply: God is not an agent like any other agent. In other words, God does not "do things" the way you and I do things. He has a unique relation to his actions. His actions spring uniquely from his nature. Finally, his actions have a unity about them not shared with other human actions. Often, however, when atonement theologians have sought to describe and explain the cross, they have made anthropomorphic assumptions about divine agency. The result has been idolatrous in ascribing to God certain qualities of human actors.

The uniqueness of divine agency, I argue, can be expressed in terms of two sorts of considerations. First, the being of God is utterly different from any other kind of being. In particular, divine attributes are identical to his being rather than components of it. Second, divine actions are utterly different from any other actions. They exhibit a particular kind of perfection, which makes all the difference in the world for the way in which we ought to describe and interpret them. I intend to unpack these claims, making a case for the so-called perfection of divine agency. Let me stress that I am not making any novel claim about the nature or attributes of God. I am simply trying to show the relevance of a classic way of thinking about God for the doctrine of the atonement.

Christian theology has always maintained that God is a simple being. The primary intention of the doctrine of simplicity is to preserve the aseity of God. It would be correct to say that simplicity is an entailment of aseity. The doctrine holds that, unlike human beings, divine attributes are not components of his being, but rather God is identical with all of his attributes. Using Aristotelian language, theologians have said that God is not "composed" of parts.

If God is good, it is not because goodness is something that can be predicated of him, that goodness has an independent existence. Remember aseity: God is utterly independent and free. Everything that now exists owes its existence to God. Traditionally theologians have held that qualities such as goodness, justice, love, and so on fall in these categories. To say that God is good is not to connect two distinct realities, predicating one of the other. That would make God dependent on a previously existing "thing" called goodness. And this would mean that God is not utterly independent, free, and self-sustaining.

Naturally it is quite difficult to wrap our minds around this idea. There are many causes for this, not least having to do with the inherent limitations of human knowledge and language. But we can perhaps get a better handle on this concept if we contrast it with the way in which we predicate moral qualities of human agents. Indeed, as I will argue, the concept of simplicity does not so much have a positive meaning but rather a negative, apophatic one, qualifying everything we say of God.

Take the case of my grading of a particular term paper. A particular student has written a paper that is slightly below my expectations for his work. I know this student well, and I know his potential. I am disappointed with his performance in this case, because I know he can do so much more. Several courses of action are open to me. I can give him a higher grade than I think he deserves because it might motivate him for better work in the future. I could also give him a lower grade than he deserves by comparison with the rest of the class, just to make a point that he has performed below expectations. Or I could give him a fair grade that reflects the level of the class as a whole. None of these courses of action are inherently compelling. There is value in all of them, in various ways. Yet in choosing, say, the first option over the third, I could say that I will have been more merciful than just. In choosing the third

242 ATONEMENT, LAW, AND JUSTICE

over the second, I will have been more just than perhaps wise. What this case illustrates is that our actions spring from certain moral qualities we have, but they will most often fail to integrate these qualities perfectly. Often we will feel a "strife of attributes," equally pressing demands on our choices.

I think we rightly see this as a limitation of our created and fallen natures. Yet we do not ascribe the same kind of vacillation to God. God does not sense these demands pressing on his nature from the outside, as it were. If he were to be in some actions more just than loving, for example, it would mean that there is potentiality in God, that there are some things God can be that he is not (in a particular action). The careful reader will have already sensed that this argument is immensely fertile for atonement theory. If there is no action of God that is more just than loving, or more loving than just, then we shall have to postulate that any divine action is equally motivated by all of his attributes, because it springs from his being. Failure to qualify divine actions in this way will result in reducing divine agency to the level of human agency.

I will certainly have to defend the idea of simplicity against the accusation of its being merely a metaphysical and nonbiblical construct. But for now let me just note the intention behind this doctrine: the preservation of the ontological distinction between God and humanity.

Stephen Holmes sums up the point of the doctrine: "To describe God as 'simple' means that God is ontologically basic. . . . If we accept the linked scholastic account of God's nature as dynamic, as pure act, then this doctrine means that God does one thing, and that is to be God—perfectly, eternally, and incomprehensibly."[1] As we shall see, there are some bad ways of expounding divine simplicity. But the point is to understand what the concept tries to preserve—not so much what it says directly. As Holmes hints, not only is divine simplicity relevant for understanding the being of God (the way in which his attributes are unified), but it is also a way of talking about the unity of God's action. This second dimension of simplicity will also prove extremely significant for atonement.

Holmes argues that God does one thing alone, and that is to be God: perfectly, eternally, and incomprehensibly. While there are clear difficulties with this notion, I again focus on the difference it makes between divine and human actions in general. Before entering this discussion, I stress that it is only meant to be suggestive, that is, to raise sufficient questions to make the reader understand that there is a significant difference here.

1. Stephen Holmes, "'Something Much Too Plain to Say': Towards a Defence of the Doctrine of Divine Simplicity," *Neue Zeitschrift für systematische Theologie und Religionsphilosophie* 43, no. 1 (2001): 139.

First, human action and divine action differ in terms of their relation to time. Human action is limited in such a way that there is a temporal distance between intention/willing and acting. This distance accounts for what some call "deliberation." The temporal distance is not always apparent in that we often act compulsively.

Sometimes there is also a distinction between the action and the consequences of the action in the sense that human agents have to wait for the unfolding of the results of their actions. Take, for example, the spy who pours the poison into the king's ear. It can take several days for the poison to work its effects. We are temporal beings, and our actions are stretched in time. But we view time as a limitation in the sense that time can bring all kinds of obstacles to our actions.

God, on the other hand, is not temporally constrained in the same kind of way. Now, God's particular relation to time has been a matter of considerable debate, perhaps without many illuminating results. Whether God is outside of time or belongs to a different temporality[2] is a different matter. However we construe this relationship, the Bible makes it clear that time does not impose restraints on God. He is Lord over time and is not passive in relation to it, such that time might bring about a frustration of divine plans. Thus divine actions in time are fully under the control of God, unlike human actions.

This brings me to a second, related difference. Each human action is a combination of activity and passivity. The spy's pouring the poison into the king's ear, for example, exhibits both activity as enactment of an intention, as well as passivity, in the sense of waiting for the poison to take effect. All human actions contain a necessary dimension of passivity, even at the most basic level: I am partly dependent on the well-functioning of my body in order to carry out actions, for example. There are always necessary conditions that do not depend on my control for the success of an intended action.

Divine action, however, is not contingent on anything that is independent of God's sustaining will. There is no distance between intention and actual outcome, except where God so determines that there should be. This is simply to say that whatever God intends to do, he unconditionally does. Since God is pure act, there is no distance between God's merely intending to do something and God's doing it. This is simply another way of saying that there is no potentiality in God, which is itself really another way of saying that God is fully himself and fully in control of each of his actions.

There has been some hesitation with regard to the implications of the notion of pure act. For example, does the lack of potentiality actually mean that God only does one thing? That there is a single divine action? Does this

2. See Thomas F. Tracy, *God, Action, and Embodiment* (Grand Rapids: Eerdmans, 1984), 130.

entail, ironically, that the world must be eternal, thus rendering the very concept of simplicity contradictory? I shall return to some of these questions at the point where certain objections against simplicity have to be addressed. At this point I only note that there is a possible way of rendering simplicity so as not to suggest that God does only one action. Thomas F. Tracy connects simplicity and divine action in the following way: "God is simple insofar as all his actions are drawn together in the unity of a single intention: he can enact his life without discordant or irreducibly divergent lines of action. The divine simplicity will consist in the overarching coherence of God's life as a project."[3] It is not that God does only one action. This would probably raise more issues than it could solve. But the unity of God's actions is such that he is fully in control of them. In other words, he fully enacts his intentions without sensing any pressure against his being. To go back to the three possible ways of grading the paper, I sense a real tension in making that choice partly because I am not fully in control of the outcomes of my action. I wrestle and debate because I do not know how it's all going to pan out.

This pure activity of the divine agency means that any kind of passivity and contingency is rejected. God is not dependent on a body to be able to carry out his intentions. Neither is God dependent on the cooperation of other agents, who might always potentially not deliver. I am not suggesting that God does not operate his agency through secondary human agencies. The only claim is that, unlike such human proxy agencies, he remains fully in control of his actions despite using such instruments. While a president might seek to enact a particular intention through the agency of his ambassador, he is not, strictly speaking, fully in control of the actions of his emissary. Simplicity means that God remains fully in control even when acting through such proxies.

Finally, there is a unity of agency that is perfect in the case of God, but always imperfect in the case of human agents. A human life's unity is always a question of degree. Again, this has to do with the combination of activity-passivity. An agent's projects might be more or less unified and integrated. Tracy suggests that this might be "due in part to the inherent open-endedness of an agent's life, his capacity for novelty, and it is also due, no doubt, to the limits of our perceptiveness and to our capacity of self-deception."[4] However, as Tracy continues, "God achieves a maximal harmonization of activity in the unity of a single life. God's life will display an undisrupted perfection of agent unity; he will be a self (i.e., a unified individual) in the highest degree."[5]

3. Ibid., 129.
4. Ibid., 134.
5. Ibid., 135.

For Tracy, simplicity really means the same thing as the perfection and unity of agency: "No part of his experience will simply be abandoned, left outside the integration achieved by each new phase of his activity; *rather, all that he has been will be present in the background of each of his actions, and each of his actions will affirm and advance the purposes at work in the projects that preceded it.*"[6] What Tracy has in mind here is nothing else than divine immutability. God does not change in response to the circumstances that transpire, as human agents do. There is no experience he has that he is not in control over. More importantly, everything that he is will always be in the background of all his acts.

This unity of divine action is also evident in contrast to the "composition" of human action. Human parts have components of various sorts. On the one hand, there is a bodily component in addition to a mental component. On the other hand, there are what might be called "action segments": I move my hand to flip a switch *in order* to be able to illuminate the room, *in order to* read a book, *in order to study for the exam,* and so on. Each of these actions must be successful and come to an end before I can engage in the next action. I am dependent on doing something first before I am able to do another thing. Partly this has to do with human actions being extended in time. More importantly, I think, it has to do with "power." In order to create an effect in the world, we often need to "wait our turn" in the "causal queue." But, given God's sustaining of the universe, including its causal structure, this is not the case for him. At the very least he is not necessarily bound to such a course of action. He can indeed undertake it, in his freedom, but it would still not have the open-endedness and undecidability that our actions have. My reading of the book might not happen as a result of there being no electric power.

It appears, then, that there are important disanalogies between human and divine action. My suggestion is that an understanding of the perfection of divine agency ought to place constraints on and qualify our ascriptions of the agency to God. We do not predicate actions of God in the same way as we do of human beings. The doctrine of simplicity, then, is a way of saying that (1) God's being is unlike any other being in the way in which his attributes are ordered; and that (2) God is the perfection of agency in the sense that divine actions themselves do not share in the limitations of human actions in general.

The doctrine of simplicity, however, has not been without its detractors, despite its being an important piece of doctrinal orthodoxy. In what follows I will review both its pedigree and some of its most important objections.

6. Ibid., emphasis added.

The Tradition of Simplicity and Its Detractors

Christian theologians have always insisted that God is a simple being. His simplicity was thought to be a direct consequence of his aseity. "Since there was no one greater" (Heb. 6:13), God's being could not be thought to be composed of parts. Despite all appearances to the contrary, simplicity is not a remnant of Platonism or Neoplatonism, but as I will show, its Christian version is directly intended to foreclose those philosophical assumptions. The absolute greatness and uniqueness of God (Exod. 18:11; 2 Sam 7:22) is unsearchable and unknowable (Ps. 145:3). Scripture uses not only adjectives but also substantives to denote the fullness of the life of God. God is "Righteousness" (Jer. 23:6) and "love" (1 John 4:8); Jesus declares himself to be "the way and the truth and the life" (John 14:6). Christ is further proclaimed by Paul as having "become for us wisdom from God—that is, our righteousness, holiness and redemption" (1 Cor. 1:30).

This scriptural habit does not by itself establish the doctrine of simplicity. Yet it has to be agreed that such a mode of speech is appropriate to the kind of being the Scriptures portray God to be. Simplicity is an implication of the absolute aseity and sovereignty of God. To say that God is "love" is not simply a stylistic device but especially a "revelatory metaphor" in that associating God with "love"—and any other attribute—does not so much reveal the essence of God but rather the nature of love.

The great tradition has always understood the concept of simplicity—but also other attributes such as aseity, immutability (and the derived perfection of impassibility), grounded as they are in such scriptural "divine names"—to qualify our reading of the Bible. The particular *modus significandi* of Scripture is appropriate to its subject matter, God. The language of Scripture itself has to be understood in the light of the absolute uniqueness of God.

So Irenaeus writes of God: "He is a simple, uncompounded Being, without diverse members, and altogether like, and equal to himself, since He is wholly understanding, and wholly spirit, and wholly thought, and wholly intelligence, and wholly reason, and wholly hearing, and wholly seeing, and wholly light and the whole source of all that is good—even as the religious and pious are wont to speak concerning God."[7]

Augustine, as we have already observed, assigns to simplicity an important function in his dogmatics. Simplicity does not contradict the Triune nature: "It is for this reason that the nature of the Trinity is called simple, because it has not anything which it can lose, and because it is not one thing and its contents

7. Irenaeus, *Haer* 2.13.3.

another, as a cup and the liquor, or a body and its color, or the air and the light or hat of it, or a mind and its wisdom. For none of these is what it has."[8] Augustine also concludes that the being of God must be the same as his existence:

> But it is impious to say that God subsists to and underlies his goodness, and that goodness is not his substance, or rather his being, nor is God his goodness, but it is in him as an underlying subject. So it is clear that God is improperly called substance, in order to signify being by a more usual word. He is called being truly and properly in such a way that perhaps only God ought to be called being. . . . But in any case, whether he is called being, which he is called properly, or substance, which he is called improperly, either word is predicated with reference to self, not by way of a relationship with reference to something else. So for God to be is the same as to subsist, and therefore if the Trinity is one being, it is also one substance.[9]

Aquinas seeks to maintain divine aseity by denying composition in God: "Every composite is posterior to its components: since the simpler exists in itself before anything is added to it for the composition of a third. But nothing is prior to the first. Therefore, since God is the first principle, He is not composite."[10]

The Protestant confessions pick up the notion without hesitation. The Westminster Confession of Faith declares: "There is but one only, living, and true God, who is infinite in being and perfection, a most pure spirit, invisible, without body, parts, or passions" (2.1). James Dolezal helpfully explains the importance of the doctrine:

> This curious verbiage signifies the Westminster divines' commitment to the simplicity that enables the Christian to meaningfully confess that God is most absolute in his existence and attributes. Adherents to this doctrine reason that if God were composed of parts in any sense, he would be dependent upon those parts for his very being, and thus the parts would be ontologically prior to him. If this were the case, he would not be *most* absolute, that is, wholly self-sufficient and the first principle of all other things. Thus, only if God is "without parts" can he be "most absolute."[11]

The Augsburg Confession (1530) reaffirms the doctrine: "There is one divine essence which is called God and is God: eternal, incorporeal, indivisible, of

---

8. Augustine, *City of God* 11.10.

9. Augustine, *Trin.* 7.10.

10. Thomas Aquinas, *Scriptum super libros Sententiarum* 1.8.4.1; quoted in James E. Dolezal, *God without Parts: Divine Simplicity and the Metaphysics of God's Absoluteness* (Eugene, OR: Pickwick, 2011), 2.

11. Dolezal, *God without Parts*, 1–2.

immeasurable power, wisdom, and goodness, the creator and preserver of all things, visible and invisible" (1.2).

We can conclude that there is a great consensus in the Christian tradition about this divine perfection. This does not settle the issue, however. In recent times simplicity has been attacked from a variety of angles. It is time to address some of those charges.

Let me pause again and remind the reader what I aim to accomplish by drafting my position in the concept of simplicity. I am arguing, quite simply, that an understanding of certain divine attributes—primarily though not exclusively simplicity—entails that God's agency is of a unique kind. If that is the case, then assigning actions to God needs to be carefully qualified, just as in the case of making predications of God. I am merely extending the principle of analogy from its usual employment (predicating things of God) to the ascription of agency to God. If God is indeed simple, two kinds of consequences follow for his actions: first, all of his attributes are in the background of all of his actions; and second, all of his actions will exhibit a unity and consistency worthy of perfect agency. Yet the question is, Have modern critics made the concept of simplicity untenable for this task?

There are several kinds of objections to the doctrine of simplicity. While I cannot attempt a full-scale defense of this concept, I can at least indicate why these critiques are not devastating.

The first claim I want to address is that *simplicity undermines divine personhood*. Christoph Schwöbel expresses this worry: "Agency in the sense expressed in the biblical traditions and in the discourse of Christian faith cannot be ascribed to the God who is represented in the conception of the metaphysical attributes of God."[12] Schwöbel takes to task the whole tradition of the metaphysical attributes of God, which he thinks are in conflict with the tradition's way of talking about God. This is a well-known claim. It stems from a generalized suspicion with regard to metaphysics and the appropriateness of metaphysical categories for the description of concrete life. The personal life of God entails that God ought to be able to engage in actions that are free, multiple, and different. In other words, we can only make sense of the personal agency of God if certain dimensions of human agency—such as freedom, response, contingency, and so on—also apply to divine action. The Bible itself portrays God in such a way. Such language can only be dismissed as metaphorical, analogical, or otherwise accommodated on pain of losing the personal agency of God.

Schwöbel's claim is clearly very important for my case, since my own suggestion is that in a very real sense we need to qualify precisely this "personalist"

12. Christoph Schwöbel, *God: Action and Revelation* (Kampen, NL: Kok Pharos, 1992), 52.

language that we do encounter in the Scriptures in light of certain divine metaphysical attributes. If he is right, what I am risking is the loss of God's personal agency altogether. To put it even more simply, I risk turning God into a kind of impersonal principle.

But Schwöbel makes an even more precise point. If attributes such as simplicity obtain, then it becomes impossible to individuate divine actions. Attributes such as simplicity seem to undercut the possibility of free action. Schwöbel argues that Boethius's definition of eternity as "complete possession all at once of illimitable life" makes it impossible to individuate divine actions: "Precisely what is excluded in this way, however, constitutes the necessary conditions for individuating actions and for identifying agents. It follows that the concept of God in philosophical theology, if it implies God's eternity interpreted as atemporality[,] does not permit us to conceive of divine action as the personal intentional action that the biblical writings do."[13]

This is an important claim. While Schwöbel does not directly aim at simplicity, simplicity might be thought guilty by association. Because the metaphysical attributes are so closely inherent in one another, this association is not merely accidental. Simplicity itself will feel the full force of this argument.

The argument goes something like this: if God is pure act, if his being is identical to his existence, if, as we have heard, God does only one thing, and that is to be God, then one complication occurs. How are we able to distinguish between one divine action and another? Doesn't simplicity entail that creation is identical to redemption? Perhaps even more problematically, does it entail that God's action of, say, loving the Son, is the same as his action of creating? Does this make creation itself an eternal and therefore not a free act?

Christopher Franks acknowledges that there is a problem: "A simple God acting in history appears nonsensical because simplicity would require that God's act at one time in history be identical with God's essence, which would also be identical with God's act at another time in history."[14] Is this, one wonders, what the Western principle of *omnia opera Trinitatis ad extra sunt indivisa* means? That God really only accomplishes one action in the economy?

The perceptive reader will perhaps anticipate that this critique in itself indicates something of the fecundity of the concept of simplicity for atonement. Is it a bad thing, one wonders, if simplicity entails that a particular unbreakable unity attaches to God's actions in, say, crucifixion and resurrection; justification and sanctification; divine forgiveness and divine wrath? Indeed, this is precisely

13. Ibid.
14. Christopher A. Franks, "The Simplicity of the Living God: Aquinas, Barth, and Some Philosophers," *Modern Theology* 21 (2005): 275–300 (here 283).

what I hope the concept will allow us to see. In other words, I welcome this critique because it senses precisely what I intend to argue.

Of course, it cannot be that easy. The critique also imputes to simplicity that it goes beyond simply stating that there is a unity of divine action. It takes it to imply not simply unity of action but also identity of action. And once a firm, metaphysical identity of action has been demonstrated, divine person-hood no longer makes sense. The reason for this implication is that divine personhood, or any kind of personhood for that matter, only makes sense in the context of a to-and-fro personal exchange, where agents are mutually receptive to one another.

But need simplicity make such a strong claim about the metaphysical identity of divine "actions"? Not necessarily. Eleonore Stump and Norman Kretzmann argue that God is a single, "pure act," but with various "temporal manifestations or effects." Stump and Kretzmann defend their interpretation of a Thomistic doctrine of simplicity in two articles.[15] Stump responds precisely to the objection regarding the possibility of individuating divine actions:

> God is identical with just one indivisible thing, but that one thing has different effects and appearances. God's talking to Cain is not the same as his talking to Abraham; but that undoubted distinction does not compromise God's simplicity, because these events are to be understood as various temporal effects of the single eternal act which is God. Similarly, what we call God's omnipotence or God's omniscience is the single eternal action viewed under different descriptions or picked out with reference to different kinds of manifestations of it.[16]

Stump's solution is to distinguish between the one pure act and its various temporal manifestations. In other words, God's response to the contingencies of human existence (his action in a temporal world) is simply a manifestation of his eternal act.

A more serious engagement with this particular solution and its inevitable problems will have to take place in another venue. One issue, however, seems to be that such a defense tends to construe God's response to historical contingencies in a physicalist way of stimulus and response. This model of act-manifestation does not seem to allow for the possibility that God may have open before him several courses of action. It tends to construe God's action in history as being rather automatic.

15. Eleonore Stump, "Dante's Hell, Aquinas's Moral Theory, and the Love of God," *Canadian Journal of Philosophy* 16, no. 2 (1986): 181–98; and Eleonore Stump and Norman Kretzmann, "Absolute Simplicity," *Faith and Philosophy* 2, no. 4 (1985): 352–82.

16. Stump, "Dante's Hell," 186; see also Stump and Kretzmann, "Absolute Simplicity," 356.

Thomas F. Tracy prefers to talk in terms of the unity of God's uncontradict-able action. He wishes to avoid the difficult concept of "pure act" precisely because he fears it will not allow him to preserve divine personhood. I will return to his concept of the unity of divine agency when I make some con-structive suggestions for reframing the language of simplicity.

In another salvo of arguments, simplicity is also faulted for *making impossible various predications about God*. In other words, simplicity seems to entail that there is no distinction between God's attributes. Alvin Plantinga has formulated this objection in his essay "Does God Have a Nature?"[17] He argues that if God is identical with his attributes, it follows that these attributes are identical to one another. But this means that all of these attributes are really one, and therefore God is identical with an attribute. But to say that God is an attribute clearly is to take away the personhood of God.

Now since I shall argue that God's love is inseparable from his justice, I must first respond to this apparent consequence of the so-called identity of attributes. Several writers have done an adequate job of responding to this critique. What transpires from these responses is that simplicity should not be taken to affirm a hard identity between God and his attributes. In other words, simplicity is not a positive way of telling us what God is like but is rather intended as an apophatic qualification of our God-talk. To say that God is identical with his attributes is simply to deny that there is a set of properties that exists independently of God, which then defines his being.

The doctrine has never been intended to deny that one can make multiple predications of God. Thomas Aquinas distinguishes between *modus signifi-candi* (the manner of our speech about God) and the *res significandi* (the reality signified by this speech). While it is appropriate for us to refer to God under multiple descriptions, we know that ontologically these descriptions refer to the same simple reality. These distinctions are not real but merely formal. They are appropriate ways to speak about God. But simplicity cautions us not to confuse them with real distinctions in God.

K. Scott Oliphint makes a similar case:

> We should remember here that we are discussing apophatic theology. As such we are focusing on what God is not. In other words, we are arguing that there are certain ways in which we are not to think of God. One such way is as One who has a number of parts that make up who he is. So, in arguments for sim-plicity, we are not saying that God is *unqualifiedly* identical with his attributes. Rather, the argument for simplicity is in some ways similar to the arguments for

---

17. Alvin Plantinga, "Does God Have a Nature?," in *The Analytic Theist: An Alvin Plantinga Reader*, ed. James F. Sennett (Grand Rapids: Eerdmans, 1998).

the Trinity. While we affirm the oneness of God, we at the same time note real distinctions that are not in any way different from who he essentially is, though they are, nevertheless, legitimate distinctions that must be made. So, goodness is not a property of God's that we deem identical with him; goodness is who God, the personal God, is. So also for the other attributes.[18]

Stump and Kretzmann appeal to the sense/reference distinction to make a similar point:

> According to the doctrine of simplicity, what human beings call God's omnipotence or God's omniscience is the single eternal action considered under descriptions they find variously illuminating, or recognized by them under different kinds of effects or manifestations of it. What the doctrine requires one to understand about all the designations for the divine attributes is that they are all identical in reference but different in sense, referring in various ways to the one actual entity which is God himself or designating various manifestations of it.[19]

Revisioning Simplicity

While other objections have been leveled against this doctrine, I hope to have laid to rest at least two of them: that the doctrine threatens divine personhood (1) by making it impossible to individuate divine actions, and (2) by suggesting that God is in fact an attribute. I would like to make three further points before I begin to cash out the implications for the doctrine of atonement.

First, *simplicity is grounded in the doctrine of the Trinity*. While it has often been construed as somehow threatening the doctrine of the Trinity, the historical fact is that simplicity has always been drafted in the defense of trinitarian doctrine. As Holmes notes, "The most basic knowledge of the tradition will demonstrate that the doctrine of the Trinity and the doctrine of simplicity have gone hand-in-hand for much of Christian history. [As John of Damascus argued,] divine simplicity . . . may be derived from standard Trinitarian positions. Each person expresses not a part of God's nature, but the fullness of the *ousia*; each person indwells the other two, without confusion; each person differs from the others only in one relational property that is of the hypostasis, not of the divine *ousia*."[20] Here Holmes is driving home the point that simplicity is in fact an argument that the God whom the Scriptures

---

18. K. Scott Oliphint, *God with Us: Divine Condescension and the Attributes of God* (Wheaton: Crossway, 2011), 68.
19. Stump and Kretzmann, "Absolute Simplicity," 356.
20. Holmes, "Something Much Too Plain to Say," 149.

describe is ontologically prime. Simplicity was precisely a way of preserving and affirming what the Bible argued, rather than giving in to a metaphysical temptation. What Scripture confesses can only be affirmed by consolidating the notion of ontological difference. This is pressed upon us precisely by the mysteries of the incarnation and the Trinity. Franks confirms this insight with respect to Aquinas's version of the doctrine: "Thomas' notion of simplicity is shaped by the church's reflections on trinity and incarnation."[21]

Both Franks and Holmes argue that the recent objections to simplicity are due to a failure to understand simplicity as fundamentally a negative device in the service of the trinitarian reading of Scripture. Both recent critics of the doctrine and, in Franks's opinion, some defenders of it tend to treat it as a univocally interpreted metaphysical attribute, that is, as if proponents of simplicity were making a positive claim about the nature of God. Along these lines, Franks argues that Stump and Kretzmann describe simplicity in "too univocal a fashion."[22] Holmes is perhaps overly confident to claim that "the problems—all the problems, I think—raised by the doctrine of divine simplicity are results of an improper assumption that we can understand God's essence."[23]

This brings me to the second point: *simplicity is a second-order doctrine*, or a negative rule of God-talk. Franks suggests that "for Thomas, simplicity is not an attribute of a being with no distinctions. It is the necessity of denying that any of the distinctions that help us discern created realities can possibly help us when our subject is the One who is the cause of all being. Again, simplicity is a way of ensuring that the One of whom we speak is indeed the prima causa of all things."[24] Franks is right. Simplicity is not just another one of the attributes. Neither is it the most important of them. Rather, simplicity is a way of holding the attributes together. Neither is simplicity another metaphysical attribute removed from the biblical narratives, but a qualifier of the very way in which we read those stories. As Andrew Radde-Gallwitz argues, "More fundamentally, commitment to divine simplicity does not impose upon biblical idiom but rather forces deeper and closer attention to biblical language, as it compels the reader to discover more precise and more faithful ways of explicating—albeit through a glass darkly—the consistency and unity of the God of scripture without sacrificing the sense of the words."[25] Scripture

21. Franks, "Simplicity of the Living God," 276.
22. Ibid.
23. Holmes, "Something Much Too Plain to Say," 141.
24. Franks, "Simplicity of the Living God," 279.
25. Andrew Radde-Gallwitz, *Basil of Caesarea, Gregory of Nyssa, and the Transformation of Divine Simplicity* (Oxford: Oxford University Press, 2009), 172.

applies words to God in a number of different ways. The variety of modes of scriptural signification cautions against a purely univocal approach. Indeed, it was precisely such an approach that was drafted against the doctrine of the Trinity by the likes of Eunomius in the fourth century. Simplicity does not univocally state something about the divine nature, but seeks to order our various ways of signifying that nature by pointing to their limit.

The third and final point to be made is that *simplicity does not have to be conceived in terms of pure act*. The notion of pure act as sometimes expounded by the tradition either has difficulties accounting for free divine action in response to contingent circumstances or risks one of the two following problems, which are really two sides of the same coin: making creation eternal (since there is no potentiality in God) or removing the divine freedom to create. But simplicity does not require the notion of pure act. Both Tracy and Franks leave open the possibility of talking about divine simplicity either as the "perfection of agency" or as "uncontradictable life."

Tracy is deeply troubled by the notion of God as pure actuality, which "makes it difficult to do justice . . . to the richness of the relationship between God and humankind that appears in the narrative sources and devotional traditions of Judaism and Christianity."[26] What transpires in these narratives is a divine consistency of action that is compatible with freely choosing various responses to particular circumstances. But this does not sacrifice divine sovereignty and immutability: "God is beyond change in the sense that he is capable of radical consistency in his actions."[27]

In this light, "divine simplicity will consist in the overarching coherence of God's life as a single project."[28] God is both consistent with himself and radically self-creative. In calling God self-creative, "we are not saying that the range of actions open to him is at every moment utterly unstructured and unfocused; rather, we are saying that his range of action is not rooted in a life pattern that he does not intentionally enact."[29]

Tracy also reframes simplicity in terms of "God's determinate and uncontradictable life,"[30] or by speaking of "the unity of God's uncontradictable action."[31] He argues that God's unchanging activity should not be misunderstood as some static prison that makes attributing activity to God paradoxical. God is free to determine his own life in a variety of ways.

26. Tracy, *God, Action, and Embodiment*, 129.
27. Ibid.
28. Ibid.
29. Ibid., 133.
30. Franks, "Simplicity of the Living God," 283.
31. Ibid., 280.

This brings me to the point of cashing out the significance of this concept of agency for understanding the atonement. I have sought to explain two dimensions of this doctrine of simplicity. On the one hand, simplicity means that the being of God is unique. As an agent he is the source of his actions in a way that is unique to himself. No creature shares such mastery of being and actions. On the other hand, God's actions themselves exhibit a perfection and a unity unparalleled in human actions. This makes a great deal of difference for how we interpret one particular manifestation of this divine agency: the cross.

Simplicity and Atonement

The thesis of this book is that in general we ascribe responsibility and describe actions in part on the basis of considerations about an agent's character, his or her assumed intentions and possible reasons, power, and so on. We seek to ground our ascriptions in an understanding of the agent as a self. That is because we understand actions as intentional, as springing from and grounded in a person. We assume a continuity between our actions and our character. Without such continuity there would be no sense of self. This does not mean that departure from a pattern is not possible, but these will on the whole be exceptions.

God, however, is a unique kind of self. He is the perfect agent. This means that we should expect some discontinuity between the way in which God is present in the background of his action(s) and the way human selves are sources of action. I exemplified some of those ways at the beginning of this final chapter. Simply put, God does not act in the same way we do. His agency and his actions are unique. This uniqueness does not mean that divine action is unrecognizable as action. Some critiques of simplicity fear that the concept inevitably implies loss of divine personhood, and by implication loss of divine action. I am not persuaded that this is the case. The doctrine of simplicity has a long history in the Christian tradition. Although it has often been misunderstood, or explained in much too univocal a fashion, it is an important rule of God-talk.

I now argue that atonement theory ought to have applied this rule more consistently. Theologians need to apply the principle of analogy to divine actions as well as divine attributes. The truth is that, just as with divine perfections, we have no positive knowledge of how action descriptions apply to God. We do know we have a variety of modes of signification, but the precise way in which these apply to God's agency eludes us. This does not mean that we cannot reliably describe divine action by using common descriptions for human action (intentionality, reason, temporality, etc.). But given simplicity and the perfection of divine agency, we must always be mindful of a certain disanalogy. We cannot name this disanalogy directly, but we must always approach it with caution. We can hint at it; we can qualify our ascriptions with respect to the doctrine of simplicity—even though the result will not be a perfect, exhaustive description of just how divine action in the economy is attached to the simple being of the trinitarian God. The immanent origin of divine economic action will remain a mystery. When this mystery is forgotten, the doctrine of simplicity becomes a positive rather than a negative doctrine, speculating about such notions as pure act, with all the ensuing complications.

Applying the rule of simplicity yields three kinds of considerations for atonement theory. First, it forces us to regard the unity of divine perfections as the ground of divine action. Second, it preserves a particular kind of unity of the divine action. Finally, to a certain extent it orders the relationship between divine and human agency. I will take all of these in turn.

The Unity of Divine Perfections as the Ground of Divine Action

Unlike human action, where certain character traits are not only more visible but also more actualized than others, the divine agent is always fully himself in each of his actions. This is one viable reading of the "pure act" doctrine, namely, that God does not evolve as human agents do, in the wake of their actions. God is fully himself as the background of each of his actions. While a human being might be more loving than just in some situations, God is in full possession and exercise of all of his attributes at all times. This is the direct consequence of the doctrine of simplicity: the attributes are not some order in which God himself participates, but they are identical to his very being. It is an utter impossibility for him to cease to be either loving or just. Human beings are morally imperfect. We are moral insofar as we participate or exemplify certain qualities that are definable apart from our actions. Goodness would exist as a quality even if there were no human actions from which to predicate it. We merely exemplify it: we never create it. To that extent it is always imperfectly exemplified in our actions. Divine goodness, however, simply is one dimension of the divine life. In other words, we identify goodness by abstracting from the divine life, by distilling one dimension of it among others. Yet we never assume that we have therefore picked out an entity distinct from God.

Simplicity, then, yields the following rule: in any divine action all divine attributes are present as its ground. The full divine character is constantly exhibited in everything God does. But, it might be objected, there are certain divine actions that seem, on the face of it, to exhibit one quality more than another. Take, for example, the doctrine of hell as an everlasting place of conscious torment. How can this kind of hell be a demonstration of divine love? This is a very important debate, and of course it cannot be squeezed into this space. But two brief considerations can be made. First, simplicity dictates that no matter what solution we come to on the issue of hell, we must not construe God as less loving, or more just than loving. Second, theologically, the doctrine of simplicity helps us to say that, although God is fully present in all the majesty of his attributes, in each divine action, given the contingencies of the circumstances of those actions, certain traits are more easily recognizable by human selves. Thus a consistent application of the rule of simplicity cautions us to distinguish between the phenomenal and the noumenal. While God's action appears to have a particular character, we should not allow our sensation to determine our description of such actions. It is never the case that God is more loving than just, or vice versa, in any of his actions. This only *appears* to be the case.

The first consequence of the doctrine of simplicity is that God never enacts certain traits more than others. God simply is his traits. It is not that he perfectly embodies these perfections, for they have no reality apart from his being. Rather, goodness, justice, holiness, and power ultimately get their meaning from God's action. These themselves, one might say, are second-order concepts that are instrumental in making sense of the action of God.

Christian theologians have not always been very careful with respect to this rule. Both proponents as well as critics of penal substitution are guilty of this omission. John Stott, for example, affirms that there is a strife of attributes in the life of God. Interpreting Hosea 11:8–9 ("My heart is changed within me; / all my compassion is aroused. / I will not carry out my fierce anger, / nor will I devastate Ephraim again"), Stott writes, "Here surely is a conflict of emotions, a strife of attributes, within God. The four questions beginning with the words 'how can I . . . ?' bear witness to a struggle between what Yahweh *ought* to do because of his righteousness and what he *cannot* do because of his love. And what is the 'change of heart' within him but an inner tension between his 'compassion' and his 'fierce anger'?"[32]

We have found similar misconceptions throughout the story we have told in this book, from Duns Scotus's prioritization of divine self-love, to Schleiermacher's emphasis on the experience of grace, to Ritschl's understanding of divine love as the primary attribute of God, and so on. It is not that these theologians did not have a sense of the justice of God. But they fleshed out

32. John Stott, *The Cross of Christ* (Leicester, UK: Inter-Varsity, 1986), 130.

their conception of this attribute in isolation from all the other attributes of God, including holiness.

Now the point of simplicity is precisely that one cannot do that. It rules out any prioritization of any divine attribute, whether justice or love. Stott anthropomorphically describes God as an agent caught between and deliberating over competing courses of action. But to think of God in that sense is to lose the perfection of divine agency and to imagine a divine deliberation, which introduces a gap between intention and actualization.

Neither is God less than fully loving nor less than fully just in all of his actions. As Stump and Kretzmann rightly argue, "Because God is simple, he is identical with his goodness; that is, in some sense it is true to say that the divine nature itself is preeminent goodness. Thus there is an essential relationship between God and the standard by which he judges."[33] Not only does God not dispense with his justice, which few theologians would actually dispute, but also his very justice cannot be defined in isolation from every other divine attribute, including holiness.

Thomas McCall, in a wonderful little book, *Forsaken: The Trinity and the Cross, and Why It Matters*, gives the lie to such anthropomorphic conceptions as Stott's. He argues that simplicity makes a conflict between love and wrath "impossible." While the attributes remain formally distinct, they are never competitive.[34] The implication is crucial, but we shall take it up in a section below: if there is no conflict in God between the attributes, it follows that the atonement does not deal with God's problem, but with ours.

To sum up the first implication of the rule of simplicity: the divine perfections, which lie at the basis of divine actions and which therefore serve as partial indicators of what these actions are, ought never to be set in conflict with one another. This ought to prevent us from ascribing those kinds of actions to God that would appear to either diminish some attributes or prioritize others. Any ascription of action to God must render his agency as fully consistent with itself and unified.

The Perfect Unity of God's Action in Christ

The second consequence of the rule of simplicity is that we are not able to distinguish between parts and components of divine action in the same way as we do for human actions. We have already analyzed the reasons for this disanalogy. I am not quite saying that there are no parts to divine actions

---

33. "Stump, "Dante's Hell," 186.
34. Thomas H. McCall, *Forsaken: The Trinity and the Cross, and Why It Matters* (Downers Grove, IL: IVP Academic, 2012), 80.

in history. That would be quite problematic since it would make it impossible to individuate the divine act of creation and distinguish it from the act of redemption and so on. What I have suggested, rather, is that there is an underlying and transcendent unity of what appear to be "discrete" actions in history. However, these multiple "discrete" actions are not *related* to each other in the way components of human actions are.

To anticipate where I am headed with this, a certain kind of sequentiality is denied whereby God has to do one thing before he is able to do another, much like in the case above of turning on the light, in order to be able to read, to be able to study for the exam, to be able to graduate, and so on. I am not denying all kinds of sequentiality to the divine action in history, as I've said. Rather, I am insisting that, contrary to human activity, which is fully collapsed into the present, as it were, there is a transcendent excess of divine intentionality. This is nothing other than a dimension of the doctrine of God's sovereignty. God's actions cannot be fully made sense of economically or immanently. Since God's being transcends temporal sequence, we will only have interpreted these "discrete" divine actions if we are able to account for and exhibit their transcending unity in the divine intention. This was the point about the unity of God's uncontradictable action.

True, the divine act unfolds on the historical plane in a particular sequence. But we must resist projecting this sequentiality onto God's agency along anthropomorphic lines. Echoing Stump and Kretzmann's language, this sequentiality is what this perfect divine action manifests itself before us. We should not take it as final, however. John Webster puts it this way: "What we encounter with concentrated historical force in Son and Spirit is the reality in time of a divine movement of sending which is itself the repetition of God's self."[35] This has a crucial entailment: the human history of Jesus cannot be "allowed to become in and of itself soteriologically primitive or constitutive."[36] I take this as primarily an epistemological caution against thinking that what goes on in history exhausts the divine action.

There are several important consequences of minding this discrepancy between economic sequentiality and its source in God's immanent life. Each of these implications will in fact carefully qualify the doctrine of penal substitution by removing certain caricatures. Such misconceptions of this doctrine occur precisely because of the failure to apply the rule of simplicity.

1. God does not have to punish Jesus (or do anything else) *before*, or as a *causal condition* of, his accepting us into fellowship with him. In other words,

---

35. John Webster, "'It Was the Will of the Lord to Bruise Him': Soteriology and the Doctrine of God," in *God of Salvation: Soteriology in Theological Perspective*, ed. Ivor J. Davidson and Murray A. Rae (Aldershot: Ashgate, 2011), 27.
36. Ibid., 33.

the punishment of Jesus does not affect God in such a way that only thenceforth is he able to love us or accept us. The sequentiality of human actions (flipping the switch, illuminating the room, reading the book, studying for the exam, passing the class) does not characterize divine action in the same way. Human agents are enabled by certain actions to do certain other actions. This is a result of human lack of power, of that combination of activity and passivity in each human action. However, God is fully in control of all the conditions of his actions. While he does order his actions sequentially in the economy, we must not make the mistake of deducing from this that a particular kind of condition presses on God. The ordering of the divine actions in history does not betray a limitation of God.

Moreover, the condemnation that Jesus suffered is just as much an expression of divine love as is his resurrection and glorification. The rule of simplicity cashes out here again: it is not that the crucifixion produced a change in God, from which point God was enabled to engage in another particular action. Rather, crucifixion, resurrection, glorification, as well as God's adoption of us into his Triune life—all are elements of a single, all-encompassing, utterly uncontradictable action, whose success depends in no measure on anything needing to happen from the human side that would somehow escape his control. God is fully himself in all of his actions, and this is precisely what ought to warn us against certain construals of divine action. The crucifixion does not *enable* God to so adjust his attributes that he is now able to receive us.

P. T. Forsyth is rather blunt. Without explicitly drawing on the concept of simplicity (intriguingly), he puts his finger on precisely the same problem:

> In speaking of the change in God, Christ has been represented as enabling God to forgive by enabling Him to adjust his two attributes of justice and mercy within Himself. Some theologians of the Reformation—Melanchthon for one—spoke of Christ in that fashion. But we have entirely outgrown that way of thinking and talking about it. It has produced much difficulty and scepticism. What does it proceed upon? It proceeds upon a certain definition of an attribute, as though an attribute were something loose within God which He could manipulate—as though the attributes of God were not God Himself, unchangeable God, in certain relations.[37]

There is nothing in the Bible, he argues, about the strife of attributes.

My point is that if simplicity holds, we have to resist ordering divine actions in history in a particular causal fashion.

37. P. T. Forsyth, *The Work of Christ*, 2nd ed. (London: Independent Press, 1938), 117.

2. Second, and this does not flow just from the logic of simplicity, but rather from the idea of the unity of the Trinity, *the Father does not punish the Son as a subject would punish an object*. One cannot, in other words, distinguish sharply between the action of the Father and the action of the Son. If the *omnia opera Trinitatis ad extra sunt indivisa*, to say that the Father punishes the Son— without careful qualification—is a gross distortion of the idea of substitution.

Here I make two subpoints. First, a trinitarian rendering of penal substitution is extremely important. I. Howard Marshall's recent book on the atonement goes a great length toward correcting some of these caricatures. He argues that the picture of the Son's intercession to the Father is "a condescension to human beings who might think of God as other than the Jesus they know as the friend of sinners and assures them that the Father is in agreement with him."[38] The Trinity ought to rule the way in which we ascribe agency to God: "There is an indissoluble unity between Father, Son, and Spirit in the work of redemption. The recognition that it is God the Son, that is to say quite simply God, who suffers and dies on the cross, settles the question finally. This is God himself bearing the consequences of sin, not the abuse of some cosmic child."[39]

Marshall approaches something like my position on the unity of divine action: "In the last analysis we cannot separate the operations of the Trinity and have the members of the Godhead working independently or in any kind of tension with one another, nor can we separate the divine and the human in Christ."[40] And even more explicitly on the single action of God:

> The death of Jesus is the single action of Father and Son together. We can only think of them in human terms: the Father sends the Son; the Son obeys the Father, and becomes incarnate; the Son dies on the cross. Nevertheless, the Father is in Christ reconciling the world to himself. . . . We have eliminated any understanding of the cross which depicts the Son [as] satisfying the claims of the Father and persuading the Father to do what he did not want to do.[41]

The second point is that while the death Jesus died has the quality of punishment, we have no reason to think of this punishment as being directly inflicted by God on Christ. God's "will to crush him" (Isa. 53:10) needs to be properly understood. The penal dimension remains there, but we are not required to think of it as a direct punishment by God. P. T. Forsyth expresses something similar here:

38. I. Howard Marshall, *Aspects of the Atonement: Cross and Resurrection in the Reconciling of God and Humanity* (London: Paternoster, 2007), 56.
39. Ibid.
40. Ibid.
41. Ibid., 56–57.

Get rid of the idea that judgment is chiefly retribution, and directly infliction. Realize that it is, positively, the establishing and the securing of eternal righteousness and holiness. View punishment as an indirect and collateral necessity, like the surgical pains that make room for nature's curing power. You will then find nothing morally repulsive in the idea of judgment effected in and on Christ, anymore than in the thought that the kingdom was set up in Him.[42]

Here is how my argument (which follows) coheres with Forsyth: Each divine action has to be seen as exhibiting the full being of God. The crucifixion, no less, equally demonstrates God's love, not simply his justice. God's mercy and love are equally present in that action, because such an action is not simply a component of a larger divine sequence of action, but simply because it is a necessary dimension of God's loving action in the world of sin. It is not that God punishes in order that he might be able to love, so that there might be a divine action that is driven only by some of his attributes. All of them are equally in the background, including at the cross.

To speak of the indirectness of the punishment is simply to say that punishment is the form the holy love of God had to take, given the human condition of sin and liability to punishment. This does not make the punishment any less real, any less a bruising. But it prevents us from portraying God as being *singly* interested in the just course of the law, as opposed to mercy, love, or any other attribute for that matter.

3. A third consequence, somewhat already anticipated, is that *God is not moved from wrath to mercy*. Both the concept of simplicity and the concept of divine immutability have very clear implications for this notion.

Several writers draw a similar conclusion. Forsyth has argued that "God can never be regarded as the object of some third party's intervention in reconciling. . . . [Otherwise] there would be no grace. It would be a bought thing, a procured thing, the work of a pardon broker." He then says explicitly: "Atonement was not the placating of God's anger."[43] Holmes agrees: simplicity means that God cannot be changed in his attitude, that he is not affected by something done from the outside. As he rightly stresses, the broad biblical witness points out that the atonement does something to us, not to God. Atonement effects a change of state in the creature, leading to a different relationship to God.[44]

But doesn't Paul write that "we were God's enemies" (Rom. 5:10) and "under a curse" (Gal. 3:10)? Isn't God propitiated, or appeased by what Christ

42. Forsyth, *Work of Christ*, 135–36.
43. Ibid., 89.
44. See Stephen R. Holmes, "A Simple Salvation? Soteriology and the Perfections of God," in Davidson and Rae, *God of Salvation*, 44.

does? Well, this is precisely the kind of language that the rule of simplicity would have prevented. It is a gross caricature to think of God in these terms. McCall cautions that we "must not confuse biblical propitiation with its counterparts in pagan religion."[45] The language of the Bible must be interpreted with due attention to the ontological difference between God and humanity. God is quite simply not the kind of being that is moved emotionally in that kind of way.

T. F. Torrance's posthumously published lectures on the atonement contain a similar caution against misrepresenting propitiation. "All this is an act of God, not only from the side of God, but [also] from the side of humanity. This is not humanity propitiating God. . . . How could God, God of all grace and love, allow himself to be propitiated by man, as if he needed to be propitiated before he could be gracious and forgiving? On the contrary, God is himself always *subject* throughout this act of atonement."[46]

Has something objective changed as a result of the atonement? Forsyth indicates that it is God's treatment of sinners that has changed: there has been no change in the feelings of God for humanity, but only in his treatment of humanity. If Forsyth were to draw on the concept of simplicity, he might have been able to say more than this. A change of treatment does not mean that God is now any less holy or any less just and more loving. Rather, an objective circumstance is now in place (we are now in Christ), which makes us experience God as more loving than just, even though strictly speaking nothing has changed in God.

4. A final consequence is that *the crucifixion cannot be separated from and given priority over the resurrection*, if indeed the action of God is so unified according to simplicity. The "discrete" actions of the so-called Christ event — his temptation, teaching, obedience, miracles, crucifixion, descent into hell, resurrection, glorification, ascension, return—cannot be read as stand-alone actions that achieve certain ends independently of the other "segments" and of the overarching divine intention. They all are part of a single pattern, which stretches from creation to eschatological glorification.

Thus critics like Darrin W. Snyder Belousek are only partly right in reproaching penal substitution for failing to incorporate the resurrection into its logic. Drawing on Romans 4:25, where Paul argues that Christ was "raised to life for our justification," Belousek suggests that "the penal substitution model, insofar as it grounds forgiveness of sins on the all-sufficiency of Jesus's death, cannot adequately account for Paul's emphasis on the resurrection as integral and

45. McCall, *Forsaken*, 82.
46. T. F. Torrance, *Atonement: The Person and Work of Christ* (Downers Grove, IL: IVP Academic, 2009), 121.

indispensable to God's salvation, including the forgiveness of sins."[47] Indeed, the resurrection appears to be a simple appendix, a happy ending to a horrible story, where all the wheels of redemption are turned by the crucifixion.

What simplicity, or the perfection of divine agency, helps us to understand, however, is that the most basic unit of divine action in history is not the "discrete" actions (teaching, crucifixion, resurrection, ascension), but the whole mission of God in the world. As Holmes has said: God does one thing, and that is to be himself.

The sequentiality and the apparent self-sufficiency and completeness of these segments of action are phenomenal. That is how the ultimate divine action appears in human history. But there is a unity to this action that is only partially and dimly reflected in the river of history. No "segment" of this divine action ought to be separated from and prioritized over any other segment. There is a *perichoretic unity* between these instantiations of the one redemptive action of God. The "segments" are not to be confused with one another. The resurrection is not the crucifixion; creation is not providence; justification is not sanctification. Nonetheless, none stands without the others.

Divine Agency and Law, Human and Divine

There is one final domain in which the doctrine of simplicity has to test its usefulness. If God is utterly unique, if the simplicity of his being means that there is no being like him, if God transcends in a very real sense human actions—then how is God related to law, both divine and human? What is the relationship between his justice (and love, mercy, holiness, and all his other moral attributes) and law? The previous chapter highlighted the tremendous contemporary suspicion of law and its ability to carry out justice. Despite its claims, law is allegedly unmasked as inherently unjust. This sentiment finds theological echo in many who contrast the law of God with the love of God. We have canvassed the consequences of this attitude to law for the atonement: God's redemption, instead of taking place according to law, either undermines or else transcends law itself.

Does an understanding of divine simplicity as the perfection of divine agency shed any light on this conundrum? I address this question with two sorts of considerations: (1) the relationship between God and law, whether Mosaic or the "law of Christ"; and (2) the relationship between God, justice, and human law and government.

---

47. Darrin W. Snyder Belousek, *Atonement, Justice, and Peace: The Message of the Cross and the Mission of the Church* (Grand Rapids: Eerdmans, 2011), 120.

1. God and the Mosaic Law

That there is a conundrum here is evidenced by Paul's seemingly ambivalent attitude to the law. This ambivalence is clearly reflected in the scholarly discussion of the place of the law in Paul's thought, including his theology of the atonement. While scholars such as C. E. B. Cranfield argue that law has not been abolished by Christ, Heikki Räisänen in *Paul and the Law* argues against the idea that Christ's death was rendered necessary by God's justice and holiness, which would be irreconcilable with Galatians 3:19–25 and 2 Corinthians 3. He further argues that "if that is what Paul meant then it is he, not his Jewish contemporaries, who makes God 'serve the law' or makes the law an absolute necessity between God and man." Instead, "God's action was needed because of the plight of mankind rather than dictated by the nature of the law."[48]

This, however, is not the shared opinion of most Paul scholars. George Eldon Ladd finds a permanence to the law that is connected to the will of God: "It is quite clear, however, that the permanent aspect of the law is the ethical and not the ceremonial."[49] Such a distinction between the ethical and the ceremonial is never explicit, but always implicit, and extremely important. According to Ladd and other scholars, the moral dimension of the law is directly related to the nature of God, whereas the ceremonial aspect is a contingent expression of God's will.

Leon Morris elaborates on the manner in which God always acts by law.[50] He treats law as the framework for divine-human relations. God will always act justly in relation to his creatures: "Will not the Judge of all the earth do right?" (Gen. 18:25). He also notes that the wondrous acts of God are called judgments (Exod. 6:6; 7:4; 12:12; Num. 33:4; Jer. 8:7 KJV). But this use of legal imagery is not accidental: "It corresponds to something deep-seated in Hebrew thinking. Law and the Lord went together. Law is congenial to God and it must be to his people."[51] Law is associated with God either as a code of law (Mal. 2:7) or as natural and moral law (Exod. 12:49). It is this divine constancy in abiding by the law that distinguishes God from the capricious deities of Israel's neighbors. Indeed, Morris goes as far as calling the law "a part of God"[52]—rather carelessly, given what the tradition holds about divine simplicity.

---

48. Heikki Räisänen, *Paul and the Law* (Philadelphia: Fortress, 1986), 60.

49. George Eldon Ladd, *A Theology of the New Testament* (Grand Rapids: Eerdmans, 1974), 510.

50. Leon Morris, *The Atonement: Its Meaning and Significance* (Downers Grove, IL: Inter-Varsity, 1983), 179.

51. Ibid., 181.

52. Ibid., 183.

But this does raise interesting questions: Is the law something already determined to which God himself must subscribe? Just how is the law related to the being of God? Does this mean that God is a prisoner of his law, as Räisänen suggests? Two components of this issue can be identified: First, is there something like Aquinas's *lex aeterna*, and if so, how is it related to the being of God? Second, how is *lex divina* (the Old Testament law) related to this eternal law?

This problem recalls the medieval debate between Thomist intellectualism and Scotist voluntarism. In the first option, law is directly related to the very nature of God. Given simplicity, one might say that law is identical to God himself. In the second option, law is an aspect of the will of God and therefore does not represent God's being, except insofar as it relates to God's self-love. This was Duns Scotus's position. If the latter position holds, there is no contradiction in saying that God is free to dispense with his law for the purposes of salvation, since the law in itself is not binding on God but on humanity. But if we do define goodness voluntaristically in this way, as that which God wills, "We shall be precluded from showing that there is any obligation of any sort upon anyone for being morally good. The new definition has indeed, successfully united 'goodness' to the will of God, but only at the cost of severing it completely from what is commonly known as moral obligation."[53]

The voluntaristic option is not always explicitly embraced by contemporary theologians, but it certainly seems like it is required by their stances.[54] Belousek, for example, while discussing Hebrews 9:22 ("without the shedding of blood there is no forgiveness") argues that this principle does not bind God to the "universal law." God is free to forgive apart from the law. Such a text merely describes the old covenant. To which the obvious question is, What could possibly compel God to legislate such a covenant? If there is a reason to it, it must mean that the same reason is still applicable. Are these laws merely arbitrary? Belousek contrasts the logic of exchange and retribution with the new covenant's logic of love. But he can do so only by neglecting the importance of the question I have just asked. On what basis, on what ground, does God legislate something like this "sacrificial principle"?

Other theologians formulate a similar contrast between law and love. Wolfhart Pannenberg argues that "the Gospel does not have the form of law." In contrast to the creativity of love,

53. James B. Pratt, *God and the Moral Law*, repr. from *Harvard Theological Review* 29, no. 3 (Cambridge, MA: Harvard University Press, 1935), 155.

54. There are some genuinely puzzling cases, such as Milbank, who is an otherwise devoted follower of Thomas Aquinas but who significantly departs from the latter's high view of the law in relation to God.

all law seeks to make a form of life that achieves permanence and may even of itself declare a regulation to be normative, so that it has to deal with new situations by casuistic extensions or expositions. Freedom, however, characterizes the work of love. This freedom does not consist only of doing "willingly" what is already prescribed instead of unwillingly agreeing to it. It applies not merely to the mode of action but [also] to its content. Although love must not despise orientation to given rules, agreement with them is always a free act because it is not accepted in every situation. For love each new situation is an appeal to its inventive powers. Here lies the contrast to the mere following of a law.[55]

Pannenberg wishes to disengage law from the eternal will of God, which is love. Law is secondary to what is right (justice). Law is an expression of justice. This distinction seems to be called for by the very nature of the gospel: "Uniting obedience to God's will that is still incumbent on Christians [i.e., uniting such obedience] to freedom from the law seems possible only on the premise that the righteous will of God differs from the form of law, even of natural law."[56] The Christian still has an obligation to do the will of God, but he or she is free from the law as well. This can only mean that the eternal will of God cannot be identified with law.

What then is the place of law? What is its motivation, if not the eternal will of God? Here Pannenberg moves away from Aquinas and toward Augustine and Hobbes and connects the law strictly to the fall: "The need for law expresses the imperfect state of human society in this world in which not all accept others and do what is right on their own."[57]

Some serious questions still remain, though. Doesn't the distinction between right and wrong, irrespective of the motivation, still presuppose the notion that there is a law? Unless Pannenberg is prepared to surrender the notions of objective right and wrong, he must still account for them. They are either tied to the contingent will of God—which, as James Pratt has argued, empties them of moral content—or they are related (albeit analogically) to the nature of God. In this latter case we are back to the idea that law is somehow inherent in the being of God.

The knowledge of right from wrong that Adam possessed after the fall is in itself premised on the existence of some kind of law. The difference between this kind of law and the Mosaic law (or positive law) is that the latter binds sin to death, as Paul argues (Rom. 7:13; 1 Cor. 15:56), or rather it makes that bond explicit. The difference between the natural and the positive law, then, is

55. Wolfhart Pannenberg, *Systematic Theology*, trans. Geoffrey Bromiley (Grand Rapids: Eerdmans, 1998), 3:75.
56. Ibid., 3:93.
57. Ibid., 3:94.

not that the Mosaic law stipulates (decrees) what is right and what is wrong. Rather, it connects disobedience to certain life outcomes. It connects sin and punishment. It thus binds sin to death.

But this binding of sin to death is not arbitrary. It rests on God's natural aversion to sin, which is due to his holiness. Thus the condemnation of sin, including its aspect as physical harm (retribution) and not merely the verbal expression of this condemnation (expressivist view of punishment), is the necessary outcome of sin, not because God contingently decreed that to be the case but rather because the nature of God cannot tolerate the presence of sin. There was sin, and therefore there was law before the law (Rom. 5:20; Gal. 3:19).

The law of Christ, on the other hand, retains the structure of natural law, which still represents the eternal will of God, contra Pannenberg, but since sin has been condemned in the flesh (Rom. 8:3 KJV), it no longer includes a condemnatory dimension. But the point is that Christ's redemption had to take place according to law, due to the law's inherence in the nature of God. As Stephen Westerholm puts it: law's recognition and condemnation of sin is a good and "necessary step in the ultimate banishment of all that corrupts the goodness of God's creation."[58]

It is therefore misleading to simply contrast love and law. While the law is distilled in the practice of love, the "just requirement of the law" (Rom. 8:4 NRSV) still must be met. Moreover, love itself makes no sense outside of a context of obedience (1 John 5:3), thus outside of a context of noncondemnatory law. God's eternal law, which lies at the basis of its contingent expression in the Mosaic law, has not changed. Nevertheless, Christ makes possible a new relation to this law, in virtue of his having satisfied the just requirement of the law. Being in Christ does not mean that we are no longer under any kind of law. Yet it does mean that we no longer experience the divine action as condemnation, but experience it as freedom. This is not because something in God has changed. Nor is it because God changed his approach to humanity. Rather, it is because in Christ a new ecclesial reality has been created, which changes our whole relation to the eternal law.

Divine law (the Mosaic law, to be distinguished from eternal law) is an expression of the eternal nature and will of God. Thus there are two irreducible aspects to it. It is partly necessary, in virtue of its springing from the simple nature of God; but it is also partly contingent, in that the perfect agency of God finds expression in the midst of concrete historical circumstances and

---

58. Stephen Westerholm, *Understanding Paul: The Early Christian Worldview of the Letter to the Romans*, 2nd ed. (Grand Rapids: Baker Academic, 2004), 121.

the inescapable presence of sin. Thus its contingency is double: first, in relation to the existence of sin—this relates to the condemnatory character of the law; and second, in relation to the particular historical setting, yielding the particular manner in which God determines to accomplish his will in Israel's history (ceremonial, civil, or judicial). But it is important to remember that the contingency of the law rests on the foundation of its eternal dimension.

The question remains as to whether the stipulation of death is itself a contingent aspect of the law, not tied to the eternal will of God. Yet if one considers the holiness of God, the concept in itself makes no sense except by pairing it with its consequences, including condemnation. Emil Brunner was right to connect these moral concepts into an irreducible cluster.[59] The notion of sin makes no sense apart from the notion of punishment; God's holiness makes no sense apart from the idea of divine wrath. Now this does not mean that God is inherently wrathful. Wrath remains a contingent expression of his holiness. But it means that God's holiness only acquires meaning for us, *given our sinful condition*, as condemnation. Because, as Forsyth puts it, "you cannot separate the idea of holiness and its kingdom from the idea of judgment,"[60] it follows that "the law of penalty is the expression of the personal Will of God, of the Divine Holiness itself."[61]

Positively, then, in concrete historical and cultural terms, the Mosaic law expresses both the will of God for Israel (thus assuming the reality of his holy character, but also a certain concrete historical directionality), yet also God's condemnation of sin, and more importantly his binding of sin to death. We could thus say that the Mosaic law is *an expression of God's holy condemnation of sin in concrete cultic and institutional forms.*

The foregoing accounts for Paul's ambivalence toward the law. On the one hand, "the law is holy and the commandment is holy, righteous and good" (Rom. 7:12). The law is holy because it is an *expression* of God's nature. But on the other hand, the law is a curse, a bane, because it is *a contingent expression* of God's holy nature as it confronts sinful human nature. Paul does not so much object to the law as he expresses his frustration about the concretization of the law in a human nature that mainly brings out the condemnatory dimension of law.

Simplicity allows us to create a distinction between the *noumenon* of God's holy and loving nature, and the *phenomenon* or the *expression* of this nature in the midst of a broken human nature. It bids us not to confuse the *outward form of the law* with its *nature or true content.* Similarly, it allows us to understand that the wrath of God is a contingent expression of the Trinity's holy love,

59. Emil Brunner, *The Mediator: A Study of the Central Doctrine of the Christian Faith* (Philadelphia: Westminster, 1947), 441–52.
60. Forsyth, *Work of Christ*, 127.
61. Brunner, *The Mediator*, 447.

but without its being an arbitrary attribute, which God could simply dispense with. Divine wrath is the manifestation of the presence of God in the midst of sin. As McCall puts it, "God inevitably expresses his holy and righteous love as wrath against sin."[62] Yet, while wrath is not necessary or essential to God, "within the simplicity of the divine nature, the righteous wrath of the Father, Son and Spirit is their holy love (contingently expressed against sin)."[63]

2. GOD, JUSTICE, AND HUMAN GOVERNMENT

Some of the most poignant critiques of penal substitution have censured it for legitimating mechanisms of oppression. We have already discussed this argument, and I will only summarize it briefly. If God's justice on the cross is meted out through the Roman court, this legitimizes the government's use of the sword.

It is true that theologians sympathetic with substitutionary models of the atonement have tended to lean toward conservative politics. However, when one reads the action of God in Christ through the prism of the doctrine of simplicity, such an implication is viewed as unwarranted at best and problematic at worst.

While theologians such as Anselm and Aquinas and Calvin have tended to map divine justice onto human justice, they have always insisted that the relationship between these is analogical and not univocal. The consequence, I think, is that human systems of justice can serve the realization of a divine justice, *but only partially, through a glass darkly,* as it were. I do not think that models of the atonement that elevate law and equate it with the nature of law necessarily imply the idolatrous mistake of confusing human laws and human institutions of justice with the eternal law of God. As Holmes argues, "A doctrine of analogy limits our capacity to argue from our own, more general conception of justice, for example, to what God 'must do' because he is perfectly just."[64]

The question is, How does divine agency connect to human agency? In what way, for instance, is the "will of God to crush" Christ actualized through the execution of Jesus by the Roman court? Are the Roman and Jewish accusers and executioners of Jesus still guilty and in need of forgiveness, despite their acting out the eternal plan of God (Rev. 13:8)? The apostles clearly indicate an affirmative answer to this question: "You killed the author of life" (Acts 3:15).

The doctrine of simplicity helps to explain how the cross can have this ambivalent meaning. Failure to observe it leads to either a strictly univocal confusion between the actions of the Romans and the actions of God, which

---

62. McCall, *Forsaken*, 80.
63. Ibid., 88.
64. Holmes, "A Simple Salvation," 38.

has indeed often been a historical caricature of penal substitution, or to the denial that God can be in any way identified as the source of Christ's death (the tragic-death scenario).[65] The latter case makes it impossible to find anything salvific about the cross, whereas the former mistakenly makes suffering itself redemptive. But simplicity counsels that while God must be seen as involved with these human acts, his agency transcends a mere one-to-one correlation between human actions and divine actions. It is not a direct divine punishment of Jesus that works its redemptive magic; but rather the full, unified, and uncontradictable action of God throughout history—which necessarily includes but is not exhausted by or reduced to an element of condemnation and retribution—should be considered redemptive.

There are multiple aspects of the same unified action of God. This action is executed in time, and it involves (not passively!) the activity of human agents. Thus the distinction between divine agency and human mediation of that agency must always be observed. The human mediation of that action should never be divinized. This remains a horrible, brutal act, a crime that incurs guilt. Theologians like Belousek often fail to consider that the planes of agency are different; they do not operate on the same level. Thus we cannot infer from the cross being treated as a crime (in human terms) that God himself must be opposed to it. Simplicity in fact enforces the ontological difference and cautions us against absolutizing the human dimension as soteriologically basic and perfectly revelatory of the divine plan and logic. On one level this was indeed a crime; but on another level, it was the will of God.

The fundamental mistake of philosophers and theologians all too keen on deconstructing law is that they deprive themselves of the very means of (always imperfectly) doing justice in the world. Human law and institutions of justice should neither be divinized nor discarded as inherently contrary to justice. The late Jewish-Christian philosopher Gillian Rose expressed her frustration at the replacement of law with love: "To oppose new ethics to the old city [Rose's shorthand for a politics, a legality, and an institutional structure] is to succumb to loss, to refuse to mourn, to cover persisting anxiety with the violence of a new Jerusalem masquerading as love. The possibility of structural analysis and political action are equally undermined by the evasion of anxiety and ambivalence inherent in power and in knowledge."[66] Human laws and government are not discardable for two reasons. First, love and justice must take concrete forms—even if those forms will be inherently exclusionary.

65. See V. Westhelle, *The Scandalous God: The Use and Abuse of the Cross* (Minneapolis: Fortress, 2006), 62–65.

66. Gillian Rose, *Mourning Becomes the Law: Philosophy and Representation* (Cambridge: Cambridge University Press, 1996), 38.

Exclusion, as Hans Boersma has so helpfully argued, is a necessary condition of justice in the midst of a broken world.[67] But there is a second reason as well, according to Rose. To think that it is possible to love and be just toward the other in the absence of a metaphysics is to make yourself impregnable to critique. Yet such a critique is only possible if one accepts the vision of a God who is not only concerned with love and justice but who also makes his love and justice partially transparent, in discernible ways, to his human subjects.

67. Hans Boersma, *Violence, Hospitality, and the Cross: Reappropriating the Atonement Tradition* (Grand Rapids: Baker Academic, 2004).

Ancient Sources Index

Author Index

Subject Index